Lecture Notes in Computer Science 6710

Commenced Publication in 1973
Founding and Former Series Editors:
Gerhard Goos, Juris Hartmanis, and Jan van Leeuwen

Jorge Cuellar Javier Lopez
Gilles Barthe Alexander Pretschner (Eds.)

Security
and Trust Management

6th International Workshop, STM 2010
Athens, Greece, September 23-24, 2010
Revised Selected Papers

 Springer

Volume Editors

Jorge Cuellar
Siemens AG - Corporate Technology
Otto-Hahn-Ring 6, 81730 München, Germany
E-mail: jorge.cuellar@siemens.com

Javier Lopez
University of Malaga, Computer Science Department
Campus de Teatinos, 29071 Malaga, Spain
E-mail: jlm@lcc.uma.es

Gilles Barthe
Fundación IMDEA Software, Facultad de Informática (UPM)
Campus Montegancedo, 28660 Boadilla del Monte, Madrid, Spain
E-mail: gilles.barthe@imdea.org

Alexander Pretschner
Karlsruhe Institute of Technology (KIT), Certifiable Trustworthy IT Systems
Am Fasanengarten 5, 76131 Karlsruhe, Germany
E-mail: alexander.pretschner@kit.edu

ISSN 0302-9743   e-ISSN 1611-3349
ISBN 978-3-642-22443-0   ISBN 978-3-642-22444-7 (eBook)
DOI 10.1007/978-3-642-22444-7
Springer Heidelberg Dordrecht London New York

Library of Congress Control Number: 2011931776

CR Subject Classification (1998): K.6.5, K.4.4, E.3, D.4.6, C.2

LNCS Sublibrary: SL 4 – Security and Cryptology

Typesetting: Camera-ready by author, data conversion by Scientific Publishing Services, Chennai, India

Printed on acid-free paper

Springer is part of Springer Science+Business Media (www.springer.com)

Preface

These proceedings contain the papers selected for presentation at the 6th International ERCIM Workshop on Security and Trust Management—STM 2010—held September 23–24, 2010 in Athens, Greece, and hosted by the University of Piraeus.

STM is a Working Group of ERCIM (European Research Consortium in Informatics and Mathematics) and was established in 2005 to foster collaborative work on security, trust and privacy in ICT within the European research community and to increase the co-operation between the research community and European industry. One of the means to achieve these goals is the organization of a yearly Workshop. STM 2010 was the sixth workshop in the series, following those in Milan (Italy), Hamburg (Germany), Dresden (Germany), Trondheim (Norway) and Saint Malo (France).

Focusing on high-quality, original unpublished research, case studies, and implementation experiences, STM 2010 encouraged submissions discussing the application and deployment of security technologies in practice. In response to the Call for Papers, 40 papers were submitted to the workshop. Each paper was reviewed by at least three members of the Program Committee. From the papers submitted, only 17 were selected for presentation at the workshop.

STM 2010 was fortunate to have two distinguished invited speakers, Gustav Kalbe, Deputy Head of Unit - Trust & Security - European Commission, and Martin Johns, SAP Research. We very much thank their contribution to making this event a success. Also, we would like to thank our General Chairs Gilles Barthe and Alex Pretschner, as well as Carmen Fernandez, our Publicity Chair and Web master. Additionally, we thank Costas Lambrinoudakis, Angeliki Tsochou and Pablo Najera for the local organization support. Special thanks to the members of the Program Committee and external reviewers for all their hard work during the review and the selection process. Last, but certainly not least, our thanks go to all the authors who submitted papers and all the attendees.

We hope that you find the proceedings stimulating and a source of inspiration for future research.

September 2010

Jorge Cuellar
Javier Lopez

STM 2010
6th International Workshop on Security and Trust Management

Athens, Greece
September 23–24, 2010

Organized by
Department of Digital Systems
University of Piraeus
Greece

Program Co-chairs

Jorge Cuellar   Siemens, Germany
Javier Lopez   University of Malaga, Spain

General Co-chairs

Gilles Barthe   IMDEA Software, Spain
Alex Pretschner   Karlsruhe Institute of Technology, Germany

Local Organization Chair

Angeliki Tsochou   University of Piraeus, Greece

Publicity Chair

Carmen Fernandez-Gago   University of Malaga, Spain

Program Committee

Rafael Accorsi   Freiburg University, Germany
Iliano Cervesato   Carnegie Mellon University, Qatar
Joris Claessens   Microsoft EMIC, Germany
Jim Clarke   WIT, Ireland
Cas Cremers   ETH Zurich, Switzerland
Sabrina de Capitani   Università degli Studi di Milano, Italy
Christian Damsgaard Jensen   Tecnical University of Denmark, Denmark
Holger Dreger   Siemens, Germany
Simone Fischer-Huebner   Karlstadt University, Sweden

Peter Hermann	NTNU, Norway
Sushil Jajodia	George Mason University, USA
Martin Johns	SAP Research, Germany
Guenter Karjotjh	IBM Research, Switzerland
Costas Lambrinoudakis	University of Piraeus, Greece
Daniel Le Metayer	INRIA, France
Ninghui Li	Purdue University, USA
Peng Liu	Pennsylvania State University, USA
Volkmar Lotz	SAP Research, France
Fabio Martinelli	CNR, Italy
Sjouke Mauw	University of Luxembourg, Luxembourg
Catherine Meadows	NRL, USA
Stig F. Mjolsnes	NTNU, Norway
Ricardo Neisse	Fraunhofer IESE, Germany
Michael Rusinowitch	INRIA, France
Peter Ryan	University of Luxembourg, Luxembourg
Piernagela Samarati	Univeristà degli Studi di Milano, Italy
Damien Sauveron	XLIM, University de Limoges, France
Jean-Marc Seigneur	University of Geneva, Switzerland
Ketil Stolen	SINTEF, Norway
Ulrich Ultes-Nitsche	University of Fribourg, Switzerland
Luca Viganò	Università di Verona, Italy
Bogdan Warinschi	University of Bristol, UK

External Reviewers

Achim D. Brucker
Yannick Chevalier
Lenzini Gabriele
Abdessamad Imine
Hugo Jonker
Leanid Krautsevich
Aliaksandr Lazouski
Jingqiang Lin
Gregory Neven

Guillaume Piolle
Georgios Pitsilis
Benedikt Schmidt
Daniele Sgandurra
Donghai Tian
Artsiom Yautsiukhin
Ge Zhang
Nan Zhang

Table of Contents

An Auto-delegation Mechanism
for Access Control Systems

Jason Crampton and Charles Morisset

Information Security Group,
Royal Holloway, University of London,
Egham, Surrey TW20 0EX, U.K.
`firstname.lastname@rhul.ac.uk`

Abstract. Delegation is a widely used and widely studied mechanism in access control systems. Delegation enables an authorized entity to nominate another entity as its authorized proxy for the purposes of access control. Existing delegation mechanisms tend to rely on manual processes initiated by end-users. We believe that systems in which the set of available, authorized entities fluctuates considerably and unpredictably over time require delegation mechanisms that can respond automatically to the absence of appropriately authorized users. To address this, we propose an auto-delegation mechanism and explore the way in which such a mechanism can be used to provide (i) controlled overriding of policy-based authorization decisions (ii) a novel type of access control mechanism based on subject-object relationships.

1 Introduction

An *access control system* is a mechanism that grants or denies requests made by active entities, the *subjects*, to access some passive entities, the *objects*. Such a mechanism usually consists of two parts, as shown in Fig. 1: the *Policy Decision Point* (PDP), which analyzes a request and decides whether it should be granted or not; and the *Policy Enforcement Point* (PEP), to which the access request is submitted and which grants the request based on the decision of the PDP.

Conceptually, a PDP is usually implemented as a function that takes an access request and an authorization policy as inputs and returns a decision indicating whether the request is authorized by the policy. The most well-known models for the definition of a PDP – such as Bell-LaPadula [20], RBAC [12], the Chinese Wall [3] or discretionary models [15,19] – consider an access from a "subject-centered" point of view: a subject is authorized to access an object if she is *qualified enough* and/or if granting such an access would not create an illicit information flow [11]. The notion of qualification depends on the system and the policy enforced, but usually the level of qualification of a subject is defined regardless of the other subjects. As a result, when no sufficiently qualified subject exists to access an object, this object cannot be accessed at all. The inaccessibility of certain objects, such as healthcare records or essential military intelligence, could be a severe limitation or even life-threatening in some contexts.

J. Cuellar et al. (Eds.): STM 2010, LNCS 6710, pp. 1–16, 2011.

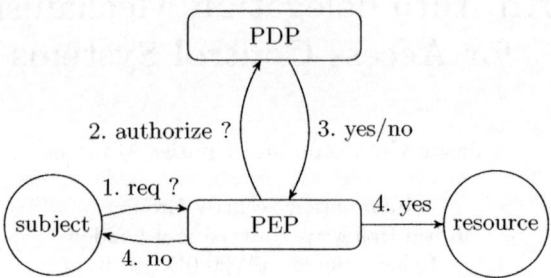

Fig. 1. Access Control System

Two different approaches exist to address this challenge. The first is to define a different authorization policy for each context, either by introducing directly the notion of context in the policy [17], or by defining specific overriding ("break-the-glass") policies to be applied when an emergency occurs [1,26]. However, these policies do not take into account the existence or availability of qualified subjects; instead they extend the set of authorized accesses for the duration of then emergency, therefore possibly allowing a (normally) unauthorized subject to access an object, even though authorized subjects are available.

The second approach is to use a delegation mechanism [6]: when a subject cannot access an authorized resource, she can delegate her right to do so to another subject.[1] Such an approach requires the delegation to be activated beforehand; that is, a subject must know when she will be unavailable in order to delegate her rights at this time. However, in some situations, the unavailability of a subject can be unexpected, for instance a subject getting injured or killed on a battlefield. In such a situation, how should the rights of this subject be delegated? Moreover, the delegating user must choose the delegate, and either the choice is not constrained, allowing the user to choose a delegate with little qualification, even though better qualified users are available, or the choice is constrained, thus requiring another policy. The approach presented here introduces, among other notions, such a policy.

In this paper, we present an automatic delegation mechanism (ADM), which is "object-centered": an object can be accessed by one of the most qualified subject available. This mechanism relies on the definition, for each object, of a partially ordered set of qualifications, each subject being assigned to a qualification. A notion of availability is also introduced, and the mechanism is implemented using either a standard access control monitor or a distribution scheme for cryptographic keys. The main contribution of this paper is thus to provide a mechanism which can automatically handle situations where no qualified user exists to perform (or to delegate) a time-critical task.

The rest of this paper is organized as follows: Section 2 introduces the ADM and illustrates it for an instance of the RBAC model and an instance of the

---

[1] We take the conventional view that a subject is a program that has been caused to execute by a human user and whose subsequent actions are controlled by that user.

Bell-LaPadula model. Section 3 describes different approaches to enforce an ADM. Section 4 describes the implementation of the mechanism. Section 5 concludes and discusses possibilities for future work.

2   An Object-Centric Auto-delegation Mechanism

We write $\mathcal{S} = \{s_1, s_2, \cdots, s_n\}$ for the set of subjects, $\mathcal{O} = \{o_1, o_2, \cdots, o_m\}$ for the set of objects and $\mathcal{A}$ for the set of access modes (*e.g.* read, write, execute). An *access* is a tuple (s, o, a), meaning that the subject s accesses the object o according to the access mode a. As we said in the introduction, an access is authorized if the subject is one of the most qualified available subject, therefore we first introduce a notion of availability and then the security policy itself based on a notion of qualification. Finally, we describe a way to build a set of qualifications for instances of the RBAC and Bell-LaPadula policies.

2.1   Availability of Subjects

The ADM makes decisions based on the *availability* of subjects. The definition of availability will be application-specific. In the context of a hospital, a physician may have authenticated to the hospital's computer systems, but may, for example, be in theater and unable to respond to any emergency that arises in relation to the care of another of her patients. In the military setting, availability may simply be whether the corresponding user is still alive.

By definition, the construction of a list of available subjects will require the run-time monitoring of the system. At its simplest, such a list might be defined by the set of users that are currently authenticated to the system.

It is likely, however, that the set of available subjects, and the meaning of "available", will be more complex. For instance, suppose we have a workflow management system (WfMS) and that there exist constraints on the execution of tasks (in the sense that if a user u performs task t in some instance of a workflow then u cannot perform some subsequent task t' in that workflow instance). Now the WfMS will maintain some authorization policy, which determines the authorized users for each task. The WfMS could also maintain an "unavailable list" for each task which is updated whenever a preceding task in the workflow is executed that affects the set of authorized users. In the above example, the unavailable list for task t' would have u added to it once u executes task t.

Hence, there will be a need for systems that can rapidly and reliably "poll" subjects to determine their availability. Whether this polling takes place periodically, or when there is a "context shift" to an emergency mode of operation, will, again, be application-dependent.

Ignoring these application-specific considerations, we assume that it is possible to identify a set of available subjects at request evaluation time, which is a subset of all subjects and is denoted by $Av(\mathcal{S})$.

2.2 The ADM Policy

Given an object $o \in \mathcal{O}$ we first define a qualification hierarchy $(Q(o), \leqslant_o)$. We then assume the existence of a qualification function $\lambda_o : \mathcal{S} \to Q(o)$, where $\lambda_o(s)$ denotes the qualification level of s, with respect to o. Given two subjects s_1 and s_2, $\lambda_o(s_1) \leqslant_o \lambda_o(s_2)$ means that s_2 is more qualified than s_1 to access o. For ease of exposition, we consider here that the qualification of a subject for an object is independent of the access mode, *i.e.* a subject is equally qualified to read, to write or to execute an object. A straight-forward way to take access modes into consideration is to define qualifications over permissions, where a permission is a pair (object, access-mode), as defined in the RBAC model. However, more elaborate approaches could be used to integrate the notion of access modes; we consider this to be future work. Henceforth, we will assume that the qualification of a subject for an object is the same for any access mode. Moreover, we will omit the subscript o except where it is necessary to distinguish between different objects.

The relation $\leqslant$ is a partial-order, therefore two qualifications q_1 and q_2 might not be comparable, in which case there is no precedence between subjects assigned to q_1 and subjects assigned to q_2. When two subjects have the same qualification with respect to an object, they are said to be equally qualified to access the object.

We define a function $Auth_{adm}$ which, given $\leqslant$, $Av(\mathcal{S})$, and an access request (s, o, a), returns an authorization decision. Specifically,

$$Auth_{adm}(\leqslant, Av(\mathcal{S}), (s, o, a))$$
$$= \begin{cases} \text{deny} & \text{if there exists } s' \in Av(\mathcal{S}) \text{ such that } \lambda(s) < \lambda(s'), \\ \text{allow} & \text{otherwise.} \end{cases}$$

In other words, a request by s to access o is allowed if s is one of the most qualified of the available subjects (and denied otherwise).

For instance, consider a UNIX-like system where the subjects are the processes, and the objects are the files. In the following, we say that s is a child of s' if s' created s, and in this case we call s' the parent of s, denoted as $s' = parent(s)$. We define the notion of sub-process inductively: s is a sub-process of s' if, and only if, s is a child of s' or if $parent(s)$ is a sub-process of s', and in this case we call s' an ancestor of s.

For each object o, we first assume a set $S_o \subseteq S$ of subjects corresponding to the most qualified subjects for o. For instance, a process belongs to S_o if, and only if, it belongs to the user owning the file, and it does not have any ancestor belonging to this user. Note that the owner of a process might be different than the owner of its parent, otherwise every process would be owned by the root.

Given an object o and a set of subject $S = \{s_1, s_2, \cdots, s_n\}$, we define $Q(o)$ as $\{q_1, q_2, \cdots, q_n\}$, such that $\lambda(s_i) = q_i$, for any $i > 0$. The partial order over $Q(o)$ is defined as follows: given two qualifications q_i and q_j, such that $\lambda(s_i) = q_i$ and $\lambda(s_j) = q_j$, $q_i \leqslant q_j$ if, and only if, s_i is a sub-process of s_j which is a sub-process of a subject in S_o, or s_i is not a sub-process of any subject in S_o. Note that if the set S changes over time, then the set $Q(o)$ also does.

If a process is one of the most qualified processes and becomes unavailable, all of its children can access the object. For instance, consider the situation described in Fig. 2, where the process s_0 is owned by the root and the processes s_1, s_2, s_3, s_4 and s_5 are owned by a user u, such that s_1 and s_4 are the children of s_0, s_2 and s_3 are children of s_1, and s_5 is a child of s_4 Given an object o owned by u, we have $S_o = \{s_1, s_4\}$. If all the processes are available, only s_1 and s_4 can access the object, according to the ADM. If s_1 becomes unavailable, then s_2 and s_3 can access the object, but not s_5. On the contrary, if s_4 becomes unavailable, s_5 can access the object, but neither s_2 nor s_3. The subject s_0 becomes the most qualified subject only if every other subject is unavailable. Note that with the underlying UNIX policy, since s_0 is owned by the root, she can access o anyway. The fact that she is the least qualified should not be seen as a constraint, but rather as the ability for s_2, s_3 and s_5 to be able to access o when s_1 or s_4 are unavailable, even though s_0 is available, thus alleviating the burden on s_0.

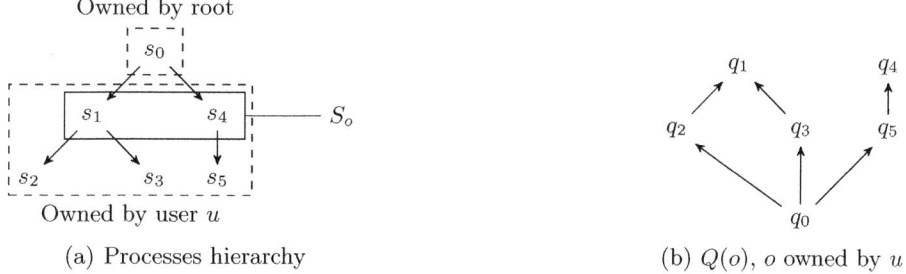

(a) Processes hierarchy   (b) $Q(o)$, o owned by u

Fig. 2. Qualifications for Processes

2.3   Applications

This section illustrates how the qualifications can be constructed for two of the most famous access control models: role-based access control (RBAC) [12] and Bell-LaPadula (BLP) [20], which have been used extensively in the medical [21,24] and the military environments, respectively.

RBAC. The RBAC96 model [25], defines a set of users $\mathcal{U}$, a partially ordered set of roles $\mathcal{R}$, a set of permissions (object-access pairs) $\mathcal{P}$, and two assignment relations, $\mathsf{PA} \subseteq \mathcal{P} \times \mathcal{R}$ and $\mathsf{UA} \subseteq \mathcal{U} \times \mathcal{R}$. The assignment relations define, respectively, the permissions for which a role is authorized and the roles for which a user is authorized. A subject, more usually called a *session* in RBAC, is associated with a user, as usual, but it may have a subset of the roles for which that user is authorized. The partial ordering on $\mathcal{R}$ (which is usually called a *role hierarchy*) extends the explicit assignments defined by UA and PA to include implicit assignments: any user assigned to r may activate any role $r' < r$ in a session and is also authorized for the permissions of r'.

We write $Perm(s)$ to denote the set of permissions for which a session is authorized, where $Perm(s)$ includes any permissions for which s is authorized by virtue of inheritance (defined by the role hierarchy). We write $\mathbf{card}(X)$ to denote the number of elements in X. First, we define a distance function $\delta_{rbac} : \mathcal{S} \to \mathcal{S} \to [0,1]$, where

$$\delta_{rbac}(s_1, s_2) = 1 - \frac{\mathbf{card}(Perm(s_1) \cap Perm(s_2))}{\mathbf{card}(Perm(s_1) \cup Perm(s_2))}$$

Hence, $\delta_{rbac}(s_1, s_2) = 1$ if $Perm(s_1) \cap Perm(s_2) = \emptyset$ (including the degenerate case when $Perm(s_1) = Perm(s_2) = \emptyset$), and $\delta_{rbac}(s_1, s_2) = 0$ if $Perm(s_1) = Perm(s_2)$.

Given an object o and the distance function δ_{rbac}, and assuming a set S_o of subjects most qualified for o, we can define $\lambda_o : \mathcal{S} \to [0,1]$ as

$$\lambda_o(s) = \min\{\delta_{rbac}(s, s_0) \mid s_0 \in S_o\}.$$

The set of qualifications Q is $[0,1]$, with the dual order relation: 0 is the highest qualification, since it is the closest from a subject in S_o, while 1 is the lowest qualification.

For instance, consider a system where there are four subjects s_1, s_2, s_3, s_4, $Perm(s_3) = Perm(s_2) \cup P$, and $Perm(s_4) = Perm(s_2) \backslash Q$, where $P \cap Perm(s_1) = \emptyset$, $Q \subseteq Perm(s_1)$ and $\mathbf{card}(P) = \mathbf{card}(Q)$. Consider also an object o such that s_1 is designated as the most qualified subject, in other words $S_o = \{s_1\}$. The qualifications for o are then defined based on the distance from each subject to s. Writing m and n for $\mathbf{card}(Perm(s_1) \cup Perm(s_2))$ and $\mathbf{card}(Perm(s_1) \cap Perm(s_2))$, respectively, and $p = \mathbf{card}(P) = \mathbf{card}(Q)$, we have

$$\delta_{rbac}(s_1, s_2) = \frac{m-n}{m}$$
$$\delta_{rbac}(s_1, s_3) = \frac{m+p-n}{m+p} = \delta_{rbac}(s_1, s_2) + \frac{pn}{m(m+p)}$$
$$\delta_{rbac}(s_1, s_4) = \frac{m-(n-p)}{m} = \delta_{rbac}(s_1, s_2) + \frac{p}{m}$$

Now $n/(m+p) < 1$ since $n \leqslant m$. Hence, $\delta(s_1, s_2) < \delta(s_1, s_3) < \delta(s_1, s_4)$. Then, as we discussed above, we can define λ_o using the distance function δ_{rbac}, as $\lambda_o(s_4) < \lambda_o(s_3) < \lambda_o(s_2) < \lambda_o(s_1)$.

We note that δ_{rbac} is not necessarily "consistent" with the role hierarchy. In particular, incomparable roles may be closer in terms of distance than junior and senior roles. For instance, a physician may be closer to a nurse, with whom she shares many permissions, than the chief medical officer, who inherits the permissions of a physician, but may have many more permissions besides.

Information Flow Policies. Reading an object can be interpreted as causing information to flow from the object (to the reader). An *information flow policy* specifies which flows of information are authorized [11]. To specify such a policy, we define:

- a partially ordered set of security labels $(L, \leqslant)$;[2]
- a set of users U and a set of objects O;
- a security function $f : U \cup O \rightarrow L$, where $f(x)$ denotes the security label of entity x.

Then a user u is authorized to read o if and only if $f(u) \geqslant f(o)$. Informally, information can only flow "upwards" with respect to L; in particular, information cannot flow from an object to a less privileged user. The standard security lattice, defined as part of the Bell-LaPadula model [20], has the form $\mathcal{C} \times 2^{\mathcal{K}}$, where $\mathcal{C}$ is a totally ordered set of security classifications (such as top secret, classified, etc.) and $\mathcal{K}$ is a set of need-to-know categories.

In the context of Bell-LaPadula (BLP), it is sufficient to define a qualification poset Q_l for each $l \in L$ and a function $\lambda_l : L \rightarrow Q_l$. Given an object, $Q(o)$ is then defined to be $Q_{f(o)}$, and for any subject s, $\lambda(s)$ is defined to be $\lambda_l(f(s))$. Although it is possible to define Q_l directly as the lattice L, such a definition would imply that users with the highest ranks are also the most qualified users, for any object. It would follow that as long as such users are available, they might have to take the responsibility to access many objects, which may prevent them from performing operations more appropriate to their seniority; in exceptional circumstances, we may wish instead to delegate such operations to unauthorized but adequately qualified users.

Instead of using the lattice L directly, we use the intuition that, for many applications, the qualification of a security level with respect to another level will be related to the proximity of the two labels in the graph of L. In particular, immediate child and parent nodes should be more qualified than other, more remote nodes. Indeed, in addition to the lattice of levels of security, users are often organised as teams or task-forces, and different members of a team might have levels of security close to each other, due to the sharing of a common subset of need-to-know categories. We believe here that, in general, if a subject is unavailable to access an object she is responsible for, another subject of the same team is more qualified to access such an object, even if she is not qualified enough, rather than a subject with a very high rank. Of course, formalising exactly this property would require a precise notion of team, which does not exist in the original BLP model, and therefore, in the following construction, we take the view that the immediate child and parent nodes of a node l are equally well qualified, to alleviate the burden on the parent nodes should all subjects associated with l be unavailable.

Given $l \in L$, we construct the (graph of the) qualification poset Q_l from the graph of the security lattice $(L, \leqslant)$ as follows:

- Set l to be the maximal node in $Q(l)$ and define $\{l\}$ to be N_c (the current-node-set) and define N_r, the remaining-node-set, to be $L \setminus N_c$.
- Define N_x, the next-node-set, to be all parent and child nodes of all nodes in N_c and add an edge from $a \in N_c$ to $b \in N_x$ if a is the parent or child of b in L.

---

[2] In other words, $\leqslant$ is a reflexive, anti-symmetric, transitive, binary relation defined on L.

- Set $N_x = N_c$.
- Repeat the above steps until $N_r = \emptyset$.

An example of the lattice is given in Fig 3, for the classifications *Pub* (Public) and *Sec* (Secret) and the set of need-to-knows categories $\mathcal{K} = \{K_1, K_2\}$, together with the corresponding poset for the level of security $(Sec, \{K_1\})$.

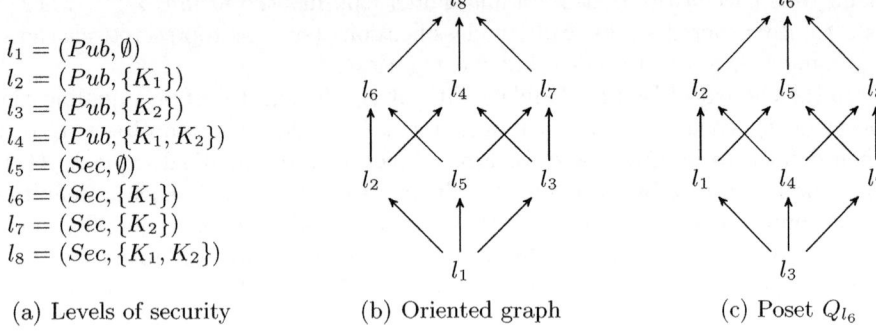

$l_1 = (Pub, \emptyset)$
$l_2 = (Pub, \{K_1\})$
$l_3 = (Pub, \{K_2\})$
$l_4 = (Pub, \{K_1, K_2\})$
$l_5 = (Sec, \emptyset)$
$l_6 = (Sec, \{K_1\})$
$l_7 = (Sec, \{K_2\})$
$l_8 = (Sec, \{K_1, K_2\})$

(a) Levels of security   (b) Oriented graph   (c) Poset Q_{l_6}

Fig. 3. Information flow lattice

3 Using the ADM

An ADM can be deployed in two different ways within an information system: either as an exception mechanism, to supplement an existing PEP/PDP, or as a standalone mechanism.

3.1 ADM as an Exception Mechanism

Most access control systems are required to be conservative, or *correct*: the PEP should not allow requests denied by the PDP. Indeed, a request denied by the PDP means that the corresponding access violates the policy enforced by the system. However, a trivially correct PEP would deny every request, therefore making the system useless. A system can also be required to be *complete*: every request authorized by the PDP should be granted by the PEP. Of course, in an ideal world, every access control system should be both correct and complete, but in practice, some exceptions have to be handled.

A *negative exception* occurs when a decision made by the PDP to authorize a request is overridden by the PEP, which denies the request. Such exceptions might occur when the PEP makes use of information received from other security systems, such as an intrusion detection system.

Conversely, a PEP may override a deny response from the PDP and grant a request. Such *positive exceptions* are needed in mission-critical systems where human lives are at stake. The main challenge here is to allow such exceptions while obeying the principle of least privilege and ensuring that unauthorized users do not acquire elevated privileges that they can abuse.

We now illustrate how our auto-delegation mechanism can be used to control positive exceptions. We assume that the access control mechanism enforces some authorization policy and that we can define a set of qualifications and a function λ on the basis of that policy. Then we have a function $Auth_{\mathrm{adm}}$ that defines whether a request is authorized by the auto-delegation mechanism. The decision returned by this function is determined by the request, λ and the set of available subjects. In other words, $Auth_{\mathrm{adm}}$ is time-dependent and is determined by the set of available subjects (assuming that λ is fixed).

In general, we would expect S_o to contain those users that are authorized for o and are "closest" or who have control over o in some sense. In a discretionary model, for example, S_o might only contain those subjects that are designated "owners" of o. In a multi-level model, S_o might contain those subjects with the same security label as o.

The purpose of ADM in this context is to provide a policy-driven way for the PEP to generate positive exceptions. In the normal course of events, the PEP accepts any PDP decision to allow. However, the PEP may choose to refer a request that is not authorized to the ADM. If there are no other suitably authorized subjects available, the ADM will return an allow decision, which the PEP may use to implement a positive exception. This architecture is illustrated in Fig 4.

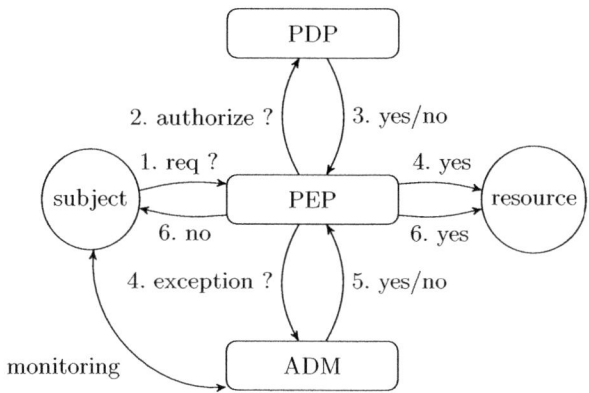

Fig. 4. Access Control System with ADM

We expect that the circumstances under which the ADM will be invoked will vary from system to system. Here we consider a few of the possibilities.

1. We define λ for a small number of objects and only invoke ADM for requests to those objects. It might be, for example, that certain objects in a mission-critical system must always be accessible to some subject.
2. We might, alternatively, only invoke the ADM when certain emergency conditions prevail. Under normal circumstances, for example, the PEP only considers the output of the PDP. However, when the context changes, the

access control mechanism transfers to a new mode, in which the ADM may be used to override deny decisions from the PDP.

3. Finally, we might have a PEP that is "aware" of the availability of subjects and the impact that this might have on the accessibility of objects. In this case, the PEP might selectively and adaptively invoke the ADM. Such an approach might be appropriate in workflow management systems to ensure that certain workflow instances can be completed (by invoking the ADM for a particular business object in the critical path of the workflow instance). Workflow satisfiability [8,27] and workflow resiliency [27] have attracted interest in the research community in recent years, and ADM may provide a way of addressing some of the issues raised by this research.

3.2   Standalone Policy

Although our original intention was to design an exception mechanism that would allow auto-delegation to override an access control policy in exceptional circumstances, we believe that the ADM can also be used as a "pure" access control mechanism.

Consider the well known "owner-group-world" access control model used in Unix and its derivatives. This could be viewed as defining a set of qualifications, and every user belongs to (precisely) one of three qualifications. These qualifications are defined by the relationship that exists between the subject and object, the relationship being determined by the UIDs (user identifiers) and GIDs (group identifiers) that are associated with the subject and object and stored in the etc/passwd and etc/group files. Of course, each qualification is now associated with a permission mask, which is an extension of our current model for auto-delegation.

We believe that this approach could be extended to any application domain in which the authorization policy is in large part determined by the relationship that exists between subjects and objects. Two obvious examples, which have been extensively used as case studies in the access control literatures, spring to mind: higher education systems and healthcare systems.

In the first example, several different relationships might exist between a piece of student coursework (a protected resource) and subjects: the student herself is the "owner" of the resource; the teaching assistant assigned to the course may be the "marker" of the resource; the professor assigned to the course may be the "grader" of the resource; and so on.

In the second example, an individual healthcare record may be the protected resource: the subject of the record is the "owner"; the personal physician is the next most privilege user with respect to this resource; then all doctors working on the patient's ward; then all nurses working on the patient's ward; then all doctors working in the hospital; and so on.

Now these relationships, in both cases, can be deduced from other information. The coursework can be identified with a particular course ID, each teaching assistant (TA) can be identified with a course ID, and so on. A healthcare management information system will define the patient-doctor relationships and the allocation of patients, nurses and doctors to wards, so all of the above relationships can (with appropriate system interaction, perhaps using web services, for example) be deduced at the time an access request is made.[3]

In this context, the auto-delegation mechanism must be extended to define the set of access rights that are associated with each qualification. In other words, we define an ADM, in which, for each protected resource we first define a set of named qualifications (owner, marker, grader, etc.); we then associate each subject with a qualification using a function defined by attributes retrieved from relevant sources; and finally we associate a permission mask with each qualification.

Space constraints do not permit a lengthy exposition of the use of ADM as an access control mechanism in its own right. This will be the subject of future research.

4   Cryptographic Implementations of ADM

Traditionally, an access control policy is enforced by a centralized mechanism (implemented in software, hardware, or both, and often called a *reference monitor*) that can evaluate every access request and permits only those requests that are authorized. The implementation of a reference monitor – commonly split into decision and enforcement modules (as shown in Fig. 1) – is well understood, and the implementation of the ADM alongside such technology appears to be straightforward. Another possibility is to use a cryptographic mechanism to enforce an authorization policy, and it is such techniques that are the focus of this section.

When using cryptographic access control, protected objects are encrypted and the authorization policy is enforced by distributing the appropriate decryption keys to authorized users (see [2,9,10,18], for example). Typically, such a mechanism is used for protected objects to which only read access is controlled and the authorization policy is static (since changes to the policy would generally require the revocation and redistribution of decryption keys and the re-encryption of protected objects). Generally, a central server acts as a repository for encrypted objects and provides them on request, the access control being realized by the ability of the end user to decrypt the object. However, this centralized approach has the disadvantage that the server may be a bottleneck and is not well-suited to distributed systems, where the mechanism becomes a single point of failure. In this section, we briefly consider the implementation of a centralized cryptographic mechanism for ADM before turning to the more interesting case of a decentralized mechanism.

---

[3] We note, in passing, that we remain unconvinced that RBAC is an appropriate solution for such applications. Most commonly, we see the use of parameterized roles [13], where we might have a personal physician role for each patient. But this, generally, results in an significant increase in the number of policy principals (roles in this case), something that RBAC, when it was introduced, was expressly seeking to avoid.

4.1   Centralized Cryptographic Implementation

Following similar work in the literature [9,10], we assume that every object o is encrypted with some symmetric encryption key $\kappa(o)$, and that every subject s shares a unique secret symmetric encryption key $\kappa(s)$ with the access control mechanism.[4]

Then the access control mechanism publishes $\mathsf{Enc}_{\kappa(s)}(\kappa(o))$ for every s that is authorized to read o, where $\mathsf{Enc}_k(m)$ denotes the (symmetric) encryption of message m with key k. Moreover, if every authorized s is unavailable, the access control mechanism can publish $\mathsf{Enc}_{\kappa(s')}(\kappa(o))$ for some appropriately qualified and available s'. Alternatively, let $q \in Q$ denote the qualification level with the property that for all $q' > q$, there is no available subject s' such that $\lambda(s') = q'$. Then the access control mechanism can publish $\mathsf{Enc}_{\kappa(s)}(\kappa(o))$ for all s such that $\lambda(s) = q$ and s is available.

Of course, once additional information is published, the original authorization policy has been overridden and o is now accessible to at least one user that was not previously able to access it. If o is ever modified at some point in the future, then it would be appropriate to: select a new key $\kappa'(o)$; re-encrypt o with the new key; and (re)publish $\mathsf{Enc}_{\kappa(s)}(\kappa'(o))$ for every authorized subject s.

4.2   Decentralized Cryptographic Implementation

The approach presented in the previous section relies on the existence of a central server that checks the availability of the subjects and distributes the key for a resource to the most qualified available subjects. The main drawback of this approach is that if this server is unavailable, then the policy can no longer be enforced. For instance, consider a military unit deployed "in theater", where the ADM is enforced within the unit. Either the server stays at the base, forcing the unit to have a permanent communication link with the base, which can be a problem if the deployment occurs far from the base or if the enemy can intercept or scramble the link, or the central server is deployed with the team, making it possible to be destroyed during an attack.

One solution is to replicate the server within the team, making it more resilient to attacks, but at the same time creating more entities with the key, therefore increasing the probability of leaking it. We propose here an approach based on secret sharing: the key is shared in several pieces, one for each subject, such that all the pieces are needed to compute the key. Each subject initially owns all the shares except those of the subjects with a strictly greater qualification, and once a subject becomes unavailable, the corresponding share is broadcast to every other subject.

More formally, given a set of subjects $\mathcal{S} = \{s_1, \cdots, s_n\}$, an object o is encrypted with a key $\kappa(o)$ such that $\kappa(o) = h(d_0, d_1, \cdots, d_n)$, where h is a hash function, d_i $(1 \le i \le n)$ denotes a "share" associated with subject s_i, and d_0

---

[4] An alternative assumption is that every subject is associated with a unique public-private key pair $(k(s), K(s))$ and that the access control mechanism possesses or can acquire an authenticated copy of the public key $k(s)$.

is a special share, corresponding to no particular subject. At initialization time, for instance before the unit is deployed on the field, each subject is assigned the special share d_0 together with all the shares of the subjects that are not better qualified than her.

Since we do not assume the existence of any central server, the unavailability of subjects must be managed directly by the subjects themselves. For each subject s_i, we introduce a broadcast unit b_i, whose only role is to broadcast the share d_i when s_i becomes unavailable. In other words, the system is organized in a P2P network, where a peer is either a subject or a broadcast unit, and where each subject owns a copy of the encrypted resource and all the shares of the subjects that are not strictly more qualified. As long as a subject s_i is available, she communicates with the corresponding broadcast unit b_i *not* to broadcast the share d_i. If s_i becomes unavailable, then she can no longer interact with b_i, which then broadcasts d_i to every other subject.

For instance, consider an object o and four subjects s_1, s_2, s_3 and s_4 such that $\lambda(s_1) \leqslant \lambda(s_3) \leqslant \lambda(s_4)$ and $\lambda(s_2) \leqslant \lambda(s_3) \leqslant \lambda(s_4)$. Then the key $\kappa(o)$ is defined to be $h(d_0, d_1, d_2, d_3, d_4)$. The shares owned by the subjects at system initialization are as follows:

$s_1:$	d_0	d_1	d_2	d_3	d_4
$s_2:$	d_0	d_1	d_2	d_3	d_4
$s_3:$	d_0			d_3	d_4
$s_4:$	d_0				d_4

The subjects s_1 and s_2 are able to decrypt o, since they have all the shares, while s_3 and s_4 are still missing some. If s_3 becomes unavailable, it will not change anything for s_1 and s_2, as they already have the share d_3, but then s_4 will only be missing d_1 and d_2. If s_1 becomes unavailable, then d_1 is broadcast to all the subjects, and therefore to s_4, but she still cannot compute $\kappa(o)$. Finally, if s_2 also becomes unavailable, then s_4 owns all the shares and can then access o.

Since the share d_0 is given to the subjects at initialization and does not correspond to any subject, this share is known by all the subjects but is never broadcast, making it impossible to get $\kappa(o)$ only by intercepting all the shares broadcast on the network. Moreover, each broadcast unit b_i only knows the share d_i, so it can be replicated to be more resilient without risking the leakage of too much information.

The main advantage of this approach is that there is no single point of failure. However, this approach is only suitable for certain applications or in certain scenarios, because it relies on cryptographic access control, which requires the re-encryption of objects when a key is compromised. In the context of ADM, a key is revealed to unauthorized users when no authorized user is available, so a decentralized approach – which cannot co-ordinate the re-encryption of objects – will only be appropriate if the re-encryption of objects is not required or if we may assume that a subject will remain unavailable once it becomes unavailable.

5   Conclusion

The main contribution of this paper is the definition of an auto-delegation mechanism (ADM), which associates each subject with a qualification for each object, and authorizes a subject to access an object if she is one of the most qualified available subjects for this object. Two concrete examples of the definition of qualifications are given, using the RBAC and the BLP models.

Related work. The advantage of this approach compared to "break-the-glass" policies [1,26] and contextual policies [17] is that the original policy is not modified, and the ADM can be (optionally) enforced on top of any policy, assuming that a notion of qualification can be defined. In [5], a notion of distance function is introduced in order to find a mentor, that is a user that can either perform the desired operation or delegate the corresponding access rights, and such a notion could be used to build directly a hierarchy of qualifications.

The implementation of "break-the-glass" policies is addressed in [4], where the notion of emergency levels represents the extension of a policy with exceptions, and an implementation in XACML is given. Traditional delegation mechanisms [6] require a subject to explicitly delegate some rights, and have been extended in [16], to introduce a notion of capability attached to roles. However, these models assume that a user must be available to make the delegation, and hence must know the delegate, whereas we propose a notion of qualification defined directly by the administrator.

Future work. As we said in Sec. 3.2, the use of ADM as an access control mechanism in its own right, in particular by associating different access modes with different qualifications, would be very appropriate within systems where the policy is determined by the relationship existing between entities. Another interesting possibility would be to use translation mechanisms between policies [14] to define the qualifications. For instance, a roles hierarchy can be automatically built from a lattice [23], therefore it would be interesting to compare the qualifications defined on such a hierarchy with the qualifications defined on the lattice.

In some contexts, when an object is accessed by a subject with a low qualification, even though this subject is the most qualified available, some parts might need to be filtered out [7,22]. For instance, if the medical record of a patient should be accessed by someone else than her physician in order to perform an emergency treatment, the sexual history can be erased from the record.

Moreover, the ADM may provide some leads in the research concerning workflow satisfiability [8,27] and workflow resiliency [27], as the notion of availability is central in these research topics.

Acknowledgements. The authors thank Pau-Chen Cheng and Pooya Farshim for enlightening discussions on this subject. We would also like to express our appreciation to the reviewers, whose remarks helped to improve the paper significantly. This research was sponsored in part by the US Army Research Laboratory and the UK Ministry of Defence and was accomplished under Agreement Number W911NF-06-3-0001. The views and conclusions contained in this document

References

1. Ardagna, C.A., De Capitani di Vimercati, S., Grandison, T., Jajodia, S., Samarati, P.: Regulating exceptions in healthcare using policy spaces. In: Atluri, V. (ed.) DAS 2008. LNCS, vol. 5094, pp. 254–267. Springer, Heidelberg (2008)
2. Blaze, M.: A cryptographic file system for UNIX. In: 1st ACM Conference on Computer and Communications Security, pp. 9–16 (1993)
3. Brewer, D.F.C., Nash, M.J.: The Chinese Wall Security Policy. In: Proceedings of the IEEE Symposium on Security and Privacy, pp. 329–339 (May 1989)
4. Brucker, A.D., Petritsch, H.: Extending access control models with break-glass. In: SACMAT 2009: Proceedings of the 14th ACM symposium on Access control models and technologies, pp. 197–206. ACM, New York (2009)
5. Brucker, A.D., Petritsch, H., Schaad, A.: Delegation assistance. In: IEEE International Workshop on Policies for Distributed Systems and Networks, pp. 84–91 (2009)
6. Chander, A., Mitchell, J.C., Dean, D.: A state-transition model of trust management and access control. In: Proceedings of the 14th IEEE Computer Security Foundations Workshop, pp. 27–43. IEEE Computer Society Press, Los Alamitos (2001)
7. Crampton, J.: Applying hierarchical and role-based access control to XML documents. In: Proceedings of 2004 ACM Workshop on Secure Web Services, pp. 41–50 (2004)
8. Crampton, J.: A reference monitor for workflow systems with constrained task execution. In: Proceedings of the 10th ACM Symposium on Access Control Models and Technologies, pp. 38–47 (2005)
9. Crampton, J., Martin, K.M., Wild, P.: On key assignment for hierarchical access control. In: Proceedings of 19th Computer Security Foundations Workshop, pp. 98–111 (2006)
10. De Capitani di Vimercati, S., Foresti, S., Jajodia, S., Paraboschi, S., Samarati, P.: Encryption policies for regulating access to outsourced data. ACM Transactions on Database Systems 35(2) (2010)
11. Denning, D.E.: A Lattice Model of Secure Information Flow. Communications of the ACM 19(5), 236–243 (1976)
12. Ferraiolo, D.F., Kuhn, D.R.: Role-based access control. In: Proceedings of the 15th National Computer Security Conference, pp. 554–563 (1992)
13. Giuri, L., Iglio, P.: Role templates for content-based access control. In: Proceedings of Second ACM Workshop on Role-Based Access Control, pp. 153–159 (1997)
14. Habib, L., Jaume, M., Morisset, C.: Formal definition and comparison of access control models. Journal of Information Assurance and Security 4, 372–381 (2009)
15. Harrison, M.A., Ruzzo, W.L., Ullman, J.D.: Protection in operating systems. Communications of the ACM 19(8), 461–471 (1976)
16. Hasebe, K., Mabuchi, M., Matsushita, A.: Capability-based delegation model in RBAC. In: SACMAT 2010: Proceeding of the 15th ACM Symposium on Access Control Models and Technologies, pp. 109–118. ACM, New York (2010)

17. Abou El Kalam, A., El Baida, R., Balbiani, P., Benferhat, S., Cuppens, F., Deswarte, Y., Miège, A., Saurel, C., Trouessin, G.: Organization based access control. In: Proceedings of Policies for Distributed Systems and Networks, Como, Italy, pp. 120–131 (June 2003)
18. Kallahalla, M., Riedel, E., Swaminathan, R., Wang, Q., Fu, K.: Plutus: Scalable secure file sharing on untrusted storage. In: Proceedings of the FAST 2003 Conference on File and Storage Technologies, pp. 29–42 (2003)
19. Lampson, B.: Protection. In: Proceedings of the 5th Annual Princeton Conference on Information Sciences and Systems, pp. 437–443. Princeton University, Princeton (1971)
20. LaPadula, L.J., Bell, D.E.: Secure Computer Systems: A Mathematical Model. Journal of Computer Security 4, 239–263 (1996)
21. Mavridis, I., Pangalos, G.: eMEDAC: Role-based access control supporting discretionary and mandatory features. In: Proceedings of 13th IFIP WG 11.3 Working Conference on Database Security, pp. 63–78 (1999)
22. G. Miklau and D. Suciu. Controlling access to published data using cryptography. In *Proceedings of 29th International Conference on Very Large Data Bases (VLDB 2003)*, pages 898–909, 2003.
23. Osborn, S.L., Sandhu, R.S., Munawer, Q.: Configuring role-based access control to enforce mandatory and discretionary access control policies. ACM Transactions on Information and System Security 3(2), 85–106 (2000)
24. Reid, J., Cheong, I., Henricksen, M., Smith, J.: A novel use of RBAC to protect privacy in distributed health care information systems. In: Proceedings of the 8th Australasian Conference on Information Security and Privacy, pp. 403–415 (2003)
25. Sandhu, R.S., Coyne, E.J., Feinstein, H.L., Youman, C.E.: Role-based access control models. IEEE Computer 29(2), 38–47 (1996)
26. Wainer, J., Barthelmess, P., Kumar, A.: W-RBAC - a workflow security model incorporating controlled overriding of constraints. International Journal of Cooperative Information Systems 12, 455–485 (2003)
27. Wang, Q., Li, N.: Satisfiability and resiliency in workflow systems. In: Proceedings of 12th European Symposium on Research in Computer Security, pp. 90–105 (2007)

Automated Symbolic Analysis
of ARBAC-Policies

Alessandro Armando[1,2] and Silvio Ranise[2]

[1] DIST, Università degli Studi di Genova, Italia
[2] Security and Trust Unit, FBK, Trento, Italia

Abstract. One of the most widespread framework for the management
of access-control policies is Administrative Role Based Access Control
(ARBAC). Several automated analysis techniques have been proposed
to help maintaining desirable security properties of ARBAC policies.
One limitation of many available techniques is that the sets of users and
roles are bounded. In this paper, we propose a symbolic framework to
overcome this difficulty. We design an automated security analysis technique, parametric in the number of users and roles, by adapting recent
methods for model checking infinite state systems that use first-order
logic and state-of-the-art theorem proving techniques. Preliminary experiments with a prototype implementations seem to confirm the scalability
of our technique.

1 Introduction

Role Based Access Control (RBAC) [16] regulates access by assigning users to
roles which, in turn, are granted permissions to perform certain operations. Administrative RBAC (ARBAC) [9] specifies how RBAC policies may be changed
by administrators; thus providing support for decentralized policy administration, which is crucial in large distributed systems. For the sake of simplicity, we
consider the URA97 component of ARBAC97 [15], which is concerned with the
management of the user-role assignment by administrative roles. The generalization to other variants of ARBAC is left to future work.

As it is almost impossible for a human to foresee the subtle interplays between the operations carried out by different administrators because of the large
number of possible interleavings. Automated analysis techniques are thus of
paramount importance to maintain desirable security properties while ensuring
flexible administration. Several techniques have been proposed, e.g., [13,19,18].
In general, security analysis problems are undecidable but become decidable under suitable restrictions. Indeed, the results of the analysis are valid under the
assumptions that make them decidable. In this respect, one of the most severe
limitations of the available techniques is that the number of users and roles is
bounded, i.e. finite and known *a priori*. So, if one has proved that a certain property holds for, say, 1000 users and 150 roles and after some times, the number of
users or roles is changed for some reason, then the result of the previous analysis
no more holds and the automated technique must be invoked again. It would be

J. Cuellar et al. (Eds.): STM 2010, LNCS 6710, pp. 17–34, 2011.
© Springer-Verlag Berlin Heidelberg 2011

desirable to have analysis techniques capable of certifying that a certain property holds regardless of the number of users or roles so to make their results more useful.

In this paper, we propose a symbolic framework to specify ARBAC policies that enables the design of parametric (in the number of users and roles) security analysis techniques. The idea is to adapt recent techniques for model checking infinite state systems [11] that use decidable fragments of first-order logic and state-of-the-art theorem proving techniques to mechanize the analysis. The paper makes two contributions towards the goal of building parametric analysis techniques for ARBAC policies. The former is a **framework for the uniform specification of a variety of ARBAC policies**. In particular, we can describe security analysis problems where users and roles are finitely many but their exact number is not known *a priori*. The second contribution is a **symbolic** backward reachability **procedure** that can be used **to solve** an important class of security analysis problems, called **user-role reachability problems**, that allow one to check if certain users can acquire a given permission or, dually, if a user can never be given a role which would give him or her a permission which is not supposed to have. The security analysis problem is iteratively reduced to a series of satisfiability checks in a decidable fragment of first-order logic. We use ideas from model theory and the theory of well-quasi-ordering [11,5] for the proof of termination of the method, which turns out to be the most substantial part of the proof of correctness. The decidability of the parametric goal reachability problem is obtained as a corollary of the correctness of the procedure.

Our decidability result is more general that those in [13,19] which assume a bounded number of users and roles. A comparison with the result in [18] is more articulated. On the one hand, we are more general in allowing for a finite but unknown number of users and roles while in [18] the users are bounded and only the roles are parametric. On the other hand, we allow for only a restricted form of negation in the preconditions of certain administrative actions while [18] seems to allow for arbitrary negation. We plan to investigate how to extend our framework to allow for arbitrary negation in the near future while in this paper we focus on the core ideas. Finally, our procedure can consider several initial RBAC policies at the same time while [13,19,18] can handle only one.

Plan of the paper. In Section 2, we formally define ARBAC policies with their user-role reachability problem. In Section 3, we present our symbolic framework for the specification of ARBAC polices. In Section 4, we design a symbolic analysis procedures of ARBAC policies. In Section 5, we discuss some preliminary experiments with a prototype of our technique. Section 6 concludes and gives some hints about future work. The omitted proofs and some additional material can be found in the extended version of the paper [7].

2   RBAC and ARBAC Policies

We assume familiarity with ARBAC (see, e.g., [9]) and many-sorted first-order logic with equality (see, e.g., [10]). Consider a signature Σ_{ARBAC} containing the sort symbols $User, Role$, and $Permission$, countably many constant symbols e_i^u, e_i^r, e_i^p (for $i \geq 0$) of sort $User$, $Role$, and $Permission$, respectively, the predicate symbols $\succeq$ (written infix), pa, and ua of arity $Role \times Role$, $Role \times Permission$, and $User \times Role$, respectively, and *no function symbols*. A $RBAC$ *policy* is a first-order structure $\mathcal{M} = (D, I)$ over this signature, where the interpretation of ua (in symbols, ua^I) is the user-role assignment relation, pa^I is the permission-role assignment, and $\succeq^I$ is the role hierarchy. Without loss of generality, we consider structures that interpret the sort symbols into (disjoint) sets of users, roles, and permissions, respectively. Our notion of state corresponds to that of miniRBAC policy in [19].

An ARBAC policy prescribes how the user-role assignment, the permission assignment, and the role hierarchy of RBAC policies may evolve. As in [19] and according to the URA97 administrative control model [15], in this paper, we assume that the interpretations of $\succeq$ and pa are constant over time and only that of ua may change. We also assume that $\succeq^I$ is a partial order and refer to $\succeq^I$ as the 'more senior than' relationship between roles. We abuse notation by denoting an interpretation $\mathcal{M} = (D, I)$ over Σ_{ARBAC} with the restriction s of I to ua when the rest of $\mathcal{M}$ is clear from the context and write $\succeq$, pa, and ua instead of $\succeq^I$, pa^I, and ua^I (or $s(ua)$), respectively.

Let s be a RBAC policy. A user u is an *explicit member* of a role r in s if $(u, r) \in s(ua)$ or, equivalently, $s \models ua(u, r)$, where '$\models$' is the standard satisfaction relation of many-sorted first-order logic. Similarly, u is an *implicit member* of r in s if $(u, r') \in s(ua)$ for some r' which is more senior than r or, equivalently, $s \models ua^*(u, r)$ where $ua^*(u, r)$ abbreviates the formula $\exists r'.(r' \succeq r \wedge ua(u, r'))$. Thus, u is *not* a member of r (neither implicit nor explicit) if for all role r' more senior than r, we have $(u, r') \notin s(ua)$ or, equivalently, $s \models \forall r'.(r' \succeq r \Rightarrow \neg ua(u, r'))$.

A *can_assign* action is a tuple $\langle r_a, C, r' \rangle$ such that r_a, r' are roles and C is a (possibly empty) finite set of *role expressions* of the form r or $\bar{r}$ where r is a role. Sometimes, along the lines of [13], a set T of users can be attached to a can_assign action; in this case, users in T are assumed not to initiate any role assignment. A *can_revoke* action is a pair $\langle r_a, r' \rangle$ such that r_a, r are roles. A *user u satisfies a role expression ρ in a RBAC policy s* if u is an implicit member of role r in s when ρ is r (or, equivalently, $s \models ua^*(u, r)$) and u is not a member of role r in s when ρ is $\bar{r}$ (or, equivalently, $s \models \neg ua^*(u, r)$). A *user u satisfies the finite set $C = \{\rho_1, ..., \rho_n\}$ of role expressions in a RBAC policy s* if u satisfies ρ_i in s, for each $i = 1, ..., n$ ($n \geq 0$) or, equivalently, $s \models [\neg]ua^*(u, r_1) \wedge \cdots \wedge [\neg]ua^*(u, r_n)$, where $[\neg]ua^*(u, r_i)$ denotes $ua^*(u, r_i)$ when ρ_i is r_i and $\neg ua^*(u, r_i)$ when ρ_i is $\bar{r_i}$. If $n = 0$, then $C = \emptyset$ and any user u always satisfies it. Let s, s' be two RBAC policies. A can_assign action $\langle r_a, C, r' \rangle$ is *enabled* in s if there exist users u_a, u such that u_a satisfies r_a in s and u satisfies C in s and s' is *obtained* from s by its application if $s'(ua) = s(ua) \cup \{(u, r')\}$. A can_revoke action $\langle r_a, r' \rangle$ is *enabled* in s if there exists a user u_a such that u_a satisfies r_a in s and s' is *obtained* from s by its application if $s'(ua) = s(ua) \setminus \{(u, r')\}$. If α is a can_assign or a can_revoke action, we write $\alpha(s, s')$ to denote the fact that the action is enabled in s and s'

is obtained from s by applying α. The pair (S_0, A) is an *ARBAC policy* when S_0 is a finite set of RBAC policies, called *initial*, and A is a finite set of *can_assign* and *can_revoke* actions. Let u be a user, RP be a finite set of pairs (r, p) where r is a role and p a permission. The pair $\gamma := (u, RP)$ is called the *goal* of the *user-role reachability problem for* $\Gamma := (S_0, A)$ which consists of answering the following question: is there a sequence $s_0, ..., s_m$ of states such that $s_0 \in S_0$, for each $i = 0, ..., m - 1$, there exists $\alpha \in A$ for which $\alpha(s_i, s_{i+1})$, $(u, r) \in s_m(ua)$, and $(r, p) \in pa$ for each pair $(r, p) \in RP$. If there is no such $m \geq 0$, then the goal γ is *unreachable*; otherwise, it is *reachable* and the sequence $s_0, ..., s_m$ of states is called a *run* leading Γ from an initial RBAC policy $s_0 \in S_0$ to a RBAC policy satisfying γ.

Example 1. We formalize the running example in [13]. Let $\mathcal{M}$ be an RBAC policy such that $User := \{Alice, Bob, Carol\}$, $Permission := \{Edit, Access, View\}$, and $Role := \{Employee, Engineer, PartTime, FullTime, HumanResource, ProjectLead, and Manager\}$.[1] Every user is a member of role Employee. Managers work full-time. Project leaders are engineers. Alice is an engineer who is part-time. All employees have access permission to the office. Thus, $\mathcal{M}$ is also such that $\succeq := \{(Engineer, Employee), (PartTime, Employee), (FullTime, Employee), (ProjectLead, Engineer), (Manager, FullTime)\}$, $pa := \{(Access, Employee), (View, HumanResource), (Edit, Engineer)\}$, $ua := \{(Alice, PartTime), (Alice, Engineer), (Bob, Manager), (Carol, HumanResource)\}$.

Examples of *can_assign* are: $\langle Manager, \{Engineer, FullTime\}, ProjectLead \rangle$, $\langle HumanResource, \emptyset, FullTime \rangle$, and $\langle HumanResource, \emptyset, PartTime \rangle$. The meaning of the first action is that a manager can assign a full-time engineer to be a project leader; the second and the third ones mean that a user in the human-resources department can turn any user to be full-time or part-time. If we attach to the previous assignments, the singleton set $T = \{Carol\}$ of users; then those actions cannot be performed by Carol even if she has the appropriate roles. Examples of *can_revoke* actions are: $\langle Manager, ProjectLead \rangle$, $\langle Manager, Engineer \rangle$, $\langle HumanResource, FullTime \rangle$, and $\langle HumanResource, PartTime \rangle$. For instance, the meaning of the first is that a manager can revoke the role of project leader to any user; the meaning of the other actions is similar. □

3   Symbolic Representation of ARBAC Policies

Our framework represents (i) sets of RBAC policies as the models of a first-order theory whose signature contains only constant and predicate symbols but no function symbols, (ii) initial RBAC policies and constraints as universal formulae, and goals of reachability problems as existential formulae, and (iii) administrative actions (such as the *can_assign* and *can_revoke*) as certain classes of

---

[1] For the sake of clarity, here and the other examples of the paper, we will abuse notation by using more evocative names for constants than e_i^{α}, $\alpha \in \{u, r, p\}$ ($i \geq 0$). Also, if constants have different identifiers, then they denote distinct elements. We use the same identifiers to denote constants and the elements they denote.

formulae. The assumptions on the three components allow us to design a decision procedure for the user-role reachability problem where the number of users and roles is finite but unknown. We now describe in details these assumptions.

Formal preliminaries. A Σ-theory is a set of sentences (i.e. formulae where no free variables occur) over the signature Σ. A theory T is axiomatized by a set Ax of sentences if every sentence φ in T is a logical consequence of Ax. We associate with T the class $Mod(T)$ of structures over Σ which are models of the sentences in T. A theory is *consistent* if $Mod(T) \neq \emptyset$. A Σ-formula φ is *satisfiable modulo* T iff there exists $\mathcal{M} \in Mod(T)$ such that $\mathcal{M}$ satisfies φ (in symbols, $\mathcal{M} \models \varphi$). A Σ-formula φ is *valid modulo* T iff its negation is unsatisfiable modulo T and it is *equivalent modulo* T to a Σ-formula φ' iff the formula $(\varphi \Leftrightarrow \varphi')$ is valid modulo T. As notational conventions, the variables u, r, p and their subscripted versions are of sort $Users, Roles$, and $Permissions$, respectively; $\underline{u}, \underline{r}, \underline{p}$ denote tuples of variables of sort $Users, Roles, Permission$, respectively; $\varphi(\underline{x}, \underline{\pi})$ denotes a quantifier-free formula where at most the variables in the tuple $\underline{x}$ may occur free and at most the predicate symbols in the tuple $\underline{\pi}$ may occur besides those of the signature over which φ is built. In this paper, we consider only consistent theories axiomatized by *universal sentences* of the form $\forall \underline{x}.\varphi(\underline{x})$. In the examples, we will make frequent use of the *theory of scalar values* $v_1, ..., v_n$ *(for* $n \geq 1$*) of type* S, denoted with $SV(\{v_1, ..., v_n\}, S)$, whose signature consists of the sort S, the constant symbols $v_1, ..., v_n$ of sort S, and it is axiomatized by the following (universal) sentences: $v_i \neq v_j$ for $i, j = 1, ..., n$, $i \neq j$, and $\forall x.(x = v_1 \lor \cdots \lor x = v_n)$, where x is of sort S.

3.1 Symbolic Representation of RBAC Policies

Let T_{Role} be a Σ_{Role}-theory axiomatized by a finite set of universal sentences where Σ_{Role} contains the sort $Role$, the predicate $\succeq$, and countably many constants of sort $Role$ but no function symbol. Let T_{User} be a Σ_{User}-theory axiomatized by a finite set of universal sentences where Σ_{User} contains the sort $User$, countably many constants of sort $User$ but no function symbol. Let $T_{Permission}$ be a $\Sigma_{Permission}$-theory axiomatized by a finite set of universal sentences where $\Sigma_{Permission}$ contains the sort $Role$ and countably many constants of sort $Permission$ but no function symbol. We emphasize that the signatures of these three theories may contain finitely many predicate symbols besides those mentioned above but no function symbols.

Example 2. For the version of ARBAC we are considering, the theory T_{Role} can be axiomatized by the following three universal sentences: $\forall r.(r \succeq r)$, $\forall r_1, r_2.((r_1 \succeq r_2 \land r_2 \succeq r_1) \Rightarrow r_1 = r_2)$, and $\forall r_1, r_2, r_3.((r_1 \succeq r_2 \land r_2 \succeq r_3) \Rightarrow r_1 \succeq r_3)$. This means that $\succeq$ is interpreted as a partial order by the structures in $Mod(T_{Role})$. The set of basic roles and their positions in the partial order can be defined, when considering Example 1, as the following sentences: $Engineer \succeq Employee$, $PartTime \succeq Employee$, $FullTime \succeq Employee$, $ProjectLead \succeq Engineer$, and $Manager \succeq FullTime$. The interested reader can see [7] for a discussion on how to formalize ARBAC with parametric roles.

For the theory T_{User}, we have a similar flexibility. For example, if there is only a *finite and known* number $n \geq 1$ of users, say $e_1^u, ..., e_n^u$, then we can use the theory of a scalar value $SV(\{e_1^u, ..., e_n^u\}, User)$. Another situation is when we have a *finite but unknown* number of users whose identifiers are, for example, linearly ordered (think of the integers with the usual order relation 'less than or equal'). In this case, we add the ordering relation $\leq$ of arity $User \times User$ to Σ_{User} and the following universal sentences constrain $\leq$ to be a linear order: $\forall u.(u \leq u)$, $\forall u_1, u_2, u_3.((u_1 \leq u_2 \land u_2 \leq u_3) \Rightarrow u_1 \leq u_3)$, $\forall u_1, u_2.((u_1 \leq u_2 \land u_2 \leq u_1) \Rightarrow u_1 = u_2)$, and $\forall u_1, u_2.(u_1 \leq u_2 \lor u_2 \leq u_1)$. If $T_{User} = \emptyset$, then the identifiers e_i^u of users can be compared for (dis-)equality and there is again a *finite but unknown* number of users.

Similar observations also hold for $T_{Permission}$. Often, there is only a finite and known number of permissions that can be associated to roles. For example, continuing the formalization of Example 1, recall that we have only three permissions: Access, View, and Edit. So, $T_{Permission} := SV(\{Access, View, Edit\}, Permission)$. $\square$

As shown by the example above, the flexibility of our approach allows us to go beyond standard ARBAC policies by specifying the domains of users, roles, and permissions enjoying non-trivial algebraic properties which are useful to model, e.g., property-based policies [12]. We leave a detailed analysis of the scope of applicability of our framework to future work (as a first step in this direction, see [6]).

Now, we define $\Sigma_{ARBAC} := \Sigma_{Role} \cup \Sigma_{User} \cup \Sigma_{Permission} \cup \{pa, ua\}$ and let $T_{ARBAC} := T_{Role} \cup T_{User} \cup T_{Permission} \cup PA$, where PA is a set of (universal) sentences over $\Sigma_{Role} \cup \Sigma_{Permission} \cup \{pa\}$ characterizing the permission assignment relation.

Example 3. Consider again Example 1. The permission-role assignment is axiomatized by $PA := \{\forall p, r.(pa(p, r) \Leftrightarrow ((p = Access \land r = Employee) \lor (p = View \land r = HumanResource) \lor (p = Edit \land r = Engineer))\}$. $\square$

Observe that a structure in $Mod(T_{ARBAC})$ over Σ_{ARBAC} is a RBAC policy.

3.2 Symbolic Representation of Initial RBAC Policies, Constraints, and Goals

Since no axiom involving ua is in T_{ARBAC}, the interpretation of ua is arbitrary. We consider the problem of how to constrain the interpretation of ua by means of an example.

Example 4. We specify the user-role assignment of Example 1. Let T_{User}, T_{Role}, and $T_{Permission}$ be as in Example 3. Consider the formula $In(ua)$:

$$\forall u, r.(ua(u, r) \Leftrightarrow ((u = Alice \land r = PartTime) \lor (u = Alice \land r = Engineer) \lor$$
$$(u = Bob \land r = Manager) \lor (u = Carol \land r = HumanResource))).$$

(Notice that $In(ua)$ can be seen as the Clark's completion [8] of the facts: $ua(Alice, PartTime)$, $ua(Alice, Engineer)$, $ua(Bob, Manager)$, and $ua(Carol,$

HumanResource).) It is easy to see that the interpretation considered in Example 1 satisfies $In(ua)$. □

Since the formula $In(ua)$ used in the example above belongs to the class of universal sentences containing the state variable ua, we will use such a class of formulae, and denote it with ∀-*formulae*, to symbolically specify initial RBAC policies.

Example 5. Although in Example 4 the numbers of users and roles are fixed to certain values, our framework does not require this. For example, recall the discussion in Example 2 and take $T_{User} = \emptyset$, $T_{Role} = \emptyset$. Then, consider the following ∀-formula: $\forall u, r.(ua(u, r) \Leftrightarrow (u \neq e_0^u \wedge r \neq e_0^r))$. A RBAC policy s satisfying the formula is such that $(e_0^u, e_0^r) \notin s(ua)$ and $(e_i^u, e_j^r) \in s(ua)$ for every pair (i, j) of natural numbers with $i, j \neq 0$. Thus, there is no bound on the number of pairs (e_i^u, e_j^r) in $s(ua)$. □

Notice that ∀-formulae are not only useful to describe initial RBAC policies but also to express constraints on the set of states that *can_assign* and *can_revoke* actions must satisfy. As an example, consider RBAC policies with separation of duty constraints, i.e. a user cannot be assigned two given roles. This can be enforced by using *static mutually exclusive roles* (SMER) *constraints* that require pairs of roles with disjoint membership (see, e.g., [19]). Formulae representing SMER constraints are ∀-formulae with the following form: $\forall u. \neg(ua(u, e_i^r) \wedge ua(u, e_j^r))$, for $i, j \geq 0$ and $i \neq j$. Notice that other kinds of constraints can be specified in our framework as long as they can be expressed as ∀-formulae.

Example 6. Let us consider again the situation described in Example 1. One may be interested in knowing if user Alice can take role FullTime and have permission Access. This property can be encoded by the following formula:

$$\exists u, r, p.(ua(u, r) \wedge pa(p, r) \wedge u = Alice \wedge r \succeq FullTime \wedge p = Access). \quad □$$

Generalizing this example, we introduce ∃-*formulae* of the form $\exists \underline{u}, \underline{r}, \underline{p}.\varphi(\underline{u}, \underline{r}, \underline{p})$.

3.3   Symbolic Representation of Administrative Actions

A *policy literal* is either $ua(u, r)$, $\neg ua(u, r)$, a literal over Σ_{User} (e.g., $u = e_i^u$ or $u \neq e_i^u$ for $i \geq 0$), or a literal over Σ_{Role} (e.g., $r = e_j^r$, $r \succeq e_j^r$, or their negations for $j \geq 0$). A *policy expression* is a finite conjunction of policy literals. Administrative actions are represented by instances of formulae of the following form:

$$\exists u, r, u_1, r_1, r_2, ..., r_k. \ (C(u, r, u_1, r_1, r_2, ..., r_k) \wedge ua' = ua \oplus (u_1, e_i^r)) \quad (1)$$
$$\exists u, r, u_1. \ (C(u, r, u_1) \qquad\qquad\qquad \wedge ua' = ua \ominus (u_1, e_i^r)) \quad (2)$$

where $k, i \geq 0$, C is a policy expression called the *guard* of the transition, primed variables denote the value of the state variable ua after the execution of the transition, $ua \odot (u, e_i^r)$ abbreviates

$$\lambda w, v.(if \ (w = u \wedge v = e_i^r) \ then \ b \ else \ ua(w, v)),$$

and b is *true* when $\odot$ is $\oplus$ and it is *false* when $\odot$ is $\ominus$.[2] It is possible to symbolically represent *can_assign* actions as formulae of the form (1) and *can_revoke* actions as formulae of the form (2). We illustrate this with an example.

Example 7. We specify in our framework the administrative actions given in Example 1. The *can_assign* action $\langle Manager, \{Engineer, FullTime\}, ProjectLead \rangle$ corresponds to the following instance of (1):

$$\exists u, r, u_1, r_1, r_2. \left(\begin{array}{l} ua(u,r) \wedge r \succeq Manager \wedge u \neq Carol \wedge \\ ua(u_1, r_1) \wedge r_1 \succeq Engineer \wedge ua(u_1, r_2) \wedge r_2 \succeq FullTime \wedge \\ ua' = ua \oplus (u_1, ProjectLead) \end{array} \right).$$

Two observations are in order. First, the literal $u \neq Carol$ disables the transition when u is instantiated to *Carol*. This allows us to model the set $T = \{Carol\}$ of users that are prevented to execute assignments. Second, by simple logical manipulations and recalling the definition of the abbreviation ua^* introduced in Section 2, it is possible to rewrite the guard of the transition as $ua^*(u, Manager) \wedge ua^*(u_1, Engineer) \wedge ua^*(u_1, FullTime) \wedge \neq Carol$. The simpler *can_assign* rules $\langle HumanResource, \emptyset, FullTime \rangle$ and $\langle HumanResource, \emptyset, PartTime \rangle$ can be specified by the following two instances of (1):

$$\exists u, r, u_1. \left(\begin{array}{l} ua(u,r) \wedge r \succeq HumanResource \wedge u \neq Carol \wedge \\ ua' = ua \oplus (u_1, FullTime) \end{array} \right)$$

$$\exists u, r, u_1. \left(\begin{array}{l} ua(u,r) \wedge r \succeq HumanResource \wedge u \neq Carol \wedge \\ ua' = ua \oplus (u_1, PartTime) \end{array} \right).$$

Following [13], we call *AATU* (an abbreviation for 'assignment and trusted users') the set containing the above three formulae.

The *can_revoke* action $\langle Manager, ProjectLead \rangle$ is formalized by the following instance of (2): $\exists u, r.(ua(u,r) \wedge r \succeq Manager \wedge ua' = ua \ominus (u_1, ProjectLead))$. The remaining three *can_revokes* can be obtained from the formula above by simply replacing Manager and ProjectLead with Manager and Engineer for $\langle Manager, Engineer \rangle$, with HumanResource and FullTime for $\langle HumanResource, FullTime \rangle$, and with HumanResource and PartTime for $\langle HumanResource, PartTime \rangle$.   □

Notice that the guards of the transitions of the form (1) do not correspond exactly to those introduced in Section 2. On the one hand, policy expressions give us the possibility to require a user u to be an explicit member of a certain role r in the guard of transition (by writing $ua^*(u,r)$) while preconditions of a *can_assign* can only require a user to be an implicit member of a role (i.e. $ua^*(u,r)$). On the other hand, it is not possible, in general, to express $\neg ua^*(u,r)$ (i.e. u is neither an explicit nor an implicit member of r), although it is possible to use $\neg ua(u,r)$ (i.e. u is not an explicit member of r). This is so because to

---

[2] We use λ-notation here for the sake of readability only. The same formulae can be easily recast in pure first-order logic. For example, (1) can be written as $\exists u, r, r_1, ..., r_k.(C(u, r, r_1, ..., r_k) \wedge \forall w, r.(ua'(w,r) \Leftrightarrow ((w = u \wedge r = e^r) \vee ua(w,r))))$.

express $\neg ua^*(u,r)$, a universal quantification is required; recall from Section 2 that $\neg ua^*(u,r)$ abbreviates $\forall r'.(r' \succeq r \Rightarrow \neg ua(u,r))$. In other words, only a limited form of negation can be expressed in the guards of our formalization of a *can_assign* action. This simplifies the technical development that follows, in particular the proof of termination of the procedure used to solve the user-role reachability problem (see Section 4 for details). We plan to adapt a technique used in infinite state model checking for handling global conditions to allow $\neg ua^*(u,r)$ in the guards of transitions (see, e.g., [4]) but leave this to future work. Here, we observe that in many situations of practical relevance, it is possible to overcome this difficulty. For example, when there are only finitely many roles ranging over a set R, it is possible to eliminate the hierarchy as explained in [17] so that the framework proposed in this paper applies without problems. It is worth noticing that although the set of roles has been assumed to be bounded, our framework supports the situation where the set of users can be finite but its cardinality is unknown.

3.4   Reachability and Satisfiability Modulo T_{ARBAC}

At this point, it should be clear that the (algebraic) structures of users, roles, and permission can be specified by suitable theories; that we can symbolically represent RBAC policies and goals by using $\forall$-formulae and $\exists$-formulae, respectively, *can_assign* actions by formulae of the form (1), and *can_revoke* actions by formulae of the form (2). As a consequence, we can rephrase the user-goal reachability problem introduced in Section 2 as follows.

Let T_{ARBAC} be a Σ_{ARBAC}-theory given as described above and specifying the structure of users, roles, permission, role hierarchy, and the permission-role relation. If $\Gamma := (S_0, A)$ is an ARBAC policy together with a set $\mathcal{C}$ of constraints on the set of states that the actions of the system must satisfy (e.g., SMER), then derive the associated *symbolic ARBAC policy* $\Gamma_s := (In(ua), Tr, C)$ as explained above, where In is a $\forall$-formula representing the initial set S_0 of RBAC policies, Tr is a finite set of instances of (1) or of (2) corresponding to the actions in A, and C is a finite set of $\forall$-formula representing constraints in $\mathcal{C}$. Furthermore, let γ_s be an $\exists$-formula of the form

$$\exists u_1, r_1, p_1, ..., u_n, r_n, p_n. \bigwedge_{i=1}^{n} (ua(u_i, r_i) \wedge r_i \bowtie e_{j_i}^r \wedge p_i = e_{j_i}^p), \tag{3}$$

called a *symbolic goal* and corresponding to a goal $RP := \{(e_{j_i}^r, e_{j_i}^p) \mid i = 1, ..., n\}$, where $\bowtie \in \{=, \succeq\}$. Then, it is easy to see that the user-role reachability problem for Γ with RP as goal is solvable iff there exists a natural number $\ell \geq 0$ such that the formula

$$In(ua_0) \wedge \bigwedge_{i=0}^{\ell} (\iota(a_i) \wedge \tau(ua_i, ua_{i+1}) \wedge \iota(a_{i+1})) \wedge \gamma_s(ua_\ell) \tag{4}$$

is satisfiable modulo T_{ARBAC}, where τ is the disjunction of the formulae in Tr, and ι is the disjunction of those in C. Notice that the (big) conjunction over ℓ

with In in (4) can be seen as a characterization of the set of states (forward) reachable from the initial set of states. Symmetrically (and more interestingly for the rest of this paper), the (big) conjunction over ℓ with γ_s in (4) characterizes the set of states backward reachable from the goal states. We observe that when $\ell = 0$, no actions must be performed and already some of the states in In satisfies γ_s, thus, formula (4) simplifies to $In(ua_0) \wedge \iota(ua_0) \wedge \gamma_s(ua_0)$.

Example 8. We illustrate the check for satisfiability of the formula (4) for $\ell = 0$ by reconsidering the situation described in Example 6. The problem was to establish if the formula $In(ua)$ of Example 4 and the goal formula of Example 6 are satisfiable modulo the theory T_{ARBAC} in Example 3. We assume that the set of constraints of the symbolic ARBAC polices is empty. In this context, the formula (4) above can be written as follows:

$$PO := \forall u, r. (ua(u,r) \Leftrightarrow \begin{pmatrix} (u = Alice \wedge r = PartTime) & \vee \\ (u = Alice \wedge r = Engineer) & \vee \\ (u = Bob \wedge r = Manager) & \vee \\ (u = Carol \wedge r = HumanResource) \end{pmatrix}) \wedge$$

$$\exists u_1, r_1, p_1. (ua(u_1, r_1) \wedge pa(p_1, r_1) \wedge u_1 = Alice \wedge r_1 \succeq FullTime \wedge p {=} Access) \ ,$$

where the existentially quantified variables in the goal have been renamed for clarity. The problem is to establish the satisfiability of PO modulo the theory T_{ARBAC} in Example 3. As it will be seen below, there exists an algorithm capable of answering this question automatically. For PO, the algorithm would return 'unsatisfiable,' entitling us to conclude that the set of initial states considered in Example 4 do not satisfy the goal of allowing Alice, who is a full-time employee, to get access to a certain resource.   □

If we were able to automatically check the satisfiability of formulae of the form (4), an idea to solve the user-role reachability problem for ARBAC policies would be to generate instances of (4) for increasing values of ℓ. However, this would not give us a decision procedure for solving the goal reachability problem but only a semi-decision procedure. In fact, the method terminates only when the goal is reachable from the initial state, i.e. when, for a certain value of ℓ, the instance of the formula (4) is unsatisfiable modulo T_{ARBAC}. When, instead, the goal is not reachable, the check will never detect the unsatisfiability and we will be forced to generate an infinite sequence of instances of (4) for increasing values of ℓ. In other words, the decidability of the satisfiability of (4) modulo T_{ARBAC} is only a necessary condition for ensuring the decidability of the user-role reachability problem. Fortunately, is possible to stop enumerating instances of (4) for a certain value $\bar{\ell}$ of ℓ when the formula characterizing the set of reachable states for $\ell = \bar{\ell} + 1$ implies that characterizing the set of reachable states for $\ell = \bar{\ell}$; i.e. we have detected a *fixed-point*. We explore this idea in the following section.

4   Symbolic Analysis of ARBAC Policies

A general approach to solve the user-role reachability problem is based on computing the set of backward reachable states. It is well-known that the computation of

function BReach(Γ : (In, Tr, C), γ : $\exists$-formula)

1    $P \longleftarrow \gamma$; $B \longleftarrow false$; $\tau \longleftarrow \bigvee_{t \in Tr} t$; $\iota \longleftarrow \bigwedge_{i \in C} i$;

2   **while** ($\iota \wedge P \wedge \neg B$ is satisfiable modulo T_{ARBAC}) **do**

3   **if** ($In \wedge P$ is satisfiable modulo T_{ARBAC})

        then return reachable;

4      $B \longleftarrow P \vee B$;

5      $P \longleftarrow Pre(\tau, P)$;

6   **end**

7   **return** unreachable;

Fig. 1. The basic backward reachability procedure

sets of backward (rather than forward) reachable states is easier to mechanize. For $n \geq 0$, the *n-pre-image* of a formula $K(ua)$ is a formula $Pre^n(\tau, K)$ recursively defined as follows: $Pre^0(\tau, K) := K$ and $Pre^{n+1}(\tau, K) := Pre(\tau, Pre^n(\tau, K))$, where[3]

$$Pre(\tau, K) := \exists ua'.(\tau(ua, ua') \wedge K(ua')). \tag{5}$$

The formula $Pre^n(\tau, \gamma)$ describes the set of states from which it is possible to reach the goal γ in $n \geq 0$ steps. At the n-th iteration of the loop, the *backward reachability algorithm* depicted in Figure 1, stores the formula $Pre^n(\tau, \gamma)$ in the variable P and the formula $BR^n(\tau, \gamma) := \bigvee_{i=0}^n Pre^i(\tau, \gamma)$ (representing the set of states from which the goal γ is reachable in *at most* n steps) in the variable B. While computing $BR^n(\tau, \gamma)$, BReach also checks whether the goal is reachable in n steps (cf. line 3, which can be read as $In \wedge Pre^n(\tau, \gamma)$ is satisfiable modulo T_{ARBAC}) or a fixed-point has been reached (cf. line 2, which can be read as $\neg((\iota \wedge BR^n(\tau, \gamma)) \Rightarrow BR^{n-1}(\tau, \gamma))$ is unsatisfiable modulo T_{ARBAC} or, equivalently, that $((\iota \wedge BR^n(\tau, \gamma)) \Rightarrow BR^{n-1}(\tau, \gamma))$ is valid modulo T_{ARBAC}). Notice that $BR^{n-1}(\tau, \gamma) \Rightarrow BR^n(\tau, \gamma)$ is valid by construction; thus, if $((\iota \wedge BR^n(\tau, \gamma)) \Rightarrow BR^{n-1}(\tau, \gamma))$ is a logical consequence of T_{ARBAC}, then also $((\iota \wedge BR^n(\tau, \gamma)) \Leftrightarrow BR^{n-1}(\tau, \gamma))$ is so and a fixed-point has been reached. The invariant ι is conjoined to the set of backward reachable states when performing the fixed-point check as only those states that also satisfies the constraints are required to be considered. When BReach returns unreachable (cf. line 7), the variable B stores the formula describing the set of states which are backward reachable from γ which is also a fixed-point. Otherwise, when it returns reachable (cf. line 3) at the n-th iteration, there exists a run of length n that leads the AR-BAC policy from a RBAC policy in In to one in γ. We observe that for BReach to be an effective (possibly non-terminating) procedure, it is mandatory that (i) the formulae used to describe the set of backward reachable states are closed

---

[3] In (5), we use a second order quantifier over the relation symbol ua, representing the state of the system. This should not worry the reader expert in first-order theorem proving since a higher-order feature is only used to give the definition of pre-image. We will see that we can compute a first-order formula logically equivalent to (5) so that only first-order techniques should be used to mechanize our approach.

under pre-image computation and (ii) both the satisfiability test for safety (line 3) and that for fixed-point (line 2) are effective.

Regarding (i), it is sufficient to prove the following result.

Property 1. Let K be an $\exists$-formula. If τ is of the form (1) or (2), then $Pre(\tau, K)$ is equivalent (modulo T_{ARBAC}) to an effectively computable $\exists$-formula.

Proof. Let $K(ua) := \exists \tilde{u}, \tilde{r}.\gamma(\tilde{u}, \tilde{r}, ua(\tilde{u}, \tilde{r}))$, where γ is a quantifier-free formula. By definition, $Pre(\tau, K)$ is $\exists ua'.(\tau(ua, ua') \wedge K(ua'))$ and there are two cases to consider. The former is when τ is of the form (1). In this case, $\exists ua'.(\tau(ua, ua') \wedge K(ua'))$ is equivalent to

$$\exists u, r, u_1, r_1, r_2, ..., r_k. \left(\begin{array}{c} C(u, r, u_1, r_1, r_2, ..., r_k) \wedge \\ \exists \tilde{u}, \tilde{r}.\gamma(\tilde{u}, \tilde{r}, (ua \oplus (u_1, e^r))(\tilde{u}, \tilde{r})) \end{array} \right)$$

by simple logical manipulations and recalling the definition of K. In turn, this can be expanded to

$$\exists u, r, u_1, r_1, r_2, ..., r_k.(C(u, r, u_1, r_1, r_2, ..., r_k) \wedge$$
$$\exists \tilde{u}, \tilde{r}.\gamma(\tilde{u}, \tilde{r}, (\lambda w, r.(if \ (w = u \wedge r = e^r) \ then \ true \ else \ ua(w, r)))(\tilde{u}, \tilde{r})))$$

by recalling the definition of $\oplus$. It is possible to eliminate the λ-expression by observing that each of its occurrence will be applied to a pair of existentially quantified variables from $\tilde{u}, \tilde{r}$ so that β-reduction can be applied. After this phase, the 'if-then-else' expressions can be eliminated by using a simple case-analysis followed by the moving out of the existential quantifiers that allows us to obtain an $\exists$-formula. This concludes the proof of this case. The second case, i.e. when τ is of the form (2), is omitted because almost identical to the previous. □

Observe also that $Pre(\bigvee_{i=1}^{n} \tau_i, K)$ is equivalent to $\bigvee_{i=1}^{n} Pre(\tau_i, K)$ for τ_i of forms (1) and (2), for $i = 1, ..., n$.

Example 9. To illustrate Property 1, we consider one of the transitions written in Example 7 and the goal in Example 6. We compute the pre-image w.r.t. the second transition in $AATU$ (where HR stands for $HumanResource$ and FT for $FullTime$), i.e.

$$\exists u, r, p.(ua'(u, r) \wedge pa(p, r) \wedge u = Alice \wedge r \succeq FT \wedge p = Access) \wedge$$
$$\exists u_1, r_1, u_2.(ua(u_1, r_1) \wedge r_1 = HR \wedge u_1 \neq Carol \wedge ua' = ua \oplus (u_2, FT)),$$

where ua' is implicitly existentially quantified. By simple logical manipulations, we have

$$\exists u, r, p, u_1, r_1, u_2.(pa(p, r) \wedge (if \ u = u_2 \wedge r = FT \ then \ true \ else \ ua(u, r)) \wedge$$
$$u = Alice \wedge r \succeq FT \wedge p = Access \wedge ua(u_1, r_1) \wedge r_1 = HR \wedge u_1 \neq Carol),$$

which, by case analysis and some simplification steps, can be rewritten to

$$\exists u, r, p, u_1, r_1, u_2.(pa(p, r) \wedge (r = FT \wedge u_2 = Alice \wedge p = Access \wedge$$

$$ua(u_1, r_1) \wedge r_1 = HR \wedge u_1 \neq Carol) \vee$$
$$(pa(p,r) \wedge u \neq u_2 \wedge ua(u,r) \wedge u = Alice \wedge r \succeq FT \wedge p = Access \wedge$$
$$ua(u_1, r_1) \wedge r_1 = HR \wedge u_1 \neq Carol) \vee$$
$$(pa(p,r) \wedge r \neq FT \wedge ua(u,r) \wedge u = Alice \wedge r \succeq FT \wedge p = Access \wedge$$
$$ua(u_1, r_1) \wedge r_1 = HR \wedge u_1 \neq Carol)) \ ,$$

which is an $\exists$-formula according to Property 1.   □

Concerning the decidability of the satisfiability tests for safety and fixed-point in the backward reachability algorithm in Figure 1 (point (ii) above), we observe that the formulae at lines 2 and 3 can be effectively transformed to formulae in the form $\exists \underline{x} \forall \underline{y}.\varphi(\underline{x}, \underline{y}, ua)$ where $\underline{x}$ and $\underline{y}$ are disjoint, which belong to the *Bernays-Schönfinkel-Ramsey* (BSR) class (see, e.g., [14]). To see how this is possible, let us consider the formulae at line 2. This is the conjunction of a $\forall$-formula (ι), an $\exists$-formula (as discussed above, the variable P stores $Pre^n(\tau, \gamma)$, which by Property 1 is an $\exists$-formula), and another $\forall$-formula (as discussed above, the variable B stores $\bigvee_{i=0}^n Pre^i(\tau, \gamma)$ whose negation is a conjunction of $\forall$-formulae by Property 1, which is a $\forall$-formula). By moving out quantifiers (which is always possible as quantified variables can be suitably renamed), it is straightforward to obtain a BSR formula. Now, let us turn our attention to the formula at line 3. It is obtained by conjoining a $\forall$-formula (In is so by assumption) and an $\exists$-formula (stored in the variable P, see previous case). Again, by simple logical manipulations, it is not difficult to obtain a formula in the BSR class. We also observe that checking the satisfiability of BSR formulae modulo T_{ARBAC} can be reduced to checking the satisfiability of formulae in the BSR class since all the axioms of T_{ARBAC} are universal sentences, i.e. BSR formulae. Collecting all these observations, we can state the following result.

Property 2. The satisfiability tests at lines 2 and 3 of the backward reachability procedure in Figure 1 are decidable.

This property is a corollary of the decidability of the satisfiability of the BSR class (see, e.g., [14]). Example 9 above contains an illustration of a satisfiability test to which Property 2 applies.

4.1   Termination

The closure under pre-image computation (Property 1) and the decidability of the satisfiability checks (Property 2) guarantee the possibility to mechanize the backward reachability procedure in Figure 1 but do not eliminate the risk of non-termination. There are various sources of diverge. For example, the existential prefix of a pre-image is extended at each pre-image computation with new variables as shown in the proof of Property 1. Another potential problem is that the fixed-point could not be expressed by using disjunctions of $\exists$-formulae (according to line 4 in Figure 1) even if it exists so that the procedure is only able to compute approximations and thus never terminates. To show that both problems can be avoided and that the procedure in Figure 1 terminates, we follow the approach proposed in [11,5] for proving the termination of backward reachability for certain classes of infinite state systems. We introduce a model-theoretic notion of certain sets of states, called *configurations*, which are the semantic counter-part of ∃-formulae, and then define a well-quasi-order on them: this, according to the results in [5], implies the termination of the backward reachability procedure. For lack of space, the full technical development is omitted and can be found in [7]; here, we only sketch the main ideas. We also point out that this result can be seen as a special case of that in [11], developed in a more general framework that allows for the formalization and the analysis of safety properties for concurrent, distributed, and timed systems as well as algorithms manipulating arrays. However, we believe worthwhile to prove termination for the procedure presented in this paper (along the lines of [11]) as some technical definitions become much simpler.

A *state of the symbolic ARBAC policy* $\Gamma := (In, Tr, C)$ is a structure $\mathcal{M} \in Mod(T_{ARBAC})$, i.e. it is an RBAC policy belonging to a certain class of first-order structures. A *configuration* of Γ is a state $\mathcal{M}$ such that the cardinality of the domain of $\mathcal{M}$ is finite. Intuitively, a configuration is a finite representation of a possibly infinite set of states that "contains at least the part mentioned in the configuration." The following example can help to grasp the underlying intuition.

Example 10. As in Example 5, let $T_{User} = \emptyset$, $T_{Role} = \emptyset$. Consider the ∃-formula: $\exists u, r.(ua(u,r) \land u = e_0^u \land r = e_0^r)$. There is no bound on the number of pairs (e_i^u, e_k^r) in a RBAC policy s satisfying the ∃-formula above provided that $(e_0^u, e_0^r) \in s(ua)$. Our procedure for the reachability problem considers (only) those RBAC policies s of the form $s(ua) = \{(e_0^u, e_0^r)\} \cup \Delta$ where Δ is a (possibly empty) set of pairs (e_i^u, e_k^r) with $i, j \neq 0$. In other words, the procedure considers all those configurations which contain at least the pair (e_0^u, e_0^r) mentioned in the ∃-formula above plus any other (finite) set Δ of pairs.   □

The idea that a configuration represents a (possibly infinite) set of RBAC policies sharing a common (finite) set of user-role assignments can be made precise by using the notion of partial order. A *pre-order* $(P, \leq)$ is the set P endowed with a reflexive and transitive relation. An *upward closed set* U of the pre-order $(P, \leq)$ is such that $U \subseteq P$ and if $p \in U$ and $p \leq q$ then $q \in U$. A *cone* is an upward closed set of the form $\uparrow p = \{q \in P \mid p \leq q\}$. We define a *pre-order on configurations* as follows. Let $\mathcal{M}$ and $\mathcal{M}'$ be configurations of Γ; $\mathcal{M} \leq \mathcal{M}'$ iff there exists an embedding from $\mathcal{M}$ to $\mathcal{M}'$. Roughly, an embedding is a homomorphism that preserves and reflects relations (see [7] for a formal definition) . A configuration is the semantic counter-part of an ∃-formula. Let $[[K]] := \{\mathcal{M} \in Mod(T_{ARBAC}) \mid \mathcal{M} \models K\}$, where K is an ∃-formula.

Lemma 1. *The following facts hold: (i) for every ∃-formula K, the set $[[K]]$ is upward closed and (ii) $[[K_1]] \subseteq [[K_2]]$ iff $(K_1 \Rightarrow K_2)$ is valid modulo T_{ARBAC}, for every pair of ∃-formulae K_1, K_2.*

An upward closed set U is *finitely generated* iff it is a finite union of cones. A pre-order $(P, \leq)$ is a *well-quasi-ordering (wqo)* iff every upward closed sets of P is finitely generated. This is equivalent to the standard definition of wqo, see [11] for a proof. The idea is to use only finitely generated upward closed sets as configurations so that their union is also finitely generated and we can conclude that the backward reachability procedure in Figure 1 is terminating because of the duality between configurations and $\exists$-formulae (Lemma 1).

Theorem 1. *The backward reachability procedure in Figure 1 terminates.*

As a corollary, we immediately obtain the following fact.

Theorem 2. *The user-role reachability problem is decidable.*

This result is more general that those in [13,19] which assume a bounded number of users and roles. We are more general than [18] in allowing for a finite but unknown number of users and roles while in [18] the users are bounded and only the roles are parametric. However, we allow for only a restricted form of negation in the preconditions of *can_assign* actions while [18] seems to allow for arbitrary negation. Moreover, our procedure can consider several initial RBAC policies at the same time while [13,19,18] can handle only one.

Finally, notice that we can reduce other analysis problems (e.g., role containment) to user-role reachability problems and thus show their decidability. For lack of space, this can be found in [7].

5   Preliminary Experiments

We briefly discuss some experiments with a prototype implementation of the symbolic reachability procedure in Figure 1 that we call ASSA, short for Automated Symbolic Security Analyser. We consider the synthetic benchmarks described in [19] and available on the web at [2] whereby both the number of users and roles is bounded. We perform a comparative analysis between ASSA and the state-of-the-art tool in [19], called Stoller below. Our findings shows that ASSA scales better than Stoller on this set of benchmarks; the experiments were conducted on an Intel(R) Core(TM)2 Duo CPU T5870, 2 GHz, 3 GB RAM, running Linux Debian 2.6.32.

A client-server architecture is the most obvious choice to implement the proposed symbolic backward reachability procedure. The client generates the sequence of formulae representing pre-images of the formula representing the goal. In addition, the client is also assumed to generate the formulae characterising the tests for fix-point or for non-empty intersection with the initial set of policies. The server performs the checks for satisfiability modulo T_{ARBAC} and can be implemented by using state-of-the-art automated deduction systems such as automated theorem provers (in our case, SPASS [3]) or SMT solvers (in our case, Z3 [1]). Although these tools are quite powerful, preliminary experiments have shown that the formulae to be checked for satisfiability generated by the client quickly become very large and are not easily solved by available state-of-the-art tools. A closer look at the formulae reveals that they can be greatly simplified with substantial speed-ups in the performances of the reasoning systems. To

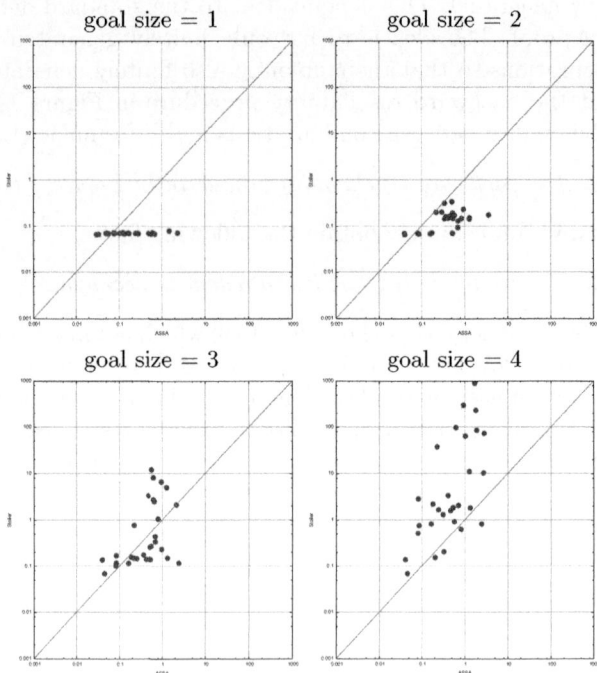

Fig. 2. Comparison between ASSA and Stoller on some benchmarks from [19,2]

this end, some heuristics have been implemented whose description is not possible here for lack of space; the interested reader is pointed to [6] for a complete description and more experiments.

We consider the randomly generated benchmarks in [2], where only the user-role assignment relation ua can be modified by can_assign or can_revoke actions (as assumed in Section 2). These benchmarks were generated under two additional simplifying assumptions: (i) a fixed number of users and roles, and (ii) absence of role hierarchy (this is without loss of generality under assumption (i) as observed in [19]). Besides the number of roles, one of the key parameter of the benchmarks (according to the parametrised complexity result derived in [19]) is the *goal size*, i.e. the number of roles in the set RP of a goal reachability problem (as defined at the end of Section 2) or, equivalently, the number of constants of sort *Role* occurring in the symbolic goal (3) of Section 3.4. The benchmarks are divided in five classes. The first and the second classes were used to evaluate the worst-case behavior of forward search algorithms (i.e. when the goal is unreachable) described in [19]. Our backward procedure (almost) immediately detects unreachability by realizing that no action is backward applicable. The fourth and fifth classes of benchmarks fix the goal size to one while the values of other parameters (e.g., the cardinality of the set R of roles) grow. In particular, the fourth class was used to show that the cost of analysis grows very slowly as a function of the number of roles while the fifth aimed to compare the performances of an enhanced version of the forward and the backward algorithms of [19]. For both classes, ASSA confirms that its running time grows very slowly according to the results reported in [19]. However, ASSA is slightly slower than Stoller because of the overhead of invoking automated reasoning systems for checking for fix-points instead of the *ad hoc* techniques of [19]. The most interesting class of problems is the third, which was used to evaluate the scalability of the backward reachability algorithm of [19] with respect to increasing values of the goal size $1, 2, 3,$ and 4. Figure 2 shows four scatter plots for values $1, 2, 3,$ and 4 of the goal size: the X and Y axes report the median times of ASSA and Stoller, respectively (logarithmic scale), to solve the 32 reachability problems in the third class of the benchmarks. A dot above the diagonal means a better performance of ASSA and viceversa; the time out was set to $1, 800$ sec. Although, both Stoller and ASSA were able to solve all the problems within the time-out, our tool is slower for goal sizes 1 and 2, behaves as Stoller for goal size 3, but outperforms this for goal size 4. These results are encouraging and seem to confirm the scalability of our techniques. For a detailed description of the implementation of ASSA and a more comprehensive experimental evaluation (confirming these results), the reader is pointed to [6].

6   Discussion

We have proposed a symbolic framework for the automated analysis of ARBAC policies that allowed us to prove the decidability of the parametric reachability problem. We used a decidable fragment of first-order logic to represent the states and the actions of ARBAC policies to design a symbolic procedure to explore the (possibly infinite) state space. Preliminary results with a prototype tool implementing the backward reachability procedure in Figure 1 are encouraging. A detailed description of the implementation of the prototype and an extensive experimental analysis is available in [6].

There are two main directions for future work. First, it would be interesting to study to what extent other variants of ARBAC can be formalized in our framework, e.g., for UARBAC [12]. Second, we want to adapt techniques developed in the context of infinite state model checking to eliminate universal quantifiers in guards of administrative actions (called global conditions, see, e.g., [4]), to allow for unrestricted negation in *can_assigns*.

Acknowledgements. This work was partially supported by the "Automated Security Analysis of Identity and Access Management Systems (SIAM)" project funded by Provincia Autonoma di Trento in the context of the "team 2009 - Incoming" COFUND action of the European Commission (FP7), the FP7-ICT-2007-1 Project no. 216471, "AVANTSSAR: Automated Validation of Trust and Security of Service-oriented Architectures," and the PRIN'07 Project 20079E5KM8 (Integrating automated reasoning in model checking: towards push-button formal verification of large-scale and infinite-state systems) funded by MIUR. Francesco Alberti must be thanked for his effort in implementing and benchmarking ASSA.

References

1. http://research.microsoft.com/en-us/um/redmond/projects/z3
2. http://www.cs.stonybrook.edu/~stoller/ccs2007
3. http://www.spass-prover.org
4. Abdulla, P.A., Delzanno, G., Rezine, A.: Parameterized verification of infinite state processes with global conditions. In: Damm, W., Hermanns, H. (eds.) CAV 2007. LNCS, vol. 4590, pp. 145–157. Springer, Heidelberg (2007)
5. Abdulla, P.A., Jonsson, B.: Model checking of systems with many identical timed processes. Theoretical Computer Science, 241–264 (2003)
6. Alberti, F., Armando, A., Ranise, S.: Efficient Symbolic Automated Analysis of Administrative Role Based Access Control Policies. In: Proc. of 6th ACM Symp. on Info. Computer and Comm. Security, ASIACCS 2011 (2011)
7. Armando, A., Ranise, S.: Automated Symbolic Analysis of ARBAC-Policies, (Extended version) (2010), http://st.fbk.eu
8. Clark, K.: Negation as failure. In: Logic and Databases, pp. 293–322. Plenum Press, New York (1978)
9. Crampton, J.: Understanding and developing role-based administrative models. In: Proc. 12th ACM Conf. on Comp. and Comm. Security (CCS), pp. 158–167. ACM Press, New York (2005)
10. Enderton, H.B.: A Mathematical Introduction to Logic. Academic Press, Inc., London (1972)
11. Ghilardi, S., Nicolini, E., Ranise, S., Zucchelli, D.: Towards SMT model checking of array-based systems. In: Armando, A., Baumgartner, P., Dowek, G. (eds.) IJCAR 2008. LNCS (LNAI), vol. 5195, pp. 67–82. Springer, Heidelberg (2008)
12. Li, N., Mao, Z.: Administration in Role Based Access Control. In: Proc. ACM Symp. on Information, Computer, and Communication Security, ASIACCS (2007)
13. Li, N., Tripunitara, M.V.: Security analysis in role-based access control. ACM Transactions on Information and System Security (TISSEC) 9(4), 391–420 (2006)
14. Piskac, R., de Moura, L., Bjoerner, N.: Deciding Effectively Propositional Logic Using DPLL and Substitution Sets. J. of Autom. Reas. 44(4), 401–424 (2010)
15. Sandhu, R., Bhamidipati, V., Munawer, Q.: The ARBAC97 model for role-based control administration of roles. ACM Transactions on Information and System Security (TISSEC) 1(2), 105–135 (1999)
16. Sandhu, R., Coyne, E., Feinstein, H., Youmann, C.: Role-Based Access Control Models. IEEE Computer 2(29), 38–47 (1996)
17. Sasturkar, A., Yang, P., Stoller, S.D., Ramakrishnan, C.R.: Policy analysis for administrative role based access control. In: Proc. of the 19th Computer Security Foundations (CSF) Workshop, IEEE Computer Society Press, Los Alamitos (July 2006)
18. Stoller, S.D., Yang, P., Gofman, M.I., Ramakrishnan, C.R.: Symbolic Reachability Analysis for Parameterized Administrative Role Based Access Control. In: Proc. of. SACMAT 2009, pp. 445–454 (2007)
19. Stoller, S.D., Yang, P., Ramakrishnan, C.R., Gofman, M.I.: Efficient policy analysis for administrative role based access control. In: Proc. of the 14th Conf. on Computer and Communications Security (CCS). ACM Press, New York (2007)

Influence of Attribute Freshness on Decision Making in Usage Control*

Leanid Krautsevich[1], Aliaksandr Lazouski[1], Fabio Martinelli[2],
and Artsiom Yautsiukhin[2]

[1] Department of Computer Science, University of Pisa, Pisa, Italy
{krautsev,lazouski}@di.unipi.it
[2] Istituto di Informatica e Telematica, Consiglio Nazionale delle Ricerche, Pisa, Italy
{fabio.martinelli,artsiom.yautsiukhin}@iit.cnr.it

Abstract. The usage control (UCON) model demands for continuous control over objects of a system. Access decisions are done several times within a usage session and are performed on the basis of mutable attributes. Values of attributes in modern highly-dynamic and distributed systems sometimes are not up-to-date, because attributes may be updated by several entities and reside outside the system domain. Thus, the access decisions about a usage session are made under uncertainties, while existing usage control approaches are based on the assumption that all attributes are up-to-date.

In this paper we propose an approach which helps to make a rational access decision even if some uncertainty presents. The proposed approach uses the continuous-time Markov chains (CTMC) in order to compute the probability of unnoticed changes of attributes and risk analysis for making a decision.

Keywords: usage control, freshness of attributes, risk, continuous-time Markov chains.

1 Introduction

The usage control (UCON) model, proposed by Sandhu and Park [20], is a successor of access control which unifies recent advances in access control in one solid model. Access decisions in UCON are based on the values of attributes, similar to the attribute-based access control model [25]. The main peculiarity of UCON is the assumption that some attributes may change after granting access to a subject [16]. Thus, the access decision has to be made not only before a session, but also during the session. These principles of UCON are known as mutability of attributes and continuity of control.

The model works well until we are sure that values of attributes we have are the real current values. In fact, in some cases values of attributes used for the access decision making are old. Such situation happens because these attributes

---

* This work was partly supported by EU-FP7-ICT CONSEQUENCE and EU-FP7-ICT NESSoS projects.

J. Cuellar et al. (Eds.): STM 2010, LNCS 6710, pp. 35–50, 2011.

might be checked only in some discrete points of time. The real values of the attributes between these points of time are unknown. Natural solution can be to reduce the interval between these points, but this is often impossible because of the cost of the checks (in terms of additional resources, bandwidth, CPU cycles required for getting and processing new data, etc.). Sometimes it is simply impossible to get fresh values of attributes because of natural delays of delivery (e.g., rating of an on-line seller is several weeks old because buyers provide their feedback only after some time after a deal is accomplished). Thus, we have to make an access decision using old, not fresh values.

Krautsevich et al. [13] proposed an approach based on risk analysis which helps to predict when possible losses caused by an incorrect decision overcome possible benefits in the presence of uncertainty. The authors proposed to exploit the discrete-time Markov chains in order to estimate the probability of a violation of security policies. The discrete-time Markov chains are well suited when the number of changes of an attribute is known (e.g., in an on-line auction, a number of accomplished deals is known, even if not all feedbacks have been uploaded). The authors also considered a simple policy: policy consisted of rules that contained one attribute and a threshold. Note, that risk in such approach arises because of imperfect system (impossibility to get fresh values of attributes) rather than because of existing threats for a system, as risk is usually used in the security community [23,9,5,22,7,19].

The main contribution of this paper is the approach which is more suitable for the attributes for which we do not know how many times the attributes have changed, but know the time elapsed since the last check (when the exact value was known). Moreover, the current approach is applicable to more complex policies composed of atomic rules that makes the analysis more practical. We have shown that policies can be analysed in two different ways depending on the cause of losses (losses caused by failure of an attribute or failure of the whole policy).

The rest of the paper is organised as follows. We provide basic information about UCON, risk, and considered uncertainties in Section 2. Section 3 describes the running example used in the paper. We present a method for risk-aware decision-making on the basis of CTMC in Section 4. Section 5 describes the risk-aware decision-making for complex policies of several attributes. Possible risk mitigation strategies are outlined in Section 6. We conclude the paper with the related work (Section 7) and the conclusion and future work (Section 8).

2 Background

2.1 UCON

The most important features of the UCON model in the context of our paper are mutability of attributes and continuity of control. Mutability of attributes means that attributes required for making an access decision can change during a usage session. Therefore, it is not enough to evaluate attributes once before the access is granted, but continuous evaluation is also required when the usage session is active.

Next to usual authorisations the UCON model also checks for conditions and obligations. Authorisations are the logical predicates which depend on attributes of subject and object (location of the subject, size of the object, etc.). Other attributes (of the environment in general) which can affect access decisions are taken into account in conditions (e.g., amount of space left on the hard disk, time of the access, etc.). Obligations are the actions which must be fulfilled (e.g., a subject must sign an agreement before accessing a resource). In this work we concentrated on authorisations and conditions only.

2.2   Risk Analysis

Risk is a well-known instrument for assessment for making decisions when some uncertainties present. The idea is to assess possible losses and compare them with possible benefits. In most cases risk is used to judge if a system is secure enough or some additional controls should be installed. Uncertainties in this cases are expressed as average probability that a threat will occur. The following well-known formula is used for computation of risk [9,23,1]:

$$Risk = Probability\_of\_event \times Impact\_of\_event \qquad (1)$$

In our paper we consider uncertainties about the actual values of attributes which are required for making an access decision.

2.3   Uncertainties

There are two types of unintentional uncertainties which arise during collecting of attributes: timeliness and currency [4]. These uncertainties may lead to incorrect decisions, i.e., allow access when it should be forbidden or grant access to an unauthorised party. Timeliness means that we cannot check an attribute very frequently because of some reasons (e.g., it is simply impossible, or impractical, or too costly, etc.). An example of such attribute could be position of a person every half an hour. Sending such information every minute will consume too much power, bandwidth, and CPU cycles of a monitoring system. Currency is a problem of other kind: there is a natural delay in the delivery of a fresh value. After accomplishing a deal an on-line buyer waits for the delivery, tests a product, and only then submits its feedback. All this time other buyers see the old reputation value of the seller. In our approach we take these two uncertainties into account by predicting a real value of an attribute and checking if access policies are satisfied.

Our approach can be also applied to some intentional uncertainties, though the problem has to be stated a bit differently. Imagine, we have one trustworthy value at some point of time. When we get a new value we may have some doubts about its trustworthiness, i.e., we believe that there is a possibility that the value is fake. Then, our task is to check how trusted is the recently sent value.

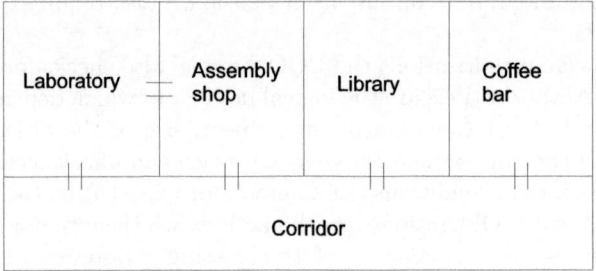

Fig. 1. Structure of the R&D department

3   Running Example

As a running example, we consider a research and development (R&D) department of a small company, which develops and produces prototypes of novel
electronic devices. The department consists of a laboratory, an assembly shop, a
library, a coffee bar, and the corridor, which connects all these rooms. There is
an additional direct door from the laboratory to the shop. The structure of the
company is presented in Figure 1.

In the example, we consider an engineer who works on a new project and uses
a tablet computer for this purpose. In order to protect secrets about new devices
from a possible leakage, the personnel is not allowed to access and use sensitive
information outside of the laboratory and the assembly shop. The engineer is
allowed to use his device outside of the laboratory and the assembly shop for
any other purposes but for working on the project.

The position of any person which has access to trade secrets is controlled
by a location tracking system. A special sensor is implanted into the tablet
laptops which sends the information about the position of the device every 15
minutes. It has been found that often the engineers go to the coffee bar to take
some coffee and do not close the usage session of projects. Thus, sometimes
they have access to the secrete information outside of the allowed rooms, while
sessions are still active and the next position check will be only several minutes
afterwards. Reducing the period between position checks results in more power
and bandwidth consumptions. Thus, there is a need for rational determination
of the time when the check has to be scheduled.

4   Risk-Aware Decision for Policy of One Attribute

In this section we consider the usage of an object that is controlled by a policy of
one rule that constraints one attribute. The generalisation for policies of several
rules is done in Section 5. We assume that we know a precise value of an attribute
in some point of time in the past and would like to tell if we should continue
the session or should stop it, even if there is some uncertainty about the current

value. In order to make a rational decision, we, first, compute the probability that the attribute has changed and its current value violates the policy. Then we apply risk management (using Formula 1) to make a decision under this uncertainty.

4.1   Computation of Probability

We start with the evaluation of the probability of policy violation. We consider a discrete attribute and assume that attribute satisfies the Markovian property, which means that a future attribute value depends only on the present value and does not depend on its previous values. Another assumption is that the average time between changes of attribute value exponentially distributed with the rate parameter v. These assumptions allow modelling the behaviour of attribute values using a CTMC.

The Markov chain contains states and transitions between states. The states of the chain represent the values of the attribute, and the transitions describe the changes of the attribute. The values of attribute can be grouped into two domains: the "bad" domain B and the "good" domain G. If the attribute takes a value from the "bad" domain then the policy is violated and the usage session should be revoked. If the attribute takes a value from the "good" domain then the policy holds and the usage is continued. The states of Markov chain can be gathered into two groups I_B and I_G respectively. The set of all values of attribute is $X = B \cup G$ and the appropriate set of states is $I = I_B \cup I_G$. In addition, we define the following variables:

- $x \in X$ is a value of the attribute. By x_i we denote the value of the state i;
- v_i is the rate parameter of exponential distribution for the time of jumping from state i to another state, the value $\frac{1}{v_i}$ is the average life-time of the attribute with the value x_i;
- p_{ij} is the one-step transition probability (the probability that the process makes a direct jump from the state i to j without visiting any intermediate state);
- t_0 is the time when we know the exact value of the attribute;
- t' is the time, when we make an access decision about the usage session. The last update of the attribute was at t_0.

We assume that the values v_i and p_{ij} can be determined and adjusted using statistical methods during the analysis of the past behaviour of the system. The history of an attribute changes between possible states is require for this purpose. Using v_i and p_{ij} we can evaluate the probability of policy violation on the basis of the approach described below.

The transitions between the states are described with the infinitesimal transition rates ($q_{ij} \in Q$). The infinitesimal transition rates are defined as

$$q_{ij} = v_i p_{ij}, \ \forall i, j \in I \text{ and } i \neq j. \tag{2}$$

The infinitesimal transition rates uniquely determine the rates v_i and one-step transition probabilities p_{ij}:

$$v_i = \sum_{\forall j \neq i} q_{ij}. \tag{3}$$

$$p_{ij} = \frac{q_{ij}}{v_i}. \tag{4}$$

Suppose, the value of an attribute is $x_i \in G$ (we are in state $i \in I_G$) at time t_0. We need to find the probability of $x_j \in B$ ($j \in I_B$) during the period from t_0 till t'. This problem is solved by replacing "bad" states with an absorbing state. An absorbing state is the state which the process can not leave. The way to model an absorbing state is to set leaving rates to zero. In our case the whole subset of states I_B should be replaced with one adsorbing state a. The modified Markov chain can be seen as

$$I^* = (I_G) \cup \{a\} \text{ and } v_i^* = \begin{cases} v_i, & \forall i \in I_G; \\ 0, & i = a. \end{cases} \tag{5}$$

The modified infinitesimal transition rates correspondingly:

$$q_{ij}^* = \begin{cases} q_{ij}, & \forall i, j \in I_G \text{ with } i \neq j; \\ \sum_{k \in I_B} q_{ik}, & \forall i \in I_G, \ j = a; \\ 0, & i = a, \ \forall j \in I_G. \end{cases} \tag{6}$$

In the sequel, all indicators with $*$ refer to the Markov chain with absorbing states (e.g., q_{ij}^*, v_i^*, etc).

Example 1. The location attribute in the R&D department is a Markov chain of five states (see Figure 2a). However, the number of states can be modified, because the access to the database should be forbidden if the researcher is in the library, the coffee bar, or the corridor. Thus, these states could be replaced with one absorbing state a. The modified Markov chain is presented in Figure 2b. The following one-step transition probabilities (P) and rates (V) have been determined according to the past observations.

$$P = \begin{bmatrix} 0 & 0.7186 & 0 & 0 & 0.2814 \\ 0.7200 & 0 & 0 & 0 & 0.2800 \\ 0 & 0 & 0 & 0 & 1.0000 \\ 0 & 0 & 0 & 0 & 1.0000 \\ 0.4976 & 0.4976 & 0.0021 & 0.0028 & 0 \end{bmatrix}, \quad V = \begin{bmatrix} 0.0167 \\ 0.0250 \\ 0.0083 \\ 0.0333 \\ 2.0098 \end{bmatrix}. \tag{7}$$

In the example we consider that time is measured in minutes. So the rate $v_1 = 0.0167$ means that the chain leaves state 1 with the average time $t_{avg} = \frac{1}{v_1} = 60$ minutes.

Let the matrix Q of the infinitesimal transition rates q_{ij} for initial chain be computed using Equation 2.

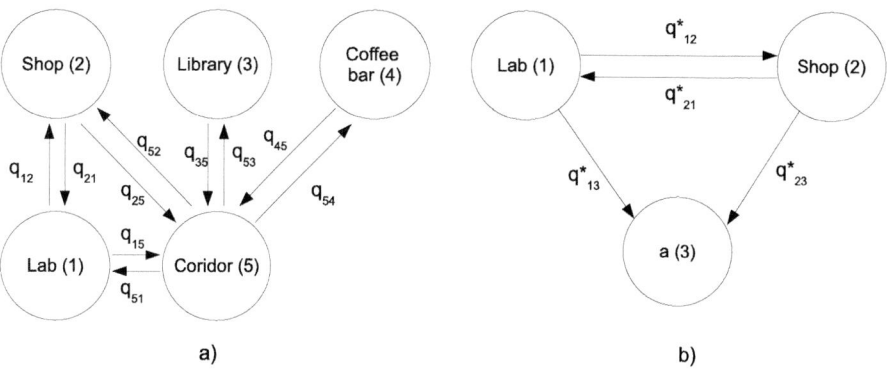

Fig. 2. Markov chains for User Location

$$Q = \begin{bmatrix} 0 & 0.0120 & 0 & 0 & 0.0047 \\ 0.0180 & 0 & 0 & 0 & 0.0070 \\ 0 & 0 & 0 & 0 & 0.0083 \\ 0 & 0 & 0 & 0 & 0.0333 \\ 1.0 & 1.0 & 0.0042 & 0.0056 & 0 \end{bmatrix}. \tag{8}$$

The matrix Q^* of the modified infinitesimal transition rates after inserting of the absorbing state according to Formula 6 is given by:

$$Q^* = \begin{bmatrix} 0 & 0.0120 & 0.0047 \\ 0.0180 & 0 & 0.0070 \\ 0 & 0 & 0 \end{bmatrix}. \tag{9}$$

The matrix V^* of the modified according to Formula 3 rates given by:

$$V^* = \begin{bmatrix} 0.0167 \\ 0.0250 \\ 0 \end{bmatrix}. \tag{10}$$

Now we need to find transient probabilities from the initial state i into absorbing state a, i.e., the probaility of policy violation. We apply the uniformisation method to compute transient state probabilities p_{ij}^* [12,24]. The uniformisation method replaces a CTMC by a discrete-time analogue, which is more suitable for numerical computations. The uniformisation is done by replacing the transition rates of Markov chain v_i^* with a sole transition rate v^* such as

$$v^* \geq v_i^*, \; \forall i \in I. \tag{11}$$

Usually, the following strategy is applied:

$$v^* = \max_{\forall v_i^* \in V^*} v_i^*. \tag{12}$$

The discrete-time Markov chain makes a transition from a state with probabilities

$$\overline{p^*}_{ij} = \begin{cases} \frac{v_i^*}{v^*} p_{ij}^* = \frac{q_{ij}^*}{v^*}, & \forall\, i \ne j; \\ 1 - \frac{v_i^*}{v^*}, & \forall i = j. \end{cases} \tag{13}$$

Now we have all required parameters and we can skip the mathematical proofs, which can be found here [24, pages 167-168]. Finally, the transition state probabilities can be found as

$$p_{ij}^*(t') = \sum_{n=0}^{\infty} e^{-v^*(t'-t_0)} \frac{(v^*(t'-t_0))^n}{n!} \overline{p^*}_{ij}^{(n)}, \ \forall i, j \in I \text{ and } t' > t_0. \tag{14}$$

where $\overline{p^*}_{ij}^{(n)}$ can be recursively computed from

$$\overline{p^*}_{ij}^{(n)} = \sum_{x_k \in I} \overline{p^*}_{ik}^{(n-1)} \overline{p^*}_{kj}, \ n = 1, 2... \tag{15}$$

starting with $\overline{p^*}_{ii}^{(0)} = 1$ and $\overline{p^*}_{ij}^{(0)} = 0$ for $i \ne j$.

For fixed $t' > t_0$ the infinite series can be truncated because of the negligible impact of the residue. The truncation number M (upper limit of summation) in Formula 14 can be chosen as

$$M = v^*t' + c\sqrt{v^*t'} \tag{16}$$

for some c with $0 < c \le c_0(\varepsilon)$, where ε is a tolerance number [24, page 169].

Equation 14 gives a matrix of probabilities. The probability of policy violation is $p_v = p_{ia}^*(t')$ in case we consider the transition from the state i to the absorbing state a.

Example 2. We continue Example 1. Choose $v_{max}^* = \max\limits_{V^*} v_i^* = 0.025$ according to Formulas 12 and 10. The matrix $\overline{P^*}$ of transition probabilities for the discrete-time Markov chain according to Formula 13 is given by:

$$\overline{P^*} = \begin{bmatrix} 0.33 & 0.48 & 0.19 \\ 0.72 & 0 & 0.28 \\ 0 & 0 & 1 \end{bmatrix}. \tag{17}$$

Suppose that we know that an engineer is in the lab (state 1) at time $t_0 = 0$. Using Formulas 14 and 15 we find that at $t_1' = 7$ minutes the probability that the engineer has left allowed area is $p_v^1 = p_{13} = 0.0330$, while the same probability after $t_2' = 14$ minutes is $p_v^2 = p_{13} = 0.0659$.

4.2 Decision Making

Two possible decisions about the further access are to continue or to revoke the access. Therefore, possible outcomes of such decisions under uncertainty are:

Table 1. Decision matrix

	Satisfied policy	Failed policy
Continue access	C^{CS}	C^{CF}
Revoke access	C^{RS}	C^{RF}

- usage session is continued when it should be continued;
- usage session is continued when it should be revoked;
- usage session is revoked when it should be continued;
- usage session is revoked when it should be revoked.

Every outcome either results in some benefits or losses. Therefore, we assign a cost to every outcome (see Table 1). The cost is a qualitative value (e.g., the amount of money) which represents the utility of the outcome for the company. We assume that the cost is positive if the right decision is made (e.g., the resource owner gains benefits allowing usage for a unauthorised subject). The cost is negative in the case of wrong decisions (e.g., the resource owner suffers losses if the access is granted erroneously).

Usually, the benefit of allowing the access to a right user is a fixed value, e.g., a user pays money for the usage of a resource to the resource provider. The benefit of revocation of the access to a malicious user often is zero, because there is no explicit benefit of such action. The loss of allowing access to a malicious user is either policy specific or depends on the nature of the attributes (see Section 5.2). The loss of revoking access of a regular user is, usually, results in some loss of reputation, however sometimes losses caused by revoking access to a regular user are significant since in this case we also have loss of productivity.

There is a well developed decision theory [11] that allows making a decision under risk and uncertainty. We apply the probability-weighted utility theory for analysis of alternatives. The idea is to compare risks of allowing access and risk of denying access.

We know the probability of policy violation $p_v(t')$ at the moment of time t' which has been found in Section 4.1. According to the Formula 1 the possible benefit of allowing further access is $(1-p_v(t'))*C^{CS}$. On the other hand, allowing access we also suffer some losses: $p_v(t') * C^{CF}$. The same logic can be applied to another alternative (to revoke access). Thus, the access should be allowed if:

$$(1 - p_v(t')) * C^{CS} - p_v(t') * C^{CF} > p_v(t') * C^{RF} - (1 - p_v(t')) * C^{RS} \quad (18)$$

Example 3. The example of the decision matrix is presented in Table 2. Suppose the company gains $C^{CS} = 20$ Euro in average per one access of a trusted user to the database, and the access of a malicious user results in losses C^{CF} of 2000 Euro. If the work on the project is idle because the access of the trusted user is revoked the company loses 100 Euro (C^{RS}). If the malicious user is prevented of accessing the database the company gains no benefits and suffers no losses ($C^{RF} = 0$).

Table 2. Example of the decision matrix

	Satisfied policy	Failed policy
Continue access	20	-2000
Revoke access	-100	0

The probability of policy violation after $t_1' = 7$ minutes is $p_v^1 = 0.0330$. When we apply Formula 18 we see that $-46.6 > -96.7$, and the usage session can be continued. When we consider this inequality after $t_2' = 14$ minutes ($p_v^2 = 0.0659$) we see the opposite situation: $-113 < -93.4$, and the usage session should be revoked or some mitigation strategy should be applied.

The start of a process from different states can lead to different decisions about the usage session. The probability of policy violation after $t_3' = 10$ minutes is $p_v^3 = 0.0471$ if the process start from the state 1 (the engineer is in the laboratory), in this case $-75.1 > -95.3$ and the access can be continued. The probability of policy violation after $t_3' = 10$ minutes is $p_v^3 = 0.0658$ if the process starts from the state 2 (the engineer is in the assembly shop), in this case $-113 < -93.4$ and some mitigation strategies should be applied.

5   Risk of Violation of Complex Policy

Frequently, a policy consists of a number of complex usage rules. A complex rule contains several atomic rules, that constrain different attributes of a subject, an object, and an environment. In our paper we consider only the following three operators for aggregation of rules: conjunction (AND), disjunction (OR), and negation (NOT). These are basic operators, though the approach can be extended for specific operators if needed (e.g., using the operations from [3]).

We assume that the attributes are statistically independent. This property can be guaranteed by the policy designer that should choose attributes in a proper way. In case when dependent rules (i.e., rules which are constructed using the same attributes) appear in the same complex policy conditional probabilities have to be used (i.e., probability of failure of one rule with the condition that another rule fails).

5.1   Combination of Probabilities

The probability that a complex rule does not hold can be assessed using the probabilities that atomic rules do not hold. An atomic rule r constrains one attribute and the probability p_r of rule violation is assessed using CTMC or any other method. Consider two simple rules α and β with probabilities of violation p_α and p_β. The probability of violation p_γ of the complex rule γ is computed as follows:

$\gamma = \alpha \ AND \ \beta$ **:** the rule γ fails in three cases: when the rule α fails and the rule β holds, when the rule β fails and the rule α holds, or when they both fail simultaneously. Therefore, the probability of the failure of the complex rule γ is a summation on the probabilities of each case.

$$
\begin{aligned}
p_\gamma &= p_\alpha \oplus p_\beta \\
&= p_\alpha * (1 - p_\beta) + (1 - p_\alpha) * p_\beta + p_\alpha * p_\beta \\
&= p_\alpha + p_\beta - p_\alpha * p_\beta
\end{aligned}
\tag{19}
$$

$\gamma = \alpha \ OR \ \beta$: the rule γ fails only if both rules α and β fail. Thus, the probability of failure of the complex rule γ is a multiplication of probabilities of failure of the rule α and the rule β.

$$
p_\gamma = p_\alpha \otimes p_\beta = p_\alpha * p_\beta
\tag{20}
$$

$\gamma = NOT \ \alpha$: the rule γ holds, when the rule α fails. Thus,

$$
p_\gamma = \neg p_\alpha = 1 - p_\alpha
\tag{21}
$$

Example 4. Consider the following situation. An engineer involved in one project requires access to the data of another on-going project. A complex policy allows to do this only if the engineer is in the laboratory and either the manager of another project or the engineer's supervisor is in the laboratory as well. The simple rules are

- α is "the engineer is in the lab";
- β_1 is "the manager of the another project is in the lab";
- β_2 is "the engineer's supervisor is in the lab".

The complex rule γ can be seen as $\gamma = \alpha \ AND \ (\beta_1 \ OR \ \beta_2)$. The probability of violation of the complex rule is p_γ.

$$
\begin{aligned}
p_\gamma &= p_\alpha \oplus (p_{\beta_1} \otimes p_{\beta_2}) \\
&= p_\alpha \oplus (p_{\beta_1} * p_{\beta_2}) \\
&= p_\alpha + p_{\beta_1} * p_{\beta_2} - p_\alpha * p_{\beta_1} * p_{\beta_2}
\end{aligned}
\tag{22}
$$

5.2   Combination of Losses and Benefits

There are two possibilities for assigning costs to a complex rule. The first one is when four costs for the decision matrix (see Table 1) are assigned for the whole complex policy. This situation is applicable if the costs do not depend on the cause of policy failure. Thus, it does not matter which atomic rule fails, because we suffer the same amount of losses. This situation is easy for policy-makers, because only 4 costs are required for computations. The risk-aware decision about a usage session for the complex rule is done in the same way as for a policy of an atomic rule. The only difference is that probabilities have to be computed using the formulas given in Section 5.1.

The second possibility is applicable when a more fine-grained analysis is required. In such case we need to distinguish between losses caused by a failure of one attribute or another one. Such situation usually happens when satisfaction of one rule is much more important for us than the satisfaction of another one. C^{CS} is assigned to the whole policy because we get this benefit only if all rules are satisfied. It also does not matter why access to a honest user has been revoked. Therefore, this loss (C^{RF}) is also rule-independent and should be assigned to the whole policy. We also assume that there is no difference why we revoked access of unauthorised person (C^{RS}).

The rule-dependent cost is the cost of a violation when the access has not been prevented (but is had to be). If one rule is more important than another one, we have to consider different losses (C^{CF}) caused by violation of corresponding rules. Thus, we should combine risks to tackle this issue.

$\gamma = \alpha \ AND \ \beta :$ The risk of failure of the complex rule γ in case of conjunction is a summation of risks. Here we follow the same strategy which is applied in usual risk assessment methodologies (e.g., [23,1]) when there are several independent risks which should be considered together.

$$R_\gamma^{CF} = C_\alpha^{CF} * p_\alpha + C_\beta^{CF} * p_\beta. \tag{23}$$

When we combine other complex rules we do not already have separate costs. On the other hand here we simply should sum up all (n) risks:

$$R_{complex}^{CF} = \sum_{i=1}^{n} R_i^{CF}. \tag{24}$$

$\gamma = \alpha \ OR \ \beta :$ The risk of failure of the complex rule γ in case of disjunction is equal to summed up losses when all atomic rules fail. The idea behind this combination is the following. We suffer losses only when all rules fail, but in this case we suffer losses from failure of all rules.

$$R_\gamma^{CF} = (C_\alpha^{CF} + C_\beta^{CF}) * p_\alpha * p_\beta. \tag{25}$$

Combination of risks of complex rules if we have n or-brunches is

$$R_{complex}^{CF} = (\sum_{i=1}^{n} C_i^{CF})(\prod_{j=1}^{n} p_j) = (C_1^{CF} * p_1) \prod_{j=2}^{n} p_j + \dots$$
$$+ (C_n^{CF} * p_n) \prod_{j=1}^{n-1} p_j = R_1^{CF} \prod_{j=2}^{n} p_j + \dots + R_n^{CF} \prod_{j=1}^{n-1} p_j \tag{26}$$

$\gamma = NOT \ \alpha :$ Negation influence only probability and, therefore, should be eliminated before considering losses. We propose to use Morgan laws in order to leave negations only for atomic rules where they can be easily used for changing probabilities as it is shown in Section 5.1.

Example 5. Consider the same example we had in Example 4, but let now the costs of violation be different. As it has been explained above, the following costs are assigned for the whole complex policy: C_γ^{CS}, C_γ^{RF}, C_γ^{RS}. Costs of failure of each atomic rule are: C_α^{CF}, $C_{\beta1}^{CF}$, $C_{\beta1}^{CF}$. The possible losses (R_γ^{CF}) caused by granting an access when, in fact, some rule has failed are:

$$
\begin{aligned}
R_\gamma^{CF} &= R_\alpha^{CF} + R_\beta^{CF} * p_{\beta2} + R_{\beta2}^{CF} * p_{\beta1} \\
&= C_\alpha^{CF} * p_\alpha + C_\beta^{CF} * p_{\beta1} * p_{\beta2} + C_{\beta2}^{CF} * p_{\beta1} * p_{\beta2}
\end{aligned}
\tag{27}
$$

6 Possible Mitigation Strategies

In this section we discuss what to do when the condition of Equation 18 fails. Naturally, the simplest solution which comes to the mind is to revoke the further access. However, this simplest solution is not applicable in all situations and, often, by far not the best one. Note, that we make a decision based on probabilities and this means that we can be wrong.

Other mitigation strategies are possible. First of all, the current session can be simply suspended unless a fresh value is received and a solid decision can be made. Another possibility is simply to ask for a fresh value right in the moment when Equation 18 fails. This is, probably, is the best strategy in our running example. When none of the proposed strategies are applicable an additional attribute may be requested, which somehow mitigates a possibility of granting the access to an unauthorised subject. One more strategy is to rise an alarm which notifies a responsible person that a suspicious operation has taken place. This could be a message to an administrator or a marked event in a log file.

As you see an immediate revocation of an access is not the only possibility which can be followed by noticing a suspicious usage session. These strategies should help administrators to react appropriately depending on the environment where our risk-based decision making approach is applied.

7 Related Work

Risk has been used by several researchers for empowering access control. In all these papers risk is used to make an access decision taking into account that granting the access is connected with some threat. This source of risk is different from the one we use in our paper (uncertainties associated with a current value of an attribute).

Some authors use risk as a static parameter which simply helps to assign correct privileges taking into account possible losses [15,10,21]. For example, Skalka et al. [21] discussed an approach for risk evaluation of authorisations, the formal approach is used to assess and combine the risks of assertions that is used in authorisation decision. Other authors use risk as a dynamically changing value which depends on the current value of possible losses and benefits as well as on the probability of abusing granting privileges by a concrete subject [26,7,17,6]. Deip et al. [7] show how risk of granting access can be computed and a decision is made if risk is less than a threshold. McGraw [17] pointed out that risk should be compared with operational needs. Unfortunately, the author did not provide any information about how this risk and operational needs can be calculated. Zhang et al. [26] also did not show how risk is computed but stated that risk should be compared with possible benefits. The authors paid more attention to propagation of risk and benefits through a trust chain. Ni et al. [19] consider the parameters required for computation of risk as static, but use a notion of "access quota", which is given to a subject and reduces with access of subjects to some resources according to a risk level.

Several authors paid more attention to incorporating risk semantics in access policies rather than to the computation of risk. For example, the policy language, proposed by Aziz et al. [2], contains three types of risks: operational, combinatorial, and conflict of interest. Dimmock et al. [8] show how OASIS access control system and its role-based policy language can be extended with trust and risk analysis.

Krautsevich et al. [14] also applied risk analysis for usage control model in order to select the less risky data processor in service-oriented architecture. The authors also indicated how risk can change after granting access to a data processor and how the data processor can reduce its risk level to provide a better service.

Trustworthiness of policy arguments and update mechanisms have been also investigated by several authors. Nauman et al. [18] provide a way to verify the attribute update behaviour (together with information flow behaviour) and showed how this behaviour can be measured and analysed against UCON policies.

8   Conclusion and Future Work

In this paper we presented an approach which helps to make decisions even if values of attributes are not up-to-date. In this approach we do not need to know the amount of changes of attributes, but just time passes after the last update. Mutability of attributes was modelled by means of CTMC where states are possible attribute values, and transitions are possible changes of the attribute. This improvement makes the approach more realistic. We also considered more complex policies and determined how risk should be computed in such settings. We discovered that the cost of violation sometime depends on the attribute which can take an unwanted value or on the violation of the policy itself. In both cases aggregation of losses must be done differently. We suppose that in most cases the simplest analysis (e.g., when costs assigned to the whole policy) is applied and only in very specific situations the fine-grained analysis is required.

As the future work we would like to make the approach more effective by using the values (probabilities) found during the previous access check rather than recomputing the values from the beginning. Such on-line approach should significantly reduce computational cost. Another possible direction of the model improvement is to consider cases of dependent attributes. This issue requires complex mathematical models for implementing correlated Markov chains. In addition, we are going to elaborate the model for applying mitigation strategy and incorporate it in the overall framework more formally. Finally, we are going to make a prototype of the proposed usage control model in order to estimate possible overhead in the decision making process.

Acknowledgments. We would like to thank the anonymous reviewers for their helpful comments.

References

1. Alberts, C.J., Dorofee, A.J.: OCTAVE Criteria. Technical Report CMU/SEI-2001-TR-016, CERT (December 2001)
2. Aziz, A.B., Foley, A.S., Herbert, A.J., Swart, A.G.: Reconfiguring role based access control policies using risk semantics. Journal of High Speed Networks 15(3), 261–273 (2006)
3. Bonatti, P., De Capitani di Vimercati, S., Samarati, P.: An algebra for composing access control policies. ACM Transactions on Information and System Security 5(1), 1–35 (2002)
4. Bouzeghoub, M., Peralta, V.: A framework for analysis of data freshness. In: Proceedings of the International Workshop on Information Quality in Information Systems, pp. 59–67 (2004)
5. Butler, S.A.: Security attribute evaluation method: a cost-benefit approach. In: Proceedings of the 24th International Conference on Software Engineering (ICSE 2002), pp. 232–240. ACM Press, New York (2002)
6. Cheng, P.-C., Rohatgi, P., Keser, C., Karger, P.A., Wagner, G.M., Reninger, A.S.: Fuzzy multi-level security: An experiment on quantified risk-adaptive access control. In: Proceedings of the 2007 IEEE Symposium on Security and Privacy, pp. 222–230. IEEE Computer Society, Washington, DC, USA (2007)
7. Diep, N.N., Hung, L.X., Zhung, Y., Lee, S., Lee, Y.-K., Lee, H.: Enforcing access control using risk assessment. In: Proceedings of the Fourth European Conference on Universal Multiservice Networks (ECUMN 2007), pp. 419–424. IEEE Computer Society, Washington, DC, USA (2007)
8. Dimmock, N., Belokosztolszki, A., Eyers, D., Bacon, J., Moody, K.: Using trust and risk in role-based access control policies. In: Proceedings of the 9th ACM Symposium on Access Control Models and Technologies, pp. 156–162. ACM, New York (2004)
9. Gordon, L.A., Loeb, M.P.: Managing Cybersecurity Resources: a Cost-Benefit Analysis. McGraw Hill, New York (2006)
10. Han, Y., Hori, Y., Sakurai, K.: Security policy pre-evaluation towards risk analysis. In: Proceedings of the 2008 International Conference on Information Security and Assurance (ISA 2008), pp. 415–420. IEEE Computer Society, Washington, DC, USA (2008)
11. Hanson, S.O.: Decision theory: A brief introduction (August 1994)
12. Ibe, O.C.: Markov processes for stochastic modeling. Academic Press, London (2009)
13. Krautsevich, L., Lazouski, A., Martinelli, F., Yautsiukhin, A.: Risk-aware usage decision making in highly dynamic systems. In: Proceedings of the The Fifth International Conference on Internet Monitoring and Protection, Barcelona, Spain (May 2010)

14. Krautsevich, L., Lazouski, A., Martinelli, F., Yautsiukhin, A.: Risk-based usage control for service oriented architecture. In: Proceedings of the 18th Euromicro Conference on Parallel, Distributed and Network-Based Processing. IEEE Computer Society Press, Los Alamitos (2010)
15. Li, Y., Sun, H., Chen, Z., Ren, J., Luo, H.: Using trust and risk in access control for grid environment. In: Proceedings of the 2008 International Conference on Security Technology, pp. 13–16. IEEE Computer Society, Washington, DC, USA (2008)
16. Martinelli, F., Mori, P., Vaccarelli, A.: Towards continuous usage control on grid computational services. In: Proceedings of the Joint International Conference on Autonomic and Autonomous Systems and International Conference on Networking and Services, ICAS/ICNS 2005 (2005)
17. McGraw, R.W.: Risk-adaptable access control (radac) (6/08/09), http://csrc.nist.gov/news_events/privilege_management_workshop/radac-Paper0001.pdf
18. Nauman, M., Alam, M., Zhang, X., Ali, T.: Remote attestation of attribute updates and information flows in a ucon system. In: Chen, L., Mitchell, C.J., Martin, A. (eds.) Trust 2009. LNCS, vol. 5471, pp. 63–80. Springer, Heidelberg (2009)
19. Ni, Q., Bertino, E., Lobo, J.: Risk-based access control systems built on fuzzy inferences. In: Proceedings of the 5th ACM Symposium on Information, Computer and Communications Security, pp. 250–260. ACM, New York (2010)
20. Park, J., Sandhu, R.: Towards usage control models: beyond traditional access control. In: Proceedings of the 7th ACM Symposium on Access Control Models and Technologies, pp. 57–64. ACM, New York (2002)
21. Skalka, C., Wang, X.S., Chapin, P.: Risk management for distributed authorization. J. Comput. Secur. 15(4), 447–489 (2007)
22. Stolen, K., den Braber, F., Dimitrakos, T., Fredriksen, R., Gran, B.A., Houmb, S.-H., Lund, M.S., Stamatiou, Y., Aagedal, J.O.: Model-based risk assessment - the coras approach. In: Proceedings of the Norsk Informatikkkonferanse, Tapir, pp. 239–249 (2002)
23. Stoneburner, G., Goguen, A., Feringa, A.: Risk management guide for information technology systems. Technical Report 800-30, National Institute of Standards and Technology (2001), http://csrc.nist.gov/publications/nistpubs/800-30/sp800-30.pdf (13/05/2009)
24. Tijms, H.C.: A First Course in Stochastic Models. Wiley, Chichester (2003)
25. Wang, L., Wijesekera, D., Jajodia, S.: A logic-based framework for attribute based access control. In: Proceedings of the 2004 ACM workshop on Formal methods in security engineering (FMSE 2004), pp. 45–55. ACM, New York (2004)
26. Zhang, L., Brodsky, A., Jajodia, S.: Toward information sharing: Benefit and risk access control (barac). In: Proceedings of the 7th International Workshop on Policies for Distributed Systems and Networks, pp. 45–53. IEEE Computer Society, Washington, DC, USA (2006)

Rewrite Specifications of Access Control Policies in Distributed Environments

Clara Bertolissi[1] and Maribel Fernández[2]

[1] LIF, Université de Provence, Marseille, France
Clara.Bertolissi@lif.univ-mrs.fr
[2] King's College London, Dept. of Computer Science, London WC2R 2LS, U.K.
Maribel.Fernandez@kcl.ac.uk

Abstract. We define a *metamodel* for access control that takes into account the requirements of *distributed* environments, where resources and access control policies may be distributed across several sites. This distributed metamodel is an extension of the *category*-based metamodel proposed in previous work (from which standard centralised access control models such as MAC, DAC, RBAC, Bell-Lapadula, etc. can be derived). We use a *declarative formalism* in order to give an *operational semantics* to the distributed metamodel. We then show how various distributed access control models can be derived as instances of the distributed metamodel, including distributed models where each site implements a different kind of local access control model.

Keywords: Security Policies, Distributed Access Control, Operational Semantics, Rewriting.

1 Introduction

Using a formal specification for defining access control models and policies is particularly important in distributed contexts. The first attempts to develop formal theories to define and validate security policies (see, for instance, [16]) have used first-order theorem provers, purpose-built logics, or flow-analysis, but these approaches have limitations (as discussed for instance in [24]). More recently, rewriting techniques have been fruitfully exploited in the context of security protocols (see [6,22,2]), security policies controlling information leakage (see [21]), and access control policies (see [35,12]). Along these lines, rewriting systems appear to be well adapted for providing a semantics for distributed access control mechanisms.

Over the last few years, a variety of access control models and languages for access control policy specification have been developed, often motivated by particular applications. We can mention the ANSI (hierarchical) role-based access control (H-RBAC) model [1], further extended with time and location constraints [17], the mandatory access control (MAC) model [9], the event-based access control (DEBAC) model [12], etc. A unifying metamodel for access control, which can be specialised for domain-specific applications, has been recently

J. Cuellar et al. (Eds.): STM 2010, LNCS 6710, pp. 51–67, 2011.

proposed in [4]. This unifying approach has advantages: for example, by identifying a core set of principles of access control, one can abstract away many of the complexities that are found in specific access control models; this, in turn, helps to simplify the task of policy writing. A rewrite-based operational semantics for this metamodel was described in [14], where the expressive power of the metamodel is also demonstrated by showing that the above mentioned access control models can be derived as specific instances of the metamodel.

Based on the work reported in [14], in this paper we define a category-based access control metamodel for *distributed environments* where each component of the system preserves its autonomy, and provide a formal specification of access control evaluation using a declarative framework. The notion of distributed environment that we consider here is related to the notion of *federation* developed in the context of database systems (see for example [28,19]), where a federated system integrates several databases while preserving their autonomy. In this paper we see a distributed system consisting of several sites, each with its own resources to protect, as a federation, and we focus on access control. More precisely, we define a framework for the specification (and enforcement) of global access control policies that take into account the local policies specified by each member of the federation.

A key aspect of our approach to access control, following [4], is to focus attention on the notion of a *category*. We regard categories as a primitive concept and we view classic types of groupings used in access control, like a role, a security clearance, a discrete measure of trust, etc., as particular instances of the more general notion of category. Here we will adapt the idea of categorisation to a distributed, federative setting. In a system with dispersed resources, classifications of entities may depend on the site to which the entity belongs. Moreover, permissions associated to categories of entities may also depend on the site where the category is defined. Therefore, we may want to use a distributed access control evaluation method, in addition to the central one proposed in [14], or we may want to combine the two.

In this paper, we first axiomatise a *distributed access control metamodel*, then give a rewrite-based operational semantics for this metamodel using the techniques introduced in [13], which allow us to deal in a uniform way with distributed systems where different access control policies are maintained locally. The rewrite-based specification that we describe enables access control policies to be defined in a declarative way and permits properties of access control policies to be proved.

Summarising, the main contributions of this paper are:

- the axiomatisation of a category-based access control metamodel that takes into account the requirements of distributed systems seen as federations in which each component preserves its autonomy;
- a declarative, rewrite-based operational semantics for the distributed access control metamodel (extending [14] to incorporate the notion of site and policies distributed across several sites);

– a formal operational semantics for access request evaluation, in centralised as well as in distributed contexts where information is shared;
– the generalisation of access request evaluation by integrating in the meta-model mechanisms for the resolution of policy conflicts.

The remainder of the paper is organised as follows. In Section 2, we recall some basic notions in term rewriting, and describe the centralised access control meta-model. In Section 3, we define the extension of the metamodel for distributed environments. In Section 4 we specify its operational semantics as a rewrite system. In Section 5, we show examples of combinations of access request answers issued by different sites using different local policies. We describe techniques for proving properties of access control policies in Section 6. In Section 7, we discuss related work. In Section 8, conclusions are drawn, and further work is suggested.

2   Preliminaries

2.1   Term Rewriting

A *signature* $\mathcal{F}$ is a finite set of *function symbols*, each with a fixed arity. $\mathcal{X}$ denotes a denumerable set of *variables* $X_1, X_2, \ldots$. The set $T(\mathcal{F}, \mathcal{X})$ of *terms* built up from $\mathcal{F}$ and $\mathcal{X}$ can be identified with a set of finite trees in the usual way. *Positions* are strings of positive integers denoting a path from the root to a node in the tree. The *subterm* of t at position p is denoted by $t|_p$ and the result of replacing $t|_p$ with u at position p in t is denoted by $t[u]_p$. This notation is also used to indicate that u is a subterm of t. $\mathcal{V}(t)$ denotes the set of variables occurring in t. A term is *linear* if variables in $\mathcal{V}(t)$ occur at most once in t. A term is *ground* if $\mathcal{V}(t) = \emptyset$. Substitutions are written as in $\{X_1 \mapsto t_1, \ldots, X_n \mapsto t_n\}$ where t_i is assumed to be different from the variable X_i. We use Greek letters for substitutions and postfix notation for their application.

Definition 1 (Rewrite step). *Given a signature $\mathcal{F}$, a* term rewrite system *on $\mathcal{F}$ is a set of rewrite rules $R = \{l_i \to r_i\}_{i \in I}$, where $l_i, r_i \in T(\mathcal{F}, \mathcal{X})$, $l_i \notin \mathcal{X}$, and $\mathcal{V}(r_i) \subseteq \mathcal{V}(l_i)$. A term t rewrites to a term u at position p with the rule $l \to r$ and the substitution σ, written $t \to_p^{l \to r} u$, or simply $t \to_R u$, if $t|_p = l\sigma$ and $u = t[r\sigma]_p$. Such a term t is called* reducible. *Irreducible terms are said to be in* normal form.

We denote by $\to_R^+$ (resp. $\to_R^*$) the transitive (resp. transitive and reflexive) closure of the rewrite relation $\to_R$. The subindex R will be omitted when it is clear from the context.

Example 1. Consider a signature for lists of natural numbers, with function symbols z (with arity 0) and s (with arity 1) to build numbers; nil (with arity 0), cons (with arity 2) and append (with arity 2) to build lists, $\in$ (with arity 2) to test the membership of a number in a list. The list containing the numbers 0 and 1 is written then as cons(z, cons(s(z), nil)), or simply [z, s(z)] for short. We can specify list concatenation with the following rewrite rules: append(nil, X) $\to X$

and $\mathsf{append}(\mathsf{cons}(Y,X),Z) \to \mathsf{cons}(Y,\mathsf{append}(X,Z))$. Then we have a reduction sequence: $\mathsf{append}(\mathsf{cons}(\mathsf{z},\mathsf{nil}),\mathsf{cons}(\mathsf{s}(\mathsf{z}),\mathsf{nil})) \to^* \mathsf{cons}(\mathsf{z},\mathsf{cons}(\mathsf{s}(\mathsf{z}),\mathsf{nil}))$.

Boolean operators, such as disjunction, conjunction, and a conditional, can be specified using a signature that includes the constants true and false. The notation *if b then s else t* is syntactic sugar for the term if-then-else(b,s,t), with the rewrite rules: if-then-else$(\mathsf{true},X,Y) \to X$ and if-then-else$(\mathsf{false},X,Y) \to Y$.

For example, we can define the membership operator "$\in$" as follows: $\in (X,\mathsf{nil}) \to \mathsf{false}$, $\in (X,\mathsf{cons}(H,L)) \to$ *if $X = H$ then* true *else* $\in (X,L)$, where we assume "=" is a syntactic equality test defined by standard rewrite rules. We will often write $\in$ as an infix operator.

A term rewriting system R is *confluent* if for all terms t, u, v: $t \to^* u$ and $t \to^* v$ implies $u \to^* s$ and $v \to^* s$, for some s; it is *terminating* if all reduction sequences are finite. If all left-hand sides of rules in R are linear and rules are non-overlapping (i.e., there are no superpositions of left-hand sides) then R is orthogonal. Orthogonality is a sufficient condition for confluence [30].

For the approach to distributed access control that we propose later, we use distributed term rewrite systems (DTRSs) introduced in [12]. DTRSs are term rewrite systems where rules are partitioned into modules, each associated with a unique identifier, and function symbols are annotated with such identifiers. In a DTRS, we can associate a module to each site of a distributed system. For example, we may write f_ν to refer to the definition of the function symbol f in the site ν, where ν is a site identifier. We say that a rule $f(t_1,\ldots,t_n) \to r$ defines f; all the functions defined in a module are annotated with the same identifier. If a symbol is used in a rule without a site annotation, we assume the function is defined locally.

For more details on DTRSs, the reader can refer to [12].

2.2 Category-Based Metamodel

We briefly describe below the key concepts underlying the category-based metamodel of access control, henceforth denoted by $\mathcal{M}$. We refer the reader to [4] for a detailed description.

Informally, a category is any of several distinct classes or groups to which entities may be assigned. Entities are denoted uniquely by constants in a many sorted domain of discourse, including: a countable set $\mathcal{C}$ of categories, denoted $c_0, c_1, \ldots$, a countable set $\mathcal{P}$ of principals, denoted $p_0, p_1, \ldots$, a countable set $\mathcal{A}$ of named *actions*, denoted $a_0, a_1, \ldots$, a countable set $\mathcal{R}$ of *resource identifiers*, denoted $r_0, r_1, \ldots$, a finite set $\mathcal{A}uth$ of possible *answers* to access requests and a countable set $\mathcal{S}$ of *situational identifiers*. Situational identifiers are used to denote contextual or environmental information. We assume that principals that request access to resources are pre-authenticated. In the metamodel, the answer to a request may be one of a series of constants. For instance, the set $\mathcal{A}uth$ might include {grant, deny, grant-if-obligation-is-satisfied, undetermined}.

In addition to the different types of entities mentioned above, the metamodel includes the following relations:

- *Principal-category assignment:* $\mathcal{PCA} \subseteq \mathcal{P} \times \mathcal{C}$, such that $(p,c) \in \mathcal{PCA}$ iff a principal $p \in \mathcal{P}$ is assigned to the category $c \in \mathcal{C}$.
- *Permissions:* $\mathcal{ARCA} \subseteq \mathcal{A} \times \mathcal{R} \times \mathcal{C}$, such that $(a,r,c) \in \mathcal{ARCA}$ iff the action $a \in \mathcal{A}$ on resource $r \in \mathcal{R}$ can be performed by principals assigned to the category $c \in \mathcal{C}$.
- *Authorisations:* $\mathcal{PAR} \subseteq \mathcal{P} \times \mathcal{A} \times \mathcal{R}$, such that $(p,a,r) \in \mathcal{PAR}$ iff a principal $p \in \mathcal{P}$ can perform the action $a \in \mathcal{A}$ on the resource $r \in \mathcal{R}$.

Thus, $\mathcal{PAR}$ defines the set of authorisations that hold according to an access control policy that specifies $\mathcal{PCA}$ and $\mathcal{ARCA}$, as follows.

Definition 2 (Axioms). *The relation $\mathcal{PAR}$ satisfies the following core axiom, where we assume that there exists a relationship $\subseteq$ between categories; this can simply be equality, set inclusion (the set of principals assigned to $c \in \mathcal{C}$ is a subset of the set of principals assigned to $c' \in \mathcal{C}$), or an application specific relation may be used.*

$(a1)$ $\forall p \in \mathcal{P},\ \forall a \in \mathcal{A},\ \forall r \in \mathcal{R},\ \forall c \in \mathcal{C},$
$\quad (p,c) \in \mathcal{PCA} \wedge (\exists c' \in \mathcal{C}, c \subseteq c'\ \wedge (a,r,c') \in \mathcal{ARCA}) \Rightarrow (p,a,r) \in \mathcal{PAR}$

The category-based metamodel of access control is based on the core axiom $(a1)$ in Def. 2. Operationally, this axiom can be realised through a set of function definitions, as shown in [14], where the information contained in the relations $\mathcal{PCA}$ and $\mathcal{ARCA}$ is modelled by functions pca and arca, respectively. The function pca returns the list of categories assigned to a principal, e.g. $pca(p) \rightarrow [c]$, and arca returns a list of permissions assigned to a category, e.g. $arca(c) \rightarrow [(a_1, r_1), \ldots, (a_n, r_n)]$.

Definition 3. *The rewrite-based specification of the axiom $(a1)$ in Def. 2 is given by the rewrite rule:*

$(a2)$ $par(P, A, R) \rightarrow if\ (A, R) \in arca^*(contain(pca(P)))\ then\ \mathsf{grant}\ else\ \mathsf{deny}$

As the function name suggests, contain *computes the set of categories that contain any of the categories given in the list* $pca(P)$. *For example, for a category* c, *this can be achieved by using a rewrite rule* $contain([c]) \rightarrow [c, c_1, \ldots, c_n]$. *The function* $\in$ *is a membership operator on lists (see Section 2),* grant *and* deny *are answers, and* $arca^*$ *generalises the function* arca *to take into account lists of categories:*

$$arca^*(nil) \rightarrow nil \qquad arca^*(cons(C, L)) \rightarrow append(arca(C), arca^*(L))$$

For optimisation purposes, one can compose the standard list concatenation operator append with a function removing the duplicate elements in the list.

An access request by a principal p to perform the action a on the resource r can then be evaluated simply by rewriting the term $par(p, a, r)$ to normal form.

A range of access control models can be represented as specialised instances of the metamodel: see [14] for the specifications of traditional access control models, such as RBAC, DAC and MAC, (including the well-known Bell-LaPadula model), as well as the event-based model DEBAC.

The category-based metamodel defined in this section does not take into account distributed issues, such as conflicts that may arise between different local policies: all the relations defined are monolithic, and the axioms defining authorisations are valid in the whole system. In the next section we will extend and refine the metamodel in order to deal in a uniform way with access control policies for distributed systems.

3   A Distributed Category-Based Metamodel

We consider the same sets of entities as in the centralised metamodel $\mathcal{M}$. The set $\mathcal{S}$ of situational identifiers will now include identifiers for sites (or locations) which will be associated to resources or policies. For simplicity we will assume that $\mathcal{S}$ is just the set of locations that compose the distributed system. In other words, each $s \in \mathcal{S}$ identifies one of the components of the distributed system, seen as a federation. The set $\mathcal{P}$ includes the principals registered in any of the sites of the system. We assume that principals identities are globally known in the federation.

In addition to principal-category assignments, permissions, and authorisations (relations $\mathcal{PCA}$, $\mathcal{ARCA}$ and $\mathcal{PAR}$), we define a notion of forbidden operation (or banned action), modelled by the relation $\mathcal{BARCA}$, and a notion of non-authorised access, modelled by the relation $\mathcal{BAR}$:

- *Banned actions on resources:* $\mathcal{BARCA} \subseteq \mathcal{A} \times \mathcal{R} \times \mathcal{C}$, such that $(a, r, c) \in \mathcal{BARCA}$ iff the action $a \in \mathcal{A}$ on resource $r \in \mathcal{R}$ is forbidden for principals assigned to the category $c \in \mathcal{C}$.
- *Barred access:* $\mathcal{BAR} \subseteq P \times A \times \mathcal{R}$, such that $(p, a, r) \in \mathcal{BAR}$ iff performing the action $a \in \mathcal{A}$ on the resource $r \in \mathcal{R}$ is forbidden for the principal $p \in \mathcal{P}$.

Additionally, a relation $\mathcal{UNDET}$ could be defined if $\mathcal{PAR}$ and $\mathcal{BAR}$ are not complete, i.e., if there are access requests that are neither authorised nor denied (thus producing an undeterminate answer). These notions are not essential in centralised systems, but they are necessary in distributed systems for integrating partially specified policies, i.e. policies that may be "not applicable" to requests on resources that are out of their jurisdiction. Moreover, to take into account the fact that the system may be composed of several sites, with different policies in place at each site, we consider families of relations $\mathcal{PCA}_s$, $\mathcal{ARCA}_s$, $\mathcal{BARCA}_s$, $\mathcal{BAR}_s$, $\mathcal{UNDET}_s$ and $\mathcal{PAR}_s$ indexed by site identifiers. Intuitively, $\mathcal{PAR}_s$ (resp. $\mathcal{BAR}_s$) denotes the authorisations (resp. prohibitions) that are valid in the site s. The relation $\mathcal{PAR}$ defining the global authorisation policy will be obtained by composing the local policies defined by the relations $\mathcal{PAR}_s$ and $\mathcal{BAR}_s$ as indicated below. For instance, $\mathcal{PAR}$ could be defined as a union, but more sophisticated combinations are possible, in particular if policies in different sites may contain conflicting information.

The axioms for the distributed metamodel are given below; they can be seen as an extension of the axioms that define $\mathcal{M}$ (see Definition 2).

Definition 4 (Distributed Axioms). *In a distributed environment, the category based metamodel is defined by the following core axioms where we assume that there exists a relationship $\subseteq$ between categories; this can simply be equality, set inclusion (i.e., the set of principals assigned to $c \in \mathcal{C}$ is a subset of the set of principals assigned to $c' \in \mathcal{C}$), or an application specific relation may be used.*

$(b1)\ \forall p \in \mathcal{P},\ \forall a \in \mathcal{A},\ \forall r \in \mathcal{R},\ \forall c \in \mathcal{C},\ \forall s \in \mathcal{S}$
$\quad (p,c) \in \mathcal{PCA}_s \wedge (\exists c' \in \mathcal{C}, c \subseteq c'\ \wedge (a,r,c') \in \mathcal{ARCA}_s) \Rightarrow (p,a,r) \in \mathcal{PAR}_s$

If the relation $\mathcal{BARCA}$ is admitted in a site s, then the following axioms should be included:

$(c1)\ \forall p \in \mathcal{P},\ \forall a \in \mathcal{A},\ \forall r \in \mathcal{R},\ \forall c \in \mathcal{C},\ \forall s \in \mathcal{S}$
$\quad (p,c) \in \mathcal{PCA}_s \wedge (\exists c' \in \mathcal{C}, c \subseteq c'\ \wedge (a,r,c') \in \mathcal{BARCA}_s) \Rightarrow (p,a,r) \in \mathcal{BAR}_s$

$(d1)\ \forall p \in \mathcal{P},\ \forall a \in \mathcal{A},\ \forall r \in \mathcal{R},\ \forall c \in \mathcal{C},\ \forall s \in \mathcal{S}$
$\quad (p,c) \in \mathcal{PCA}_s\ \wedge\ (a,r,c) \notin \mathcal{ARCA}_s\ \wedge\ (a,r,c) \notin \mathcal{BARCA}_s \Rightarrow$
$\qquad\qquad\qquad\qquad\qquad\qquad\qquad (p,a,r) \in \mathcal{UNDET}_s$

$(e1)\ \forall s \in \mathcal{S},\quad \mathcal{ARCA}_s \cap \mathcal{BARCA}_s = \emptyset$

Finally, the axioms below describe the global authorisation relation in terms of the local policies defined at each site:

$(f1)\ \forall p \in \mathcal{P},\ \forall a \in \mathcal{A},\ \forall r \in \mathcal{R},$
$\quad (p,a,r) \in \mathcal{OP}_{par}(\{\mathcal{PAR}_s, \mathcal{BAR}_s \mid s \in \mathcal{S}\}) \Rightarrow (p,a,r) \in \mathcal{PAR}$
$(g1)\ \forall p \in \mathcal{P},\ \forall a \in \mathcal{A},\ \forall r \in \mathcal{R},$
$\quad (p,a,r) \in \mathcal{OP}_{bar}(\{\mathcal{PAR}_s, \mathcal{BAR}_s \mid s \in \mathcal{S}\}) \Rightarrow (p,a,r) \in \mathcal{BAR}$
$(h1)\ \mathcal{PAR} \cap \mathcal{BAR} = \emptyset$

According to these axioms, the result of an access request may be different depending on the site where the request is evaluated (since each site has its own authorisation policy defined by the local relation $\mathcal{PAR}_s$). The relation $\mathcal{UNDET}_s \subseteq \mathcal{P} \times \mathcal{A} \times \mathcal{R}$ is such that $(p,a,r) \in \mathcal{UNDET}_s$ iff the action $a \in \mathcal{A}$ on resource $r \in \mathcal{R}$ is neither allowed nor forbidden for the principal $p \in \mathcal{P}$ at site $s \in \mathcal{S}$. The final authorisation is computed specialising the definition of the operators $\mathcal{OP}_{par}$ and $\mathcal{OP}_{bar}$, according to the application requirements. For instance, consider a system with two sites $s, t \in \mathcal{S}$, we may have $\mathcal{OP}_{bar} = (\mathcal{BAR}_s \vee \mathcal{BAR}_t)$ and $\mathcal{OP}_{par} = ((\mathcal{PAR}_s/\mathcal{BAR}_t) \vee (\mathcal{PAR}_t/\mathcal{BAR}_s))$. This corresponds to a union operator giving priority to deny, according to the "deny takes precedence principle" [26] (i.e. access is denied if it is denied by any of the component policies).

Also, if the information available in a site s is not sufficient to grant a principal the right to access a certain resource, but does not ban the access either (i.e., the outcome of the request evaluation cannot be determined at s), then the access request may need to be processed in another site of the system. We can model this kind of policy definition with the axioms above using the operator $\mathcal{OP}_{par} = (\mathcal{PAR}_s \vee (\mathcal{PAR}_t/\mathcal{PAR}_s))\}$ and $\mathcal{OP}_{bar} = (\mathcal{BAR}_s \vee (\mathcal{BAR}_t/\mathcal{BAR}_s))$. This corresponds to the precedence operator, as defined e.g. in [15].

The distributed metamodel refines and extends $\mathcal{M}$ as defined in Section 2.2 because different access control policies (possibly using *different access control models*) may be defined at different sites, and access requests can be evaluated using any combination of local access control policy as well as a global, centrally defined policy (for instance, if the system has a central policy at site ς, then $\mathcal{OP}_{par} = (\mathcal{PAR}_\varsigma)$ and $\mathcal{OP}_{bar} = (\mathcal{BAR}_\varsigma))$.

Intuitively, the axioms preclude inconsistent specifications (axioms $e1$ and $h1$) and define authorised actions as follows:

> *A principal $p \in \mathcal{P}$ is permitted to perform an action $a \in \mathcal{A}$ on a resource $r \in \mathcal{R}$ if*
> i) *at the site where the request is evaluated, p is assigned to a category $c \in \mathcal{C}$ to which a access on r has been locally assigned (axiom b_1), or*
> ii) *in the global policy, p is assigned to a category $c \in \mathcal{C}$ to which a access on r has been granted (axiom f_1).*

4   Operational Semantics

The operational semantics of the distributed model will be defined by extending the functions presented in Definition 3 and in addition a new function barca, corresponding to the relation $\mathcal{BARCA}$ in Section 3, will be introduced to represent explicitly forbidden actions on resources. We recall that functions with no site annotations are assumed to be defined locally. The function barca_s returns the list of prohibitions assigned to a category in a site s:
$$\mathsf{barca}_s(\mathsf{c}) \rightarrow [(\mathsf{a_1, r_1)}, \ldots, (\mathsf{a_n, r_n})].$$

If for a given category c, a pair (a, r) is neither in $\mathsf{arca}_s(c)$ nor in $\mathsf{barca}_s(c)$, then we say that such access privilege is undefined and consequently the corresponding access request is *undeterminate*. This permits a finer-grained evaluation of access requests: the constant undet is a possible answer, at the same level as grant and deny. We assume that, in a correct specification, for the same category c, $\mathsf{arca}_s(c)$ and $\mathsf{barca}_s(c)$ do not have elements in common, i.e., if $(a_i, r_j) \in \mathsf{arca}_s(c)$, then $(a_i, r_j) \notin \mathsf{barca}_s(c)$, and viceversa, for any $i, j \in \mathbb{N}$, as required by axiom $(e1)$. The rewrite-based specification of the extended axioms of Section 3 follows.

Definition 5. *In a distributed environment, the rewrite-based specification of the axiom $(b1)$ in Def. 4 is given by the rewrite rule:*

$(b2)$ $\mathsf{par}_s(P, A, R) \rightarrow if\ (A, R) \in \mathsf{arca}_s^*(\mathsf{contain}(\mathsf{pca}_s(P)))$ *then* grant *else* deny

where the function $\in$ is a membership operator on lists (see Section 2), grant *and* deny *are answers, and arca_s^* is the function defining the assignment of privileges to categories, as in the previous section.*

If we consider the extended axioms $(c1)$, $(d1)$ in Def. 4, which involve a $\mathcal{BARCA}$ relation, the function par *is defined as:*

$(c2, d2)$ $\mathsf{par}_s(P, A, R) \rightarrow if\ (a, r) \in \mathsf{arca}_s^*(\mathsf{contain}(\mathsf{pca}_s(p)))\,then$ grant *else*
$\qquad\qquad\qquad\qquad if\ (a, r) \in \mathsf{barca}_s^*(\mathsf{contain}(\mathsf{pca}_s(p)))\,then$ deny *else* undet

where barca$^*_s$ *generalises the previously mentioned function* barca$_s$ *to take into account lists of categories instead of a single category:*

$$\text{barca}^*(\text{nil}) \rightarrow \text{nil} \qquad \text{barca}^*(\text{cons}(C, L)) \rightarrow \text{append}(\text{barca}(C), \text{barca}^*(L))$$

As already mentioned, the functions arca$_s$ *and* barca$_s$ *should satisfy axiom (e1), but note that even if axiom (e1) is not satisfied, the operational semantics defined for* par *above is consistent: it gives priority to positive authorisations.*

The axioms (f1) and (g1) are realised by the following rewrite rule (implementing $\mathcal{OP}_{par}$):

$$(f2, g2) \; \text{authorised}(P, A, R, s_1, \ldots, s_n) \rightarrow \text{fauth}(op, \text{par}_{s_1}(p, a, r), \ldots, \text{par}_{s_n}(p, a, r))$$

where the function fauth *combines the results into a final access authorisation according to the operator op.*

The axioms (f1) and (g1) can be implemented in several ways. The version chosen in the definition above corresponds to a very general rewrite rule that can be used for evaluating an access request in a single central site, if $n = 1$ and the operator op is the identity, as well as for evaluating combinations of answers (with a suitable operator op) from n different local policies. An alternative can be to specify an authorised rewrite rule for any specific combination operator. For example, if we consider two sites s_1 and s_2, for the precedence operator previously mentioned, we may have

$$\begin{aligned} \text{authorised}(P, A, R, S_1, S_2) \rightarrow \; &\textit{if } \; \text{par}_{s_1}(P, A, R) = \text{grant } \textit{or } \text{par}_{s_1}(P, A, R) = \text{deny} \\ &\textit{then } \; \text{par}_{s_1}(P, A, R) \; \textit{else } \; \text{par}_{s_2}(P, A, R) \end{aligned}$$

In this case priority is given to local evaluation in site s_1, external evaluation in site s_2 being executed only when the local policy in s_1 is not able to give as answer grant or deny. However, when dealing with policy combinations, it is unlikely to find a unique evaluation strategy that works for every possible scenario. A suitable policy integration mechanism depends on the requirements of the application and the involved parties. Distributed evaluation of access requests and combination of authorisation answers is further discussed in the next section. An overview of the rules modelling the distributed version of $\mathcal{M}$ is given in Table 1.

4.1   Evaluating Access Requests

The novelty of the distributed metamodel lies in the fact that different local policies can be defined and combined in this framework in a smooth and uniform manner.

Evaluation initially takes place in the site where the request is issued, using the local function authorised (see rule *Aut* in Table 1). The local rule *Aut* specifies a number of sites s_i, $i = 1 \ldots n$, where the request may be passed and evaluated by the corresponding function par$_{s_i}$. For defining the sites of the evaluation, we may use functions like e.g. psite(p), which returns the site where the principal p

is registered, or rsite(r) which returns the site where the resource r is located. In this way, access requests can be evaluated in a predefined central site, or priority can be given to local evaluation, or more elaborated combinations of access answers can be implemented.

In order to specify a particular policy at a site s, e.g. RBAC, MAC or DEBAC, it is sufficient to specialise locally the functions arca$_s$, barca$_s$, pca$_s$, contain$_s$. Their definition in Table 1 can be adapted to the application we want to consider. Thus, for example, if we want to express a hierarchical RBAC policy at site s, the function arca$_s$ will return the permissions associated to each defined role and contain$_s$ will return the roles senior to a given role, according to the hierarchy specified in the model (see [14] for more application examples).

Thus, in the distributed metamodel, the request can be passed to other sites (with possibly different local policies) and evaluated in a distributed way. The generic rule (Aut), implementing the axioms of Section 3, will then integrate the different local access request answers to provide a final authorisation decision. More precisely, the distributed answers are collected and combined by using the specific rule ($Fauth$) which is locally defined for an operator op. For example, consider a principal in an international organisation belonging to the U.K division and asking for access to the French division. In this case, we want to evaluate the access authorisation in the U.K. site, where the principal is registered, and also in the French site, the two sites possibly having different policies. Access will be permitted if the policies in both sites return a grant answer (denied if at least one policy denies the access). In our metamodel, we can combine evaluations from different sources in a flexible way by refining the definition of the fauth function (rule $Fauth$). In our example, we would use a fauth function with a union operator:

$$\text{fauth}(\text{union}, \text{deny}, X) \rightarrow \text{deny} \qquad \text{fauth}(\text{union}, X, \text{deny}) \rightarrow \text{deny}$$
$$\text{fauth}(\text{union}, \text{undet}, \text{undet}) \rightarrow \text{undet} \qquad \text{fauth}(\text{union}, \text{grant}, \text{grant}) \rightarrow \text{grant}$$
$$\text{fauth}(\text{union}, \text{undet}, \text{grant}) \rightarrow \text{undet} \qquad \text{fauth}(\text{union}, \text{grant}, \text{undet}) \rightarrow \text{undet}$$

Following the same idea, the rewrite system can be adapted to a variety of algebraic commutative and associative operators, as well as operators in the style of those defined in [15] (Subtraction, Precedence, etc.). For more elaborated operators, higher-order features can be added to the model, along the lines of [10].

5   Examples

We give next more detailed examples to demonstrate the expressive power of the distributed metamodel.

Example 2. (Combining RBAC and DEBAC policies) Consider an organisation composed of several commercial branches, all depending from a central department. Assume a principal p is the director of the London branch and has currently been assigned the management of a project Proj involving several U.K. branches. The information on the project is stored at the departmental level.

Table 1. Rewrite specification of the metamodel

Par_s	$\mathsf{par}(P, A, R)$	$\rightarrow$ if $(A, R) \in \mathsf{arca}^*(\mathsf{contain}(\mathsf{pca}(P)))$ then grant else
		if $(A, R) \in \mathsf{barca}^*(\mathsf{contain}(\mathsf{pca}(P)))$ then deny else undef
$Arca^*$	$\mathsf{arca}^*(\mathsf{cons}(C, L))$	$\rightarrow \mathsf{append}(\mathsf{arca}(C), \mathsf{arca}^*(L))$
$Arca^*$	$\mathsf{arca}^*(\mathsf{cons}(C, \mathsf{nil}))$	$\rightarrow \mathsf{nil}$
$Barca^*$	$\mathsf{barca}^*(\mathsf{cons}(C, L))$	$\rightarrow \mathsf{append}(\mathsf{barca}(C), \mathsf{barca}^*(L))$
$Barca^*$	$\mathsf{barca}^*(\mathsf{cons}(C, \mathsf{nil}))$	$\rightarrow \mathsf{nil}$
Pca	$\mathsf{pca}(\mathsf{p})$	$\rightarrow [\mathsf{c}]$
$Arca$	$\mathsf{arca}(\mathsf{c})$	$\rightarrow [(\mathsf{a_1, r_1}), \ldots, (\mathsf{a_k, r_k})]$
$Barca$	$\mathsf{barca}(\mathsf{c})$	$\rightarrow [(\mathsf{a_l, r_l}), \ldots, (\mathsf{a_t, r_t})]$
$Contain$	$\mathsf{contain}(\mathsf{c})$	$\rightarrow [\mathsf{c, c_1}, \ldots, \mathsf{c_n}]$

Aut	$\mathsf{authorised}(P, A, R, s_1, \ldots, s_n)$	$\rightarrow$
		$\mathsf{fauth}(op, \mathsf{par}_{s_1}(P, A, R), \ldots, \mathsf{par}_{s_n}(P, A, R))$
$Fauth$	$\mathsf{fauth}(op, \mathsf{par}_{s_1}(p, a, r), \ldots, \mathsf{par}_{s_n}(p, a, r)) \rightarrow \mathsf{answ}$	with $\mathsf{answ} \in \mathcal{A}ut$

Assume a principal wants to read the balance sheet of the project, and, according to the policy of the organisation, only the leader of the project has the right to access it. In our model, this corresponds to the presence of the pair (read, balanceProj) in the privileges associated to the category "leader of the project", $\mathsf{arca}_\delta(\mathsf{leaderProj}) \rightarrow [(\mathsf{read, balanceProj}), \ldots]$, stored at the departmental site δ.

In the distributed evaluation model, the request from p to read the balance of Proj is first treated by the site ν where the request is issued, which passes it to the local branch where p is registered, say π, and to departmental site δ.

$$\mathsf{authorised}_\nu(\mathsf{p, read, balanceProj, psite(p), dept(p))}) \rightarrow$$
$$\mathsf{authorised}_\nu(\mathsf{p, read, balanceProj}, \pi, \delta)$$

Suppose the organisation implements locally for each branch a role-based policy and at the departmental level an event-based policy, to deal with dynamic changes. We refer to [14] for the definition of individual RBAC and DEBAC policies in the metamodel. Here we consider the distributed model where the function fauth combines policies according to the precedence operator (see Section 4), focusing on the evaluation of the access request locally. Assume we have

$$\mathsf{pca}_\pi(\mathsf{p}) \rightarrow [\mathsf{director}]$$
$$\mathsf{arca}_\pi(\mathsf{director}) \rightarrow [(\mathsf{read, report}), (\mathsf{write, report}), \ldots,]$$
$$\mathsf{barca}_\pi(\mathsf{director}) \rightarrow [(\mathsf{delete, trail}), \ldots,]$$

No privileges associated to the project Proj are present in the policy defined for branch π. Therefore, the local request evaluation will produce as result undef: local information is not sufficient to produce an authorisation or a denial of access, $\mathsf{par}_\pi(\mathsf{p, read, balanceProj}) \rightarrow^* \mathsf{undef}$.

The request is then evaluated at the departmental site by the function par_δ which calls again the function pca to compute the category associated to principal p. The difference with respect to the local par_π function is that the policy associated to the central site is a DEBAC policy, and thus the resulting category associated to p may be different. The DEBAC policy defined in δ computes the category of a principal according to a history of events h_δ. In such history, among others, we have recorded the events relevant to the project Proj, such as the nomination of the managers and participants to the project. Thus p's category in site ς may be computed using rules:

$$pca(P) \rightarrow categ(P, h)$$
$$categ(P, nil) \rightarrow Participant$$
$$categ(P, cons(event(E, P, inchargeProj, T), H)) \rightarrow if\ P \in Managers(Proj)$$
$$then\ [LeaderProj])$$
$$else\ [ParticipantProj]$$

meaning that the events that happened at some previous time t involving p in the project Proj determine the category of p. Managers(P) returns the list of managers associated to project P that we suppose registered locally in site δ.

So, according to the DEBAC policy, we have $pca_\varsigma(p) \rightarrow [LeaderProj]$ because in the history of events there is a tuple indicating that p became a leader of the project, and since the pair (read, balanceProj) is in the privileges of the category LeaderProj, we have $par_\varsigma(p, read, balanceProj) \rightarrow^*$ grant and thus finally the reduction $authorised_\nu(p, read, balanceProj, \pi, \delta) \rightarrow^*$ grant.

Example 3. (Combining RBAC and Bell-Lapadula policies)

Consider a principal working in an organisation where employees share an electronic agenda a, maintained on a server ν. Suppose this organisation adopts an RBAC policy for the employees, and moreover uses a specific Bell-Lapadula policy on the agenda in site ν. Consider the request of editing the agenda by the principal p. In this case, p has to be an employee of the organisation to access the agenda and moreover p must respect the "no read up" and "write only at the subject level" rules of the Bell-Lapadula policy in order to edit it. In the metamodel, we will use a union operator giving priority to deny (see Section 4.1) to meet the requirements of this distributed scenario. At the local level, we have an RBAC policy implemented in the site where the principal is registered, say π. The policy provides rules such as

$$pca_\pi(p) \rightarrow [employee]$$
$$arca_\pi(employee) \rightarrow [(read, report), (write, a_{all}), (read, a_{all}]$$
$$barca_\pi(employee) \rightarrow [(write, report), \dots,]$$

where *all* stands for any section of the agenda. We have in addition a Bell-Lapadula policy local to site ν. Assume we have three different levels (top-secret, secret and public) and three different sections of the agenda ts, s and p that can be modified according to the category associated to the principal. The privileges depend thus on the secrecy level:

$$\mathsf{arca}_\nu(\mathsf{top\_secret}) \rightarrow [(\mathsf{read}, a_{\mathsf{ts}}), (\mathsf{write}, a_{\mathsf{ts}}), (\mathsf{read}, a_{\mathsf{s}}), (\mathsf{read}, a_{\mathsf{p}}),]$$
$$\mathsf{barca}_\nu(\mathsf{top\_secret}) \rightarrow [(\mathsf{write}, a_{\mathsf{s}}), (\mathsf{write}, a_{\mathsf{p}})]$$

. . .

$$\mathsf{arca}_\nu(\mathsf{public}) \rightarrow [(\mathsf{write}, a_{\mathsf{p}}), (\mathsf{read}, a_{\mathsf{p}}),]$$
$$\mathsf{barca}_\nu(\mathsf{public}) \rightarrow [(\mathsf{write}, a_{\mathsf{s}}), (\mathsf{write}, a_{\mathsf{ts}}), (\mathsf{read}, a_{\mathsf{s}}), (\mathsf{read}, a_{\mathsf{ts}})]$$

Assume p is assigned to the public level, $\mathsf{pca}_\nu(\mathsf{p}) \rightarrow [\mathsf{public}]$, and asks for editing a section a_{s} in the agenda.

The request evaluation starts by calling the authorised function local to the site where the request is issued

$$\mathsf{authorised}(\mathsf{p}, \mathsf{write}, a_{\mathsf{s}}, \mathsf{psite}(\mathsf{p}), \mathsf{rsite}(a))$$
$$\rightarrow^* \mathsf{fauth}(\mathsf{union}, \mathsf{par}_\pi(\mathsf{p}, \mathsf{write}, a_{\mathsf{s}}), \mathsf{par}_\nu(\mathsf{p}, \mathsf{write}, a_{\mathsf{s}}))$$

We consider first the evaluation of the request in the site $\mathsf{psite}(\mathsf{p}) \rightarrow \pi$. In this case, we have $\mathsf{par}_\pi(\mathsf{p}, \mathsf{write}, a_{\mathsf{s}}) \rightarrow^*$ grant since p is indeed an employee of the organisation and as such has access to the shared agenda. We consider now the finer-grained evaluation of the request which is performed locally to site ν. We have $\mathsf{par}_\nu(\mathsf{p}, \mathsf{write}, a_{\mathsf{s}}) \rightarrow^*$ deny since the pair $(\mathsf{write}, a_{\mathsf{s}})$ is in the list of prohibitions of the category public to which the principal belongs. Thus finally the access to principal p at the secret section of the agenda will be denied

$$\mathsf{authorised}(\mathsf{p}, \mathsf{write}, a_{\mathsf{s}}, \mathsf{psite}(\mathsf{p}), \mathsf{rsite}(a)) \rightarrow^* \mathsf{fauth}(\mathsf{union}, \mathsf{grant}, \mathsf{deny}) \rightarrow^* \mathsf{deny}$$

6   Policy Analysis: Proving Properties of Policies

Specifying access control policies via term rewriting systems, which have a formal semantics, has the advantage that this representation admits the possibility of proving properties of policies, and this is essential for policy acceptability [34]. Rewriting properties may be used to demonstrate satisfaction of essential properties of policies, such as:

Totality: Each access request from a valid principal p to perform a valid action a on a resource r receives an answer (e.g., grant, deny, undeterminate).

Consistency: For any $p \in \mathcal{P}$, $a \in \mathcal{A}$, $r \in \mathcal{R}$, at most one result is possible for an authorisation request $\mathsf{par}(p, a, r)$.

Soundness and Completeness: For any $p \in \mathcal{P}$, $a \in \mathcal{A}$, $r \in \mathcal{R}$, an access request by p to perform the action a on r is granted if and only if p belongs to a category that has the permission (a, r).

Totality and consistency can be proved, for policies defined as term rewriting systems, by checking that the rewrite relation generated by the rules used in a specific instance of the metamodel is confluent and terminating. Termination ensures that all access requests produce a result (e.g. a result that is not grant or deny is interpreted as undet) and confluence ensures that this result is unique. The soundness and completeness of a policy can be checked by analysing the normal forms of access requests.

Confluence and termination of rewriting are undecidable properties in general, but there are several results available that provide sufficient conditions for these properties to hold. For instance, a *hierarchical* term rewriting system is terminating if the basis of the hierarchy is terminating and non-duplicating (i.e., rules do not duplicate variables in the right-hand side) and in the next levels of the hierarchy the recursive functions are defined by rules that satisfy a general scheme of recursion, where recursive calls on the right-hand sides of rules are made on subterms of the left-hand side and there are no mutually recursive functions [23]. Using the metamodel, the full definition of the policy can be seen as a hierarchical rewrite system, where the basis includes the set of constants identifying the main entities in the model (e.g., principals, categories, etc.) as well as the set of auxiliary data structures (such as booleans, lists) and functions on these data structures. The next level in the hierarchy contains the parameter functions of the model, namely pca, arca, barca, arca*, barca*, contain. Finally the last level of the hierarchy consists of the definition of the function par, and the functions authorised and fauth.

For instance, for the examples in this paper, provided the auxiliary functions in the basis of the hierarchy are defined by non-duplicating and terminating rewrite rules, the system is terminating (notice that the functions par, authorised and fauth are not recursive).

Confluence can be proved in various ways. Orthogonal systems are confluent, as shown by Klop [30]. A less restrictive condition, for systems that terminate, is the absence of critical pairs (the latter, combined with termination implies confluence by Newman's lemma [33]).

7   Related Work

There are several works in the literature using term rewriting to model access control problems. Koch et al. [31] use graph transformation rules to formalise RBAC, and more recently, [5,35,12] use term rewrite rules to model particular access control models and to express access control policies. Our work addresses similar issues to [5,31,35,12], but is based on a notion of a meta-model of access control for distributed environments, from which various models can be derived, instead of formalising a specific kind of model such as RBAC or DEBAC.

Several proposals for general models and languages for access control have already been described in the literature, but neither of them provides the level of generality of the category-based approach. For example, the Generalised TRBAC model [29] and ASL [25] aim at providing a general framework for the definition of policies, however they focus essentially on the notion of users, groups and roles (interpreted as being synonymous with the notion of job function). Li et al.'s *RT* family of role-trust models [32] provides a general framework which can be specialised for defining specific policy requirements (in terms of credentials). The category-based metamodel, however, can be instantiated to include concepts like times, events, actions and histories that are not included as elements of RT.

The metamodel defined in [4] incorporates the notion of site like our distributed metamodel, but there is no explicit definition of "forbidden" action and the issue of combinations of different policies is not addressed.

The metamodel that we have described is more expressive than any of the Datalog-based languages that have been proposed for distributed access control (see [3,27,20,7]); these languages, being based on a monotonic semantics, are not especially well suited for representing dynamically changing distributed access request policies.

Another work dealing with decentralised systems is reported in [8], where the authors propose the constraint logic programming language SecPal for specifying a wide range of authorisation policies and credentials, using predicates defined by clauses. Inspired by this work, the DKAL authorisation language was proposed, based on existential fixed-point logic. In our approach, we focus on the definition of a general metamodel suitable for distributed systems rather than on the design of a specification language, but we give an operational semantics for the metamodel which can be instantiated further to derive specific access control models and policies.

The notion of Federated Systems can also be related to our work. In [28,19] local systems evolving independently cooperate in a distributed architecture called federation. In our model, we can simulate this behaviour specifying local sets of registered users and defining rules for treating requests from external users at the federation level (associated to a remote site).

8   Conclusions and Further Work

We have given a rewrite-based specification of a distributed metamodel of access control that is based on general, common concepts of access control models. The term rewriting approach can be used to give a meaningful formal semantics to policies in the case of both centralised and distributed computer systems. In addition, operators for defining combinations of policies can be smoothly integrated in our framework. In future work, we plan to develop the algebra of operators used for integrating policies, along the lines of [10,15], in order to express arbitrary combinations of policies at a finer granularity.

Rewrite rules provide a declarative specification of access control requirements which facilitates the task of proving properties of policies. Also, term rewriting rules provide a well-defined, executable specification of the access control policy. We plan to investigate the design of languages for policy specification and the practical implementation of category-based policies, defined as instances of our metamodel; in particular, an access control policy may be transformed into a MAUDE [18] program by adding type declarations for the function symbols and variables used and by making minor syntactical changes (see [11]). The distributed features, like the notion of site and local evaluation, can be reproduced in different Maude modules in which rewrite rules are partitioned.

References

1. ANSI. RBAC, INCITS 359-2004 (2004)
2. Armando, A., et al.: The AVISPA tool for the automated validation of internet security protocols and applications. In: Etessami, K., Rajamani, S.K. (eds.) CAV 2005. LNCS, vol. 3576, pp. 281–285. Springer, Heidelberg (2005)
3. Bacon, J., Moody, K., Yao, W.: A model of OASIS RBAC and its support for active security. TISSEC 5(4), 492–540 (2002)
4. Barker, S.: The next 700 access control models or a unifying meta-model? In: Proc. of ACM Int. Conf. SACMAT 2009, pp. 187–196. ACM Press, New York (2009)
5. Barker, S., Fernández, M.: Term rewriting for access control. In: Proc. of DBSec 2006 Data and Applications Security. LNCS, Springer, Heidelberg (2006)
6. Barthe, G., Dufay, G., Huisman, M., Melo de Sousa, S.: Jakarta: a toolset to reason about the JavaCard platform. In: Attali, S., Jensen, T. (eds.) E-smart 2001. LNCS, vol. 2140, p. 2. Springer, Heidelberg (2001)
7. Becker, M., Sewell, P.: Cassandra: Distributed access control policies with tunable expressiveness. In: Proc. of POLICY 2004, pp. 159–168 (2004)
8. Becker, M.Y., Fournet, C., Gordon, A.D.: SecPAL: Design and Semantics of a Decentralized Authorization Language. Journal of Computer Security 18(4), 597–643 (2010)
9. Bell, D.E., LaPadula, L.J.: Secure computer system: Unified exposition and multics interpretation. MITRE-2997 (1976)
10. Bertolissi, C., Fernández, M.: A rewriting framework for the composition of access control policies. In: Proc. of PPDP 2008, Valencia. ACM Press, New York (2008)
11. Bertolissi, C., Fernández, M.: Time and location based services with access control. In: Proc. of NMTS 2008. IEEEXplore (2008)
12. Bertolissi, C., Fernández, M., Barker, S.: Dynamic event-based access control as term rewriting. In: Barker, S., Ahn, G.-J. (eds.) Data and Applications Security 2007. LNCS, vol. 4602, pp. 195–210. Springer, Heidelberg (2007)
13. Bertolissi, C., Fernández, M.: Distributed event-based access control. International Journal of Information and Computer Security, Special Issue: selected papers from Crisis 2008 3 (2009)
14. Bertolissi, C., Fernández, M.: Category-based authorisation models: Operational semantics and expressive power. In: Massacci, F., Wallach, D., Zannone, N. (eds.) ESSoS 2010. LNCS, vol. 5965, pp. 140–156. Springer, Heidelberg (2010)
15. Bonatti, P., de Capitani di Vimercati, S., Samarati, P.: A modular approach to composing access control policies. In: Proc. of CCS 2000, pp. 164–173. ACM Press, New York (2000)
16. Bonatti, P.A., Samarati, P.: Logics for authorization and security. In: Logics for Emerging Applications of Databases, pp. 277–323. Springer, Heidelberg (2003)
17. Chandran, S.M., Joshi, J.B.D.: Lot-rbac: A location and time-based rbac model. In: WISE 2005. LNCS, vol. 3806, pp. 361–375. Springer, Heidelberg (2005)
18. Clavel, M., Durán, F., Eker, S., Lincoln, P., Martí-Oliet, N., Meseguer, J., Talcott, C.: The Maude 2.0 system. In: Nieuwenhuis, R. (ed.) RTA 2003. LNCS, vol. 2706, pp. 76–87. Springer, Heidelberg (2003)
19. De Capitani di Vimercati, S., Samarati, P.: Authorization Specification and Enforcement in Federated Database Systems. Journal of Computer Security 5, 155–188 (1997)
20. DeTreville, J.: Binder, a logic-based security language. In: Proc. IEEE Symposium on Security and Privacy, pp. 105–113 (2002)

21. Echahed, R., Prost, F.: Security policy in a declarative style. In: Proc. of PPDP 2005. ACM Press, New York (2005)
22. Escobar, S., Meadows, C., Meseguer, J.: A Rewriting-Based Inference System for the NRL Protocol Analyzer and its Meta-Logical Properties. In: Theoretical Computer Science, vol. 367(1-2), pp. 162–202. Elsevier, Amsterdam (2006)
23. Fernández, M., Jouannaud, J.-P.: Modular termination of term rewriting systems revisited. In: Reggio, G., Astesiano, E., Tarlecki, A. (eds.) Abstract Data Types 1994 and COMPASS 1994. LNCS, vol. 906. Springer, Heidelberg (1995)
24. Jagadeesan, R., Saraswat, V.: Timed Constraint Programming: A Declarative Approach to Usage Control. In: Proc. of PPDP 2005. ACM Press, New York (2005)
25. Jajodia, S., Samarati, P., Sapino, M., Subrahmaninan, V.S.: Flexible support for multiple access control policies. ACM TODS 26(2), 214–260 (2001)
26. Jajodia, S., Samarati, P., Subrahmanian, V.S., Bertino, E.: A unified framework for enforcing multiple access control policies. SIGMOD Rec. 26(2), 474–485 (1997)
27. Jim, T.: SD3: A trust management system with certified evaluation. In: IEEE Symp. Security and Privacy, pp. 106–115 (2001)
28. Jonscher, D., Dittrich, K.: An approach for building secure database federations. In: Proc. of VLDB 1994, ACM Trans. on Internet Technology, vol. 8(1) (1994)
29. Joshi, J., Bertino, E., Latif, U., Ghafoor, A.: A generalized temporal role-based access control model. IEEE Trans. Knowl. Data Eng. 17(1), 4–23 (2005)
30. Klop, J.-W., van Oostrom, V., van Raamsdonk, F.: Combinatory reduction systems, introduction and survey. TCS 121, 279–308 (1993)
31. Koch, M., Mancini, L., Parisi-Presicce, F.: A graph based formalism for Rbac. In: SACMAT 2004, pp. 129–187 (2004)
32. Li, N., Mitchell, J.C., Winsborough, W.H.: Design of a role-based trust-management framework. In: IEEE Symposium on Security and Privacy, pp. 114–130 (2002)
33. Newman, M.H.A.: On theories with a combinatorial definition of equivalence. Annals of Mathematics 43(2), 223–243 (1942)
34. Department of Defense. Trusted computer system evaluation criteria, DoD 5200.28-STD (1983)
35. Santana de Oliveira, A.: Réécriture et Modularité pour les Politiques de Sécurité. PhD thesis, Université Henri Poincare, Nancy, France (2008)

A Case Study in Decentralized, Dynamic, Policy-Based, Authorization and Trust Management – Automated Software Distribution for Airplanes

Peter Hartmann[1], Monika Maidl[2], David von Oheimb[2], and Richard Robinson[3]

[1] Landshut University of Appl. Sciences, Am Lurzenhof 1, 84036 Landshut, Germany
peter.hartmann@fh-landshut.de
[2] Siemens Corporate Technology, Otto-Hahn Ring 6, 80200 München, Germany
{monika.maidl,david.von.oheimb}@siemens.com
[3] Boeing Research & Technology, P.O. Box 3707, MC 7L-70, Seattle, WA 98127-2207, USA
richard.v.robinson@boeing.com

Abstract. We apply SecPAL, a logic-based policy language for decentralized authorization and trust management, to our case study of automated software distribution for airplanes. In contrast to established policy frameworks for authorization like XACML, SecPAL offers constructs to express trust relationships and delegation explicitly and to form chains of trusts. We use these constructs in our case study to specify and reason about dynamic, ad-hoc trust relationships between airlines and contractors of suppliers of software that has to be loaded into airplanes.

Keywords: Authorization, trust management, security-tokens, logic, software-distribution.

1 Why do We Need Dynamic, Decentralized Authorization and Trust Management?

Electronically collaboration increasingly takes place not only within security domains, but between enterprises and individuals with no pre-established trust relationships. The application areas comprise industrial applications, energy management and distribution, transportation systems, healthcare, and many others. The use case we focus on is the distribution of software 'parts' to airplanes. The challenge is not only to transport such software parts from the airline to the airplane, but that a range of other parties – suppliers, the airplane manufacturer, and service providers – are involved. There is a strong security requirement that only unmodified parts that have been released by trusted producers are loaded into the airplane.

Triggered by the increasing demand for electronic communication and collaboration over the Internet, there is also a strong trend towards using standard protocols and frameworks as a uniform interface to existing computer systems and programming frameworks, based on standardized XML messages that are exchanged between various parties. In particular, grid computing and web services, based on XML/SOAP are used in scientific computing, automated business to business and

J. Cuellar et al. (Eds.): STM 2010, LNCS 6710, pp. 68–83, 2011.

business to customer scenarios (services) or cloud scenarios like Software-as-a Service. The use of web services has been standardized by the WS-* family of standards [1].

Many of these use cases have strong security requirements, and the classic security mechanisms based on enterprise perimeters protection (firewalls, DMZ etc.) are not suitable for dynamic, perimeter-crossing collaborations. In particular, mechanisms for the authentication of externals are required, as incorporating externals into the internal user management is considered to be inflexible and costly: accounts and access rights have to be managed, in case of changes in positions at a business partner, and accounts have to be removed when employees leave a company.

So new security models on top of http and web services communication have been developed, in particular SAML, the WS-* security specifications, XACML and CardSpace [1,2]. The core of these approaches is the use of *security tokens*. Security tokens, e.g. SAML tokens, WS-Security tokens, or InfoCards, are short-lived, signed expressions that are used to transfer authentication status and attributes across domain boundaries. This means that the authentication decision is delegated to an external party, namely the one issuing the security token. We will discuss in Section 1.2 how security tokens form the basis of dynamic, decentralized authentication.

1.1 Authorization

Just as with authentication, established domain-centric security mechanisms do not fit the requirements of cross-domain collaboration. Authorization has to be decided by the local authority, i.e. the owner of the application or resource. Typically, this is done by ACL (access control lists) on operating system level, or by application-specific authorization models like RBAC (e.g. in SAP). When externals are involved, both approaches do not work, as externals are typically not covered by the provisioning processes of an enterprise.

In contrast to authorization within an enterprise, authorization decisions for externals critically depend on trust. There are many aspects of trust decisions: whether to trust the authentication mechanism, to what extent the individual or their organization is trusted, the criticality of the application or action that is requested, and so on. In addition, in many scenarios including our case study, chains of trusts are formed. Today, authorization and trust often is handled implicitly. An example is that users implicitly trust all the root certificates contained in the certificate store of their operating system or browser. Typically, such a certificate store contains up to several hundreds of certificates, and decisions which of these are still trusted are difficult and unreliable. [3] discusses this problem and describes possible attacks.

Hence in order to handle authorization in cross-domain collaboration scenarios, a flexible language is required to explicitly address authorization in the context of trust relationships. In the next section we explain the difference between long-term trust and dynamic, ad-hoc trust relationships in order to make clear what features such a language should have.

1.2 Dynamic Ad-Hoc Trust Relationships

It is important to distinguish between *stable trust relationships*, which are often bilateral, and those relationships that are set up in a *dynamic, ad-hoc way*. Typically, users have a stable trust relationship within their domain. Typical features of long-term stable relationships are:

-   Authentication by long-term credentials (password, PKI certificate, …).
-   User accounts are managed (change of password, roles, etc.).
-   User accounts are removed only when the user leaves the domain.

PKI (Public Key Infrastructure) certificates are also security tokens in the sense discussed above, in that they provide transferable proof of identity. However, PKI certificates are only issued within a stable trust relationship, as PKI certificates typically have a validity time of up to several years, and accordingly are issued under strict procedures and rules only. Inter-domain use of PKI certificates is also long-term, by formally setting up cross certification or bridge CAs, or implicitly by inserting root CA certificates in certificate stores of operating systems or browsers.

In contrast, the trust relationship between e.g. a user and a service provider, or two businesses which want to collaborate is often dynamic and ad-hoc. As already mentioned, short-lived security tokens can be used in such settings to transfer authentication status and other attributes between business partners or services without having stable trust relationships in place beforehand.

The issuer of a security token could be the organization of the individual whose identity or other attributes are stated, or a third party that is trusted by both the individual's organization and the recipient. For example, an owner of an airplane that needs software updates might not directly trust the supplier of the airplane manufacturer, but trusts the manufacturer. So the manufacturer can issue a signed security token to the supplier, stating the supplier's identity, and the supplier sends this security token to the airplane owner. That establishes a dynamic trust relationship between the supplier and the airline.

Dynamic trust might be established in chains, i.e. dynamic trust relationships might again be used to set up other dynamic relationships. As an example, a supplier might have contractors to develop software, and issue security tokens for the contractor. Using this token, the dynamic trust relationship between the supplier and the airline can be used to set up a dynamic trust relationship between the contractor and the airline.

The recipient of a short-term security token relies on the information conveyed in the token to verify the PKI signature of the token and trusts the signer to make these statements, so long-term PKI trust has to be established. The issuer can only issue tokens to an individual or an organization that it can authenticate reliably. So ultimately, dynamic trust relationships ultimately have to be built on stable trust relationships.

Security tokens can carry more information than just authentication information. Any sort of statement could be made, e.g. that a company is an official supplier of another company, or that an employee has certain responsibilities. Using such attributes plays an important part in trust decisions because such statements can be used as input to authorization decisions that take into account not only the identity of the subjects of the security token, but also asserted properties of them. In our case study, we use security tokens that state that a certain software part has been approved, or that a service provider is certified to handle airplanes of a certain type.

To summarize, we list typical features of dynamic, ad-hoc trust relationships:

- Authentication by short-term *security tokens*, i.e. delegation of authentication to trusted parties.
- Chains of trust.
- Attribute-based authentication.

Hence short-term *security tokens* are the basic building blocks of dynamic, ad-hoc trust relationships. For the establishment and management of dynamic relationships, a framework is required to explicitly reason about attributes, delegation and chains of trust. We will explain in Section 3.2 how SecPAL matches these requirements.

2 Case Study in Automated Software Distribution to Airplanes

In the past, distribution of embedded software packages to mobile platforms such as airplanes was accomplished manually. In a typical scenario, the owner or maintenance provider for a vehicle would receive software updates on physical media, delivered via courier. A mechanic would be given a work order that entails installing software updates directly from physical media onto the airplane systems by means of a CD drive or similar. In the near future, however, software updates will increasingly be delivered over networks in an automated way.

On the way from the software *supplier* to the target device, software items may be handled at intermediate entities: an airplane manufacturer, in our use case Boeing, typically receive software items from suppliers or their *contractors*, and send it to *airlines*, which bear responsibility for the safe operation of their *airplanes*, and have the authorization to send software there. An airline might commission local *service providers* at airports to install software on its airplanes. So the software distribution process consists of several hops, and the software distribution stretches over the IT systems related to the process at each of these entities.

The airline is the central element of the distribution system and has relations to suppliers and Boeing on the one hand and to service providers and airplanes on the other hand. The central role of the airline is justified by the fact that the airline is responsible for all software due to be installed on an airplane and has to approve these software parts.

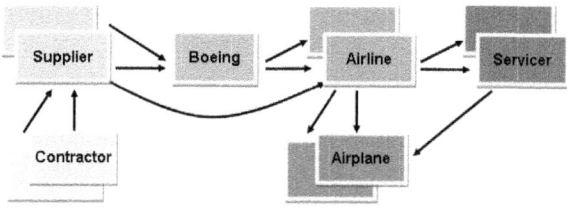

Fig. 1. Software distribution chain

In order to guarantee integrity and authenticity, software parts are signed, possibly in a nested way – e.g. a software package might be signed by a contractor, by a supplier and by the manufacturer. More details on the case study can be found in [4].

We assume that suppliers, the manufacturer, the airlines and the service providers have PKI certificates from some certificate authority, but we do not assume that each entity trusts all respective CA root certificates. In other words, we do not assume that stable trust relationships exist between all parties. This means for instance that the airline or the airplane cannot verify all signatures directly. Instead, we propose the use of ad-hoc dynamic trust relationships, managed by using SecPAL. First we discuss the stable relationships that we assume to exist in the case study.

2.1 Trust Relationships between Suppliers, Manufacturers and Airlines

We assume that there are contractual agreements and a technical set up so that suppliers are able to verify signatures of subcontractors, but neither Boeing nor the airline can. Similarly, Boeing has stable trust relations with suppliers, possibly by using a bridge CA like CertiPath Aerospace Bridge CA [5], but the airlines do not deal with suppliers or contractors directly. Instead, airlines trust Boeing to assert the identity and role of suppliers. We also assume that airlines own a trusted root certificate of Boeing's CA or use the CertiPath Trust Bridge CA, so that the airline can validate Boeing signatures and assertions.

2.2 Trust Relationships between Airline, Service Providers and Airplanes

We assume that airlines run a proprietary CA or buy commercial certificates, and that they have processes in place to equip airplanes with a trusted copy of the airline certificate, so that there is a direct stable trust relationship between the airline and its airplanes. The airplanes are maintained by local service providers who are contracted by the airline. An airline may have several service providers, responsible for maintenance of different airplane types or on different airports. The service providers use maintenance laptops to connect to the airplane or to the ground network, and will have to authenticate themselves to the airplane. As service providers contracts might be short-term, we do not assume stable trust between the airline and service providers. Instead, service providers obtain short-term security tokens from the airline that specify e.g. for which airplane types and during which time period a service provider is authorized to install software.

3 Policy-Based Authorization and Trust Management

We use a logic-based language, SecPAL, to model our use case. There are other policy languages that defined in terms of syntactic language constructs, while their semantics, i.e. the evaluation algorithm, is described in an informal way. Examples are XACML and XrML. Such description can be difficult to understand and implement, and in particular for complicated languages that include delegation, like XrML, subsequent analysis showed problems [14], which is not surprising because designers are likely to build something as complex as a logic framework from scratch. Unclear semantics also makes a language difficult to understand for users.

3.1 SecPAL - Logic-Based, Decentralized Authorization

Logic programming is well-suited for expressing trust management, because logic provides a framework for defining attributes, and enables reasoning, in particular about chains of trust.. After defining a set of statements or facts, an authorization request can be formulated and logic rules can be used to check whether the authorization request is a valid consequence of these facts.

SecPAL [6,7] is a logic-based policy language that addresses authorization and trust in distributed scenarios that involve frequent ad-hoc collaborations between entities with no pre-established trust relationships.

For example, an airline might decide to accept parts from suppliers and their contractors, where approval from contractors is sufficient for less critical parts, but critical parts require approval by suppliers. This can be expressed in SecPAL as follows:

> *Airline* says *p* is accepted if
>   *p* is type2-critical AND p is approved.
> *Airline* says *p* is accepted if
>   *p* is type1-critical AND p is supplier-approved.

Note that '*is accepted*', '*is* type1-critical' and 'is approved' are examples of attributes. In SecPAL, a wide range of attributes or authorization primitives ("can read", "is entitled to discount", "has access from [time1] to [time2]") can be defined by the author of the policy.

In our example, the airline does not want to manage the information which parts are type1-critical, and which companies are direct suppliers or contractors. Instead, the airline delegates statements about suppliers and parts to the manufacturer Boeing like the following:

> *Airline* says *Boeing* can say_0 *x* is type1-critical.
> *Airline* says *Boeing* can say_0 *x* is a supplier.

Delegation is expressed in SecPAL by the 'can say' construct.

These requirements are matched by assertions from other parties, for example:

> *Boeing* says *Part123* is type1-critical.

The suffix _0 for 'can say' means that the statement '*Boeing* says *Part123* is type1-critical' is only accepted if it is directly asserted by Boeing, and not derived by a chain of trust, as explained below.

The concept of parts being supplier-approved is defined by delegation:

> *Airline* says x can say p is supplier-approved
>   if x is a supplier.

If the following statements exist:

> *Boeing* says *Honeywell* is a supplier.
> *Honeywell* says *Part123* is supplier-approved.

then the request "*Part123* is accepted" can be derived.

Chains of trust are used to derive that a company is a contractor. The following statements are required to derive that 'FlightMedia is a contractor':

```
Airline says x can say y is a contractor till t
    if x is a supplier AND currentTime < t.
Airline says x can say that y is a contactor till t1
    if x is a contractor till t2 AND t1 < t2.
Boeing says Honeywell is a supplier.
Honeywell says EquipTech is a contractor till 2010.
EquipTech says FlightMedia is a contractor till 2009.
```

As this example shows, the requirements of dynamic trust relationships we identified in Section 1.2, namely the use of attributes, delegation to trusted parties and chains of trust can be expressed in SecPAL.

3.1.1 SecPAL Assertions

Formally, a SecPAL policy consists of several *SecPAL assertions*, which have the following form:

$$A \text{ says } fact \text{ if } fact_1 \text{ AND } ... \text{ AND } fact_n \text{ AND constraint.}$$

where *fact* is a sentence that states properties of principals. All names of principals in an assertion, like A in the example, stand for public (signature verification) keys. The principal A is the issuer of the assertion, and signs the assertion.

There are three different types of facts. The first type of *fact* is based on authorization primitives like

```
e has access from t1 to t2.
```

where e is either a name (like A) or a variable, and where authorization primitives can be defined by the user. The second type of *fact* expresses delegation in the form

e can say *fact*   (e.g. B can say c has access from date1 to date2).

Finally, facts can express principal aliasing in the form

e can act as d.

Note that delegation ('can say') may be nested, as the *fact* that is delegated can itself be a delegation expression.

Assertions are implicitly signed by the issuer, i.e. an assertion 'A says ...' is meant to be signed by A.

Assertion tokens and authorization rules

Informally, we can distinguish between SecPAL assertions that are used to prove identities, attributes or capabilities to another party, which we call *assertion tokens*, and assertions that express *authorization rules*. A service provider specifies authorization rules to state explicitly under which circumstances a user will be granted rights, and states precisely what sort of rights can be obtained. The authorization rules and the delegation rules issued by a service or communication partner together form its *local policy rules*.

In contrast, the assertion tokens are provided by the users who want to access a service in order to prove claims about themselves. Assertion tokens are typically issued by the home domain of a user, or by a trusted third party that can identify the user in a reliable way as part of a stable trust relationship. The policy engine of the service provider will use the user's assertion tokens together with the local policy rules to decide whether the access can be granted.

3.1.2 Solving SecPAL Queries

A set of SecPAL assertions, consisting of local policy rules and assertion tokens, determines whether an authorization request to a service is accepted. Authorization requests are called queries in SecPAL. An atomic request is of form

```
e says fact
```

General queries are formed from atomic queries and constraints by the logical connectives AND, OR, NOT and EXISTS x. In the example above, a useful query would be

```
Part123 is accepted.
```

In order to solve queries, SecPAL assertions are translated into a formal logic model, more precisely Datalog [8], which is a restricted logic programming language, i.e., "Prolog without function symbols". The evaluation of a query against a set of SecPAL assertion corresponds to a run of the corresponding Datalog program. During such a run, nested delegation is resolved by iteration, and suitable variable assignments are generated.

The use of an established logic model as a basis offers a clear semantics, and because logic models like Datalog have been well studied in academia, there are results on decidability (i.e. termination) and on runtime complexity. Moreover, implementation methods for such logic models have been developed and iteratively improved. More concretely, for SecPAL these results state that query evaluation is decidable with polynomial time complexity. For practical purposes, such a statement is valuable, as it guarantees that query evaluation is tractable even for the most complex policies.

3.2 Other Security Token Frameworks: SAML, WS-* Security and XACML

As already mentioned in Section 1.2, the use of security tokens is well established in by WS-* security, the SAML and the XACML standards. We briefly describe the framework in order to show how it differs from SecPAL. The token-based security model that underlies the WS-* specifications is explained in [9] and shown in Fig. 2. Security tokens are carried in messages and are used to prove *claims* about the sender of the message, e.g. the name of the sender, or roles and attributes, i.e. attribute-based authentication is possible. Before sending a message, e.g. to request a service, a user has to obtain a suitable security token from a Security Token Services (STS), which is located in the user's domain and hence can authenticate the user as part of a stable trust relationship. Authentication might be via username and password, smart cards, biometrics or any other means. The STS might impose restrictions on authentication methods, e.g. require passwords to have a certain quality, or only allow access at

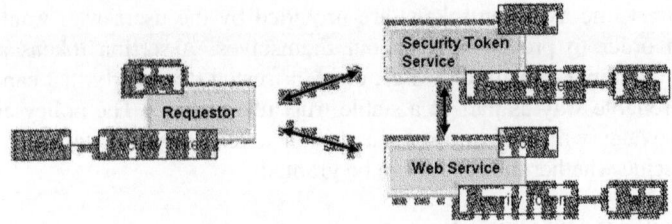

Fig. 2. The web services security model

office hours, or restrict the validity period of security tokens to one day. Such requirements form the *policy* of the STS.

After obtaining a security token, which is signed by the STS, the user can make a request to a service and include the security token into the request message. The service or application authenticates and authorizes the user by evaluating the security token. The service might impose its own restrictions, e.g. requirements on security tokens like the use of specific cryptographic algorithms, acceptable maximal validity periods and acceptable methods with which the user has been authenticated to the STS. These restrictions form the local policy of the web service.

A widely used type of security token is SAML assertions. The SAML standard also includes protocols for using SAML assertions for Single Sign-on, similar to Fig. 2, but for use in web browsers rather than web services (SOAP) messages.

Neither the WS-* security specifications nor SAML do cover authorization. The XACML standard defines an XML based policy language to describe general access control requirements, including extension points for defining new functions, data types, combining logic, etc. XACML also includes a request/response language to pose queries whether or not a given action should be allowed.

XACML can be used in conjunction with SAML, i.e. a user provides a SAML security token to a service, and based on this information and a XACML policy, the services grants access or not. In such a setting, authentication decisions can be delegated and attribute-based authentication and authorization can be used. The main difference to the SecPAL framework is that delegation is implicit, i.e. it is not specified in the local policy of a service who is trusted to make assertions, i.e. there is not equivalent to the 'can say' construct of SecPAL. Consequently, chains of trust cannot be specified. Another difference is that in XACML there is an implicit central authority that states the policy, whereas in SecPAL, the authorship is explicit, as in 'A says...'.

3.3 Other Logic-Based Authorization and Trust Policy Languages

The use of logic for authorization and delegation was pioneered by the Speaks-for Calculus [10], where the 'says' construct was introduced. Many later logic-based authorization frameworks and trust management systems are based on variants and extensions of Datalog with constraints [8], e.g. Binder [11], Delegation Logic [12], and Cassandra [13]. SecPAL differs from these languages in that is offers constructs specifically targeted for distributed authorization policies, and that it is very expressive while requiring only a small number of constructs.

Other logic frameworks that have been used to provide semantics for policy languages include first-order logic, e.g. for XrML in [14] and SPKI/SDSI [15], and pushdown automata for SPKI/SDSI [16].

The development of DKAL (Distributed-Knowledge Authorization Language) [17], another logic-based language, was by SecPAL, and had the goal to remove a potential information leak problem and to increase expressivity by allowing the free use of functions. Apart from the use of function symbols, the main difference to SecPAL is that communication is targeted, i.e. that the basic form of assertions is not 'A says ...' but 'A says ... to B'. In that way it can be avoided that confidential information is leaked by posing queries that are evaluated using confidential assertions. A revised version of DKAL, yet more expressive, is presented in [18] SecPAL can be naturally translated into DKAL, so we could have used DKAL instead of SecPAL. But as confidentiality is not relevant to our use case, and we also do not need to use free functions, we decided to use SecPAL. An important reason for our decision to use SecPAL was that an implementation is available for SecPAL, so we could build a demonstrator for our use case, described in Section 5.

4 Applying SecPAL to the Case Study

4.1 Building and Managing Trust between Airlines and Suppliers

We represent the scenario of Section 2.1 in terms of SecPAL policies. In that scenario, the airline has to make decisions on whether to accept an incoming part that originates from a supplier or the contractor of a supplier. As explained, the airline usually does not have a stable trust relationship with suppliers or contractors, and hence cannot verify supplier signatures directly. However, airlines do have a stable trust relationship with the manufacturer Boeing, and in particular airlines can verify Boeing signatures. So SecPAL assertion tokens issued by Boeing can be used to establish trust between airlines and suppliers or contractors.

In Fig. 3 we present the SecPAL assertions of the different parties in that scenario, i.e. the airline, Boeing, the supplier Honeywell, and various subcontractors of Honeywell.

The airline specifies in its authorization rules when to accept a part. We distinguish between critical software parts (type-1-critical) and less critical parts (type-2-critical). Critical parts have to be approved by a supplier, while type2-critical parts can also be approved by contractors of suppliers.

In the first of its delegation rules, the airline states that Boeing is trusted to make claims about who is a supplier. The 'can say' construct is restricted by _0, meaning that the airline does not trust statements about supplier status that Boeing might make by using itself some form of delegation rules. The second rule, which states that suppliers are trusted to make statements about their contractors, does not have the _0 suffix. A contractor is allowed to have subcontractors, as long as the validity period of the contract with the subcontractor is shorter then the validity of his own contract with the supplier. The next four delegation rules state that supplier and contractors are allowed to approve parts and that Boeing is the only party that is allowed to define the criticality type of a part. The authorization rules state that parts accepted only if they

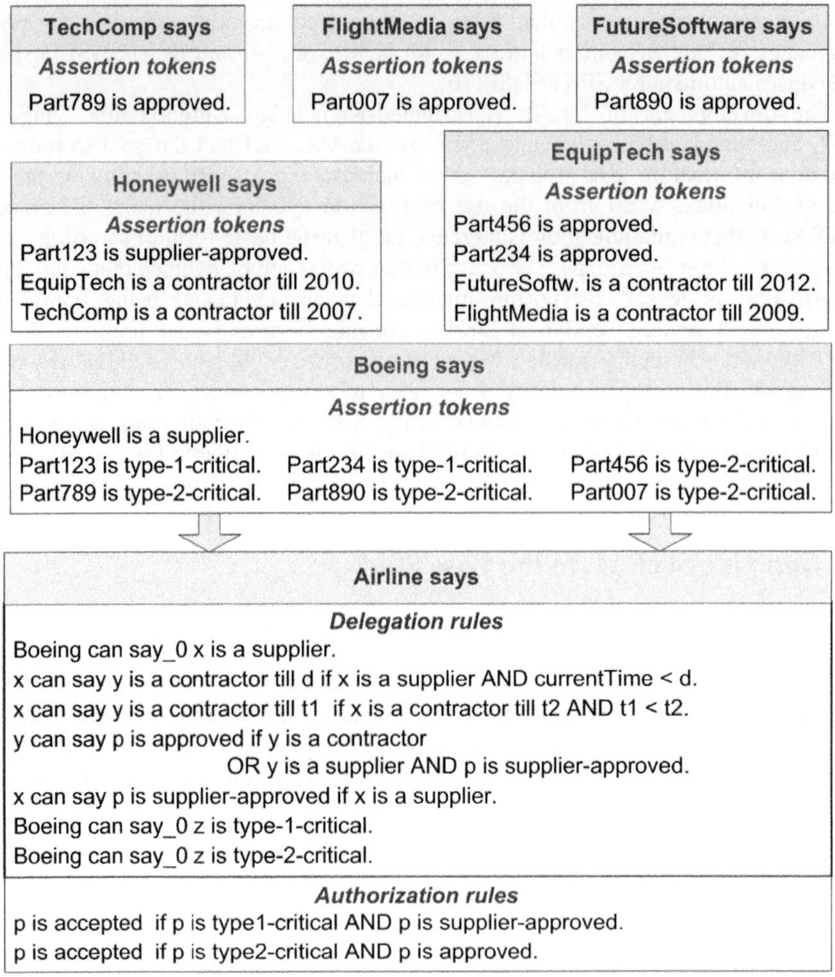

TechComp says	FlightMedia says	FutureSoftware says
Assertion tokens	*Assertion tokens*	*Assertion tokens*
Part789 is approved.	Part007 is approved.	Part890 is approved.

Honeywell says
Assertion tokens
Part123 is supplier-approved.
EquipTech is a contractor till 2010.
TechComp is a contractor till 2007.

EquipTech says
Assertion tokens
Part456 is approved.
Part234 is approved.
FutureSoftw. is a contractor till 2012.
FlightMedia is a contractor till 2009.

Boeing says

Assertion tokens

Honeywell is a supplier.

Part123 is type-1-critical.	Part234 is type-1-critical.	Part456 is type-2-critical.
Part789 is type-2-critical.	Part890 is type-2-critical.	Part007 is type-2-critical.

Airline says

Delegation rules

Boeing can say_0 x is a supplier.

x can say y is a contractor till d if x is a supplier AND currentTime < d.

x can say y is a contractor till t1 if x is a contractor till t2 AND t1 < t2.

y can say p is approved if y is a contractor

                    OR y is a supplier AND p is supplier-approved.

x can say p is supplier-approved if x is a supplier.

Boeing can say_0 z is type-1-critical.

Boeing can say_0 z is type-2-critical.

Authorization rules

p is accepted if p is type1-critical AND p is supplier-approved.

p is accepted if p is type2-critical AND p is approved.

Fig. 3. SecPAL policies for an airline accepting parts originating from suppliers

are approved by contractors or suppliers. Only the airline specifies authorization rules, all other parties issue assertion tokens. Boeing issues several assertion tokens, thereby making claims about its suppliers, and classifying the criticality of parts. Honeywell, as a supplier, issues assertion tokens about the approval of parts, and about its contractors. The various contractors issue assertion tokens about the approval of parts, and about their contractors. Note the different validity times for the contractors. We list some example queries.

"SupplierPart": A software supplier delivers a part that is type1 critical for approval by the airline.

```
Airline says Part123 is accepted.    (valid)
```

"ContractorPart": A contractor of a software supplier delivers a part that is type2 critical for approval by the airline.

`Airline` says `Part789` is accepted.   (valid)

"IllegalSubContractor": A contractor has a contract with another contractor, and the validity period of the subcontractor exceeds the validity period of the contractor's contract with the supplier. The subcontractor tries to deliver a part.

`Airline` says `Part890` is accepted.   (invalid)

"InvalidPartType": A contractor of a software supplier delivers a part which is type1 critical for approval by the airline.

`Airline` says `Part234` is accepted.   (invalid)

4.2   Authorizing Services to Perform Tasks in Airplanes

As a second example, we show how to implement the scenario from Section 2.2, an airplane granting requests to install software parts. Service providers install (load) parts from in an airplane. As service providers are contracted by airlines at various airports for a limited time, we use SecPAL assertions to authenticate service providers to airplanes.

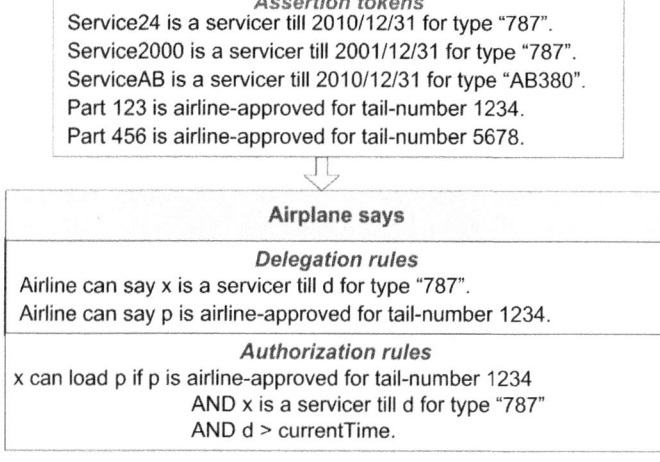

Fig. 4. SecPAL policy for an airplane accepting software part loading

As shown in Fig. 4, the authorization rules of the airplane state under which conditions a service providers is allowed to load a part into the airplane: the part has to be approved by the airline for the specific airplane and the person installing the part in the airplane has to be a service providers with a valid service provider contract with the airline. The airline is not mentioned in the authorization rules directly, but comes into play by the delegation rules or the airplane, where the airplane states that its airline is trusted to issue SecPAL assertion tokens about who is a service provider, and which parts are approved.

The airline issues a range of assertion tokens about current service providers and about approved parts. A service provider has to authenticate towards an airline in order to get an assertion token about his identity. How this is done is not addressed by the SecPAL policy – it could by done by personal exchange at some airline authority at an airport.

Note that most principal names in SecPAL assertions denote public keys and that all SecPAL assertions of the form 'A says ...' are signed with the public key of A. So in the assertion token 'Airline says Service24 is a servicer till 2010/12/31 for type "787". Service24 is a public key of a current service provider, and when the airplane receives the token, it validates the signature to verify that its airline has issued the token. As the airplane and the airline have a stable long-term relationship, the airplane knows the public key of its airline and can perform the signature verification. After accepting the token, the airplane with tail number 1234 accepts the public key of Service24, and can use this key for authentication of the service provider, e.g. by using SSL.

Again, we list example queries.

"ServicerValid": A service provider who is authorized by the airline for an airplane type wants to load a part which was approved by the airline and released for upload to the actual airplane.

> *Airline* says *Service24* can install *Part123*.   (valid)

"ServicerOutdated": A service provider whose contract with the airline has expired, wants to load a part which was approved by the airline and released for upload to the actual airplane.

> *Airline* says *Service2000* can install *Part123*.   (invalid)

"ServicerIncompetent": A service provider who has a valid contract with the airline, but for a different airplane type, wants to load a part which was approved by the airline and released for upload to the actual airplane.

> *Airline* says *ServiceAB* can install *Part123*.   (invalid)

5 Demonstrator

As part of the project, a demonstrator application has been created to show how the scenarios described in the previous section can be evaluated with SecPAL. The implementation of this demonstrator is based on the SecPAL Authorization Engine provided by Microsoft and available at [7].A Windows forms application called "QueryEditor" is also offered by Microsoft. The QueryEditor displays the assertion rules in readable language and can be used to edit and evaluate queries. If a query is accepted, the corresponding proof tree can be examined. The Query editor can save assertions as XML files. The XML representation of policies and assertions will be the basis for real world implementations of SecPAL applications that can be integrated with distributed services. The Query editor offers the user basic English language constructs to generate policies, assertions and queries, which proved to be too restricted for our case study scenarios.

The figures below are screenshots of the Query Editor application. The Principal window shows all principals that are part of this sample. Using the next two tabs, the policies and assertions of all principals can be displayed. Fig. 5 shows the tokens in the "ServicerValid" sample. The button "evaluate" starts the evaluation of the query. Using the tabulator "proof graph" tab, the proof of the evaluation can be displayed when successful (Fig. 6).

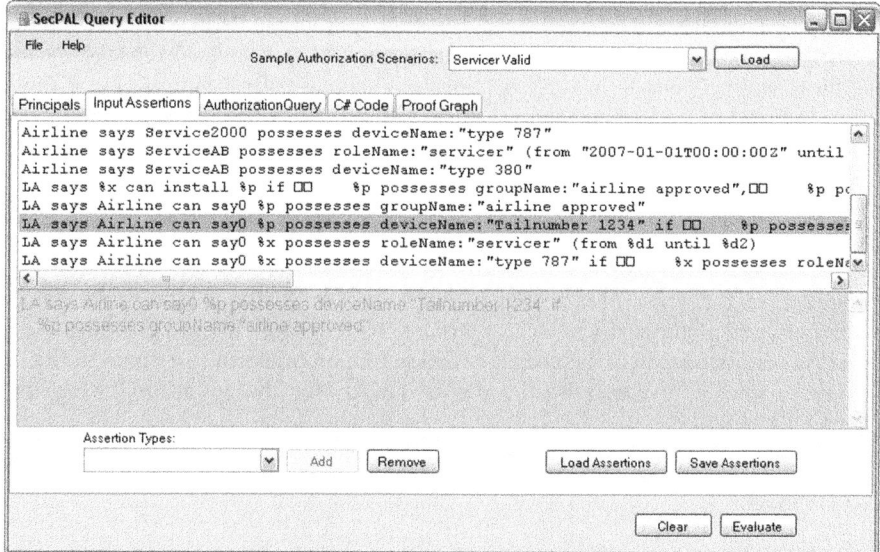

Fig. 5. QueryEditor: Assertions

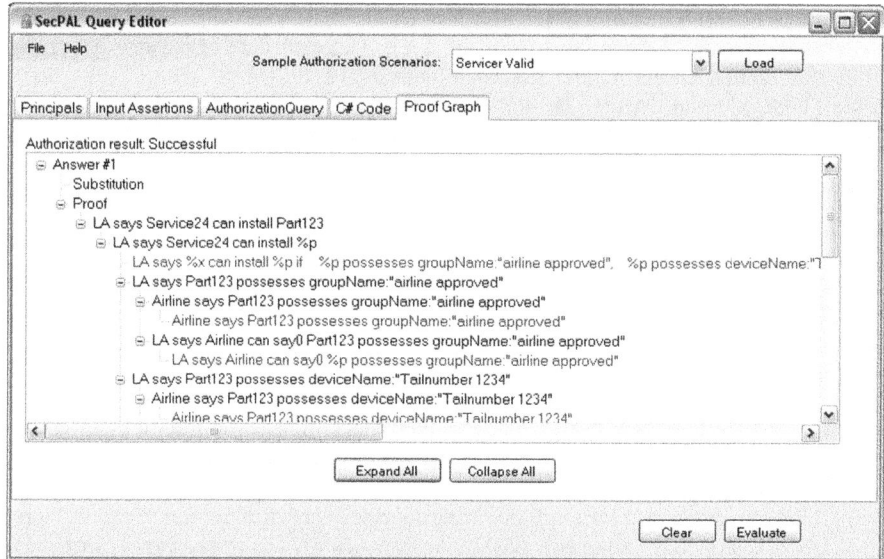

Fig. 6. QueryEditor: Proof Tree

We implemented the scenarios in C#. The source code can be viewed at the C# Code tab. There the user can also see how English language assertion statements and the query are translated to C#.

6 Conclusion

Currently trust and authorization across domain boundaries is often established by setting up contractual agreements and inserting appropriate PKI certificates into local certificate stores. Doing so will become unmanageable when data exchanges between partners without long-term trust relationships increase. By handling a real-life use case, we have convinced ourselves that logic-based policy languages for authorization and trust, in particular SecPAL, are well suited to address this challenge. We found that we could handle our case study in a straightforward way, and that the resulting policies are easy to grasp for non-experts. Microsoft's implementation of SecPAL served as a practical proof of concept. However, for a wider applicability of SecPAL or its successor languages, it would be important to have a standardization of the language in the form of a syntax coding, say, in XML, a binding to transport protocols, and a processing model, to promote wider usage. We will continue to apply SecPAL or its successor languages whenever appropriate in our future work. For instance, we are investigating the use of DKAL for the application scenarios of AVANTSSAR [19].

References

[1] The WS-*, SAML and XACML standards are,
    http://www.oasis-open.org/specs/
[2] Microsoft Corporation: Introducing Windows CardSpace,
    http://msdn.microsoft.com/en-us/library/aa480189.aspx
[3] Soghoian, C., Stamm, S.: Certified Lies: Detecting and Defeating Government Interception Attacks Against SSL. (under submission)
[4] Maidl, M., von Oheimb, D., Hartmann, P., Robinson, R.: Formal security analysis of electronic software distribution systems. In: Harrison, M.D., Sujan, M.-A. (eds.) SAFECOMP 2008. LNCS, vol. 5219, pp. 415–428. Springer, Heidelberg (2008)
[5] Nigriny, J., Phaltankar, K.: Identity Assurance in Commercial Aviation Facilitated Through a Trusted Third Party Hub. White paper of CertiPath,
    http://www.certipath.com/white-papers.htm
[6] Becker, M., Fournet, C., Gordon, A.: SecPAL: Design and Semantics of a Decentralized Authorization Language. In: 20th IEEE Computer Security Foundations Symposium, pp. 3–15. IEEE Press, New York (2007)
[7] SecPAL homepage,
    http://research.microsoft.com/en-us/projects/SecPAL/
[8] Li, N., Mitchell, J.C.: DATALOG with constraints: A foundation for trust management languages. In: Dahl, V. (ed.) PADL 2003. LNCS, vol. 2562, pp. 58–73. Springer, Heidelberg (2002)
[9] IBM Corporation and Microsoft Corporation: Security in a Web Services World: A Proposed Architecture and Roadmap (2002), http://www.ibm.com/developerworks/library/specification/ws-secmap/

[10] Abadi, M., Burrows, M., Lampson, B., Plotkin, G.: A Calculus for Access Control in Distributed Systems. ACM Transactions on Programming Languages and Systems 15(4), 706–734 (1993)

[11] DeTreville, J.: Binder, a logic-based security language. In: IEEE Symposium on Security and Privacy, pp. 105–113. IEEE Press, New York (2002)

[12] Li, N., Grosof, B., Feigenbaum, J.: Delegation Logic. ACM Trans. on Information and System Security (TISSEC) 6(1), 128–171 (2003)

[13] Becker, M., Sewell, P.: Cassandra: Flexible trust management, Applied to Electronic Health Records. In: 17th IEEE Computer Security Foundations Workshop (CSFW). IEEE Press, New York (2004)

[14] Halpern, J.Y., Weissmann, V.: A formal foundation of XrML. In: 17th IEEE Computer Security Foundations Workshop (CSFW). IEEE Press, New York (2004)

[15] Li, N., Mitchell, J.C.: Understanding SPKI/SDSI using first-order logic. In: 16th IEEE Computer Security Foundations Workshop (CSFW), pp. 89–103. IEEE Press, New York (2003)

[16] Jha, S., Schwoon, S., Wang, H., Reps, T.: Weighted Pushdown Systems and Trust-Management Systems. In: Hermanns, H. (ed.) TACAS 2006. LNCS, vol. 3920, pp. 1–26. Springer, Heidelberg (2006)

[17] Gurevich, Y., Neeman, I.: DKAL: Distributed-Knowledge Authorization Language. In: 21th IEEE Computer Security Foundations Workshop (CSFW), pp. 149–162. IEEE Press, New York (2008)

[18] Gurevich, Y., Neeman, I.: A Simplified and Improved Authorization Language. Microsoft Research Tech Report (February 2009),
http://research.microsoft.com/en-us/um/people/
gurevich/dkal.htm

[19] EU-funded project AVANTSSAR: Automated Validation of Trust and Security of Service-oriented Architectures, http://avantssar.eu/

GUTS: A Framework for Adaptive and Configureable Grid User Trust Service

Ioanna Dionysiou[1], Harald Gjermundrød[1], and David E. Bakken[2]

[1] Department of Computer Science
University of Nicosia, Nicosia, Cyprus
{dionysiou.i,harald}@unic.ac.cy
[2] School of Electrical Engineering and Computer Science
Washington State University, Pullman, WA, USA
bakken@eecs.wsu.edu

Abstract. Even though trust plays a significant role during decision-making in open collaborative environments, still Grid user trust mechanisms have not been widely deployed in Grid computing settings like Enabling Grids for E-sciencE (EGEE). In this paper, an investigation on the specification and management of user trust in Grid infrastructures is presented. The design of a novel Grid user trust service (GUTS) is introduced that aims in leveraging Grid functionality with trust mechanisms, with a special focus on achieving end-user trust in an intuitive and practical manner.

Keywords: activity-oriented trust, grid computing, user trust.

1 Introduction

Trust is an abstraction of individual beliefs that an entity has for specific situations and interactions. An entity's beliefs are not static but they change as time progresses and new information is processed into knowledge. Trust must evolve in a consistent manner so that it still abstracts the entity's beliefs accurately. In this way, an entity continuously makes informed decisions based on its current beliefs.

Trust must be managed in an appropriate and systematic manner. Trust management is a process that collects information, that is treated as evidence, to evaluate trust relationships, as well as monitor and re-evaluate the state of these trust relationships. Trust is a multifaceted concept, encompassing even more than message integrity, source authentication and reliance on other entities. There is no single correct way to determine the right level of trust, or which aspects to include. Decisions about how to weigh each aspect lie with the evaluator and can differ substantially from situation to situation.

Collaborative settings, such as Grid environments, where risk and uncertainty are inherent due to their open nature could greatly benefit from using trust as an integral part of decision-making. For example, a Grid user could choose the

J. Cuellar et al. (Eds.): STM 2010, LNCS 6710, pp. 84–99, 2011.

most *trustworthy* site from a pool of available sites to submit a job. A Grid user could specify its *trust requirements* in a parametrized job description and these requirements will be taken into consideration during job-site matching. Sites, offering computational resources, could be rated based on their *reputation* among Grid users.

To the best of our knowledge, trust tools are currently not available to the average Grid end-user. A trust management framework is needed, where trust is specified, managed and visualized in an intuitive manner; in this way Grid computing will leverage its existing security services with trust mechanisms tailored for the needs of a typical Grid e-scientist. In this paper, we present a preliminary investigation on integrating trust routines in Grid settings, focusing on intuitive and practical solutions. The design of GUTS (Grid User Trust Service) framework is introduced with a conceptual feasibility investigation on how it could be deployed in actual Grid infrastructures.

The remaining of the paper is organized as follows: Section 2 briefly discusses existing trust approaches in Grid infrastructures. Section 3 presents a trust approach applicable to Grid interactions, where multiple entities are expected to collaborate. The GUTS framework is introduced in Section 4, followed by Section 5 that analyzes the feasibility of deploying GUTS in Enabling Grids for E-sciencE (EGEE), a Grid infrastructure that serves as the exemplary Grid in this paper. Finally, Section 6 concludes.

2   Trust Management in Grid Environments

A computational Grid [13],[14],[12] is a collection of distributed, possibly heterogeneous resources that can be used as an ensemble to execute computational-intense applications, such as earth observation, climate modeling, and biology applications. The two pillars of the Grid paradigm are access to shared services and support of multi-user collaboration, while the resource owner is always in control. Figure 1 illustrates a generic Grid environment. Sites are organized in one or more virtual organizations, thus creating federations of central services, such as cross-domain authentication, authorization, job-site matching, and job dispatching. Authorized users access computational and storage resources of a site by contacting either the central services or the site itself.

The Grid must be managed to allow coordination of the dynamic cross-organizational resource sharing among virtual organizations not only in an efficient manner but securely as well. This is nontrivial to achieve, mainly due to the self-managed and unpredictable nature of the virtual organizations. Nevertheless, there are deployed mechanisms that provide a number of security services. For instance, a single sign-on authentication mechanism is already available via proxy certificates. Authorization is implemented via access control lists. X.509 certificates could be used not only to authenticate a user but to encrypt traffic flows.

Humphrey et al. [20] analyzed a comprehensive set of Grid usage scenarios with regard to security requirements. However, cryptographic algorithms and

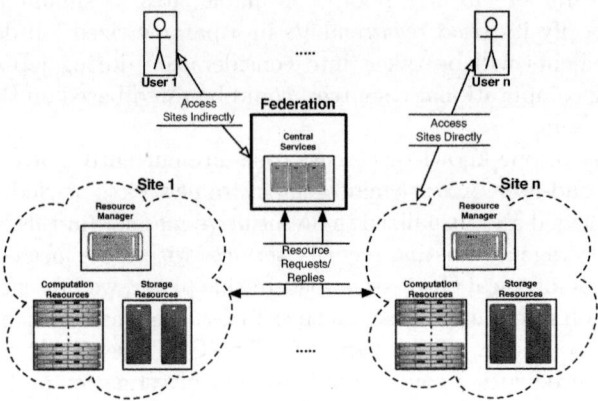

Fig. 1. Generic Grid Environment

access control schemes cannot be used to reason about the more general concept of trust, – the *belief* that an entity will behave as expected under certain conditions – as there are no provisions for a number of security, behavioral, and QoS issues such as data privacy, site administrators qualifications, and service reliability provided by the various sites. An authenticated and authorized user has no guarantees that the Grid infrastructure will successfully carry out the execution of a submitted job. The Grid user remains defenseless against job failures, which according to a recent study [24] account for a large percentage of all submitted jobs, and attempts to compensate for any potential failures by submitting the same job to multiple sites.

The failures could be attributed to security, behavioral, or QoS factors, thus making the Grid environment the ideal setting for deploying trust as an integral part of the decision-making. In the recent years, there has been an increasing interest in addressing specific trust challenges in Grid environments. However, the existing research efforts limit the trust scope to either authentication or authorization. In [26], the Trust domains establishment is mentioned as being one of the three key functions in a Grid Security Model, where virtual organizations establish trust among users and resources that is expressed in policies and proxy certificates. The authors in [5] leverage the authentication and authorization capabilities of the Grid security framework using trust negotiation with PeerTrust policy language whereas the importance of trust negotiation is reiterated in [23]. Similarly, [1] uses trust federation and dynamic authorization supported by GRIA middleware to demonstrate the dynamic federation of resources capability. The research work in [7] focuses on a decentralized resource access control scheme using trust chains and an extended SPKI/SDSI that allow intermediate levels of trust to be expressed per chain, rather a a binary model of valid or invalid.

A more general approach to trust is presented in the survey by Arenas et al. in [4], which discusses the trust classifications in Internet services [17] from the Grid perspective. Furthermore, [3] investigates the possibility of exploiting reputation systems for managing virtual organizations. Still, there is no implementation of a suite of trust mechanisms that the average Grid end-user could utilize to specify its trust requirements and incorporate them in decision-making. The proposed work in [10] investigates the emerging technological challenges associated with the support of such a comprehensive user-oriented adaptive trust framework deployed in Grid infrastructures.

3   Activity-Oriented Grid Trust Approach

Grid interactions involve the collaboration of multiple entities, and this characteristic is central in the proposed trust approach described in this section. The discussion starts with presenting the rationale behind activity-aware trust, followed by a list of requirements that a trust management system needs to meet in order to support such trust.

3.1   Activity-Aware Trust in the Grid

In a typical trust setting, there is a *trustor* and a *trustee*. A trustor is the entity that makes a trust assessment for an entity, which is the trustee. The scope of the trust relationship between a trustor and a trustee is narrowed to a specific action called *context* and is valid for a time *interval*. Each trust relationship is associated with a set of *expectations*, which are requirements that the trustor has for the particular interaction with the trustee. Formally, $\tau(\gamma, \delta, c, \lambda, \iota, \epsilon, id)$ represents a trust relationship between two entities and it is interpreted as *"trustor γ, based on γ's trusting attitude, believes that the extent to which trustee δ will act as expected for context c during time interval ι is λ, and this belief is subject to the satisfaction of expectation set ϵ. This relationship is valid for a specific interaction id"* [8].

A trust relationship may be one-to-many to cover a group of trustees, which are trusted similarly within the same context. However, such approach cannot encompass the complexity of trust in an activity that involves different contexts and trustees. An *activity* is an interaction that involves multiple trustees that assume different roles [8]. The successful outcome of an activity requires the collaboration of trustees performing functions that are not necessarily the same.

In order to illustrate the applicability of activity-aware trust in Grid settings, consider a Grid user who wants to assess the outcome from a job execution. The user has to consider all entities that are involved in this interaction. The actual site where the job execution is to be performed is a key entity, but the presence of the intermediate entity that performs the job-site matching has also an impact on the job. As a result, the user (trustor) has to make trust assessments for all interacting entities (trustees) that collaboratively execute a task and combine them in order to derive an end-to-end trust assessment about the quality of the submitted job. Consider Figure 1 again. If Grid user $User_1$ were to make a trust assessment concerning the activity of *executing job j_1 on the Grid by accessing $Site_1$ indirectly*, then the following relationships had to be examined and synthesized:

- relationship $\tau(User_1, Federation, ...)$ between $User_1$ and Federation regarding Federation's ability to *perform job-site matching* for job j_1 (note that for simplicity reasons, the remaining trust attributes are omitted)
- relationship $\tau(User_1, Site_1, ...)$ between $User_1$ and $Site_1$ regarding $Site_1$'s ability to *execute* job j_1 on its local resources (the computational and storage resources as well as the resource manager are abstracted as a single entity Site.)

3.2   Managing Grid User Trust

Trust relationships are managed by a trust management system (TMS) that supports four activities [17]. The first activity is the *Trust Evidence Collection*, which is the process of collecting evidence required to make a trust decision. The second activity, *Trust Analysis*, is the process of examining trust relationships to identify implicit relationships. *Trust Evaluation* is the third activity that evaluates evidence in the context of trust relationships. Finally, *Trust Monitoring* is the activity that is responsible for updating trust relationship based on evidence. Building a trust management service for activity-aware trust applications requires defining those issues that are necessary for extending a general trust management system to support dynamic and composable trust assessments of all entities that handle the information, not just the creator or consumer of the data. Below is an overview list of the requirements:

R1 Evidence Collection and Distribution: The TMS must support a diversity of evidence types, including recommendations, credentials, low-level instrumentation data. Diversity on evidence types allows for a more comprehensive assessment of trust. The evidence collected and distributed must be controllable by user policies, and the evidence streams must not be assumed to be static but rather changing with respect to user policies.

R2 Trust Analysis: The TMS must model time as a fundamental quantity that allows reasoning about it during the specification and analysis of trust relationships and provide the necessary constructs that will allow an end-to-end trust assessment of a chain of trust relationships.

R3 Trust Evaluation: The TMS must provide a wide range of mechanisms to aggregate evidence of the same or different type. The feedback from recommenders must be weighted based on the trust relationship between the receiver of the feedback and the recommender.

The TMS must also allow a user to express functions that map evidence to expectations. Expectation is defined as a requirement and its allowed values that a trustor has for a particular interaction with a trustee; these values are constraint by equality and inequality operators. For instance, the expectation tuple $(reliability, >=, 0.90, 0.95)$ denotes the user's requirement on the reliability as a value greater or equal to 0.90, with the current actual value to be 0.95. The observed value for an expectation is not necessarily derived directly from a single type of evidence. For example, a trustor may choose to specify the behavior expectation as a function of reputation and reliability. Behavior is not collected directly from evidence streams, but on the contrary, recommendations and reliability measurements are manipulated to derive behavioral values.

R4 Trust Monitoring: The TMS must take into consideration the dynamic nature of the domain and the dynamic behavior its participants whenever a trust assessment is made, and it must provide for different trusting attitudes. For example, new participants join the network and existing ones depart from it. Participants performance and properties change. Legal contracts may force collaborators to become competitors. Trust relationships should reflect these social, organizational, performance and network changes.

4   Grid User Trust Service (GUTS) Framework

Grid User Trust Service (GUTS) Framework, illustrated in Figure 2, is a novel trust management service tailored to the needs of a typical Grid user. It comprises of three main components:

- **Grid Middleware-Agnostic Trust Specification:** Allows a user to specify in an easy and intuitive manner the trust requirements for a Grid service.
- **Grid Middleware-Dependent Trust Specification:** Translates and maps general requirements to the specific Grid infrastructure, yielding the trust profile of a project.
- **Trust Management and Visualization:** Gathers and evaluates evidence provided by the specific Grid infrastructure, updates the trust profiles accordingly, and produces a ranking list of the various Grid sites.

The GUTS framework could be deployed by Grid client frameworks such as g-Eclipse [16] or GANGA [19] as plug-ins or could be offered as a service through Grid web portals that are developed using toolkits like OGCE [25]. Regardless the deployment avenue chosen, GUTS internal workings will remain unaffected, with the exception of slight modifications that have to take place in order to accommodate the seamless integration with the tools used by the Grid user.

4.1   Grid Middleware-Agnostic Trust Specification

The main objective of this component is to devise a middleware-agnostic trust requirements XML schema, which captures in an abstract manner the trust requirements that an e-scientist can comprehend and specify. These requirements are abstracted to the user as a set of *attributes* along with their types and associated value ranges. The XML schema will be used to instantiate valid XML trust requirements documents, one per Grid project, as various projects may have different trust requirements.

In order to demonstrate the above statement, suppose that a user creates a Grid project that applies pruning rules on a very large data set to produce a smaller one. A number of sites may have to coordinate to execute this task,

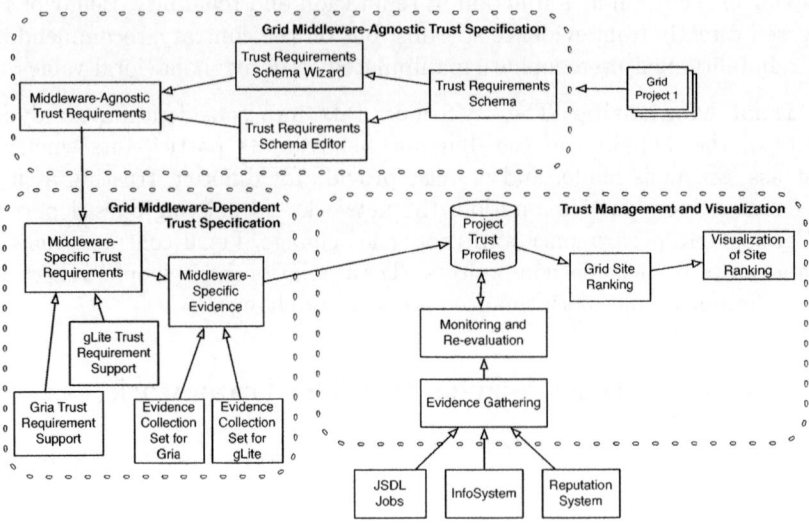

Fig. 2. Design of GUTS Framework

as each site will be assigned a subset of the data. A second project uses data mining on the generated pruned data set to derive vital conclusions. In this case, only a single site is responsible for the task execution. The trust requirements on the sites that execute the jobs associated with these projects are different; for the latter case it is required that the site meets stringent reliability, security, and privacy requirements whereas in the former case more relaxed requirements could be imposed as the various sites do not have access to the entire data set.

Some of the attributes that a Grid user could specify include the following:

- **Administrator Certification:** Is there any information publicly available that could serve as a certification for the competence and expertise of the site administrators?
- **Institute Hosting the Site:** What type of institute is hosting the site? It could be public/private university, public/private research center, public (not-for-profit) organization, etc.
- **Security Level:** Grid sites deploy a variety of security mechanisms and tools to protect themselves against malicious and accidental attacks. The e-scientist could specify the security requirements that all sites should meet.
- **Proximity to E-Scientist:** How far is the site from the user's local site?
- **Uptime:** How often and for how long does the site experience a downtime?
- **Job Failures:** What is the percentage of job failures over a given time interval?
- **Hardware Profile:** The user may only want to use sites with relative new hardware and/or hardware with special features like ECC RAM (perhaps the user is concerned with bit-flipping or other problems which may occur during the computation).

The creation of the trust requirements document that conforms to the XML schema depends on the framework that GUTS is integrated with. The generated trust requirements document is tied to a Grid project and used by GUTS to generate the middleware-specific trust requirements. In order to give more concrete details on the generation of the trust requirements document, the g-Eclipse framework is used as the exemplary framework. One of the design goals is to support e-scientists with varied levels of knowledge regarding the underlying Grid infrastructure. Thus, two different methods could be provided to help the user supply the trust requirements. For the Grid novice e-scientist, a wizard is available and for the Grid-aware e-scientist, a multi-paged editor is available:

Trust Requirements Schema Wizard: A wizard in the Eclipse [15] terminology is a set of dialog windows that guides the user to complete a specific task. Depending on the task at hand, it may be enough for the user to only fill in a few of the dialogs to meet the minimum required information. Hence, there are required dialogs and optional dialogs. As soon as the required dialogs are filled out, the user will click on a *Finish* button to complete the process.

In GUTS, the wizard concept will be used to guide the user in creating a trust requirements document and it will consist of both required and optional dialogs. The design goal will be to present the user with the absolutely necessary dialogs as to make it as simple as possible for the novice Grid user to create the initial trust requirement set. Advanced users will have at their disposal more comprehensive dialogs to set advanced options or attributes. The end result of the wizard will be an XML document that is compliant with the trust requirements schema. The generated document could be opened in the the multi-paged trust profile editor for further editing.

Trust Requirements Schema Editor: A multi-page editor in the Eclipse terminology is a multi-tabbed window that is used to edit a document. In each tab, parts of the document that are conceptually related are presented to the user in order to be edited along with an informative text. The advantage of using a multi-page editor is that the user is provided with an easy and intuitive way of editing a document with the assistance of online help and tooltips. Furthermore, the entered information is verified with appropriate error messages.

The GUTS multi-page editor will consist of a few tabs. The exact number of tabs depends on the XML schema and on the way the set of attributes can conceptually be grouped together. However, there will at least be one or two tabs where the minimum number of attributes (required) will be specified. This will be followed by a few more tabs (maybe in the range of 2-5) where the user can specify the optional attributes, or provide more refined information to the required attributes. The last tab, will present to the user the syntax-highlighted XML document where the user can edit the source of the document directly. If any editing is done here, the other tabs will be automatically updated to reflect the changes.

4.2   Grid Middleware-Dependent Trust Specification

The Grid Middleware-Dependent Trust Specification component translates the middleware-agnostic trust requirements document specified in the previous component to a middleware-specific requirement document. This translation entails the mapping of generic trust requirements into specific requirements that could be evaluated, based on the information supplied or deduced by a specific Grid middleware. The GUTS framework supports a specific Grid infrastructure/middleware only in the case where plug-ins for that specific Grid middleware are available. GUTS plug-ins and abstract interfaces will be accessible to the developer for extension as to support new Grid middleware. Needless to say, developer guidelines will be offered and special attention will be given on simplifying the task of the middleware porter.

The GUTS framework will supply a set of abstract plug-ins with clear APIs and extension points as to allow identification and specification of requirements that the Grid middleware could provide information for. This requirements set will be examined and analyzed against the middleware-agnostic trust requirement document so that the middleware specific requirements could be identified. In the case that a mapping cannot be deduced, the user will be notified about the unsuccessful translation due to lack of Grid middleware support.

Similar to the middleware specific requirements plug-ins, developers must also supply middleware specific plug-ins for gathering evidence (information) from the particular middleware. Based on the identified middleware specific requirements, the middleware will be queried as to whether or not the required evidence can be obtained through these plug-ins. It is assumed that the middleware specific plug-ins will know how to contact the specific Grid infrastructure/middleware and how the retrieved information can be parsed in order to be presented in a uniform way. The combination of the middleware specific requirements with the evidence collection set yields the Project Trust Profile, which is generated in the following manner:

- **Load Plug-ins:** As each project will be tied to a Grid instance, the middleware used for the specific instance is known from within the project. Therefore, the first step is to load the evidence collection set and middleware-specific requirements template plug-ins for the project. If no such plug-ins are available, the e-scientist will be notified via an exception message.
- **Query Plug-ins:** Once the plug-ins are loaded, they are queried. The middleware-agnostic trust requirements form the basis of the query send to the middleware evidence collection plug-ins to discover the mappings between the requirements and information that can be obtained.
- **Generate Trust Profile:** The knowledge of what evidence can be gathered is used to generate the Middleware-specific evidence profile. In this profile it will be specified which plug-ins are used, what information to gather, from where to gather this information, and how often it should be gathered.

4.3   Trust Management and Visualization

The final component is the trust management component. Project trust profiles are stored in a database, which is accessible and updated as new evidence becomes available. A Grid Site ranking list will be generated based on the current information residing in the database. The rendered list will be stored in the database for future use, in case historical ranking data is desired. Below is a discussion of the main activities of this component.

Monitoring and Re-evaluation

From the previous component, the necessary plug-ins are identified and provided along with the Project Trust profile, which contains information on how often new evidence should be collected and how to evaluate it. The collection process will be time-triggered, where at a regular interval an evidence collection sweep will be initiated and gathered data will be stored in the database. Depending on the presence of advanced settings in the middleware-agnostic profile, filtering and/or aggregation of the evidence may occur once the information becomes available and before it gets stored. The interval between each sweep for evidence may be different and depends on the requirement that it is intended to be applied for. Some information will be very static while other is going to be highly dynamic. For example, information about the physical location and type of a Grid site or its hardware profile needs to be collected only once as it remains static. Similarly, information about the the security level of the site or the certification level of the administrators could be collected on a weekly basis. On the contrary, information about failures and system loads may be needed to be collected on an hourly (or even more frequent) basis. The evidence collection frequency configurations are provided in the Project Trust Profile.

Grid Site Ranking

Trust is not useful unless it becomes part of the decision process. In the case of the Grid, an end-user could utilize trust knowledge to choose the most suitable site for the specific job. An important aspect though is the presentation of trust results to the user. Lessons and techniques from security visualization [22], [21] will affect trust visualization as well. Overall, the purpose of this module is to present the user with a list of the available sites ranked based on their compliance with the trust profile as specified by the e-scientist. The ranking list could serve multiple purposes such as becoming a decisive factor when choosing a site to submit a job and provide the current "trustworthiness" of the various Grid sites that are available to the e-scientist. In addition, the user could also initiate to view past ranking lists as well as generate list where the rank over time for a specific site is provided.

Compared to the evidence gathering which is time-driven, the Grid Site Ranking could be either time-driven or event-driven. If it is time-triggered, at a specific time interval a new raking list becomes available to the user. An event-driven ranking list is triggered by two events. First, the trust profile dictates that when a certain amount of new evidence has been gathered or the newly collected evidence modified the trust relation, a new ranking list should be generated. The second event that generates a new ranking list is having the e-scientist initiating it directly through the user interface.

Placement of Evidence Gathering Module

There are two approaches to integrate trust techniques within a Grid environment. In the first approach, the required functionality is added at the end-point application like g-Eclipse, whereas in the second approach, some of that functionality is supported by the Grid middleware. Note that enabling trust should be optional; the user should be able to turn off/on this feature per job.

The functionality that could be moved to the Grid middleware level is the Evidence Gathering module from Figure 2. If standards are defined then this module could be offered as a service by each Grid site or as a regional Grid service similar to the information service BDII that is part of the gLite middleware [6]. The advantage of doing this is that the query load on the Grid sites would be reduced as the individual client applications would use the Evidence service instead of querying/pinging various other services within a Grid site. The API provided by the service could also offer push notification compared to the standard pull, hence the traffic on the service could be reduced. A Grid client could register to have the Evidence service push the information only when a certain amount of new evidence have been gathered. This would save resources both at the client and at the Grid site as all the unnecessary pulls would be avoided.

However, the easiest way to integrate trust is to place all the trust functionality at the end-point. The reason is that no modification is required for the Grid middleware, something that may be a lengthy process and nontrivial to convince the various Grid middleware providers of its usefulness. The amount of resources that the user will need to use as well as the resources that the Grid infrastructure will need to use increases, as they will need to support all the various pull queries from a large set of user applications. Both versions are viable due to the fact that most of the Grid middleware are open source. If a region or Grid infrastructure would like to provide the evidence collection as a service, the middleware could be extended to do this.

5   Deployment of GUTS in EGEE Grid

This section demonstrates the viability of integrating GUTS framework with the g-Eclipse. In particular, it is investigated how the TMS requirements of section 3 are satisfied. The g-Eclipse framework supports Grid/Cloud middleware like gLite, GRIA, and Amazon Web Services. The EGEE Grid infrastructure uses gLite, and thus becomes accessible through g-Eclipse. Two integration approaches are demonstrated: at the client side and at the middleware.

5.1   EGEE Overview

The EGEE Grid infrastructure [11] is the largest Grid world-wide, with about 250 resource providers, 40,000 CPUs and several Petabytes of storage. The EGEE

Grid is deployed using the gLite Grid middleware [6]. Figure 3 illustrates such deployment and illustrates its main components:

- **UI:** The User Interface allows the user to log on, issue commands to create Grid proxies, submit jobs, upload/download data, etc.
- **VOMS:** The Virtual Organization Management Service provides Grid Proxies to authenticated users belonging to the Virtual Organization.
- **WMSLB Service:** The Workload Management Service & Logging and Bookkeeping service matches the functional requirements of user-submitted jobs with Grid sites and manages associated bookkeeping information for the jobs as they are handled by these sites.
- **CE Service:** The Computing Element service maintains the job queue for a specific Grid site and manages the jobs as they are executing on one or more Worker Nodes.
- **WN:** A Worker Node is the machine where the job gets executed.

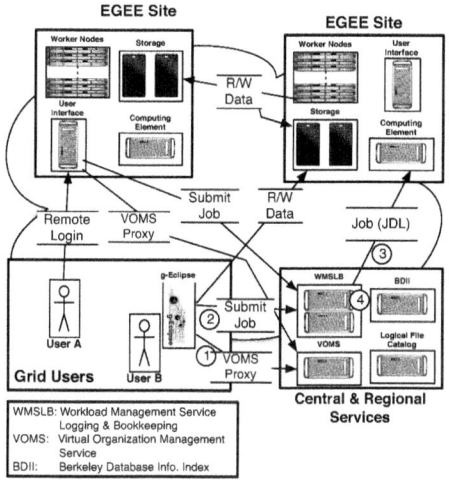

Fig. 3. EGEE Grid Deployment

As the UI only provides a CLI (Command Line Interface) other ways to interface with the Grid have been developed, like the g-Eclipse client [16] and various web portals. Using the g-Eclipse client, a job is executed as follows:

1. The User obtains a valid authentication token, which is provided by a VOMS service.
2. The User creates a job using JSDL (Job Submission Description Language), which is an extensible language encoded in XML [18]. Within the g-Eclipse environment there is a multi-page editor to help the user specify the job. Once the job is specified, it gets submitted to the Grid (automatically converted to JDL for gLite Grids), and more specifically to the WMSLB service.

3. The WMSLB service matches the requirements specified in the job with the current state of the various Grid sites that it knows about. If a match is found, the job is sent to that specific Grid site. It is also possible that the job contains parameters that specify the site that the job must be executed on. Depending on the configuration of the WMSLB, the preference may be honored. If the job fails the WMSLB may try to submit the job to another site for a specified maximum retry count.
4. Once the job is executed, the results are sent to the WMSLB. The Logging and Bookkeeping part of the WMSLB keeps track of the exit status and results of the job for a specified number of days. The user can then query for the output via g-Eclipse.

5.2   GUTS Integration with the g-Eclipse Framework

The GUTS framework could be integrated with the g-Eclipse framework and would satisfy the four trust requirements listed in Section 3 as described below:

R1. The collection of a complete evidence set at the end-point may be not feasible, however a subset could be collected. Each site already publishes its static information such as number of CPUs, RAM, storage capacity, etc. Based on this, knowledge could be deduced dynamically: if the site publishes that it has 0 CPUs or the information service cannot be queried then the site is most likely down. In addition to the static information provided by a site, there also exist centralized locations where data is published: one example of this is the GridIce site [2]. As this data is publicly available, an end-point application could collect it and use it as evidence. More specifically, the information system plug-in within g-Eclipse could be extended to collect it. This would require the end-point application to be running over an extended period of time in order to collect enough evidence for the evaluation.

R2. The conceptual framework Hestia [8] that specifies trust state using a set of requirements could be used as a starting point in specifying Grid trust relationships. The user would specify the trust requirements using an extended version of the JSDL editor. As the JSDL specification is open for extension, one such extension could be the specification of trust requirements for the job. An extra page would be added to the editor where the user specifies parameters such as site reliability, site uptime, confidentiality of data, timeliness of the result, failure rate of jobs executed on a site, etc. These parameters are embedded in the job specification.

R{3,4}. The evaluation and monitoring of the trust requirements occur simultaneously for the Grid application domain. When the user submits the job, then evidence for the trust requirements is gathered. The trust engine plug-in will take these requirements and evaluate them with the collected evidence from R1. Trust evaluation will also present the user with tradeoffs among expectations, e.g. decrease reliability in favor of increased confidentiality. When the JSDL is translated to the Grid-specific job language (JDL for gLite) the trust engine will set the *candidate host* property of the job to sites that satisfy the trust requirements of the job. In this way the WMSLB is informed about the Site preferences for the job.

The main advantage of integrating trust mechanisms at the end-point is that no modification is required at the Grid middleware. As a matter of fact, trust is a transparent service to the middleware. On the other side though, the client application becomes trust-aware with added functionality that may overpower its indented use.

5.3   GUTS Integration with the gLite Middleware

The GUTS framework could be integrated with the gLite middleware and would satisfy the four trust requirements listed in Section 3 as described below:

R1. The collection of evidence is performed by a new Grid service or is part of the WMSLB service. Being part of the middleware, each Grid site should be required to make information such as job failure rate, network failure rate, and average down time available. As the collection service would always run, a large evidence set would be collected and the long-term consistency of the various Grid sites could be evaluated and stored as historical information. The publication of this information may even be an incentive for Grid sites to improve their reliability.

R2. The user specifies the trust relation in a similar manner as described earlier for the trust integration at the client application, i.e. by using an extended version of the JSDL editor.

R{3,4}. The evaluation and monitoring of the trust relation occur simultaneously. This would be done at the WMSLB service, which would have to be able to accept jobs specified in JSDL. The service's matching algorithm would have to be extended. The trust requirements from the JSDL would be compared with the evidence collected using the method from R1, in addition to the normal matching that takes place. In this way, the sites that are selected would both satisfy the normal job requirements as well as the extended trust requirements. After the match is performed the job is submitted as any job without the extended trust requirements.

The main advantage of integrating trust mechanisms at the middleware is that a more accurate trust evaluation can be performed. This is because the middleware will have access to more data-points; it is also always running, hence it can collect very large evidence sets. From the clients point of view trust becomes almost transparent in that only the required trust level will need to be specified as part of the job description. On the other side though, the Grid site will use a substantial amount of resources in order to provide this service and it may not be willing to sacrifice its resources on a *"nice-to-have"* service.

6   Conclusion and Future Work

We expect research efforts on Grid trust to continue at an even faster pace as more users that utilize the computational capabilities of the Grid will realize the potentials of trust techniques. One of the design goals of a Grid trust framework should be to allow a typical e-scientist manage and use trust in a simple and intuitive manner. GUTS is a novel framework that aims in supplying the Grid user the means to do so. We have shown conceptually that GUTS could be deployed both at the client application and the Grid middleware.

We are currently working on implementing a g-Eclipse trust-aware client application that conforms to GUTS design guidelines. However, placeholders will be added for future features: query the collected evidence in order to produce various reports, have the users annotate the collected evidence and share it among their collaborators, gather evidence from other clients, i.e. reuse evidence that are collected by one's colleagues. GUTS could also be a candidate trust framework for Cloud computing settings, and this is a direction that will be further pursued.

References

1. Ahsant, M., Surridge, M., Leonard, T., Krishna, A., Mulmo, O.: Dynamic trust federation in grids. In: Stølen, K., Winsborough, W.H., Martinelli, F., Massacci, F. (eds.) iTrust 2006. LNCS, vol. 3986, pp. 3–18. Springer, Heidelberg (2006)
2. Andreozzi, S., De Bortoli, N., Fantinel, S., Ghiselli, A., Rubini, G.L., Tortone, G., Vistoli, M.C.: Gridice: a monitoring service for grid systems. Future Generation Computer Systems 21(4), 559–571 (2005)
3. Arenas, A., Aziz, B., Silaghi, G.C.: Reputation management in grid-based virtual organisations. In: International Conference on Security and Cryptography, SECRYPT 2008 (2008)
4. Arenas, A., Wilson, M., Matthews, B.: On trust management in grids. In: Autonomics 2007: Proceedings of the 1st international conference on Autonomic computing and communication systems, pp. 1–7. ICST, Brussels (2007)
5. Basney, J., Nejdl, W., Olmedilla, D., Welch, V., Winslett, M.: Negotiating trust on the grid. In: 2nd WWW Workshop on Semantics in P2P and Grid Computing (2004)
6. CERN. glite: Lightweight middleware for grid computing. Website, http://glite.web.cern.ch/glite/ (last accessed January 2010)
7. Braga Jr., J.d.R.P., Vidal, A.C.T., Kon, F., Finger, M.: Trust in large-scale computational grids: an spki/sdsi extension for representing opinion. In: MCG 2006: Proceedings of the 4th international workshop on Middleware for grid computing, p. 7. ACM, New York (2006)
8. Dionysiou, I., Bakken, D.: Formalizing and managing activity-aware trust in collaborative environments. In: Yan, Z. (ed.) Trust Modeling and Management in Digital Environments: from Social Concept to System Development, pp. 179–201. IGI Global (2010)
9. Dionysiou, I., Frincke, D., Hauser, C., Bakken, D.: An approach to trust management challenges for critical infrastructures. In: Lopez, J., Hämmerli, B.M. (eds.) CRITIS 2007. LNCS, vol. 5141, pp. 173–184. Springer, Heidelberg (2008)
10. Dionysiou, I., Gjermundrød, H., Bakken, D.E.: An initial approach for adaptive trust in grid environments. In: Proceedings of 1st Workshop on Computational Trust for Self-Adaptive Systems (SELFTRUST 2009), Athens, Greece, pp. 719–722 (November 2009)

11. EGEE. The enabling grids for e-science project. Website,
    http://www.eu-egee.org (last accessed January 2010)
12. Foster, I.: What is the grid? - a three point checklist. GRIDtoday 1(6) (July 2002)
13. Foster, I., Kesselman, C.: The globus toolkit. In: Foster, I., Kesselman, C. (eds.)
    The Grid: Blueprint for a New Computing Infrastructure, pp. 259–278. Morgan
    Kaufmann Publishers Inc., San Francisco (1999)
14. Foster, I.T.: The anatomy of the grid: Enabling scalable virtual organizations. In:
    Sakellariou, R., Keane, J.A., Gurd, J.R., Freeman, L. (eds.) Euro-Par 2001. LNCS,
    vol. 2150, pp. 1–4. Springer, Heidelberg (2001)
15. Eclipse Foundation. Eclipse integrated development environment. Website,
    http://www.eclipse.org (last accessed January 2010)
16. Gjermundrod, H., Dikaiakos, M.D., Stuempert, M., Wolniewicz, P., Kornmayer, H.:
    An integrated framework to access and maintain grid resources. In: Proceedings
    of the 9th IEEE/ACM International Conference on Grid Computing (Grid 2008),
    pp. 57–64 (2008)
17. Grandison, T., Sloman, M.: A survey of trust in internet applications. IEEE Com-
    munications Surveys and Tutorials 3(4), 2–16 (2000)
18. OGF JSDL Working Group. Job submission description language working group
    (jsdl-wg). open grid forum. Website,
    http://forge.gridforum.org/projects/jsdl-wg (last accessed January 2010)
19. Harrison, K., Tan, C.L., Liko, D., Maier, A., Moscicki, J.T., Egede, U., Jones,
    R.W.L., Soroko, A., Patrick, G.N.: Ganga - a grid user interface. In: Computing
    in High Energy and Nuclear Physics (CHEP 2006), Mumbai, India (2006)
20. Humphrey, M., Thompson, M.R.: Security implications of typical grid computing
    usage scenarios. Cluster Computing 5(3), 257–264 (2002)
21. Ma, K.-L.: Guest editor's introduction: Visualization for cybersecurity. IEEE Com-
    puter Graphics and Applications 26(2), 26–27 (2006)
22. Marty, R.: Applied Security Visualization. Addison-Wesley Professional, Reading
    (2008)
23. Miah, D.: A matter of trust: enabling grid security through bilateral negotiation.
    International Science Grid this week, ISGTW (2008),
    http://www.isgtw.org/?pid=1001540
24. Neokleous, K., Dikaiakos, M.D., Fragopoulou, P., Markatos, E.: Failure manage-
    ment in grids: The case of the egee infrastructure. Parallel Processing Letters 17(4),
    391–410 (2007)
25. OGCE. The open grid computing environments portal and gateway toolkit. Web-
    site, http://www.collab-ogce.org/ (last accessed January 2010)
26. Welch, V., Siebenlist, F., Foster, I., Bresnahan, J., Czajkowski, K., Gawor, J.,
    Kesselman, C., Meder, S., Pearlman, L., Tuecke, S.: Security for grid services.
    In: HPDC 2003: Proceedings of the 12th IEEE International Symposium on High
    Performance Distributed Computing, p. 48. IEEE Computer Society, Washington,
    DC, USA (2003)

Aggregating Trust Using Triangular Norms in the KeyNote Trust Management System

Simon N. Foley, Wayne Mac Adams, and Barry O'Sullivan

Cork Constraint Computation Centre,
Department of Computer Science,
University College Cork, Ireland
{s.foley,w.macadams,b.osullivan}@cs.ucc.ie

Abstract. A Trust Management model that provides a measure of the degree to which a principal is trusted for some action is proposed. At the heart of the model is the notion that triangular norms and conorms provide a natural and consistent interpretation for trust aggregation across delegation chains. It is argued that specifying how trust is aggregated is as important as specifying a degree of trust value in an attribute certificate and, therefore, in stating the degree to which a principal trusts another, the principal should also state how that trust may aggregate across delegation chains. The model is illustrated and has been implemented using a modified, but backwards-compatible, version of the KeyNote Trust Management system.

1   Introduction

Trust Management [1, 4, 9, 20], as originally defined by [5], is an approach to constructing and interpreting trust relationships between principals such as users, groups, roles, hardware-devices, etc. These *well placed trust* relationships [25], defined in terms of relatively static attributes that are perceived by a trusting party, are constructed as a graph of credentials encoding the conditions under which a principal is willing to trust some action. Trust Management systems are intended to support decentralized security: individual trust statements are encoded as cryptographic certificates that can be safely distributed across the network and reasoned over without the need for trusted authorization servers mediating over centralized policy state.

While a Trust Management system determines whether a principal is trusted (authorized) for some action, reputation (trust) schemes such as [14, 18] are used to provide some measure of the degree of trust between principals. For example, Slashdot Karma gives a measure of an individual's standing in that message board community. Many Trust Management systems provide a binary decision—whether or not a principal is trusted—and do not consider the degree to which a principle is authorized for an action. In this paper a model is developed whereby a Trust Management decision is given in terms of a measure/degree of trust.

There is much published research on how reputation trust between principals might be measured and is not the focus of this paper. In this paper we assume

J. Cuellar et al. (Eds.): STM 2010, LNCS 6710, pp. 100–115, 2011.

that principals assert subjective measures of well placed trust when defining the conditions under which they trust another principal. The challenge is then to determine how these trust values should *aggregate* across the trust relationships that make up an attribute certificate delegation graph. We argue that *Triangular Norms* provide a natural approach to aggregating trust. Triangular norms and conorms are classes of well-understood aggregation operators that are used to combine values in the metric space $[0..1]$ [8, 26] and have been used to aggregate knowledge for a variety of applications such as fuzzy-logic [8], risk management [11], multimedia databases [10] and medical decision support systems [6].

In this paper, a model of quantitative Trust Management is developed whereby delegation certificates may specify a degree of trust. Rather than prescribing specific aggregation operators, the model allows the user to also specify, as part of the delegation certificate, how the delegated trust may be aggregated. This model has been implemented in an extended version of the KeyNote Trust Management system. The extension provides backwards compatibility with the standard KeyNote system whereby KeyNote compliance values can be considered to implement degrees of trust, aggregated by Gödel fuzzy logic t-norm/conorm operators min and max.

The paper is organized as follows. Section 2 considers how triangular norms and conorms might be used to aggregate trust across a delegation network and argues that treating the calculation as an inclusion-exclusion or two-terminal network reliability style problem is not appropriate. A model for trust aggregation is described in Section 3 and Section 4 presents a series of KeyNote credentials to illustrate its use. Section 5 discusses the implementation of this model. Section 6 reviews related research and discusses the results of the paper.

2   Quantifying Trust

Let the statement $A \xrightarrow{x} B$ denote an assertion by principal A that she trusts (delegates trust to) the principal B to a degree $x : [0..1]$. We assume that A's trust of B increases linearly with the value of x, whereby $x = 0$ represents no trust and $x = 1$ denotes complete trust.

A set of trust delegation statements form a directed graph with labeled arcs between principals representing trust/delegation statements. Figure 1 illustrates a delegation graph with statements $A \xrightarrow{0.8} B$, $B \xrightarrow{0.9} D$ and so forth. Given such a graph, we are interested in determining how transitive trust, that is, the implicit degree of trust $trust(X, Y)$ from a principal X to principal Y, should be computed. For example, the implicit degree of trust from A to D in Figure 1.

2.1   Trust Aggregation Using Max and Min

One strategy for computing $trust(X, Y)$ in a delegation graph is to compute the maximum degree of trust over all delegation chains from X to Y, whereby the degree of trust for a single chain is the minimum of the degrees along its path. For example, given the graph in Figure 1, the single chain from A to D

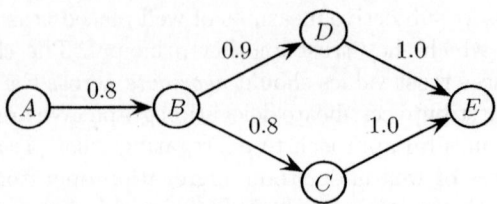

Fig. 1. Quantitative Delegation Graph

results in $trust(A,D) = \min(0.8, 0.9)$. The two chains $A \xrightarrow{0.8} B \xrightarrow{0.9} D \xrightarrow{1.0} E$ and $A \xrightarrow{0.8} B \xrightarrow{0.7} C \xrightarrow{1.0} E$ connect A and E and $trust(A,E) = \max(0.8, 0.7) = 0.8$. This max-min paths strategy is implemented as a breath first search of the delegation graph in the KeyNote Trust Management system [4] where (an enumerated set of) KeyNote compliance values can be effectively interpreted to represent degrees of trust measures.

The min operator may not always provide an intuitive aggregation of trust values along the path of a chain. For example, given Figure 1, while B considers its trust of D and C to be different, this distinction is lost in the calculation of $trust(A,D) = 0.8$ and $trust(A,C) = 0.8$, despite B's involvement in both chains. Had A's trust of B been less that 0.8 then this distinction would be apparent. An alternative operator for aggregating trust along a chain is the (probabilistic) product operator $\times$. Using this operator in Figure 1 gives $trust(A,C) = 0.64$ and $trust(A,D) = 0.72$ which could be regarded as better reflecting the knock-on effect of trust by B. Such use of probabilistic product to aggregate trust along a chain of trust is proposed as a way to provide more fine-grained treatment for GnuPGP's degree of trust measure [15].

Similarly, the max operator does not necessarily provide an intuitive operator with which to aggregate the degree of trust across multiple delegation chains. Continuing the example above, E's trust from B might be considered to be an *accumulation* of trust obtained via chains $B \xrightarrow{0.9} D \xrightarrow{1.0} E$ and $B \xrightarrow{0.7} C \xrightarrow{1.0} E$, and therefore, should be greater than $trust(B,E) = \max(0.9, 08)$. Computing $trust(B,E) = 0.9 + 0.8 - 0.8 * 0.9 = 0.98$ using probabilistic sum to aggregate trust across chains $B \xrightarrow{0.9} D \xrightarrow{1.0} E$ and $B \xrightarrow{0.8} C \xrightarrow{1.0} E$ may be regarded as better reflecting how E's trust accumulates from multiple chains. Probabilistic sum is also used in GnuPGP [15] to aggregate across different chains where the calculation of $trust(X,Y)$ is treated as an two-terminal network reliability-style problem [7, 22].

2.2   Trust Aggregation Using Triangular Norms and Conorms

Computing $trust(X,Y)$ requires selection of an operator (denoted $\otimes$) used to aggregate trust along a chain and an operator (denoted $\oplus$) used to aggregate across different chains. We argue that *triangular norms* and *triangular conorms*, respectively provide suitable aggregation operators.

A triangular norm (hereafter referred to as t-norm) operator $\otimes$ is commutative and associative; its monotonicity ensures that its use for aggregating trust values along a delegation chain does not result in an amplification of trust, that is, $x \otimes y \leq \min(x, y)$ for $x, y : [0..1]$ and min is the largest pointwise t-norm.

We use a triangular conorm (t-conorm) $\oplus$ to aggregate trust across different chains. A t-norm has a corresponding t-conorm under the DeMorgan style law: $x \oplus y = 1 - (1 - x) \otimes (1 - y)$. The max operator is the smallest t-conorm and for any t-conorm operator $\oplus$, then $x \oplus y \geq \max(x, y)$ for $x, y : [0..1]$. Thus, t-conorm based aggregation of trust chains provides monotonic trust, that is, adding further trust statements/chains to a delegation graph does not result in a decrease in the value of $trust(X, Y)$. The t-norm and t-conorm operators can be interpreted as forms of fuzzy disjunction and conjunction, respectively [8]. Table 1 includes a number of common t-norm and their respective t-conorm operators.

Table 1. Some t-norms and t-conorms

	t-norm $x \otimes y$	t-conorm $x \oplus y$
Probabilistic	$x \times y$	$x + y - x \times y$
Gödel	min	max
Lukasiewicz	$\max(0, x + y - 1)$	$\min(1, x + y)$
Drastic	if $x = 1$ then y elseif $y = 1$ then x else 0	if $x = 0$ then y elseif $y = 0$ then x else 1
Compensating Trust(e)	if $e \leq (x, y) \leq 1$ then $x \times y$ else $min(x, y)$	if $e \leq (x, y) \leq 1$ then $x + y - x \times y$ else $max(x, y)$

2.3   Accumulating Trust

The max-min style calculation of $trust(X, Y)$ as a sum (t-conorm) of products (t-norm) along the chains between X and Y does not necessarily generalize to other t-norm/conorm operators. For example, suppose that probabilistic product is used as a chain-aggregator $\otimes_p$ along paths $A \overset{0.8}{\to} B \overset{0.9}{\to} D \overset{1.0}{\to} E$ and $A \overset{0.8}{\to} B \overset{0.7}{\to} C \overset{1.0}{\to} E$ in Figure 1. This results in trust values 0.72 and 0.64, respectively; using probabilistic sum $\oplus_p$ to aggregate across these chains results in calculation $trust(A, E) = 0.899$. This calculation may not necessarily reflect the trust intentions of A, for example, E might be owned by B. In Figure 1, A states that she trusts B to degree 0.8. However, as a consequence of statements of other principals, using this calculation results in E holding more trust (0.899) from A even though it originated exclusively via B. In this case the most trust (from A) that B should be able to delegate to E should be degree 0.8.

Intuitively, we might expect to be able to address this issue by reducing the subgraph connecting B to E to a single arc and computing:

$$trust(A, E) = trust(A, B) \otimes_p trust(B, E) = 0.8 \otimes_p (0.8 \oplus_p 0.9) = 0.78$$

However, the graph in Figure 2 illustrates that such a rewriting strategy is not applicable in general. In this case it it not immediately clear how D's trust should be proportioned to C and E so as to ensure that E gets the maximal trust available while ensuring that D does not delegate more trust than the 0.9 degrees obtained from B.

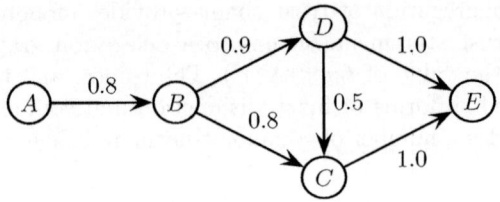

Fig. 2. Quantitative Delegation Graph

The probabilistic sum operator treats trust as a quantity that can effectively be accumulated as more statements about trust are made; the more statements that X makes delegating trust to Y then, the more that Y's trust of X accumulates, that is, $trust(X,Y)$ increases (bounded by 1). This gives rise to the following principle for computing trust.

Principle of Preservation of Trust. A principal may not delegate more trust than it has accumulated. Note that this principle is expressed as a safety property in that it does not require conservation of trust (in a liveness sense).

Trust delegation may be treated as a network flow-style problem. However, we argue that it does not correspond to the two-terminal network reliability problem [22], nor its variation suggested in [15], as both schemes can result in a 'double-counting' of trust statements. For example, using [15] to compute trust as the probabilistic sum of the trust along paths $ABDE$, $ABDCE$ and $ABCE$, results in $trust(A, E) = 0.989$. This result violates the principle of trust accumulation as it implies that B effectively delegates more trust to E (0.989) than it accumulated from A (0.8).

In the next section we propose a model in which $trust(X,Y)$ can be used with any t-norm for trust aggregation along a chain and with any t-conorm to aggregate trust across different chains, while preserving the principle of trust accumulation.

3   A Model of Trust Aggregation

The calculation of $trust(X,Y)$ treats trust as a material-like quantity that flows through the delegation graph. In many cases the degree of trust delegated is the degree of trust that flows, for example, 0.8 degrees of trust 'flows' from A to B as a consequence of the delegation $A \xrightarrow{0.8} B$ in the graph in Figure 1. Given this trust held by B, suppose that we consider that 0.9 of this flows to D as a consequence of $B \xrightarrow{0.9} D$ (under t-norm $\otimes_p$). For the reasons discussed in the previous section, permitting a further 0.8 (of the trust from A to B) to flow from B to C will violate the Principle of Preservation of Trust since probabilistic sum of A's trust flowing, via B to C and D must be less than or equal to the trust flowing to B. In this section we define the calculation of $trust(X,Y)$ in terms of a search for a set of flow of trust labels for the delegation graph that preserves the Law of Preservation of Trust.

Let $trust(X,Y)$ denote a degree of trust that arbitrary principal Y can accumulate from principal X over a delegation graph. Given nodes X, Y and Z and arc $Y \overset{x}{\to} Z$ in the delegation graph, then let the value $flow(X,Y,Z)$ represent some portion (ranging from nothing (0) to everything ($trust(X,Y)$)) of the trust that Y holds, originating from X, that is passed on to Z by Y.

The value of $trust(X,Y)$ is a solution to the following constraint problem and is based on a search for a suitable configuration of the function $flow$ that ensures the principle of preservation of trust.

- If no directed path exists in the graph from X to Y then $trust(X,Y) = 0$.
- The (cross chain aggregation of) flow from principal Y to others cannot exceed the degree of trust from X that is accumulated by Y.

$$trust(X,Y) \geq \bigoplus_{\forall Z, x | Y \overset{x}{\to} Z} flow(X,Y,Z).$$

- A node may not accumulate more trust than the cross chain aggregation of the trust that it receives from others.

$$trust(X,Y) \leq \bigoplus_{\forall Z, x | Z \overset{x}{\to} Y} (flow(X,Z,Y) \otimes x).$$

The intuition behind this calculation is to effectively find flow labelings for the graph such that a subsequent max-min/network reliability style calculation of $trust(A,B)$ preserves the principle of preservation of trust accumulation.

As an example, Figure 3 depicts a solution of this problem: each node $Z \in \{C,D,E\}$ is decorated with the value $trust(A,Z)$ and each delegation statement $X \overset{x(y)}{\to} Y$ indicates the degree of trust x and the value $flow(A,X,Y) = y$. Note that in this solution, all available trust flows from B to D to E. However, as a consequence, none of the available trust held by B may flow to C; any higher proportion and the Principle of Preservation of Trust is violated as the flow from A to B exceeds 0.8. Note that this is just one solution to the above problem, it is not necessarily optimal. Figure 4 gives an alternative solution. Section 5 considers the implementation of $trust(X,Y)$ in practice.

4   Trust Aggregation in QKeyNote

Sections 2 and 3 consider the quantification of *unconditional* trust, that is, the degree of trust delegated from one principal to another is not related to any

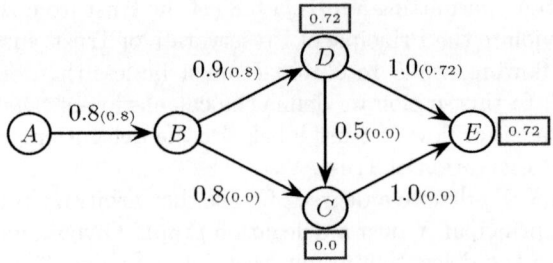

Fig. 3. Delegation graph solution including *flows* originating from A

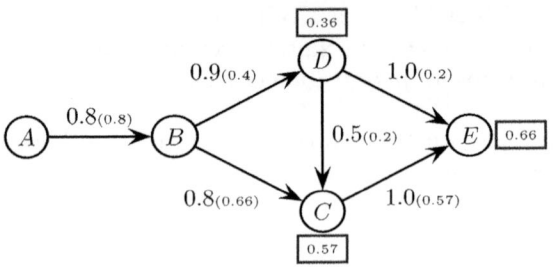

Fig. 4. Alternative solution including *flows* originating from A

particular action or attributes of the principals. In this section quantified *conditional* trust is considered whereby a delegation statement $A \overset{p:x}{\rightarrow} B$ is interpreted to mean that a principal A asserts that she trusts another principal B for permission p (related to some action) to a degree $x : [0..1]$. This section explains how the KeyNote Trust Management system [4] can be extended to support these delegation statements thereby providing decentralized support for quantitative trust management. A KeyNote delegation credential encodes the delegated 'permission' as a condition over attribute values. The approach is illustrated using examples based on a photograph sharing trust policy [13] which uses a probabilistic network to represent trust relationships between variables (attributes).

4.1   KeyNote Compliance Values as Degrees of Trust

A KeyNote credential is a statement that delegates trust from an authorizer to a licensee constrained by some condition. The condition is given using a C-like expression syntax in terms of attributes that are used to characterize action(s) for which the licensee is trusted (by the authorizer). For example, consider a server that permits trusted users access stored photographs based on image tags. The server owner specifies that Alice (public key Ka) is trusted to access photographs tagged as public. This is specified by the KeyNote policy credential:

```
Authorizer: POLICY
Licensee: Ka
Conditions: App_Domain=="PhotoShare" && Tag == "public";
```

The condition for this delegation is defined in terms of action attributes App_Domain and Tag. For the purposes of this example we assume that a photograph is tagged either as public or private. When Alice requests access to a particular photograph, the application uses the KeyNote query engine to determine whether there is a chain of trust from POLICY to the requesting key Ka with conditions satisfying the [App_Domain←"PhotoShare"; Tag←"public"].

In practice, the condition on a KeyNote credential evaluates to a value from a user-enumerated (ordinal) set of *compliance values* that range from _MIN_TRUST to _MAX_TRUST, for example, the compliance set={false,true}, for the above policy. When a return value is not specified in the condition field then the default return value is _MAX_TRUST when the condition is satisfied, otherwise _MIN_TRUST is returned. The following credential, where Alice delegates trust to Bob Kb, specifies a compliance value of 0.7. This value defines Alice's degree of trust in Bob concerning public photographs.

```
Authorizer: Ka
Licensee: Kb
Conditions: (App_Domain=="PhotoShare"
&& Tag=="public") -> 0.7;
Signature: ....
```

Compliance values in KeyNote conventionally define an enumerated and discrete datatype, for example, $\langle 0, 0.3, 0.5, 0.7, 1.0 \rangle$ with _MIN_TRUST=0.0 and _MAX_TRUST=1.0. A conventional KeyNote query corresponds to a calculation of the maximum compliance value returned over the minimum compliance value along all delegation chains whose conditions satisfy the attribute binding given in the query.

4.2   Aggregating Compliance Values in QKeyNote

The KeyNote query engine has been extended to support compliance values from the real datatype [0..1] and a revised query algorithm (QKeyNote) is used to implement $trust(X, Y)$ for computing compliance values. If operators max and min are selected as the aggregation operators then a QKeyNote query behaves as a conventional KeyNote query.

Continuing the photograph sharing example, the policy is extended to authorize Clare (Kc), who in turn, delegates authority to Bob (Kb).

```
Authorizer: POLICY
Licensee: Kc
Conditions:
(App_Domain=="PhotoShare")
-> { {Tag=="public"} -> 0.6;
     {Tag=="private"} -> 0.2; }
Signature: ....
```

```
Authorizer: Kc
Licensee: Kb
Conditions:
(App_Domain=="PhotoShare"
&& Tag=="public") -> 0.8;
Signature: ....
```

Given these and the earlier credentials, a QKeyNote query as to whether Bob is trusted for [App_Domain←"PhotoShare"; Tag←"public"] returns compliance value 0.844 when probabilistic operators are used to aggregate, that is, it calculates $trust(\text{POLICY}, \text{Kb}) = (1 \otimes_p 0.7) \oplus_p (0.6 \otimes_p 0.8) = 0.844$.

QKeyNote supports two predefined attributes that are treated similarly to other predefined attributes such as _MAX_TRUST and _ACTION_AUTHORIZERS. Attribute _TNORM specifies the t-norm operator that the QKeyNote query engine has been configured to use when aggregating trust along a chain. Attribute _TCONORM specifies the t-conorm operator that the QKeyNote query engine has been configured to use when aggregating trust across multiple chains. The default query engine configuration is _TNORM="min" and _TCONORM="max" providing the 'conventional' KeyNote query.

We argue that specifying how delegated trust is aggregated should be as important to the authorizer as is specifying the degree of trust within a credential. Therefore, a delegation of trust can be made conditional on the operators used to aggregate the trust by constraining the values of _TNORM and _TCONORM in its condition. For example, suppose that the server owner decides that Alice is trusted to access private photographs as long as probabilistic sum and product are used to aggregate this trust. This credential may be used only when the query engine is configured to use probabilistic sum and product for aggregation.

```
Authorizer: POLICY
Licensee: Ka
Conditions: (App_Domain=="PhotoShare"
&& _TNORM=="probProduct" && _TCONORM=="probSum
&& Tag=="private") -> 0.2;
Signature: ....
```

A partial order can be defined over the t-norm and t-conorm operators. Given t-norms $\otimes_t$ and $\otimes_t'$ then

$$\otimes_t \sqsubseteq \otimes_t' \equiv \forall x, y : [0,1] \bullet x \otimes_t y \leq x \otimes_t' y$$

The operator min is the top t-norm under this ordering, for example we have $\otimes_p \sqsubseteq$ min. A similar ordering exists over t-conorms with max providing the bottom t-conorm. These orderings can be used within a credential to facilitate aggregation operator selection. For example, Alice trusts Bob to share private photographs on condition that he can never use this trust with other credentials to accumulate more than 0.6 degrees of trust. In this case the t-conorm used to aggregate across chains must be the max operator, while the t-norm can be any operator less than or equal to the min operator.

```
Authorizer: Ka
Licensee: Kb
Conditions: (App_Domain=="PhotoShare"
&& _TNORM<="min"  && _TCONORM=="max"
&& Tag=="private") -> 0.6;
Signature: ....
```

This credential cannot be used if the query engine is configured with probabilistic product and sum. However, for example the condition can be satisfied the query engine is configured with probabilistic product as t-norm and max as t-conorm. If a credential condition does not refer to _TNORM and _TCONORM then the delegation is applicable for any aggregation operator. Figure 5 lists the aggregation operators (and ordering) available in our current implementation of QKeyNote. Currently values for _TNORM and _TCONORM must be provided as part of the query. We are currently investigating how search for optimal values for these operators might form part of the query $trust(X, Y)$.

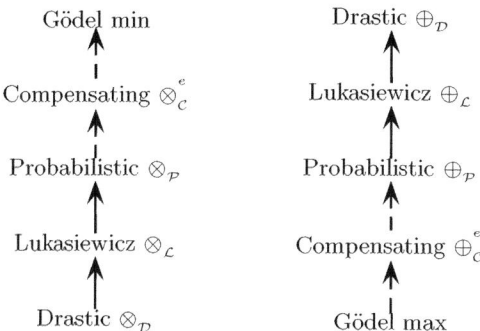

Fig. 5. Type system aggregation operator orderings $\sqsubseteq$

4.3   Accumulating Compliance Values in QKeyNote

The delegation graph built by the QKeyNote query engine supports multiple delegation statements between arbitrary principals so long as each delegation statement is unique. Credential uniqueness ensures that a malicious principal cannot accumulate more trust than he holds by presenting multiple copies of the same credential. For example, based on an evolving relationship, Alice issues a credential to Bob, every day, specifying that she incrementally trusts him to degree 0.01 to access private photographs:

```
Authorizer: Ka
Licensee: Kb
Conditions: (App_Domain=="PhotoShare"
&& _TNORM=="probProduct" && _TCONORM=="probSum"
&& Tag=="private" && Nonce = "123456"
&& Date >= "20100101" && Date<= "20101231"
&& _Action_Authorizers==Kb)  -> 0.01;
Signature: ....
```

The nonce provides credential freshness and Bob may accumulate and use multiple credentials over time, subject to an expiry date. Bob may not delegate this trust further (_Action_Authorizers==Kb). For example, Bob may present three credentials (different nonces) to prove a 0.0297 degree of trust from Alice (for accessing private photographs). In this case each delegated degree of trust is very small and could be regarded as form of *micro-trust* that can be accumulated over time into a worthwhile relationship. Rather than expending the cost of a public-key signature to generate and validate each each micro-trust statement, a hash-based micropayment scheme such as [12] could be used, whereby each micro-payment on a hash-chain corresponds to a micro-trust credential of value 0.01. Following [12], a micro-trust contract, analogous to a micropayment contract, is issued as KeyNote credential by Alice, to Bob indicating that she is willing to eventually trust Bob to a high degree, that will be accumulated as a series of micro-trust 'payments'.

4.4   Compensating Aggregation Operators

One concern over using conventional arithmetic and/or probabilistic sum is that when making decisions humans do not necessarily aggregate in a linear manner [28], that is, there may be potential for non-linearity in the way that they perceive combinations. In [6, 11, 19] a compensating uni-norm operator $\odot^e$ is described for aggregating in a non-linear manner, for neutral element $e : [0..1]$. Intuitively, this uni-norm operator may be thought of as a combination of probabilistic product when operand severity values are less than e, and probabilistic sum when operand severity values are greater than e. Using this operator, for example with $e = 0.6$, to aggregate trust along a chain causes the calculation to be less sensitive to aggregation of higher trust values along the chains. While flexible, this uni-norm does not behave exclusively as a t-norm and causes trust amplification along a chain if operand values are greater than the neutral element due to aggregation via probabilistic sum. Similarly, if the operator is used to aggregate across chains operand values that are less than the neutral element then probabilistic product may result in non-montonic trust; that is, it is not a t-conorm and adding further delegation statements cause a reduction in trust.

QKeyNote provides a t-norm operator $\otimes_c^e$, as a safe trust-aggregating version of the uni-norm $\odot^e$ that provides a degree of compensation around neutral element e. This operator is a combination of probabilistic product when operand severity values are less than e, and min when operand severity values are greater than e and is defined in Table 1. A corresponding compensating trust t-conorm operator $\oplus_c^e$ is a combination of probabilistic sum when operand severity values are greater than e, or the max operator otherwise.

Following the micro-trust example above, suppose that Alice does not want her micro-trust statements to aggregate her trust of Bob beyond 0.5 degrees. This is achieved by requiring micro-trust to be aggregated using the compensating trust t-norm configured with a neutral element of 0.5:

```
Authorizer: Ka
Licensee: Kb
Conditions: (App_Domain=="PhotoShare"
&&  _TCONORM<="compTrust(0.5)"
&& Tag=="private" && Nonce = "123456"
&& Date >= "20100101" && Date<= "20101231"
&& _Action_Authorizers==Kb)  -> 0.01;
Signature: ....
```

5 Implementing $trust(X,Y)$

There are many possible solutions for configurations of $flow$ and $trust$ that satisfy the the constraints given in Section 3. Two approaches to finding a solution are considered in this section.

Optimized Search. The problem can be expressed as a constraint satisfaction problem (CSP) [21, 23] that searches for a solution while maximizing the value of $trust(X,Y)$. This approach has been implemented using choco [27], a Java library for solving CSPs and supports optimization over real-valued variables. This implementation could be used in computing trust values in KeyNote delegation graphs. However, this search violates the principle of efficient trust evaluation [24] as it is computationally expensive and not suited to providing real-time answers involving search over large delegation graphs.

Heuristic Search. Rather than searching for values of $flow$ that yield an optimal $trust(X,Y)$, we use fixed heuristics that distribute $flow$ over outgoing arcs in the delegation graph. Given a node Z on a path between X and Y then the value of the $flow$ from Z could be based, for example, on an even distribution of the value of $trust(X,Z)$ across the cardinality of the set of individual statements $Z \xrightarrow{z} Z'$ in the graph whereby Z' is connected to Y. For example in Figure 4, the distribution (under probabilistic sum) of $trust(A,D) = 0.36$ across outgoing flows $flow(A,D,E) = 0.2$ and $flow(A,D,C) = 0.2$, en-route to destination E.

This heuristic search approach is implemented using a topological sort of the delegation graph to direct the assignment and/or division of flows within the delegation graph while preserving the principle of conservation of trust. This strategy has been used in the implementation of the QKeyNote query engine discussed in Section 4.

When a trust query is made it is possible that the $flows$ selected during a previous search may contradict choices of $flow$ from earlier trust queries. For example, assuming an optimal search across the graph in Figure 3, then an earlier query $trust(A,D)$ returning 0.72 implies that a later query $trust(A,C)$ should return 0.0. Alternatively, if $trust(A,C)$ is queried first, then it could return the optimal trust value 0.64, with the subsequent query $trust(A,D)$ returning 0.0. Thus, an implementation of $trust(X,Y)$ may be *stateful*, in the sense that past trust queries may influence the results of future queries against the graph.

Stateful Trust Compliance. Let partial function $trust_{\Sigma}(X, Y)$ record past trust queries by returning the result of the most recent trust value computed between X, Y. Given a delegation graph and $trust_{\Sigma}$, then a principal Y is trusted to at least degree x by principal X, if there exists a solution for this query such that $trust(X, Y) = x$ and for all principals Z, W then $trust_{\Sigma}(Z, W) \leq trust(Z, W)$.

Stateful trust compliance is useful for enforcing history-based security policies such as Chinese walls and dynamic separation style policies. For example, interpreting the policy in Figure 3, both D and C have the *potential* to interact with A as trusted principals. However, once A queries D's trust (presumably as a consequence of some interaction with D), then C's level of potential trust diminishes. The disadvantage of a stateful implementation of *trust* is that it requires a globally coordinated trust state, for example relying a centralized graph of delegation statements and $trust_{\Sigma}(X, Y)$ function. While a centralized approach is common in reputation trust systems, a goal of trust management is to support decentralized delegation statements in the form of cryptographic credentials. For the purposes of this paper we regard trust queries as stateless, determining the degree of trust regardless of past queries. Investigating the implementation of statefull queries is a topic for future research.

6   Discussion

This paper proposes a generalization of the KeyNote Trust Management system whereby KeyNote compliance values in the metric space $[0..1]$ can be aggregated using arbitrary triangular norms and conorms. This provides a basis for Trust Management queries that return the degree to which a principal is trusted for some action. Note that the results in this paper are not limited to KeyNote, which was chosen for the sake of ease of exposition and implementation.

We argue that specifying how trust is aggregated, both along chains and across chains, is as important as specifying a degree of trust value and therefore should form part of the trust information provided in a credential. It is not the intention of this paper to prescribe any particular aggregation operator, rather we provide a framework in which different aggregation operators can be used in a consistent way. While a relatively intuitive distinction exists between the use of the fuzzy (max/min) operators and the probabilistic operators, exploring trust-based interpretations for the other Triangular norms is a topic for future research.

By encoding degrees of trust as compliance values and by using special attributes _TNORM and _TCONORM to specify optional aggregation operators within delegation credentials it is not necessary to change the KeyNote language. While the KeyNote query engine has been modified to implement the model described in Section 3 its behavior is consistent with the standard KeyNote implementation when the aggregation operators are min/max (default). Thus, backwards compatibility is provided. Furthermore, QKeyNote credentials can be used in a standard KeyNote query, at least to the extent that standard KeyNote effectively aggregates according to min/max, thereby providing a 'safe' interpretation under the aggregation operator type ordering. The current model assumes fixed aggregation operators for any given query (subject to the credential conditions). Investigating how a query can support different aggregation operators to be simultaneously used across a graph is a topic for future research.

The current model and implementation does not currently support threshold delegation in KeyNote. We are investigating how a form of threshold delegation can be emulated by using probabilistic sum. In this case a conventional KeyNote credential that delegates authority to the conjunction of two principals can be rewritten as two individual credentials, each delegating authority to one principal, with, for example degree of trust 0.5 and probabilistic sum as _TCONORM. A KeyNote decision is considered acceptable if the degree of trust is greater than the trust of either individual 0.5.

A wide range of literature exists on many different forms of reputation trust and trust metrics and the reader is referred to [18] and [24] for an in-depth review. Closest to the underlying trust model proposed in this paper are schemes that treat the problem as an inclusion/exclusion style calculation across a probabilistic network such as [15, 22]. However, Section 2 demonstrates the problem of double-counting trust when performing such a calculation. Furthermore, [15, 22] does not generalize to arbitrary t-norm/conorm aggregation operators and does not consider integration with a Trust Management system.

The heuristic search described in Section 5 provided the basis for a proof of concept implementation of QKeyNote. Future research will investigate whether more effective algorithms exist for computing trust while preserving the Principle of Preservation of Trust. Jøsang et. al. [17] avoid double-counting by removing weakest (trust) delegation statements from the graph until a series of delegation chains remain that can be safely aggregated, resulting in a sub-optimal trust calculation. In [16] an improved strategy is proposed that uses edge-splitting to transform a delegation-statement (shared across different chains) into separate statements, one for each path, with the trust of the original statement distributed across the separate statements. We conjecture that these strategies also uphold the Principle of Preservation of Trust; investigating the use of these strategies in an alternative implementation of the QKeyNote interpreter is a topic for future research.

Bistarelli et. al. use multi-trust [2, 3] to model reputation trust within the RT Trust Management language. In the multi-trust model trust relationships are represented in terms of the degree of trust from a single trustor to a group of trustees; a c-semiring defines how the trust should be aggregated, using probabilistic product along chains and max for aggregating trust across separate chains. Adapting this model to the trust calculation scheme described in Section 3, and thereby supporting other t-norms and t-conorms, is a topic for future research.

Acknowledgments. This research is supported by Science Foundation Ireland grant 08/SRC/11403. The authors would like to thanks the anonymous reviewers and the workshop participants for their helpful feedback.

References

1. Becker, M., Fournet, C., Gordon, A.: Design and semantics of a decentralized authorization language. In: 20th IEEE Computer Security Foundations Symposium (January 2007)
2. Bistarelli, S., Martinelli, F., Santini, F.: A semantic foundation for trust management languages with weights: An application to the RT family. In: Rong, C., Jaatun, M.G., Sandnes, F.E., Yang, L.T., Ma, J. (eds.) ATC 2008. LNCS, vol. 5060, pp. 481–495. Springer, Heidelberg (2008)
3. Bistarelli, S., Santini, F.: Propagating multitrust within trust networks. In: SAC 2008: Proceedings of the 2008 ACM symposium on Applied computing, pp. 1990–1994. ACM, New York (2008)
4. Blaze, M., Feigenbaum, J., Ioannidis, J., Keromytis, A.D.: The Keynote trust-management system, version 2, IETF RFC2704 (September 1999)
5. Blaze, M., Feigenbaum, J., Lacy, J.: Decentralized trust management. In: Proceedings of the IEEE Symposium on Research in Security and Privacy, pp. 164–173. IEEE Computer Society Press, Oakland (1996)
6. Buchanan, B., Shortliffe, E.: Ruled Based Expert Systems, The MYCIN Experiment of the Stanford Heuristic Programming Project. Addison-Wesley, Reading (1984)
7. Colbourn, C.: The Combinatorics of Network Reliability. Oxford University Press, Oxford (1987)
8. Dubois, D., Prade, H.: A review of fuzzy sets aggregation connectives. Information Sciences 36, 85–121 (1985)
9. Ellison, C., Frantz, B., Lampson, B., Rivest, R.L., Thomas, B., Ylonen, T.: SPKI certificate theory, IETF RFC2693 (September 1999)
10. Fagin, R.: Fuzzy queries in multimedia database systems. In: PODS 1998: Proceedings of the seventeenth ACM SIGACT-SIGMOD-SIGART symposium on Principles of database systems, pp. 1–10. ACM, New York (1998)
11. Foley, S.N.: Security risk management using internal controls. In: WISG 2009: Proceedings of the first ACM workshop on Information security governance, pp. 59–64. ACM, New York (2009)
12. Foley, S.N.: Using trust management to support transferable hash-based micropayments. In: Proceedings of the 7th International Financial Cryptography Conference, FWI, Gosier (January 2003)
13. Foley, S.N., Rooney, V.: Qualitative analysis for trust management: Towards a model of photograph sharing indiscretion. In: Seventeenth International Security Protocols Workshop. LNCS. Springer, Heidelberg (April 2009) (post-proceedings forthcoming)
14. Gilbert, E., Karahalios, K.: Predicting tie strength with social media. In: Proceedings of the 27th international conference computer-human interaction (January 2009)
15. Haenni, R., Jonczy, J.: A new approach to PGP's web of trust. In: EEMA 2007: European e-Identity Conference, Paris, France (2007)
16. Jøsang, A., Bhuiyan, T.: Optimal trust network analysis with subjective logic. In: Second International Conference on Emerging Security Information, Systems and Technologies (SECURWARE), pp. 179–184 (2008)
17. Jøsang, A., Hayward, R., Pope, S.: Trust network analysis with subjective logic. In: ACSC: Proceedings of the 29th Australasian Computer Science Conference, pp. 85–94 (2006)

18. Jøsang, A., Ismail, R., Boyd, C.: A survey of trust and reputation systems for online service provision. Decis. Support Syst. 43(2), 618–644 (2007)
19. Klement, E.P., Mesiar, R., Pap, E.: On the relationship of associative compensatory operators to triangular norms and conorms. International Journal of Uncertainty, Fuzziness and Knowledge based Systems 4(2) (1996)
20. Li, J., Li, N., Winsborough, W.: Automated trust negotiation using cryptographic credentials. In: Proceedings of the 12th ACM conference on Computer and Communications Security (January 2005)
21. Mackworth, A.: Constraint satisfaction. In: Shapiro, S. (ed.) Encyclopedia of AI, 2nd edn, pp. 285–293. John Wiley & Sons, Chichester (1992)
22. Mahoney, G., Myrvold, W., Shoja, G.: Generic reliability trust model. In: Proceedings of the 3rd Annual Conference on Privacy, Security and Trust (PST), 3rd edn, vol. 5 (2005)
23. Montanari, U.: Networks of constraints: Fundamental properties and applications to picture processing. Information Science 7, 95–132 (1974)
24. Reiter, M., Stubblebine, S.: Authentication metric analysis and design. ACM Trans. Inf. Syst. Secur. 2(2), 138–158 (1999)
25. Riegelsberger, J., Sasse, M., McCarthy, J.: The mechanics of trust: A framework for research and design. Int. J. Hum.-Comput. Stud. 62(3), 381–422 (2005)
26. Schweizer, B., Sklar, A.: Probabilistic metric spaces. North Holland, New York (1983)
27. Team Choco: choco: an open source java constraint programming library. In: Third International CSP Solver Competition, Website, http://www.choco.emn.fr (2008)
28. Zimmermann, H.J., Zysno, P.: Latent connectives in human decision making. Fuzzy Sets and Systems 4, 37–51 (1980)

An Authentication Trust Metric
for Federated Identity Management Systems

Hidehito Gomi

Yahoo! JAPAN Research, 9-7-1 Akasaka, Minato-ku, Tokyo 107-6211, Japan
hgomi@yahoo-corp.jp

Abstract. A formalisation of authentication trust is proposed for federated identity management systems. Identity federation facilitates user interaction with Web services that control access, but it is more difficult for a service provider to evaluate the assurance of a user's identity if the creation and propagation of user authentication assertions involve different authentication authorities and mediators. On the basis of this formal representation, an aggregated trust value is calculated for evaluating the trustworthiness of a user's identity from the user's authentication assertions propagated through multiple entities.

Keywords: trust metric, identity federation.

1 Introduction

Identity federation is a scheme in which an identity provider (IdP) provides a service provider (SP) with an assertion about a user's information such as authentication events or personal attributes beyond security domains [1, 2, 3]. The SP decides to grant or deny user access to resources on the basis of the assertion obtained from the IdP without directly authenticating him or her. This decision depends on the credibility of the assertion and the trustworthiness of the IdP. Thus, trust plays a crucial role in identity federation as an underlying concept.

This paradigm facilitates user interaction with Web services that control access, but it is more difficult for an SP to evaluate the assurance of a user's identity if the creation and propagation of user authentication assertions involve different IdPs and intermediaries in different domains. In addition, in recent years many types of authentication methods have been deployed in practical systems and multifactor authentication is also required from increasing demands on strong authentication in some environments. Consequently, a trust metric is needed to evaluate propagated authentication assertions for federated identity management (FIM) systems in an open and distributed network.

In this paper, the formalisation of authentication trust is proposed for FIM systems where an authentication assertion is propagated through business partners. On the basis of the trust model, a trust metric is described to quantitatively calculate a trust value for a user's identity from the user's multiple authentication assertions using a logic reasoning approach.

J. Cuellar et al. (Eds.): STM 2010, LNCS 6710, pp. 116–131, 2011.

The rest of this paper is organised as follows: Section 2 reviews related work. Section 3 describes the trust model and its formal representation. Section 4 examines the metric for deriving authentication trust value. Section 5 describes the application of the proposed authentication trust calculation. Section 6 discusses several issues and Section 7 concludes the paper with a summary of the key points.

2   Related Work

There has been much work on trust models, metrics and formalisation in the literature. Prior work on general trust has focused on defining the semantics of trust and modelling trust-based systems. There have been a variety of trust classes and types and reputation systems [4]. Agudo et al. [5] analysed a general model of trust based on graph theory.

Existing work on trust formalisation focuses on assigning numerical values of trustworthiness to paths representing relationships between entities [6,7,8]. Beth et al. [6] presented a formal representation of trust relationships and algorithms for deriving them to estimate the trustworthiness of entities in open networks. Reiter and Stubblebine [7] developed a set of guiding principles for the design of authentication metrics. Huang and Nicol [8] introduced a formal representation of trust in a public key infrastructure (PKI) and proposed a mechanism for quantifying trust in certificate chains. They presented a general model and a metric with logical rule inferences. The work described here specifically focuses on authentication trust evaluation for FIM systems while taking a relevant approach to formalisation using logical rules for trust relationships. Abadi et al. [9] described the general concepts and algorithms for access control in distributed systems based on a modal logic approach whereas the work here proposes the derivation of authentication trust from propagated authentication assertions in distributed systems.

Prior work on FIM systems deals with trust management issues since trust is an important building block for identity management. Thomas et al. [10] defined the semantics of the authentication trust level on the basis of a mathematical model and provided a method for combining two trust levels to express the effect of a multifactor authentication in a FIM environment. Although the work proposed here is related in that it examines the authentication trust level, it focuses on evaluating the aggregated authentication level when multiple types of authentication assertions are available and each authentication level is given, by analysing the similarity of the assertions. Alenárez et al. [11] analysed the existing identity federation frameworks and identified the drawbacks to be deployed in dynamic open environments. They also proposed a SAML [1] extension for dynamic federation that dynamically establishes trust between entities.

Other relevant works are end-to-end trust establishment methods. Seigneur et al. [12] proposed an entity recognition approach in which dynamic enrollment enables spontaneous interactions with unknown entities in a certain context such as pervasive computing environments. They clarify two layers of trust— trust in technical infrastructure and trust between entities—whereas the trust definitions in this paper encompass both layers of trust and represent each trust semantic in the application level.

3 Formal Representation of Trust for Authentication

This section describes the formal representation of authentication trust for FIM systems. This paper gives trust specific definitions from the practical viewpoint of FIM. The concept of identity is introduced into a trust model, which consists of entities that exchange a user's assertion with other entities. All the entities are capable of authenticating other entities or end-users by means of authentication schemes.

3.1 Trust Semantics

The model's trust relationships are defined as follows.

Definition 1 (Identity Trust). *Identity trust is the certainty that the identity of an entity is identical to the identity claimed by the entity itself or by other parties regarding the entity.*

Identity trust is a foundation for authorising an interacting entity to access restricted resources or for regulating interactions with the entity in trust-based systems including FIM systems. Identity trust in an entity is established as a result of authentication procedures in which the entity presents a credential such as a password or an X.509 certificate proclaiming its identity to an authenticating entity using a predefined authentication protocol. The authenticating entity verifies the presented credential and determines the trustworthiness of the entity with some level of certainty depending on the above authentication method.

Accordingly, the semantics of identity trust can be defined as follows:

$$trust^{(i)}(p, q) \equiv authn(p, q) \tag{1}$$

where $trust^{(i)}(p, q)$ expresses that entity p has identity trust in entity q and $authn(p, q)$ means that entity p authenticates entity q by means of an authentication method. This axiom plays the role of a practical procedure for entity authentication in FIM systems associated with the identity trust relationship in this trust model.

Many metrics for evaluating this trust relationship have already been proposed. For example, many PKI trust models focus on the relationships among certification authorities for X.509 certificates. Instead, the proposed trust model focuses on the chain of user authentication information that comprises a certification trust evaluation.

The following definitions are related to the identity trust deriving capabilities that are specific to FIM systems.

Definition 2 (Attestation Trust). *Attestation trust is the certainty about the entity's capability to accurately create and assert information necessary for a recipient in a format appropriate for the recipient and to securely transmit the information to the recipient.*

Based on the above definition, if $trust^{(a)}(p, q, x)$ designates the attestation trust of trustor p for trustee q regarding information x, its semantics is formally given in first-order logic as

$$trust^{(a)}(p, q, x) \equiv assert(q, x) \Rightarrow accept(p, x) \tag{2}$$

where $assert(q, x)$ means that q creates an assertion containing information x and $accept(p, x)$ represents that p accepts that x is true. The $\Rightarrow$ operator designates the implication that whenever the consequent (expression to the left of the operator) is true, the antecedent (expression to the right of the operator) is true.

For example, if an authentication authority issues an assertion in a format such as SAML [1] or OpenID [2] stipulating that it authenticated a user by using a particular authentication method at a specified time, then an SP with attestation trust in that authority accepts the information represented in the assertion format as credible.

The functionalities required for attesting in FIM systems include not only selective information encoding but also identity mapping. An attesting entity specifies a user in attested information using a corresponding identifier for a recipient associated with the user's local identifier in the attesting entity. This functionality is important from the viewpoint of privacy because the recipient's identifier may differ from the local one and be unique to the pair of recipient and attesting entity.

Definition 3 (Mediation Trust). *Mediation trust is the certainty about the entity's capability to verify the accuracy and reliability of information created by another entity and securely transmit the information to the recipient without modification.*

Let $trust^{(m)}(p, q, x)$ denote the mediation trust of trustor p in trustee q regarding information x. Its semantics is formally expressed as

$$trust^{(m)}(p, q, x) \equiv accept(q, x) \Rightarrow accept(p, x). \tag{3}$$

This axiom means that if q accepts that information x is true, then p also accepts that x is true.

For example, a "proxying IdP" in SAML can act as a "trust mediating" entity. If it receives an authentication request regarding a user from an SP and cannot directly authenticate the user, it asks another IdP to authenticate the user and then returns the authentication assertion obtained from the authenticating IdP to the SP.

Note that in the above definition a trust mediating entity does not create an assertion by itself, but forwards it, whereas the entity shares responsibility

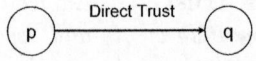

Fig. 1. Direct Trust for Authentication

for its trustworthiness with the entity providing it. In the above example, if the proxying IdP produces a new assertion by transforming identifiers used in the original information obtained from another IdP into the ones for the SP, then the proxying IdP corresponds to a "trust attesting" entity described in Definition 2.

3.2   Inference Rules

On the basis of the above trust semantics, the following inference rules for attestation and mediation trust are introduced using modus ponens to applied Axioms (2) and (3).

$$accept(p, x) \Leftarrow trust^{(a)}(p, q, x) \land assert(q, x). \tag{4}$$

$$accept(p, x) \Leftarrow trust^{(m)}(p, q, x) \land accept(q, x). \tag{5}$$

These logical rules enable information asserted by an entity to propagate via trusted entities in a network. Specifically, once an authentication authority has authenticated a user and asserted that the information about an authentication event regarding the user is true, the asserted information can propagate among trusted entities in FIM systems.

3.3   Direct Trust and Propagation Trust for Authentication

For entity authentication, there are two types of trust: *direct trust* and *propagation trust*. To trust an entity directly means to confirm its identity. This means that direct trust for authentication corresponds to identity trust in Axiom (1), which is represented by $trust^{(i)}(p, q)$ for trustor p and trustee q. A case of direct trust is shown in Fig. 1; here, entity p directly authenticates entity q, as indicated by the solid line from p to q. In the remainder of this paper, this relationship is represented by symbol $p \rightarrow q$.

Propagation trust expresses the certainty with which an entity accepts as trustworthy the information propagated from another entity having that information. The information refers to an entity other than the ones sending and receiving it. The trustworthiness of the information for its receiver depends on the trustworthiness of its sender because the sender holds and accepts the information. Propagation trust is categorised into two modes: *attestation mode* and *mediation mode*.

In the attestation mode of the propagation trust relationship between trustor p and trustee q, it is q that produces the information propagated to p. An attestation mode example of propagation trust is illustrated in Fig. 2; here, entity p has propagation trust in entity q, which is represented by the dotted

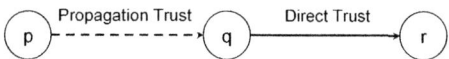

Fig. 2. Propagation Trust for Authentication in Attesting Entity $(p \rightsquigarrow q)$

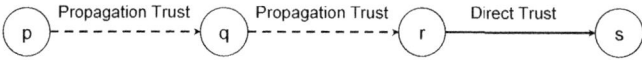

Fig. 3. Propagation Trust for Authentication via Mediating Entity $(p \rightsquigarrow q)$

line from p to q, while q has direct trust in entity r. In the remainder of this paper, this propagation trust relationship is represented by $p \rightsquigarrow q$. In Fig. 2, trustee q directly authenticates the other entity r and produces an authentication assertion regarding r. From this observation, the following axiom is defined for the attestation mode of propagation trust using Axioms (1) and (2).

$$trust^{(i,a)}(p,q,x) \equiv trust^{(i)}(p,q) \land trust^{(a)}(p,q,x). \tag{6}$$

In this axiom, $trust^{(i,a)}(p,q,x)$ denotes the attestation mode of propagation trust from p to q regarding information x that q propagates to p. This means that p has attestation trust in q regarding information x and p also has identity trust in q.

In the mediation mode of propagation trust, a mediating entity does not produce propagated information but accepts and transfers the information to another entity. A mediation mode example of propagation trust is illustrated in Fig. 3; here, entity q mediates to entity p the assertion created by entity r about an event that r authenticated entity s.

In this example, q does not authenticate s directly, but accepts the authentication information about s from r and mediates it to p. In the same way as in attestation mode, the mediation mode also needs the assumption of identity trust from p to q for information propagation. In this sense, the following axiom is defined using Axioms (1) and (3):

$$trust^{(i,m)}(p,q,x) \equiv trust^{(i)}(p,q) \land trust^{(m)}(p,q,x) \tag{7}$$

where $trust^{(i,m)}(p,q,x)$ denotes the mediation mode of propagation trust from p to q regarding information x. This means that p has both mediation and identity trust in q.

3.4 Derivation of Direct Trust and Propagation Trust

The above representation of trust for authentication can be used to derive a new trust relationship by aggregating individual trust relationships when corresponding authentication information is propagated (*serial aggregation*). This formalisation of trust rules is based on the *trust transitivity* principle [4], which leads to an inference about whether propagated information such as authentication result through entities is accurate.

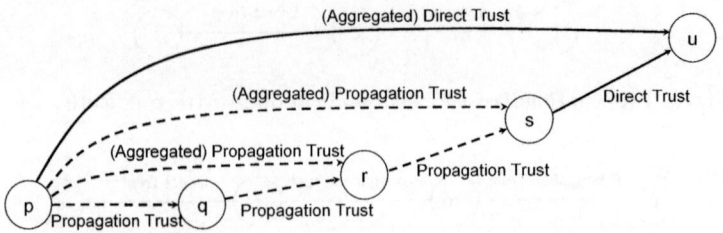

Fig. 4. Aggregation of Direct Trust and Propagation Trust

As shown in Fig. 4 for entities p, q, r, s, and u, there exists authentication trust path $p \rightsquigarrow q \rightsquigarrow r \rightsquigarrow s \rightarrow u$. For the circumstances assumed here, consider the derivation of the aggregated direct trust relationship $p \rightarrow u$ and propagation trust relationships $p \rightsquigarrow r$ and $p \rightsquigarrow s$. Note that this illustration is for the reader's intuitional understanding of the derived rules, which are general rules that are not specific to the case shown.

Let $trust^{(i)}(p, u, x)$ denote aggregated direct trust from entity p to entity u with information x, where p indirectly authenticates u on the basis of x. Using Axioms (1) and (6), the rule for direct trust derivation is given as follows.

Rule 1 (Direct Trust Derivation)

$$trust^{(i)}(p, u, x) \Leftarrow trust^{(i,a)}(p, s, x) \wedge trust^{(i)}(s, u). \tag{8}$$

This rule means that p has assurance in authentication assertion x regarding u attested by s since p trusts in s's identity and attestation capability. It clearly explains a typical identity federation scenario in which p, s, and u correspond to an SP, IdP, and end-user, respectively, in FIM systems.

Next, consider the derivation of aggregated propagation trust $p \rightsquigarrow r$. Regarding $p \rightsquigarrow q$ and $q \rightsquigarrow r$, p has assurance in information x since q has assurance in x and propagates it to p as credible information obtained from r. In other words, the assurance in x propagates from q to p. This observation leads to the following rule for serial aggregation of propagation trust relationships involving mediation using Axiom (7).

Rule 2 (Propagation Trust Derivation for Mediation)

$$trust^{(i,m)}(p, r, x) \Leftarrow trust^{(i,m)}(p, q, x) \wedge trust^{(i,m)}(q, r, x). \tag{9}$$

The derivation of $p \rightsquigarrow s$ is similar to that of $p \rightsquigarrow r$, which was explained above, since both are propagation trust relationships. In the case where $p \rightsquigarrow s$, trustee s propagates its attestation about s's authentication activity while in the case where $p \rightsquigarrow r$, trustee r mediates the information obtained from another entity. A trustor p can have assurance in an attestation that was originally asserted by s and then propagated by mediating entity r. This trust derivation is represented by the following rule using Axioms (6) and (7).

Rule 3 (Propagation Trust Derivation for Attestation)

$$trust^{(i,a)}(p,s,x) \Leftarrow trust^{(i,m)}(p,r,x) \land trust^{(i,a)}(r,s,x). \tag{10}$$

These rules enable us to logically derive aggregated direct trust for FIM systems in which assertions are propagated among multiple entities.

4 Authentication Trust Quantification

This section describes a formal algorithm for trust aggregation based on the axioms and rules described in Section 3.

4.1 Authentication Trust Value

A direct authentication takes place if an entity authenticates a user by means of an authentication method. The value of entity p's direct authentication trust in entity q, $v^{(i)}(p,q)$, is defined on the basis of the semantics of Axiom (1) as

$$v^{(i)}(p,q) \stackrel{\text{def}}{=} \Pr(authn(p,q)). \tag{11}$$

This trust value can be a probability derived from the data accumulated in transactions between p and q. Alternatively, p's administrator can set a value as a subjective probability or give a value as an assurance level in the range [0,1]. For example, the Liberty Alliance Identity Assurance Framework [13] and National Institute of Standards and Technology (NIST) 800-63 [14] describe four assurance levels for the certainty values associated with an identity assertion according to the types of authentication mechanisms.

For propagation authentication trust, the acceptance of propagated information depends on the authentication of the entity propagating the information. On the basis of the relationship between probability and conditionals and the semantics of Axiom (2) and (3), the following values of authentication trust for attestation and mediation are defined.

$$v^{(a)}(p,q,x) \stackrel{\text{def}}{=} \Pr(accept(p,x)|assert(q,x) \land authn(p,q)), \tag{12}$$

$$v^{(m)}(p,q,x) \stackrel{\text{def}}{=} \Pr(accept(p,x)|accept(q,x) \land authn(p,q)). \tag{13}$$

Let $v^{(i,a)}(p,q,x)$ and $v^{(i,m)}(p,q,x)$ be the authentication trust values for $trust^{(i,a)}(p,q,x)$ and $trust^{(i,m)}(p,q,x)$, respectively, in Axioms (6) and (7). For simplicity, suppose that $v^{(*)}(p,q)$ is used to denote $v^{(*)}(p,q,x)$ by omitting x since x is authentication result information and it is common to all axioms in this context. Then, the following equations are obtained:

$$v^{(i,a)}(p,q) = v^{(i)}(p,q) \cdot v^{(a)}(p,q), \tag{14}$$

$$v^{(i,m)}(p,q) = v^{(i)}(p,q) \cdot v^{(m)}(p,q). \tag{15}$$

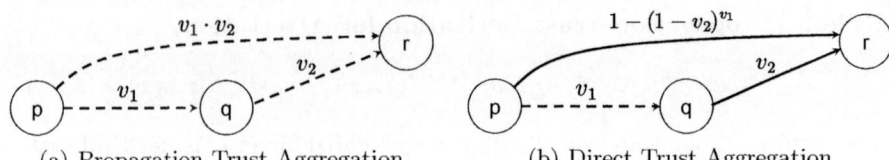

(a) Propagation Trust Aggregation   (b) Direct Trust Aggregation

Fig. 5. Serial Trust Aggregation with Beth-Borcherding-Klein Metric

4.2 Trust Value Calculation

On the basis of the above definitions of authentication trust values, the Beth-Borcherding-Klein metric [6, 7] is applied as an instance to calculate the values of direct and propagation trust (Fig. 5).

Serial Trust Aggregation. Serial trust aggregation creates a new trust relationship from two existing trust relationships and assigns it a new trust value.

If there is a path $p \rightsquigarrow \cdots \rightsquigarrow q$ with propagation trust value $v^{(i,m)}(p,q)$ and a propagation edge $q \rightsquigarrow r$ with value $v^{(i,m)}(q,r)$, then the propagation trust value for path $p \rightsquigarrow \cdots \rightsquigarrow q \rightsquigarrow r$ is expressed using Eq. (15) as follows (see Fig. 5(a)).

$$v^{(i,m)}(p,r) = v^{(i,m)}(p,q) \cdot v^{(i,m)}(q,r). \tag{16}$$

If there is a path $p \rightsquigarrow \cdots \rightsquigarrow q$ with propagation value $v^{(i,a)}(p,q)$ and a direct edge $q \rightarrow r$ with value $v^{(i)}(q,r)$, then the direct trust value for the path $p \rightsquigarrow \cdots \rightsquigarrow q \rightarrow r$ is expressed using Eqs. (11) and (14) as follows (see Fig. 5(b)).

$$v^{(i)}(p,r) = 1 - (1 - v^{(i)}(q,r))^{v^{(i,a)}(p,q)}. \tag{17}$$

Thus, if, in general, there exists propagation path $p \rightsquigarrow q$ and path q to r, then the aggregated trust value $v(p,r)$ is obtained from Eqs. (16) and (17) as

$$v(p,r) = \begin{cases} v^{(i,m)}(p,r) & \text{for mediator } q, \\ v^{(i)}(p,r) & \text{for attester } q. \end{cases} \tag{18}$$

Parallel Trust Aggregation. Since, in general, there exist multiple propagation paths, there will be multiple (aggregated) direct trust relationships as a result of serial trust aggregation. Parallel trust aggregation derives a new trust value for a path between two entities when there are multiple direct trust relationships between them. The case where there are N (aggregated) direct trust relationships between p and q ($p \rightarrow q$) and the k-th relationship has direct trust value v_k is illustrated in Fig. 6.

Here, consider calculating a combined trust value from all the existing (aggregated) direct trust relationships and their assigned trust values using the *weighted aggregation* approach. If w_k denotes the weight for trust value $v_k(p,q)$, then aggregated direct trust value $v(p,q)$ is given by

$$v(p,q) = \sum_{k=1}^{N} w_k \cdot v_k(p,q). \tag{19}$$

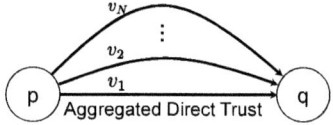

Fig. 6. Multiple Aggregated Direct Trust Relationships

How much value is assigned to each weight depends on its parallel aggregation policy. The following policies are examined according to what kind of factor takes precedence:

- The equality of each transaction. Each path is equally assigned the same weight.
- The strength of authentication. The path involved with a stronger authentication event has more weight.
- The freshness of authentication events. The path that has more recent authentication event has more weight.
- The depth of authentication trust paths. The path that is involved with more attesting and mediating entities has less weight.
- The number of accumulated transactions. Suppose that the k-th path $(p \rightarrow q)$ has had n_k events in the history of accumulated transactions between p and q. In this case, w_k is calculated as $w_k = n_k(p,q)/n^*(p,q)$, where its total number $n^*(p,q)$ is given by $n^*(p,q) = \sum_{k=1}^{N} n_k(p,q)$.

Since the above policies indicate typical concepts for assigning weight, the combination of several policies can actually be considered in accordance with practical requirements.

Similarity of Authentication Trust Paths. The above trust aggregation has *sensitivity* to misbehaviour or threats that attempt to manipulate the output of trust values to increase the user's identity assurance [7]. This sensitivity issue is illustrated as an example in Fig. 7.

Entity p has a mediation mode of propagation trust relationships with entities q, r, and s that have an attestation mode of propagation trust for entity t. Here, t is the only attesting entity for q, r, and s that directly authenticates u, but q, r, and s receive the same authentication information from t: the aggregation approach sums up the values. In addition, entities h_1, h_2, and h_3 correspond to the same attesting entity h but have different authentication events. Attesting entity h can increase its aggregated propagation trust value for $g \rightarrow u$ by increasing the number of authentication events if the weight values for the corresponding trust paths relatively increase in Eq. (19).

As a solution to the sensitivity problem, the approach of discovering *similar authentication trust paths* is proposed as an extension of the weighted aggregation. If there are similar authentication trust paths (e.g., $p \rightsquigarrow q \rightsquigarrow t$, $p \rightsquigarrow r \rightsquigarrow t$, and $p \rightsquigarrow s \rightsquigarrow t$), they are aggregated into one path (e.g., $p \rightsquigarrow q \rightsquigarrow t$) with an aggregated value to avoid an excessive weight value being assigned. This similarity of trust paths is detected through the following evaluation measures:

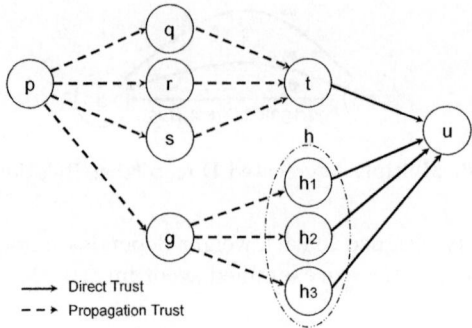

Fig. 7. Graph Example

- Authentication events: Regarding two authentication events, if their authentication methods are the same or similar in their authentication trust, or if the times when they take place are the same or their difference is within a specific time period, they can be regarded as similar.
- Attestations: For two authentication assertions, if they are issued by the same attesting entity at the same time for similar authentication events, they can be regarded as similar attestations.
- Mediations: For two mediation events of authentication assertions, if the assertions are similar and if the events are executed by the same mediating entity, the events can be regarded as similar.

On the basis of the above measures, similar authentications, attestations, and mediations are categorised into the same one. This approach provides trust values to appropriately assess authentication trust.

Aggregation Algorithm. A direct acyclic graph (DAG) is considered to aggregate a trust value between two entities using the above metric. Algorithm 1 shows a procedure for calculating the aggregated direct trust between SP p and user u $(p \rightarrow u)$ in DAG G that recursively simplifies its graph by replacing multiple paths with a single trust path labelled with a new trust value. This algorithm enhances and formalises the aggregating approach shown in [8]. Let E and A denote entities and arcs in G, respectively.

$N(u)$ denotes u's neighbours that have direct trust relationships with u (step 1). If path (p, u) is the only path from p to u in G, nothing is done (steps 2–3). reachable(p, q) denotes a utility function that returns true if there is path p to q. Step 4 checks whether p has only one path to u. If this holds true, then serial aggregation is executed; the last arc is deleted and a new trust path with its trust value is added to G (steps 5–6). Step 7 checks whether p has multiple nonintersecting paths to u. If this is true, parallel aggregation is performed; the aggregated trust value is calculated using the weighted aggregation approach in calcWeightedAggregatedTrust with an aggregation policy for discovering the similarity of trust paths (step 8), the last arcs in all paths from p to u are deleted

---

Algorithm 1. aggregate(p, u, G, agg_policy)

Require: $p, u \in E$; $A \in E \times E$, $G = (E, A)$
1: $N(u) \leftarrow \{e_i | (e_i, u) \in A\}$
2: **if** $N(u) = \{p\}$, **then**
3:      do nothing
4: **else if** $N(u) = \{e_i\}$, $e_i \neq p$, reachable(p, e_i), $(e_i, u) \in A$,
     $\neg\{\exists e_j \in E;$ reachable(p, e_j), $(e_j, e_i) \in A$, $e_i \neq e_j\}$, **then** {serial aggregation}
5:      del$((e_i, u), G)$
6:      add$((p, u), v(p, u), G)$
7: **else if** $\forall e_i; \in N(u); e_i \neq p, N(e_i) = \{p\}$, **then** {parallel aggregation}
8:      $v(p, u) \leftarrow$ calcWeightedAggregatedTrust$(N(u)$, $agg\_policy)$
9:      **for all** i such that $e_i \in N(u)$ **do**
10:         del$((e_i, u), G)$
11:      **end for**
12:      add$((p, u), v(p, u), G)$
13: **else** {recursive aggregations for sub-graphs}
14:      **for all** i such that $e_i \in N(u)$, $e_i \neq p$ **do**
15:         aggregate(p, e_i, G, agg_policy)
16:      **end for**
17: **end if**
18: **return**

(steps 9–11) and a new aggregated trust path with its trust value is added to G (step 12). Otherwise, the above procedure is recursively called for each sub-graph (steps 13–17). Finally, this procedure is completed (step 18).

Trust Aggregation Example. The example shown in Figs. 8 to 9 demonstrates the trust aggregation procedure starting with the trust relationships shown in Fig. 7. The procedure applies Algorithm 1 to obtain the aggregated direct trust value of $p \rightarrow u$. In Fig. 7, u has neighbours t, h_1, h_2, and h_3.

The result of parallel aggregation between p and t is shown in Fig. 8(a). Since t's neighbours q, r, and s have one neighbour p, parallel aggregation is applied for the sub-graph of G with p as the source and t as the sink. The aggregated trust $p \rightsquigarrow t$ is created and combined from three serial trust aggregations $p \rightsquigarrow q \rightsquigarrow t$, $p \rightsquigarrow r \rightsquigarrow t$, and $p \rightsquigarrow s \rightsquigarrow t$. After the combination, arcs $q \rightsquigarrow t$, $r \rightsquigarrow t$, and $s \rightsquigarrow t$ are removed, and arc $p \rightsquigarrow t$ is added with its aggregated trust value.

The result of serial aggregations for the sub-graphs $p \rightsquigarrow g \rightsquigarrow h_1$, $p \rightsquigarrow g \rightsquigarrow h_2$, and $p \rightsquigarrow g \rightsquigarrow h_3$ are shown in Fig. 8(b). In Fig. 8(a), g is a mediating entity of p that has trust relationships with attesting entities h_1, h_2, and h_3. Three aggregated trust relationships $p \rightsquigarrow h_1$, $p \rightsquigarrow h_2$, and $p \rightsquigarrow h_3$ are created and arcs $g \rightsquigarrow h_1$, $g \rightsquigarrow h_2$, and $g \rightsquigarrow h_3$ are removed. Now u has four neighbours (t, h_1, h_2, and h_3), each of which has only one neighbour p.

The result of parallel aggregation between p and u is shown in Fig. 9. After four serial trust aggregations $p \rightsquigarrow t \rightarrow u$, $p \rightsquigarrow h_1 \rightarrow u$, $p \rightsquigarrow h_2 \rightarrow u$, and $p \rightsquigarrow h_3 \rightarrow u$, aggregated direct trust $p \rightarrow u$ and its trust value are added, and arcs $t \rightarrow u$, $h_1 \rightarrow u$, $h_2 \rightarrow u$, and $h_3 \rightarrow u$ are removed. As a result, the aggregated direct trust value for $p \rightarrow u$ is obtained.

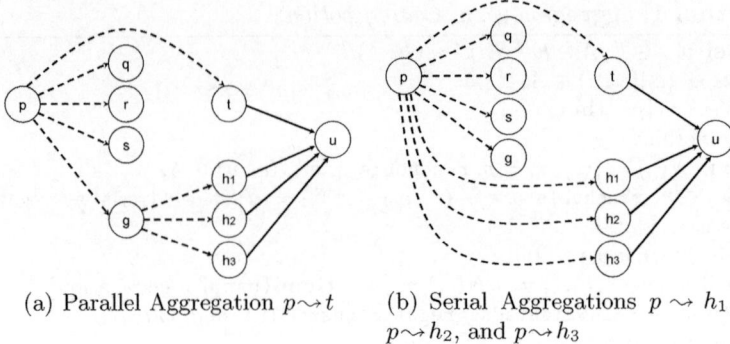

(a) Parallel Aggregation $p \rightsquigarrow t$ (b) Serial Aggregations $p \rightsquigarrow h_1$, $p \rightsquigarrow h_2$, and $p \rightsquigarrow h_3$

Fig. 8. Example: Trust Aggregation—Parallel and Serial Aggregations

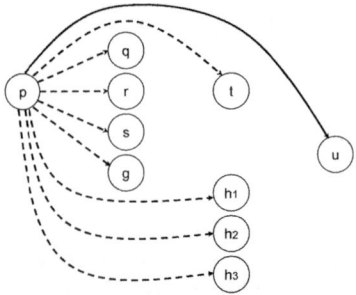

Fig. 9. Example: Trust Aggregation—Parallel Aggregation $p \rightarrow u$

5   Authentication Trust Assessment

This section shows how the derived values of aggregated trust are used to assess the trustworthiness of an entity in several use cases.

Authorisation for Multifactor Authentication Assertions. If an IdP has multiple types of authentication methods and issues authentication assertions regarding a user to an SP, the SP can assess the user's identity assurance by deriving the trust value and decide whether to grant the user access to a particular resource by comparing the value with a predefined threshold value.

A use case in which IdP h provides SP p with authentication assertions regarding user u by means of two authentication methods—a basic authentication (using a password) and biometric authentication (using a fingerprint)—is shown in Fig. 10(a). Since different authentication methods are provided by the same entity, the figure represents the IdP as two different attesting entities h_1 and h_2. The value allocated to each path represents the trust value for that path. Namely, $v^{(i,a)}(p, h_1)$, $v^{(i,a)}(p, h_2)$, $v^{(i)}(h_1, u)$, and $v^{(i)}(h_2, u)$ are equal to 0.90, 0.90, 0.60, and 0.90, respectively. In this case, since biometric authentication is known as a stronger authentication method than the basic authentication,

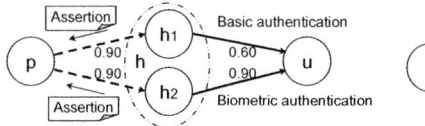

(a) Multifactor Authentication Assertions   (b) Multiauthority Authentication Assertions

Fig. 10. Use Cases: Authorisation by Accessing Multiple Assertions

$v^{(i)}(h_2, u)$ is larger than $v^{(i)}(h_1, u)$, whereas the trust values for attestation are the same. From Eq. (17), the aggregated trust value $v_k^{(i)}(p, u)$ for $k = 1, 2$ is obtained as $v_k^{(i)}(p, u) = 1 - (1 - v^{(i)}(p, h_k))^{v^{(i,a)}(h_k, u)}$. In applying Eq. (19), if $(w_1, w_2) = (0.5, 0.5)$ is assumed, then the aggregated trust value $v(p, u)$ is obtained as

$$v(p, u) = w_1 \cdot v_1^{(i)}(p, u) + w_2 \cdot v_2^{(i)}(p, u)$$
$$= 0.50 \cdot \underbrace{\{1 - (1 - 0.60)^{0.90}\}}_{0.56} + 0.50 \cdot \underbrace{\{1 - (1 - 0.90)^{0.90}\}}_{0.87} = 0.72.$$

Consider that p's administrator sets threshold values to 0.5 and 0.7 in u's profile information to grant u permission to "read" and "write", respectively. In this case, u is denied permission to update u's profile if p has only an authentication assertion regarding u from h_1 whereas u is granted permission to do so if p additionally obtains another authentication assertion from h_2.

Authorisation for Assertions from Multiple Authorities. Figure 10(b) shows different IdPs q and r issuing authentication assertions regarding user u to SP p using the aforementioned basic and biometric authentication methods, respectively. The trust values $v^{(i,a)}(p, q)$, $v^{(i,a)}(p, r)$, $v^{(i)}(q, u)$, and $v^{(i)}(r, u)$ are 0.90, 0.60, 0.60, and 0.90, respectively. With these assumptions, and in the same way as for the above use case, the aggregated trust value $v_*^{(i)}(p, u)$ for $* = q, r$ is obtained as $v_*^{(i)}(p, u) = 1 - (1 - v^{(i)}(p, *))^{v^{(i,a)}(*, u)}$. If the weights for trust values are assumed to be $(w_q, w_r) = (0.5, 0.5)$, then the aggregated trust value $v(p, u)$ for this use case is obtained as

$$v(p, u) = w_q \cdot v_q^{(i)}(p, u) + w_r \cdot v_r^{(i)}(p, u)$$
$$= 0.50 \cdot \underbrace{\{1 - (1 - 0.60)^{0.90}\}}_{0.56} + 0.50 \cdot \underbrace{\{1 - (1 - 0.90)^{0.60}\}}_{0.75} = 0.66.$$

Like in the above use case, an SP can determine its authorisation decision for a user on the basis of a quantitative evaluation of authentication trust for the case in which multiple authentication authorities are involved.

Although the above two use cases are very simple because there are two attesting entities, it is possible to treat more complicated cases having multiple mediating entities and the combination of those entities.

Selection of Authentication Authority and Method. The proposed trust value calculation enables an entity to estimate an appropriate authentication authority and method, and assertion propagation path when the entity needs to authenticate a user. For example, when SP p receives an access request from user u for a restricted resource, p needs the appropriate assurance of identity trust in u. If p can authenticate u directly with a basic authentication method, but the evaluated trust value for the authentication is below the threshold value, p can optionally choose an authentication authority (IdP) to authenticate u indirectly with a stronger authentication method than the basic one. Here, p simulates and evaluates the aggregated trust values of possible authentication methods and authorities from accumulated experience in order to obtain an appropriate aggregated trust value that exceeds the threshold value. This is cost effective in FIM systems because an SP can selectively depend on an IdP for authentication of appropriate strength even if the SP itself does not have that capability.

6   Discussion

FIM systems typically focus on the trust relationships between authentication authorities (IdPs) and collaborative partners (SPs); i.e., they are *relationship-focused*. In such a system, an online IdP dynamically issues short-term security tokens while restricting its transitivity on the basis of the relationships between the issuer and recipient in contrast to a *credential-focused* system in which long-term, non-transitive cryptographic credentials such as X.509 are issued without involving the original IdP [15]. The proposed trust model reflects the above characteristic and thus introduces entity-to-entity relations to quantitatively evaluate the identity assurance of an entity through multiple assertions.

In practical authentication systems, the trustworthiness of an entity decays with the time after the system has authenticated the entity, whereas the proposed trust model does not incorporate such a notion: that remains for future work. Other topics for future work include examining the appropriateness of a trust value assigned to each identity trust and establishing weights for trust aggregation with possible aggregation policies. Further, performing a feasibility study of the proposed trust value calculation is also an open issue.

7   Conclusion and Future Work

This paper defined the semantics of authentication trust and described formal rules for deriving authentication trust using a trust reasoning approach for federated identity management systems. In addition, on the basis of the proposed representation, it quantitatively derived aggregated trust for authentication trust from a user's authentication assertions propagated through multiple entities in order to evaluate the trustworthiness of the user's identity. Future work includes the incorporation of trust decay with the passage of time and the establishment of a method for assigning weights for trust aggregation with its policies.

References

1. OASIS: Assertions and Protocol for the OASIS Security Assertion Markup Language (SAML) V2.0 (2005),
   http://www.oasis-open.org/committees/tc_home.php?wg_abbrev=security
2. OpenID: OpenID Authentication 2.0 - Final (2007), http://openid.net/
3. IBM, Microsoft, BEA, RSA, VeriSign: Web Services Federation Language (2003)
4. Jøsang, A., Ismail, R., Boyd, C.: A Survey of Trust and Reputation Systems for Online Service Provision. Decision Support Systems 43(2), 618–644 (2007)
5. Agudo, I., Fernandez-Gago, C., Lopez, J.: A model for trust metrics analysis. In: Furnell, S.M., Katsikas, S.K., Lioy, A. (eds.) TrustBus 2008. LNCS, vol. 5185, pp. 28–37. Springer, Heidelberg (2008)
6. Beth, T., Borcherding, M., Klein, B.: Valuation of Trust in Open Networks. In: Gollmann, D. (ed.) ESORICS 1994. LNCS, vol. 875, pp. 3–18. Springer, Heidelberg (1994)
7. Reiter, M., Stubblebine, S.: Authentication Metric Analysis and Design. ACM Transactions on Information and System Securiry 2(2), 138–158 (1999)
8. Huang, J., Nicol, D.: A Calculus of Trust and Its Application to PKI and Identity Management. In: Proceedings of the 8th Symposium on Identity and Trust on the Internet (IDtrust 2009), pp. 23–37 (2009)
9. Abadi, M., Burrows, M., Lampson, B., Plotkin, G.: A Calculus for Access Control in Distributed Systems. ACM Transactions on Programming Languages and Systems 15(4), 706–734 (1993)
10. Thomas, I., Menzel, M., Meinel, C.: Using Quantified Trust Levels to Describe Authentication Requirements in Federated Identity Management. In: Proceedings of the 2008 ACM Workshop on Secure Web Services (SWS 2008), pp. 71–80 (2008)
11. Almenárez, F., Arias, P., Marín, A., Díaz, D.: Towards Dynamic Trust Establishment for Identity Federation. In: Proceedings of the 2009 Euro American Conference on Telematics and Information Systems (EATIS 2009), pp. 1–4 (2009)
12. Seigneur, J.M., Farrell, S., Jensen, C.D., Gray, E., Chen, Y.: End-to-End Trust Starts with Recognition. In: Proceedings of the 1st International Conference on Security in Pervasive Computing (SPC 2003), pp. 130–142 (2003)
13. Liberty Alliance Project: Liberty Identity Assurance Framework (2008),
    http://www.projectliberty.org/specs
14. Burr, W., Dodson, D., Polk, W.: Electronic Authentication Guideline (2006),
    http://csrc.nist.gov/publications/nistpubs/800-63/SP800-63V1_0_2.pdf
15. Bhargav-Spantzel, A., Camenish, J., Gross, T., Sommer, D.: User Centricity: A Taxonomy and Open Issues. Journal of Computer Security 15(5), 493–527 (2007)

A Trust-Augmented Voting Scheme for Collaborative Privacy Management

Yanjie Sun[1,2], Chenyi Zhang[1,3], Jun Pang[1],
Baptiste Alcade[1,*], and Sjouke Mauw[1]

[1] University of Luxembourg, L-1359, Luxembourg
[2] Shandong University, Jinan, 250101, China
[3] University of New South Wales, Sydney 2052, Australia

Abstract. Social networks have sprung up and become a hot issue of current society. In spite of the fact that these networks provide users with a variety of attractive features, much to users' dismay, however, they are likely to expose users private information (unintentionally).

In this paper, we propose an approach which is intended for addressing the problem of collaboratively deciding privacy policies for, but not limited to, shared photos. Our proposed algorithm utilizes trust relations in social networks and combines it with the Condorcet preferential voting scheme. An optimization is developed to improve its efficiency. Experimental results show that our trust-augmented voting scheme performs well. An inference technique is introduced to infer a best privacy policy for a user based on his voting history.

1   Introduction

Social networking is one of the greatest inventions on the Internet during the last ten years. Social network sites provide users platforms to socialize both in the digital world and in the real world, for making friends, information exchange and retrieval, and entertainment. Some of the largest ones, such as Facebook [1] and MySpace [2], provide services to hundreds of millions of registered users. However, partly due to the intention to attract as many users as possible for their commercial success, social networks tend to intentionally or unintentionally expose private information of existing users. User privacy has become an important and crucial research topic in social networks. A number of scholars have studied it from different viewpoints, e.g. [3,4,5,6,7,8]. Moreover, the excessively expanded number of users also bring difficulties into the management of these sites, so that designing effective mechanisms to coordinate users' opinions over their privacy becomes an emerging issue.

As a shared platform, resources in a social network may be co-owned by a number of users. For instance, documents can be co-authored and several users may appear in a same photo. Such co-ownership might cause breach of privacy.[1]

---

* Supported by the grant TR-PDR BFR08-038 from the Fonds National de la Recherche, Luxembourg.

[1] Determining the co-owners requires some content recognition or manual tagging mechanisms.

J. Cuellar et al. (Eds.): STM 2010, LNCS 6710, pp. 132–146, 2011.
© Springer-Verlag Berlin Heidelberg 2011

For example, suppose user Alice wishes to publish on her personal page a picture which contains Bob's image, this action may cause exposure of Bob's privacy, regardless of Bob's personal will. In response to this issue, most of the social network sites choose to place the burden of privacy setting solely on the owners of the resources, to which we hold a different stance. We believe it might be more desirable to let all co-owners participate in the privacy setting. In this paper, we mainly focus on the particular problem of how to merge privacy opinions from co-owners of shared resources.

Voting is a natural choice to build a mechanism which takes individual's preferences on their privacy policies into a joint decision reflecting the "general will" of the group of people who are sharing a piece of data. Siquicciarini *et al.* [9] propose a game theoretical method based on the Clarke-Tax mechanism [10], which can maximize the social utility function by encouraging truthfulness among people in the group. This induces a nice property that the final decision cannot be manipulated by individuals, as users express their true opinions about the privacy preference. However, their method is not as simple as it is claimed to be, as it requires each user to compute a value for each different preference and the user-input values are essential for their method to derive a joint decision. We argue that this requirement is not realistic and it makes users less interested in participating collaborative privacy control.

Instead, in this paper we propose a different but novel solution, by combining trust in social networks with a well-known preferential voting scheme. The trust relations are inherent in social networks and can be easily derived among users, for example, by comparing user profiles or computing the distance of users in a social network. We believe that trust should play an important role especially when users cooperate to decide the privacy policy on a shared resource. In a preferential voting scheme users are required to give an order of their privacy preferences rather than only select a single choice. This allows users to express their opinions on different privacy policies in a more comprehensive way. Moreover, users are not required to associate values to preferences. Comparing to the method of Siquicciarini *et al.* [9], ours is simple to use. The above discussion reflects the two design rationales *expressiveness* and *simplicity of use* in our mind – these considerations lead us to a method for collaborative privacy control which is as simple as possible without losing its expressive power.

The rest of the paper is organized as follows. Sect. 2 introduces notions of trust in social networks and Condorcet's preferential voting scheme. In Sect. 3 we propose a new algorithm that enhances traditional Condorcet's voting scheme by taking the trust relation into account. We also propose a heuristic to improve the performance of this new algorithm. Sect. 4 presents experimental data on comparing the algorithms previously introduced, which also justifies the correctness of our heuristic approach. Sect. 5 provides an inference technique to automatically recommend a default vote for a user based on his profile setting and voting history. We conclude the paper in Sect. 6.

2   Preliminaries

2.1   Trust in Social Networks

Literature shows that social life is simply not possible without trust [11,12]. In particular, trust relations are central to cooperation, i.e., the social process aiming at the increase or preservation of the partners' power, wealth, etc. Online social networks reflect human social relations in the Internet, allowing users to connect to people they know, to share data (e.g., video, photos, text), and to have group activities (e.g., games, events). A number of social structures have been introduced in social networks, such as friendship, group membership and virtual family. The notion of trust is naturally present in social networks, and moreover, in contrast to real life, it can be quantified and made explicit.

Trust has been defined in several different ways. The definition of trust adopted here, first formulated by Gambetta [13], is often referred to as "reliability trust". Thus, we define *trust* as the belief or subjective probability of the *trustor* that the *trustee* will adequately perform a certain action on which the trustor's welfare depends. Trust is hence a quantifiable relation between two agents. There are mainly two approaches to trust quantification, namely by the evaluation of the similarity, or by an analysis of relevant past events (stored in a history) between two entities.

The similarity between two entities is a distance function that can take various attributes into account, such as *social* (e.g., gender, location, company, etc.), and *behavioral* (e.g., the way one ranks or buys) attributes. Intuitively, the closer the two entities are w.r.t. an attribute (i.e., the distance is small), the more likely the trust relation will be strong. In practice, a social network like Facebook implements a *social similarity* mechanism in order to suggest to the user people that she might consider as friends. For instance, if Alice and Bob both have Clare and Danny in their friend list but Bob also has Elisabeth as a friend, then Elisabeth might be suggested to Alice.

In the second approach, a sequence of past events concerning a specific action can be analyzed to predict the likelihood that the same action will be correctly performed if requested. This analysis can consist in checking a property over the history [14,15], or the computation of a probability (e.g., Hidden Markov Models [16]). Moreover, trust transitivity can be used when an entity wants to evaluate the trust in an unacquainted entity, e.g., when the trustor does not have access to the trustee's profile, or has never interacted with her. Trust transitivity is defined as the possibility for the trustor to use trust information from other entities in order to infer a trust evaluation towards the trustee, i.e., derive a trust value from a trust graph. In social networks, we can use the trust over friendship relations as transitive relations. Computational models for trust transitivity can be found in the literature [17,18,19,20], and can be applied to social networks.

Our main motivation to incorporating trust in collective privacy management is that people's opinion in a social network can be evaluated by taking trust relations into account. For instance, when Alice rates a video that is made by Bob, Clare evaluates this data item through the trust she has assigned to Alice (as a referee) and Bob (as a film-maker). Similarly, combining users' opinions is usually required to decide privacy policies of shared contents, which leads us to a trust-augmented voting scheme. In the following sections, we define trust as a function that assigns a value in $[0, 1]$ to every (ordered) pair of users, and assume that trust values among users can be efficiently computed in social networks by using the approaches as discussed above. The meaning of a value 0 is that a trustor fully distrusts a trustee such that his opinion will be completely disregarded, while 1 means that a trustor fully trusts a trustee.

2.2 Privacy Policies

In this paper, we simply refer to privacy policies as the set of users who are allowed access to shared resources. For instance, for a co-owner picture, the available policies are (i) visible only to the owner (P_1), (ii) visible only to those tagged, also called co-owners, in the picture (P_2), (iii) visible to friends of the tagged users (P_3) and (iv) available to everyone (P_4). Throughout the paper, we use $P_1, P_2, \ldots, P_n$ to range over such policies.[2]

2.3 Condorcet's Preferential Voting Scheme

There exist a number of voting systems in the literature. In single candidate systems each vote refers to a single choice, which sometimes may not be able to encode more comprehensive opinions. For example, a voter cannot express that he is initially willing to vote for Alice, but in case that Alice fails to be elected, he will vote for Bob among the rest of the candidates. In such a situation preferential systems can be applied to express more precise and more comprehensive ideas from the voters. In this paper we present a preferential voting scheme which is extended from a system that is originally developed by Condorcet in late eighteenth century. For a complete description of Condorcet's voting system we refer to [21], which also explains why in a certain sense Condorcet's scheme may be regarded as 'optimal'.

In a preferential voting system, a ballot consists of a (preferential) list of all candidates. For every pair of candidates appearing in the list, say C_1 and C_2, their relative positions reflect the voter's preference, e.g., the case that C_1 precedes C_2 in the list indicates that the voter prefers C_1 to C_2. Such a list implies a total order on the set of candidates expressing the complete opinion from a particular voter. A *voting profile* is a collection (or a multi-set) of all the cast ballots.

A voting profile may also be described as a *weighted matrix* of size $|\mathbb{C}| \times |\mathbb{C}|$, where $\mathbb{C}$ is the set of candidates. A cell in a weighted matrix with row C_1 and column C_2 is filled with $w(C_1, C_2)$, which is the number of votes that prefer C_1 to C_2. We further define a *Condorcet directed graph* $G = (V, E, W)$ such

---

[2] We assume that privacy policies are independent from each other. To model and capture dependencies among policies is not considered in this paper, it will be an interesting topic for the future.

that $V = \mathbb{C}$ is the set of vertices, and E is the set of edges, which is defined as the set $\{(C_1, C_2) \in V \times V : w(C_1, C_2) \geq w(C_2, C_1)\}$. The function $W : E \to \mathbb{N}$, determines the labelings of the edges and is defined by $W(C_1, C_2) = w(C_1, C_2) - w(C_2, C_1)$, i.e., the difference between the votes preferring C_1 to C_2 and the votes that prefer C_2 to C_1. At the end of a voting procedure, a voting profile (or equivalently, a weighted matrix) needs to be evaluated in a certain way, in order to get a final result. There is a famous criterion applied in the calculation of a final winner as originally advocated by Condorcet.

Principle 1. *(Condorcet Winner) If there is a candidate that beats every other candidate in one-to-one comparison, that candidate should be the winner.*

Plainly, a Condorcet winner is a vertex in the Condorcet directed graph with out-degree $|\mathbb{C}| - 1$. We illustrate Condorcet's method in the following example.

Example 1. Suppose there are three users Alice (C), Bob (B) and Clare (C) tagged in a picture owned by Alice. Alice wants to publish the picture on her personal page in the network, therefore she needs to negotiate with Bob and Clare to reach an agreement on the privacy policy associated to the picture. Suppose the available policies are defined in Sect. 2.2. A (preferential) voting form is made for Alice, Bob and Clare in which they fill in their preferential list on the available policies, as shown in the voting profile on the left of Fig. 1.

Voter \ Policy	P_1	P_2	P_3	P_4
A	1	2	3	4
B	2	3	1	4
C	3	1	2	4

	P_1	P_2	P_3	P_4
P_1	–	2	1	3
P_2	1	–	2	3
P_3	2	1	–	3
P_4	0	0	0	–

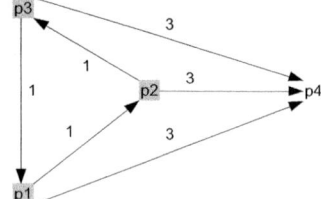

Fig. 1. A Condorcet voting example: the voting profile (left), the weighted matrix (middle), and the Condorcet directed graph (right)

The weighted matrix and the Condorcet directed graph are also sketched in Fig. 1. As one can see, P_4 is the least preferred by all users. However, there exists a *general tie* between policies P_1, P_2 and P_3. This situation is referred to as the *Condorcet paradox*, meaning that the generated Condorcet directed graph is cyclic on its top vertices, and unfortunately, as we will show, the traditional method of Condorcet is unable to break such tie in this example.

Condorcet's method adopts what is known as *maximum likelihood estimation*. A philosophical assumption is that there exists an invisible total ranking, reflecting the true capabilities of all the candidates in an election. In this paper we adopt such mechanism on selecting optimal privacy policies. For every pair of policies P_1 and P_2, such that P_1 precedes P_2 on the (invisible) ranking list, a user is more likely to vote for P_1 than P_2. As Condorcet assumes, each user will choose a better option (P_1 in this case) with some fixed probability p, where

$\frac{1}{2} < p < 1$. Taking Example 1, the likelihood of the total order $P_1P_2P_3P_4$ to be the same as the true invisible ranking order, denoted by $L(P_1P_2P_3P_4)$, is calculated by combining the likelihood of every P_i beating P_j with $i < j$ (note that there are six preferential pairs in this case). If "$P_1P_2P_3P_4$" is the true ordering on the candidates, then the chance that we get the current voting profile can be calculated as

$$L(P_1P_2P_3P_4) = L(P_1P_2) \cdot L(P_2P_3) \cdot L(P_1P_3) \cdot L(P_1P_4) \cdot L(P_2P_4) \cdot L(P_3P_4)$$
$$= \binom{3}{2}\left(p^2(1-p)^1\right) \cdot \binom{3}{2}\left(p^2(1-p)^1\right) \cdot \binom{3}{1}\left(p^1(1-p)^2\right) \cdot$$
$$\binom{3}{3}\left(p^3(1-p)^0\right) \cdot \binom{3}{3}\left(p^3(1-p)^0\right) \cdot \binom{3}{3}\left(p^3(1-p)^0\right)$$

where $\binom{m}{n} = \frac{m!}{n!(m-n)!}$ for non-negative $m \geq n$. The expression for $L(P_1P_2)$, for example, follows from the fact that 2 out of 3 voters ranked policy P_1 higher than P_2, and thus voted in accordance with the hypothetical true ranking order $L(P_1P_2P_3P_4)$.

It has been pointed out that in practice when comparing the likelihood of two possible orderings, the combinatoric coefficients can be safely ignored [21], given the same voting profile. The only part that needs to be taken into account consists of the exponents over p (note that $\frac{1}{2} < p < 1$). In the case of $L(P_1P_2P_3P_4)$, the power over p is 14. One may also find that the power over p for $L(P_4P_3P_2P_1)$ is 4, thus $P_1P_2P_3P_4$ is more likely to be the true ordering over the privacy policies than $P_4P_3P_2P_1$ by Condorcet's method. As we have mentioned above, in this example we can compute the likelihood for every sequence that is a permutation of the set $\{P_1, P_2, P_3, P_4\}$. In fact, we have $L(P_1P_2P_3P_4) = L(P_2P_3P_1P_4) = L(P_3P_1P_2P_4)$ and it is larger than the likelihood of any other sequence. This means that Condorcet's method might select *multiple winners*, as P_1, P_2 and P_3 are all selected in Example 1.

Condorcet voting algorithm. The Condorcet voting algorithm is detailed as in Alg. 1. The algorithm takes a voting profile as input and produces a set of winners as output. Function *getCondorcetWeightedMatrix* translates a voting profile into a weighted matrix, and then in the next step function *getCondorcetDirectedGraph* converts the weighted matrix into a Condorcet directed graph.[3] For example, as shown in Fig. 1, the algorithm translates the voting profile on the left part into the weighted matrix in the middle, and then into the Condorcet directed graph on the right. The rest of the algorithm focuses on how to select a set of top vertices in the Condorcet directed graph. By definition, the set of Condorcet winners are vertices that have an outgoing edge to every other vertex, although in the real world such sets are singletons in most cases. Such set will be returned by function *getWinners*. If *getWinners* returns an empty set, i.e., no Condorcet winners exist, the algorithm will compute the likelihood of all possible sequences and maintain the set of those with the maximal likelihood, and return their first elements as winners.

---

[3] We represent directed graphs as two-dimensional arrays. For example, if there is a directed edge from i to j with weight $n \geq 0$, then $cdg[i][j]$ has value n, and $cdg[j][k] = -1$ means that there is no edge from j to k.

Algorithm 1. The Condorcet voting algorithm

---

input : *votingprofile* : VotingProfile;
output : *winners* : set ⟨*string*⟩;
var *cwm*   : int[ ][ ]   **init**   null
       cdg   : int[ ][ ]   **init**   null
       tlv   : int[ ]   **init**   null
       sql   : int   **init**   0
       ml   : int   **init**   0
       ms   : set ⟨*string*⟩ **init**   ∅

begin
cwm := getCondorcetWeightedMatrix(*votingprofile*);
cdg := getCondorcetDirectedGraph(*cwm*);
winners := getWinners(*cdg*);
if *winners* = ∅ **then**
    tlv := findTopLevelVertices(*cdg*);
    for each sequence *sq* which is a permutation of *tlv* **do**
        sql := computeSequenceLikelihood(*sq*, *cwm*);
        if *sql* > *ml* **then**
            ml := *sql*;
            ms := {*sq*};
        else if *sql* = *ml* **then**
            ms := *ms* ∪ {*sq*};
        end if
    end for
    winners := getFirstElements(*ms*);
end if
end

In the above algorithm, not all sequences are required to be involved in the comparison of likelihoods. As a Condorcet directed graph imposes a topological order, the top level vertices compose a subgraph which is a strongly connected component (SCC) in the original graph. Function *findTopLevelSCC* returns the set of vertices that form the SCC. One may easily find that the set of winners can only come from the SCC, thus we only need to compute the sequences initialized by permutations of vertices in the SCC.[4] As in Example 1, only six three-element sequences need to be taken into account: $P_1P_2P_3$, $P_1P_3P_2$, $P_2P_1P_3$, $P_2P_3P_1$, $P_3P_1P_2$ and $P_3P_2P_1$, as P_4 can only be the least preferred. The algorithm will pick up three (total) sequences, $P_1P_2P_3P_4$, $P_2P_3P_1P_4$ and $P_3P_1P_2P_4$, which are with the most likelihood, and produce the winner set $\{P_1, P_2, P_3\}$ by taking the first elements (by the function *getFirstElements*). The restriction to the top-level SCC effectively narrows the range of winners we need to consider, which greatly improves the performance of the selection procedure. It is easy to see that the

---

[4] There is no need to compute a whole sequence containing elements not in the SCC, as Condorcet's methods is *locally stable* [21], the particular order of less preferred candidates would not influence the final voting result.

running time of the algorithm has an upper bound in $O(|V|!)$, due to checking the likelihood of all possible sequences of nodes in the SCC.

3   A Trust-Augmented Voting Scheme

3.1   Incorporating Trust as Weighted Votes

In some situations not all voters are equal. Typical examples include decision-makings in a shareholder's meeting where the weight of each voter corresponds to his volume of share. Likewise in social networks, users' opinions on deciding a privacy policy do not necessarily carry the same weight. For example, Alice has a picture in which there are Bob, Clare, Danny and Elisabeth, and she wants to publish that picture in her album. She is willing to give right to the co-owners of the picture, i.e. Bob, Clare, Danny and Elisabeth, on deciding whether the privacy level of that picture is P_1 or P_2 (see their definitions in Sect. 2.2). Here we suppose that Bob is a friend of Alice and Clare is a friend of Bob but not a direct friend of Alice, i.e., Clare is a friend of a friend of Alice. Similarly, Danny is a friend of Alice and Elisabeth is a friend of a friend of Alice. In this case it seems more reasonable to give Bob's and Danny's opinion more weight than Clare's and Elisabeth's. In this section we propose an extension of Condorcet's voting system for weighted votes. The weight of each vote reflects the trust level of the owner of the shared resource having on the co-owners in their votes for setting a privacy policy for publishing the resource.

Voter \ Policy	P_1	P_2
A	1	2
B	2	1
C	1	2
D	2	1
E	1	2

Voter(trust) \ Policy	P_1	P_2
A (1.0)	1	2
B (0.9)	2	1
C (0.2)	1	2
D (0.8)	2	1
E (0.3)	1	2

Fig. 2. An example: The effect of trust in collaborative privacy management

We sketch the voting results from this scenario in Fig. 2, and it is easy to find that P_1 is the winner according to the left table, as it receives three votes while P_2 only receives two. However, if weights (interpreted as the trust level of Alice in the co-owners to make the right decision on privacy preferences) are associated to votes, then P_2 is the winner, as it is supported by 1.7 weighted votes while P_1 supported only by 1.5. This example clearly shows that trust relations in social networks, if carefully incorporated into decision making procedures, can affect the results in collaborative privacy management.

In the original Condorcet voting system all votes carry the same weight, and the preferential orders can be compared by only looking at the (integer) exponents of p regarding to their likelihoods. In this paper we measure the likelihoods of these orders by allowing discounted votes to reflect the degree of trust of a user by the owner of a resource, so that each vote carries a real valued weight in $[0, 1]$ instead of always being an integer 1.

Algorithm 2. A trust-augmented Condorcet voting algorithm

---

input : *trustvotingprofile* : VotingProfile;
output : *winners* : set $\langle string \rangle$;
var *cwm*   : double[ ][ ]   **init**   null
     cdg   : int[ ][ ]   **init**   null
     tlv   : int[ ]   **init**   null
     sql   : double   **init**   0.0
     ml   : double   **init**   0.0
     ms   : set $\langle string \rangle$ **init** $\emptyset$

begin
cwm := getCondorcetWeightedMatrix(*trustvotingprofile*);
cdg := getCondorcetDirectedGraph(*cwm*);
winners := getWinners(*cdg*);
(* the rest is the same as Alg. 1 *)
end

Trust-augmented Condorcet voting algorithm. The trust-augmented Condorcet voting algorithm is detailed as in Alg. 2. The whole procedure of calculation is exactly the same as that of Alg. 1, except that now the sequence likelihood (*sql*) and maximal likelihood (*ml*) are of real valued type instead of integer type, as shown above. A trust-based voting profile, which includes the preference lists and trust level for each participant, is taken as input by the algorithm (e.g., left part of Fig. 3), while the output, a set of winners, remains unchanged. In Fig. 3, we assume that A, as the owner of the picture, fully trusts himself, i.e., his trust value is 1.0. The trust of A in other participants (0.8 for B and 0.6 for C) is also shown in the table. From the trust-based voting profile, the revised Condorcet weighted matrix is obtained (e.g., middle part of Fig. 3). The weighted matrix is slightly different from that in Example 1 in the way that simply counted (integer) votes are replaced by accumulated trust values throughout the table. From the Condorcet directed graph in the right part of Fig. 3, we can find a unique winner P_1, after computing the likelihood of all sequences of nodes in the top level SCC (containing P_1, P_2 and P_3). This can be easily verified since the likelihood of the sequence $P_1 P_2 P_3 P_4$, as calculated as follows, is greater than the likelihood of every other sequence. Note that here we replace the number of votes as integer exponents over "p" and "$1 - p$" by their corresponding sums of trust values.

$$L(P_1 P_2 P_3 P_4) = L(P_1 P_2) \cdot L(P_2 P_3) \cdot L(P_1 P_3) \cdot L(P_1 P_4) \cdot L(P_2 P_4) \cdot L(P_3 P_4)$$
$$= \binom{3}{2} \left(p^{1.8}(1-p)^{0.6} \right) \cdot \binom{3}{2} \left(p^{1.6}(1-p)^{0.8} \right) \cdot \binom{3}{1} \left(p^{1.0}(1-p)^{1.4} \right) \cdot$$
$$\binom{3}{3} \left(p^{2.4}(1-p)^{0} \right) \cdot \binom{3}{3} \left(p^{2.4}(1-p)^{0} \right) \cdot \binom{3}{3} \left(p^{2.4}(1-p)^{0} \right)$$

It is easy to see that this algorithm has the same time complexity upper bound $O(|V|!)$ as Alg. 1.

As we have seen so far, the trust level indeed has an impact on collaborative privacy management. Moreover adding trust makes the algorithm better adopted

Voter\policy	P_1	P_2	P_3	P_4
A (1.0)	1	2	3	4
B (0.8)	2	3	1	4
C (0.6)	3	1	2	4

	P_1	P_2	P_3	P_4
P_1	–	1.8	1.0	2.4
P_2	0.6	–	1.6	2.4
P_3	1.4	0.8	–	2.4
P_4	0.0	0.0	0.0	–

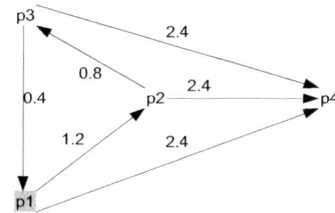

Fig. 3. A trust-augmented Condorcet voting example: the voting profile (left), the weighted matrix (middle), and the Condorcet directed graph (right)

in social networks, since in the real life, advices from different friends affect one's decision differently, depending on the social relationship between the person and his friends. Introducing a trust relation also expands the value space to avoid clashes, as we are going to show experimentally later. In Alg. 2 it is less likely to have unsolved cases as well as multiple winner cases than in Alg. 1. Similar to Alg. 1, the algorithm always selects Condorcet winners whenever they exist. However, in order to decide winners, both Alg. 1 and Alg. 2 may require a calculation of likelihoods for all permutations from the top-level SCC, which potentially takes running time exponential to the number of policies. This fact leads us to the search of more applicable algorithms.

3.2 A Heuristic Algorithm

The algorithm presented in this section provides another way to resolve general ties in the top-level SCC, as well as to reduce the computational time. A comparison between all the algorithms is conducted in Sect. 4.

Taking a Condorcet directed graph, first we have the following arguments. Suppose $w(P_i, P_j)$ is close to 0, it is very likely to be the case that the voters are relatively indifferent with respect to the two policies P_i and P_j. Therefore, regarding to Condorcet's assumption, P_i does not have a significant chance to precede P_j in the underlying invisible order. This justifies our choice in the following algorithm to weaken such difference by adding another (reversing) edge in the graph from P_j to P_i. By doing this, we *equalize* the votes between policies P_i and P_j. Technically, we only apply this operation within the top-level SCC, gradually by starting from the pairs (P_i, P_j) with least $w(P_i, P_j)$, then the pairs with second least weight, and so on. Each time we add new edges it is required to check whether a set of Condorcet winners have been generated in the new graph. The running time of the algorithm has an upper bound of $O(|V|^2)$, where V is the set of vertices of the Condorcet directed graph, which is much faster than Alg. 2. Nevertheless, the experimental results in Sect. 4 reveal strong similarity with respect to the results of Alg. 3 and Alg. 2, which provides a concrete support to the applicability of Alg. 3.

Optimized trust-augmented Condorcet voting algorithm. Similar to Alg. 2, Alg. 3 takes a voting profile as input and produces a set of winning privacy policies. The

---

Algorithm 3. Optimized trust-augmented Condorcet voting algorithm

---

input : *trustvotingprofile*: VotingProfile;
output : *winners* : set ⟨*string*⟩;
var *cwm*   : int[ ][ ]   **init**   null
        cdg   : int[ ][ ]   **init**   null
        tls   : int[ ][ ]   **init**   null
        lwes   : set ⟨*string*⟩ **init**   ∅
        nodes   : set ⟨*string*⟩ **init**   ∅

begin
cwm := getCondorcetWeightedMmatrix(*trustvotingprofile*);
cdg := getCondorcetDirectedGraph(*cwm*);
winners := getWinners(*cdg*);
if *winners* = ∅ **then**
    tls := findTopLevelSCC(*cdg*);
    while true **do**
        lwes := findLowestWeightEdges(*tls*);
        addReverseEdges(*lwes*, *cdg*);
        nodes := findNodeN-1OutDegree(*cdg*);
        if *nodes* ! = ∅ **then**
            winners := *nodes*;
            return
        end if
    end while
end if
end

---

first part of the algorithm is exactly the same as in the above two algorithms. However, if Alg. 3 cannot find Condorcet winners, it will extract the whole top-level SCC into a subgraph *tls*. Then by starting from the lowest weighted edges, it adds reverse edges into the original Condorcet directed graph *cdg*, and searches for Condorcet winners in the modified graph. This will repeat until Condorcet winners are found in *cdg*. The algorithm is guaranteed to terminate before every pair of vertices in the top-level SCC has two connecting edges pointing to each other. Therefore it is bounded by $O(|V|^2)$ where V is the set of vertices in *cdg*. An application of Alg. 3 on Example 1 with additional trust values (as data shown in Fig. 3) has been depicted in Fig. 4.

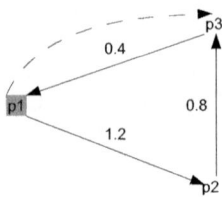

Fig. 4. An example: adding a reverse edge

4   Experimental Results

We have implemented a program to test the three algorithms. In our test, the voting profiles and the trust levels are randomly generated.[5] The experimental results are obtained from 10,000 cases. We set the policy number in the range of [3, 10], while the number of voters ranging in [3, 100]. The optimized algorithm (Alg. 3) can perform well even in the case of a large number of policies due to its improved time complexity.

From Fig. 5, we can find that the number of cases where we cannot find a Condorcet winner in Alg. 2 and Alg. 3 is much less (12%) than that in Alg. 1. This is due to the incorporation of trust. Based on this we can conclude that trust can have a big impact on the voting results. It is also clear that the cases with multiple winners as output is on a steady decrease (15%), which means that the adoption of a trust relation, to a large extent, can effectively increase the possibility of having a unique winner. Moreover, we only see a slight increase in the number of cases with multiple winners for Alg. 3 compared to Alg. 2. Besides, we measured the similarity among the outputs of Alg. 3 and Alg. 2. In 9,519 out of 10,000 cases (i.e., > 95%) they produce the same results. Since theoretically Alg. 2 always generates the best privacy policy, we can conclude that our optimization (Alg. 3) can also produce the best privacy policy for most cases in practice.

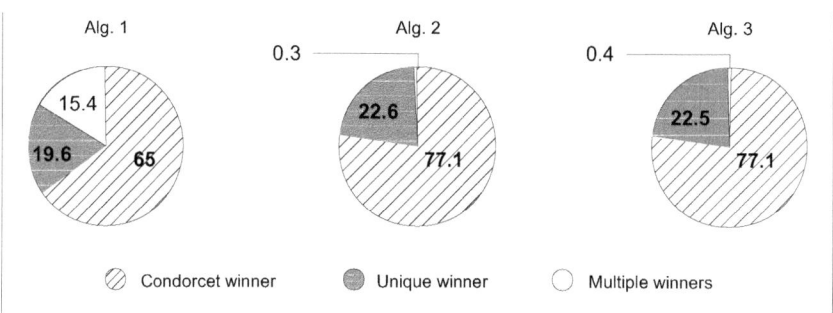

Fig. 5. Case analysis on outputs of the algorithms

Next, we have built a different set of experiments to compare the performance of Alg. 2 and Alg. 3. For each number of policies [5, . . . , 10], we test the two algorithms on 1,000 randomly generated voting profiles. We calculated the average CPU time for each algorithm to produce an output. From Table 1, it is clear that our optimized algorithm greatly improves the efficiency of Alg. 2 – the performance of Alg. 2 degrades largely when the number of policies increases. All experiments are conducted on a Dell laptop with Intel Core(TM) 2 Duo CPU (2.26GHz) and 1.95GB of RAM under light load.

---

[5] Alg. 1 does not take the trust levels into account.

Table 1. Average CPU time consumption (ms) w.r.t. policy numbers

Algorithm/#Policy	5	6	7	8	9	10
Alg. 2	100	304	2, 289	54, 361	334, 260	7, 597, 046
Alg. 3	75	77	80	82	84	91

5   Inference of Privacy Policies

When setting collective privacy management issues among users, each user is required to feed input into the social network system, as complete voting profiles are necessary for the algorithms. This may quickly become a cumbersome job of users over time, as the number of co-owned resources increases rapidly. In this section, we introduce an inference technique to automatically suggest suitable preferential votes to the users, which thus relieves the burden of tedious manual inputs. This algorithm only provides a *default vote* for a user, and if he disagrees, it is possible for the user to specify his preferred vote.

In social networks there always exists an initial privacy setting as specified by each user. The proposed inference technique compares a user's initial setting with his history votes, trying to guess his future votes by picking up a vote from the history with the most similarity to the initial privacy setting. Let a user profile's privacy preferential list be a vector $\overrightarrow{P} = \langle p_1, p_2, \ldots, p_n \rangle$, and the privacy preference of a co-owned resource be $\overrightarrow{C} = \langle c_1, c_2, \ldots, c_n \rangle$. Our inference technique picks up an element from a collection of preferences $\{\overrightarrow{C_1}, \ldots, \overrightarrow{C_m}\}$ that has the most similarity to $\overrightarrow{P}$. First, we calculate the cosine similarity [22] between the privacy preference $\overrightarrow{P}$ of a user's profile setting and every $\overrightarrow{C_i}$ in his history votes

$$s_i := cos(\overrightarrow{P}, \overrightarrow{C_i}) = \frac{\sum_{k=1}^{n} p_k \cdot c_{ik}}{\sqrt{(\sum_{k=1}^{n} p_k^2) \cdot (\sum_{k=1}^{n} c_{ik}^2)}}$$

We use $\bar{s}$ to denote the average similarity $\bar{s} = \frac{1}{m} \sum_{k=1}^{m} s_i$. Then the default vote is set as $\overrightarrow{C_i}$ with $|s_i - \bar{s}|$ being the smallest.

Example 2. Suppose there are three users, Alice (A), Bob (B) and Clare (C), each of which has three co-owned pictures. Their profile settings and history decisions are shown in Fig. 6. Here we apply the inference technique on user Alice. The cosine similarity between $\overrightarrow{P} (\langle 1, 2, 3, 4 \rangle)$ and A's historical decisions $\overrightarrow{C_1} (\langle 2, 4, 3, 1 \rangle)$, $\overrightarrow{C_2} (\langle 1, 2, 3, 4 \rangle)$ and $\overrightarrow{C_3} (\langle 3, 1, 4, 2 \rangle)$ can be calculated as $23/30$, 1 and $25/30$, respectively. The average similarity is $26/30$, to which $\overrightarrow{C_3}$ is the closest and thus is recommended to Alice. We can perform a similar calculation for Bob and Clare.

Voter/Preference	P	C_1	C_2	C_3
A	$\langle 1, 2, 3, 4 \rangle$	$\langle 2, 4, 3, 1 \rangle$	$\langle 1, 2, 3, 4 \rangle$	$\langle \mathbf{3}, \mathbf{1}, \mathbf{4}, \mathbf{2} \rangle$
B	$\langle 2, 3, 1, 4 \rangle$	$\langle 1, 3, 2, 4 \rangle$	$\langle \mathbf{4}, \mathbf{1}, \mathbf{2}, \mathbf{3} \rangle$	$\langle 2, 4, 3, 1 \rangle$
C	$\langle 4, 3, 2, 1 \rangle$	$\langle \mathbf{4}, \mathbf{2}, \mathbf{1}, \mathbf{3} \rangle$	$\langle 3, 4, 1, 2 \rangle$	$\langle 1, 2, 3, 4 \rangle$

Fig. 6. An example of the inference of policy preferences

6   Discussion and Conclusion

Privacy in social networks is a rather complicated issue [23], from which many hot research issues have emerged in different areas such as economics, social science, computer science, and law. In this paper, we have proposed a trust-augmented voting scheme to solve the particular problem of collective privacy management for shared contents in social networks. Our main idea is to incorporate trust relations among users in social networks as vote weights in the Condorcet preferential voting algorithm. The motivation comes from the facts that trust is naturally inherent in social networks and that a preferential voting scheme is an expressive but simple way for users to formulate their privacy concerns on shared contents. To make the algorithm both efficient and effective, we have developed a heuristics for the algorithm to deal with the case when the number of privacy policies is large. An inference technique is used to relieve the users from the burden of manually inputing their privacy preference for each picture.

The algorithms in this paper have been developed mainly from a technical point of view and one can reasonably argue that voting is not the ideal approach to collective privacy management. In the end, the owner of a picture will have to decide for herself whether and how she wants to publish a picture, possibly taking into account the interests of concerned people. For example, a different approach proposed by Sarrouh et al. [8], gives a single user complete control over the picture she is co-owner. In our voting scheme, occasionally a group decision may override an owner's decision. If an owner does not feel comfort with the outcome of the voting, in reality she can contact a trusted third party or the social network site, which will then decide whether and how to publish the picture. However, a reasonable social decision is only required to be 'fair' with a certain degree of confidence. We believe that heuristic and algorithmic support to this process will result in a more transparent and hopefully more fair decision process. In the future, we want to build an application as a proof-of-concept for our proposal.

References

1. Facebook:, http://www.facebook.com
2. MySpace, http://www.myspace.com
3. Gross, R., Acquisti, A., John Heinz III, H.: Information revelation and privacy in online social networks. In: Proc. 2005 ACM Workshop on Privacy in the Electronic Society, pp. 71–80. ACM, New York (2005)
4. Ellison, N.B., Steinfield, C., Lampe, C.: Benefits of Facebook Friends: Social capital and college students' use of online social network sites. Journal of Computer Mediated Communication-Electronic 12(4) (2007)

5. Rosenblum, D.: What anyone can know: The privacy risks of social networking sites. IEEE Security and Privacy 5(3), 40–49 (2007)
6. Carminati, B., Ferrari, E.: Privacy-aware collaborative access control in web-based social networks. In: Atluri, V. (ed.) DAS 2008. LNCS, vol. 5094, pp. 81–96. Springer, Heidelberg (2008)
7. Grossklags, J., Christin, N., Chuang, J.: Secure or insure?: a game-theoretic analysis of information security games. In: Proc. 17th Conference on World Wide Web, pp. 209–218. ACM, New York (2008)
8. Sarrouh, N., Eilers, F., Nestmann, U., Schieferdecker, I.: Defamation-free networks through user-centered data control. In: Cuellar, J., Lopez, J., Barthe, G., Pretschner, A. (eds.) STM 2010. LNCS, vol. 6710, pp. 179–193. Springer, Heidelberg (2011)
9. Squicciarini, A.C., Shehab, M., Paci, F.: Collective privacy management in social networks. In: Proc. 18th International Conference on World Wide Web, pp. 521–530. ACM, New York (2009)
10. Clarke, E.H.: Multipart pricing of public goods. Public Choice 11, 17–33 (1971)
11. Good, D.: Individuals, interpersonal relations, and trust. In: Gambetta, D. (ed.) Trust: Making and Breaking Cooperative Relations, Department of Sociology, University of Oxford (1988)
12. Luhmann, N.: Trust and Power. John Wiley and Sons Inc., Chichester (1979)
13. Gambetta, D. (ed.): Trust: Making and breaking cooperative relations. Department of Sociology, University of Oxford, University of Oxford (1988)
14. Krukow, K., Nielsen, M., Sassone, V.: A logical framework for history-based access control and reputation systems. Journal of Computer Security 16(1), 63–101 (2008)
15. Eilers, F., Nestmann, U.: Deriving trust from experience. In: Degano, P., Guttman, J.D. (eds.) FAST 2009. LNCS, vol. 5983, pp. 36–50. Springer, Heidelberg (2010)
16. ElSalamouny, E., Sassone, V., Nielsen, M.: HMM-based trust model. In: Degano, P., Guttman, J.D. (eds.) FAST 2009. LNCS, vol. 5983, pp. 21–35. Springer, Heidelberg (2010)
17. Gray, E., Seigneur, J.-M., Chen, Y., Jensen, C.: Trust propagation in small worlds. In: Nixon, P., Terzis, S. (eds.) iTrust 2003. LNCS, vol. 2692, pp. 239–254. Springer, Heidelberg (2003)
18. Jøsang, A., Marsh, S., Pope, S.: Exploring different types of trust propagation. In: Stølen, K., Winsborough, W.H., Martinelli, F., Massacci, F. (eds.) iTrust 2006. LNCS, vol. 3986, pp. 179–192. Springer, Heidelberg (2006)
19. Dong, C., Russello, G., Dulay, N.: Trust transfer in distributed systems. In: Proc. Joint iTrust and PST Conferences on Privacy, Trust Management and Security. IFIP, vol. 238, pp. 17–30. Springer, Heidelberg (2007)
20. Alcalde, B., Mauw, S.: An algebra for trust dilution and trust fusion. In: Degano, P., Guttman, J.D. (eds.) FAST 2009. LNCS, vol. 5983, pp. 4–20. Springer, Heidelberg (2010)
21. Young, H.P.: Condorcet's theory of voting. The American Political Science Review 82(4), 1231–1244 (1988)
22. Tan, P.B., Steinbach, M., Kumar, V.: Introduction to Data Mining. Addison-Wesley, Reading (2005)
23. Bonneau, J., Preibusch, S.: The privacy jungle: On the market for privacy in social networks. In: Proc. 8th Workshop on the Economics of Information Security (2009)

Universally Composable NIZK Protocol in an Internet Voting Scheme

Md. Abdul Based and Stig Frode Mjølsnes

Department of Telematics
Norwegian University of Science and Tenchnology (NTNU)
{based,sfm}@item.ntnu.no

Abstract. We use the Universally Composable (UC) framework to evaluate our Non-Interactive Zero-Knowledge (NIZK) protocol for verifying the validity of the ballot in an Internet voting scheme. We first describe the Internet voting scheme followed by the explanation of the NIZK protocol for ballot verification in that voting scheme. We then define the ideal functionalities using the UC framework and evaluate the NIZK protocol by using these ideal functionalities. We find that this NIZK protocol is secure in the UC framework in the presence of malicious and adaptive adversaries.

1 Introduction

We define an Internet voting scheme as an electronic voting scheme where voters cast their ballots through voter computers to counting servers over Internet. Internet voting has become a very important research topic in recent years, because many countries are considering electronic voting and are planning to deploy it. Estonia ran an electronic voting over Internet in the year 2007. Norway is preparing for an Internet voting pilot for the general election in 2011. If the trial gives positive result, the Norwegian government is interested to deploy a full Internet voting scheme by 2017.

There are two approaches to networked voting in terms of control of terminal and people: voting remotely or voting from polling booth. Voting remotely is also called remote Internet voting or voting from home. There is no cryptographic way to protect the voter from physical coercion when voting from home. One possible way to handle the problem of coercion in a remote voting is to allow the voters to vote multiple times. This approach is called revoting, where only the final ballot is included in the tally. In a polling booth based Internet voting scheme, the voter first goes to the polling booth for identification and authentication, and then he/she casts the ballot without physical coercion.

We present an Internet voting scheme here that is suitable for both voting remotely and voting from polling booth. In our scheme, the counting servers publish the nonces that are included in the ballot by means of a bulletin board. The content of the bulletin board is the nonce values which all voters can see. The voters verify the ballots by the nonces published by the counting servers. Hence, our scheme is *voter verifiable*.

J. Cuellar et al. (Eds.): STM 2010, LNCS 6710, pp. 147–162, 2011.

148   Md.A. Based and S.F. Mjølsnes

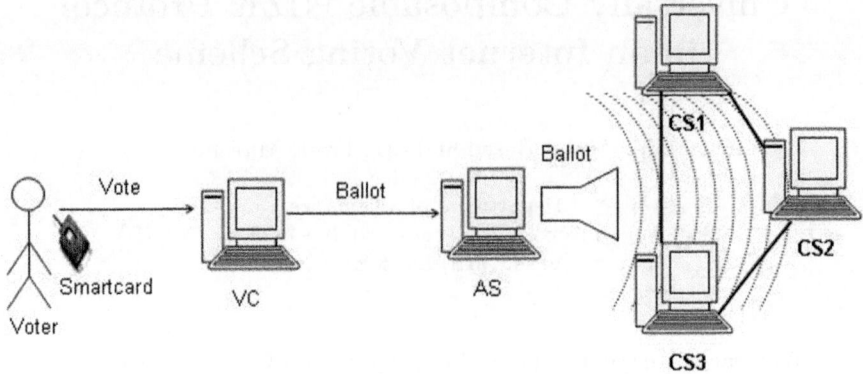

Fig. 1. The Internet voting scheme exemplified with 3 counting servers. The voter chooses a vote for a particular candidate and delegates the remaining tasks to the Voter Computer (VC). The VC computes the ballot from this vote and sends the ballot to the Authentication Server (AS). The AS forwards the ballot to all the Counting Servers (CS).

In general, the security requirements and their evaluation is a very complex task for networked voting. For this reason, we choose the UC framework to define and evaluate the security of our voting scheme. In particular, in this paper, we are presenting a NIZK protocol to verify the validity of the ballot and evaluating the security of this protocol in the UC framework.

The structure of the paper is as follows: Section 2 presents published papers related to our work. The voting scheme is presented in Section 3 (A pictorial view of this scheme is shown in Fig. 1), and the NIZK protocol is described in Section 4. We describe the universal composability of the NIZK protocol in Section 5. Various ideal functionalities for this NIZK protocol are also defined in this section. This paper concludes with Section 6 where the final comments are presented.

2   Related Work

We use the definitions of the UC framework presented in [1] to define ideal functionalities for our commitment scheme, common random string, and non-interactive zero-knowledge proof protocol. In [2], Groth investigates the existing voting schemes based on homomorphic threshold encryptions and evaluates the security of the schemes in the UC framework. The author also proposes some modifications to make the voting schemes secure against active adversaries. Some research works on zero-knowledge proofs and homomorphic cryptosystems are published in [2,3,4,5]. The UC framework for two-party and multiparty secure computations are presented in [6], including the description of zero-knowledge proof protocols for a prover broadcasting one commitment to many verifiers (one-to-many scheme). In [7], the author presents the UC framework ideas for a non-interactive zero-knowledge protocol in a mix-net. Universally composable

VC   AS   CS

$[\{[\{B, Nonce\}Sign_{Group}]E_{PubCS}\}Sign_{Voter}]E_{PubAS}$

$[\{B, Nonce\}Sign_{Group}]E_{PubCS}$

Fig. 2. The message sequence diagram between Voter Computer (VC), Authentication Server (AS), and Counting Servers (CS)

commitments are presented in [8]. A non-interactive zero-knowledge protocol for Internet voting is presented in [9], but the scheme presented in that paper is not voter verifiable. The basic and expanded security properties for secure and practical Internet voting systems are published in [14].

We evaluate our Non-Interactive Zero-Knowledge (NIZK) protocol using the UC framework ideas presented in [1,6,8]. The commitment and zero-knowledge scheme in the NIZK protocol are also one-to-many, since every voter commits to the value of a ballot and proves the validity of the ballot to j counting servers.

3   The Internet Voting Scheme

3.1   Security Requirements

The security and privacy requirements of Internet voting system can be classified as basic and advanced [14]. The basic requirements include authentication of the voter, confidentiality and integrity of the ballot, privacy of the voter, fairness and soundness of the counting process. The advanced requirements are validity of the ballot, verifiability of the counting process, receipt-freeness, and coercion-resistance. Fairness of the counting process means no partial results should be published before the final tallying. Otherwise, the partial results may affect the intentions of the voters who have not cast their ballots before knowing the partial results. Soundness ensures that the counting process should count only valid ballots. The NIZK protocol presented in Section 4 verifies every ballot before counting and discards invalid ballots, and thus the counting process contains only valid ballots. Also, the counting servers only publish the final tally and the nonces, and the voters can verify these nonces.

The Internet voting scheme presented in this paper aims to satisfy all these basic and advanced security requirements.

3.2   The Scheme

The voting scheme is shown in Fig. 1 and the corresponding message diagram is shown in Fig. 2. The assumptions of this voting scheme are as follows:

- The unidirectional channel from the Authentication Server (AS) to the Counting Servers (CS) is a broadcast channel by some mechanism not discussed here.
- A Public Key Infrastructure (PKI) is assumed in the voting scheme, but we do not describe the key distribution and key management issues here.

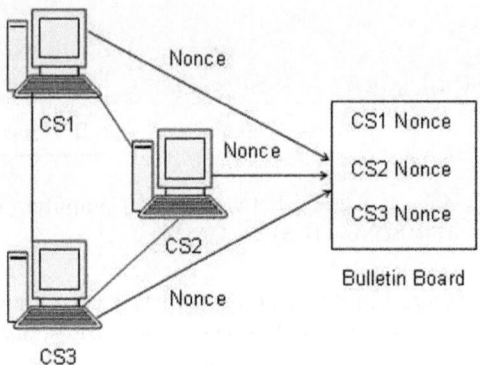

Fig. 3. Voter verifiability. The Counting Servers (CS) publish the nonces that were added with the ballots. Every voter can verify the nonces.

– A smartcard is distributed to each voter before the Election Day. The voter list and the candidate list are also prepared before that day. The smartcard contains the private key for the group signature, the private key of the voter, the public key of the authentication server, the public key of the counting servers, and the fingerprint features of the voter. Only the eligible voters can make a group signature.

Voter authentication is done by using a smartcard with local biometric identification (fingerprint) technology, as it is proposed in [9] and [10]. The voter first inserts the smartcard into a smartcard reader. Then the voter identifies himself/herself by the fingerprint scanner on the smartcard and the web server authenticates the smartcard, and the voter gets access to the voting web page. The voter chooses a vote for a particular candidate and delegates the remaining tasks to the Voter Computer (VC). The VC computes the ballot from the vote. The VC also generates a random number (nonce) and appends it to the ballot. The VC displays this nonce to the voter, and the voter must remember this nonce in order to verify his/her ballot after the counting process. It is important that the length of this nonce is sufficiently long to avoid collision between nonce values. For example, if the length of the nonce is 64 bits, this gives probability $\frac{1}{2^{64}}$ that two VCs will choose the same nonce.

The message construction between VC, AS, and CS is shown in Fig. 2. The voters' smartcard sign and encrypt the ballot, first using the private key for the group signature, then the CS public key, then the private key of the voter, and finally the public key of the AS. The VC sends this encrypted and signed ballot to the AS. The AS decrypts and verifies the signature of the voter, and forwards the encrypted ballot (encrypted with the CS public key) to all the counting servers. The AS maintains a list of the voters and the encrypted ballots, and forwards only the latest ballot to the CS after the voting period is over.

The counting servers decrypt and verify the group signature by using the Group Public Key to see whether the ballot is from an eligible voter. The CSs can only verify the group signature, but, can not know who the actual voter is because the group signature only proves the identity of the group of voters, but does not provide any identity of the voter. The counting servers discard all ballots with duplicate nonces. Then the counting servers count the ballots and publish the nonces (Shown in Fig. 3). A voter can now verify his/her ballot by the nonces published by the counting servers. If a voter cannot see the nonce, he/she can appeal by revealing the identity and showing the nonce. Note that the same nonce is published by j counting servers (or t counting servers in a t-threshold homomorphic scheme). So no counting server can alter or delete any nonce without detection.

The AS can only forward ballots generated by the voter computer to the counting servers since all ballots must be signed with the private key of the group signature. Also, the AS can not modify ballots, because the ballots are encrypted with the CS public key by the voter. Since the voter knows his/her nonce value, the AS can not drop or replay a ballot without detection.

4   Ballot Verification Using NIZK Protocol

4.1   Introduction

A zero-knowledge proof protocol is classified as interactive or non-interactive. An interactive zero-knowledge protocol requires interaction between the prover and the verifier. On the other hand, a Non-Interactive Zero-Knowledge (NIZK) protocol allows the prover to prove the statement without interaction with the verifier. So, a NIZK protocol is usually faster and efficient, since it requires no online communication between the prover and the verifier. But, a NIZK protocol requires that both the prover and verifier share a common random string, usually provided by a trusted third party and a pre-arranged use of this random string is required.

In any zero-knowledge protocol, the interaction between the prover and the verifier can be replaced by sharing a common random string [13]. We use this idea to modify the interactive zero-knowledge protocol [3] as a Non-Interactive Zero-Knowledge (NIZK) protocol to prove the validity of the ballot in our Internet voting scheme.

4.2   The NIZK Protocol

The Voter Computer (VC) plays the role of the prover and the Counting Servers (CS) play the role of the verifiers, where the VC proves the validity of the ballot to the counting servers. Here, the counting servers verify that the ballot is valid. Note that in our voting scheme the counting servers are offline. So the counting servers must verify the ballot without any interaction with the voter computer. Hence our protocol needs to be a non-interactive zero-knowledge protocol. Here, there is no interaction between the voter computer and the counting servers.

Smartcard. The j public values $((e, g_1, n_1), (e, g_2, n_2), \ldots, (e, g_j, n_j))$ are stored in the smartcard. Here, j is the number of counting servers, e is a prime number agreed by all the counting servers. Let g_j be an element in $\mathbf{Z}^*_{n_j}$ such that

e divides the order of g_j, and $n_j = p_j.q_j$. Here, p_j and q_j values are chosen by server j such that e divides $(p_j - 1)$, but does not divide $(q_j - 1)$. The p_j and q_j values are private to server j. The value of e must be larger than the total number of eligible voters.

Computations at the VC. The VC picks the random values $(r_{11}, r_{21},\ldots,r_{j1})$ which are elements of $\mathbf{Z}^*_{n_1}$, $(r_{12}, r_{22},\ldots,r_{j2})$ which are elements of $\mathbf{Z}^*_{n_2}$, and similarly $(r_{1j}, r_{2j},\ldots,r_{jj})$ which are elements of $\mathbf{Z}^*_{n_j}$.

Then the VC generates the random string $R = (r_1, r_2,\ldots,r_j)$, where

$$r_1 = \sum_{i=1}^{j} r_{i1} \ (\mathrm{mod}\ e)$$
$$r_2 = \sum_{i=1}^{j} r_{i2} \ (\mathrm{mod}\ e)$$
$$\ldots$$
$$\ldots$$
$$\ldots$$
$$r_j = \sum_{i=1}^{j} r_{ij} \ (\mathrm{mod}\ e)$$

The VC uses these random values to compute the ballot $B = (b_1, b_2,\ldots,b_j)$, such that

$$b_1 = (g_1^{r_{11}} \ (\mathrm{mod}\ n_1), g_2^{r_{12}} \ (\mathrm{mod}\ n_2),\ldots, g_j^{r_{1j}} \ (\mathrm{mod}\ n_j))$$
$$b_2 = (g_1^{r_{21}} \ (\mathrm{mod}\ n_1), g_2^{r_{22}} \ (\mathrm{mod}\ n_2),\ldots, g_j^{r_{2j}} \ (\mathrm{mod}\ n_j))$$
$$\ldots$$
$$\ldots$$
$$\ldots$$
$$b_j = (g_1^{r_{j1}} \ (\mathrm{mod}\ n_1), g_2^{r_{j2}} \ (\mathrm{mod}\ n_2),\ldots, g_j^{r_{jj}} \ (\mathrm{mod}\ n_j))$$

Here, a ballot is sent as secret shares to j servers. The random values are chosen such that a vote $V = (v_1, v_2,\ldots,v_j)$, where

$$v_1 = \sum_{i=1}^{j} r_{1i} \ (\mathrm{mod}\ e)$$
$$v_2 = \sum_{i=1}^{j} r_{2i} \ (\mathrm{mod}\ e)$$
$$\ldots$$
$$\ldots$$
$$v_j = \sum_{i=1}^{j} r_{ji} \ (\mathrm{mod}\ e)$$

The construction of the ballot shares $b_1, b_2, \ldots, b_j$ is valid if all of $v_1, v_2,\ldots,v_j$ are either 0 or 1 (mod e). If all of $b_1, b_2, \ldots, b_j$ are valid, and if $\sum_{i=1}^{j} v_i = 1$ (mod e), then the ballot $B = (b_1, b_2, \ldots, b_j)$ is valid . Here, v_1 is the vote for candidate 1, v_2 is the vote for candidate 2, and so on. We assume that a voter can vote only for one candidate and the candidate with most votes will be elected. That is, if a voter wants to cast the ballot for candidate 1, the value of v_1 must be 1. If the voter wants to cast the ballot for candidate 2, the value of v_2 must be 1, and so on.

The VC picks $((\alpha_{11}, \alpha_{21}, \ldots, \alpha_{k1}),(\beta_{11}, \beta_{21}, \ldots, \beta_{k1}))$ values which are elements of $\mathbf{Z}^*_{n_1}$, $((\alpha_{12}, \alpha_{22}, \ldots, \alpha_{k2}),(\beta_{12}, \beta_{22}, \ldots, \beta_{k2}))$ values which are elements of $\mathbf{Z}^*_{n_2}$, and so on. Here, k is a security parameter of the system. Let $\alpha = (\alpha_1, \alpha_2, \ldots, \alpha_k)$ values, and $\beta = (\beta_1, \beta_2, \ldots, \beta_k)$ values, where

$$\alpha_1 = (\alpha_{11}, \alpha_{12}, \ldots, \alpha_{1j})$$
$$\alpha_2 = (\alpha_{21}, \alpha_{22}, \ldots, \alpha_{2j})$$
$$\ldots$$
$$\ldots$$
$$\ldots$$
$$\alpha_k = (\alpha_{k1}, \alpha_{k2}, \ldots, \alpha_{kj})$$

and

$$\beta_1 = (\beta_{11}, \beta_{12}, \ldots, \beta_{1j})$$
$$\beta_2 = (\beta_{21}, \beta_{22}, \ldots, \beta_{2j})$$
$$\ldots$$
$$\ldots$$
$$\ldots$$
$$\beta_k = (\beta_{k1}, \beta_{k2}, \ldots, \beta_{kj})$$

Here, the value of each $\alpha_1, \alpha_2, \ldots, \alpha_k$ is 0 (mod e), and the value of each β_1, $\beta_2, \ldots, \beta_k$ is 1 (mod e).

For $i = 1$ to k, the VC picks a random bit, if the bit equals to 0 then the VC computes $pair_i = (x_i, y_i)$ else $pair_i = (y_i, x_i)$, where

$$x_i = (g_1^{\alpha_{i1}} \ (\text{mod } n_1), g_2^{\alpha_{i2}} \ (\text{mod } n_2), \ldots, g_j^{\alpha_{ij}} (\text{mod } n_j))$$

and

$$y_i = (g_1^{\beta_{i1}} \ (\text{mod } n_1), g_2^{\beta_{i2}} \ (\text{mod } n_2), \ldots, g_j^{\beta_{ij}} (\text{mod } n_j)).$$

The ballot B and $\{pair_i\}_{i \leq k}$ are sent to the counting servers by the VC via the Authentication Server (AS).

We assume that a trusted third party will provide the $k-bit$ random challenge string c that will be used by both VC and counting servers. We also assume that the VC sends $[B, \text{and } pair]$ values before the random string is provided. This implies that the claim is chosen before the random string is presented to the prover [11]. That is, this NIZK protocol is a non-interactive zero-knowledge protocol with preprocessing according to Feige et al. [12]. In the preliminary stage (before the random string is provided), the voter computer and the counting servers agree on the value of the ballot shares (either 0 or 1), and then the VC sends $[B, \text{and } pair]$ values to the counting servers via the AS. The third party sends the random challenge string c to the voter computer after the $[B, \text{and } pair]$ values are sent to the counting servers. Then, for each ballot, the VC follows the following procedure.

For ballot share b_1, the VC checks the challenge bit c_i ($i = 1$ to k) of the random string, and answers with d_i ($i = 1$ to k). The VC computes $d_i = ((\alpha_{i1}, \alpha_{i2}, \ldots, \alpha_{ij}), (\beta_{i1}, \beta_{i2}, \ldots, \beta_{ij}))$, if $c_i = 0$. The VC computes $d_i = (r_{11}+\alpha_{i1}, r_{12}+\alpha_{i2}, \ldots, r_{1j}+\alpha_{ij})$, if $c_i = 1$ and $v_1 = 1$ (mod e). The VC computes $d_i = (r_{11}+\beta_{i1}, r_{12}+\beta_{i2}, \ldots, r_{1j}+\beta_{ij})$, if $c_i = 1$, but $v_1 = 0$ (mod e). The VC sends the d_i value to the counting servers via the AS.

The VC repeats the same procedure for each ballot share, and finally, the VC sends the random string R to the counting servers via the AS.

Computations at the CS. The counting servers check the challenge bit c_i ($i = 1$ to k) of the random string after receiving [B, *pair*, d, and R] values. If the value of c_i is 0, the servers first check that $d_i[1,1] + d_i[1,2] + \ldots + d_i[1,j] = 0$ (mod e), and $d_i[2,1] + d_i[2,2] + \ldots + d_i[2,j] = 1$ (mod e), and the servers then check that $pair_i = ((g_1^{d_i[1,1]}, g_2^{d_i[1,2]}, \ldots, g_j^{d_i[1,j]}), (g_1^{d_i[2,1]}, g_2^{d_i[2,2]}, \ldots, g_j^{d_i[2,j]}))$ or $((g_1^{d_i[2,1]}, g_2^{d_i[2,2]}, \ldots, g_j^{d_i[2,j]}), (g_1^{d_i[1,1]}, g_2^{d_i[1,2]}, \ldots, g_j^{d_i[1,j]}))$. The servers become sure that *pairs* were computed correctly if both of these calculations are correct.

If the value of $c_i = 1$, the counting servers first check that ($\sum_{m=1}^{j} d_i[1,m] = 1$ (mod e), $\sum_{m=1}^{j} d_i[2,m] = 1$ (mod e), $\ldots$, $\sum_{m=1}^{j} d_i[j,m] = 1$ (mod e)), and the servers then check that ($g_1^{d_i[1]}, g_2^{d_i[2]}, \ldots, g_j^{d_i[j]}$) = $b_m.pair_i[1]$ or $b_m.pair_i[2]$ ($m = 1$ to j, $i = 1$ to k). Here,

$$d_i[1] = r_{11}+\alpha_{i1}, r_{12}+\alpha_{i2}, \ldots, r_{1j}+\alpha_{ij} \text{ or } r_{11}+\beta_{i1}, r_{12}+\beta_{i2}, \ldots, r_{1j}+\beta_{ij}$$
$$d_i[2] = r_{21}+\alpha_{i1}, r_{22}+\alpha_{i2}, \ldots, r_{2j}+\alpha_{ij} \text{ or } r_{21}+\beta_{i1}, r_{22}+\beta_{i2}, \ldots, r_{2j}+\beta_{ij}$$

$$\ldots$$
$$\ldots$$
$$\ldots$$

$$d_i[j] = r_{j1}+\alpha_{i1}, r_{j2}+\alpha_{i2}, \ldots, r_{jj}+\alpha_{ij} \text{ or } r_{j1}+\beta_{i1}, r_{j2}+\beta_{i2}, \ldots, r_{jj}+\beta_{ij}$$

The counting servers become sure that each of the ballot shares $b_1, b_2, \ldots, b_j$ was computed correctly if these calculations are correct.

The counting servers finally check (from the R value) that $\sum_{i=1}^{j} r_i = 1$ (mod e), and $g_i^{r_i} = \prod_{i=1}^{j} b_j[i]$, and if these calculations are correct the servers become sure that only one of $b_1, b_2, \ldots, b_j$ is 1, and all others are 0. Thus, the ballot B is validated.

The above computations both at the VC and at the CS non-interactively prove the validity of a ballot without revealing anything about a particular choice of a voter in that ballot.

We skip the ballot counting part in this paper since this is outside the scope of the paper.

The computations at the VC are dominated by the modular exponentiations, which is of complexity $\mathcal{O}(\log n)$ [3] of modular multiplications. The time complexity for the VC is $\mathcal{O}(kj^2\log n) = \mathcal{O}(\log n)$ [3], and the time complexity for the counting servers is also $\mathcal{O}(kj^2\log n) = \mathcal{O}(\log n)$ [3]. Since time-consuming computations can be done offline, and all computations at the VC can be done without any interaction with the counting servers, the NIZK protocol is very efficient.

4.3   The Security Properties of the NIZK Protocol

The security properties of this non-interactive protocol are described as follows:

Completeness. By completeness of zero-knowledge protocol we assume that both the prover (voter computer) and the verifier (counting servers) will follow the normal protocol. If both parties follow the protocol properly, the valid ballot cast by authenticated voter can be accepted by the counting servers with probability one.

Soundness. Soundness means, if at least one of the counting servers is honest (follow the protocol), then with overwhelming probability, a dishonest Voter Computer (VC) will not be able to cheat by sending an invalid ballot. Overwhelming probability means the probability is 1 - a negligible probability [3].

In our voting scheme, the VC sends a signed and encrypted ballot to the counting servers via the authentication server. The counting servers verify the group signature and check for duplicate nonce values. Also, the VC sends the d values. From the d values, the counting servers check the validity of the pair values, and the validity of the ballot shares $b_1, b_2, \ldots, b_j$. Each of $b_1, b_2, \ldots, b_j$ will be valid (valid means either 0 or 1) if the VC can answer with d_i for both $c_i = 0$ and $c_i = 1$. Suppose, $c_i = 0$, the counting servers accept the first checks if and only if $d_i[1, 1] + d_i[1, 2] + \ldots + d_i[1, j] = 0 \pmod{e}$, and $d_i[2, 1] + d_i[2, 2] + \ldots + d_i[2, j] = 1 \pmod{e}$. Similarly, suppose $c_i = 1$, the counting servers accept the first check if and only if $(\sum_{m=1}^{j} d_i[1, m] = 1 \pmod{e}, \sum_{m=1}^{j} d_i[2, m] = 1 \pmod{e}, \ldots, \sum_{m=1}^{j} d_i[j, m] = 1 \pmod{e})$.

Now, for ballot share b_1, if the counting servers accept the second checks for both $c_i = 0$ and $c_i = 1$, then this implies that

$$d_i[1, 1] \ (c_i = 1) \equiv r_{11} + d_i[1, 1] \ (\text{mod } \psi(n), \text{ and } c_i = 0) \text{ or } r_{11} + d_i[2, 1] \ (\text{mod } \psi(n), \text{ and } c_i = 0)$$

$$d_i[1, 2] \ (c_i = 1) \equiv r_{12} + d_i[1, 2] \ (\text{mod } \psi(n), \text{ and } c_i = 0) \text{ or } r_{12} + d_i[2, 2] \ (\text{mod } \psi(n), \text{ and } c_i = 0)$$

$$\ldots$$
$$\ldots$$
$$\ldots$$

$$d_i[1, j] \ (c_i = 1) \equiv r_{1j} + d_i[1, j] \ (\text{mod } \psi(n), \text{ and } c_i = 0) \text{ or } r_{1j} + d_i[2, j] \ (\text{mod } \psi(n), \text{ and } c_i = 0)$$

This condition holds since for two elements f_1 and f_2 in $\mathbf{Z}^*_{\psi(n)}$, if $g^{f_1} = g^{f_2}$, then $f_1 = f_2$ [3], where, $\psi(n) = (p - 1) (q - 1)$, when n is a product of two primes p and q.

If $c_i = 1$, then $\sum_{m=1}^{j} d_i[1, m] = 1 \pmod{e}$ and this means that for $c_i = 0$,

$$(r_{11} + d_i[1, 1], r_{12} + d_i[1, 2], \ldots, r_{1j} + d_i[1, j]) = 1 \pmod{e}$$

or

$$(r_{11} + d_i[2, 1], r_{12} + d_i[2, 2], \ldots, r_{1j} + d_i[2, j]) = 1 \pmod{e}.$$

Since $d_i[1, 1] + d_i[1, 2] + \ldots + d_i[1, j] = 0 \pmod{e}$, and $d_i[2, 1] + d_i[2, 2] + \ldots + d_i[2, j] = 1 \pmod{e}$, this shows that the value of $b_1 = v_1 = 0$ or 1.

The counting servers thus check the validity of each ballot. Here, to cheat the counting servers with this proof, the VC has to guess the challenge bit c_i from the random string c. The VC can do no better guessing than with probability $\frac{1}{2}$, and for a $k - bit$ random string the probability is reduced to $\frac{1}{2^k}$.

Now, the validity of the whole ballot B depends on the validity of each of the ballot shares $b_1, b_2, \ldots, b_j$ and the value of R. So, if each of $b_1, b_2, \ldots, b_j$ is valid and $R = \sum_{i=1}^{j} r_i = 1 \pmod{e}$, then the ballot B is valid. If at least one counting server is honest, it will be able to detect the invalid ballot. Thus, there is no way for a dishonest voter to succeed with an invalid ballot.

Zero-Knowledgeness. By zero-knowledgeness we mean that no information what-soever except the validity of the prover's claim flows to the verifier, in that the verifier's view can be well simulated. In our NIZK protocol, the verifiers view1 = $\{pair_i, c_i, d_i\}$ ($i = 1$ to k) can be simulated by the probabilistic Turing machine M constructed in [3], that on input (B, k) runs in expected polynomial time to construct view2 which is computationally indistinguishable from view1. Our NIZK protocol is simpler in that there is no interaction between the prover and the verifier. We do not have to worry about the possible cheating by the verifier to obtain a "more interesting view" [13]. In this protocol, the VC sends [B, *pair*, R, and d] values to the counting servers via the authentication server, where the ballot B is sent as ballot shares $(b_1, b_2, \ldots, b_j)$. Also, each of these ballot shares is further divided into shares, for example, $b_1 = (g_1^{r_{11}} \pmod{n_1}, g_2^{r_{12}} \pmod{n_2}, \ldots, g_j^{r_{1j}} \pmod{n_j})$, and sent to j counting servers. So, a single counting server can not discover the value of the ballots without cooperating with other counting servers. But, every counting server can verify the d values to validate the ballots. After ballot verification, the counting servers cooperate to count the ballots and publish the results. That is, a counting server receives only the necessary values to individually prove the validity of the ballots, but can not reveal the value of the ballots without cooperating with other counting servers, and this fulfills the zero-knowledgeness property of the protocol.

5   Universally Composable NIZK Protocol

In this section, we describe the UC framework for representing and analyzing the NIZK protocol in our voting scheme.

5.1   The UC Framework

In the UC framework, we define the ideal functionality $\mathcal{F}$ which is also called the trusted party. All parties hand their inputs to this incorruptible trusted party for evaluating some function f. The ideal functionality locally computes the outputs, and hands each party the prescribed outputs. Here, the adversary is limited to interacting with the ideal functionalities in the name of the corrupted parties.

According to UC framework [1,6], a protocol π securely evaluates a function f if for any adversary $\mathcal{A}$ (that interacts with the protocol) there exists an ideal-process adversary $\mathcal{S}$ such that no environment $\mathcal{Z}$ can tell with non-negligible probability whether it is interacting with π and $\mathcal{A}$ or with $\mathcal{S}$ and the ideal process for f. Here, the environment $\mathcal{Z}$ and the adversary $\mathcal{A}$ are allowed to interact, that is, they can exchange information after each message or output generated by a party running the protocol. If π securely realizes f with this type of interaction with $\mathcal{Z}$ then we say that π UC-realizes f.

The ideal functionalities handle everything taking place in the protocol. The parties hand their inputs from $\mathcal{Z}$ directly and securely to $\mathcal{F}$. $\mathcal{F}$ computes the outputs and sends the outputs to the parties. $\mathcal{S}$ is restricted to corrupting some of the parties and blocking messages from $\mathcal{F}$ to the honest parties [2].

One main characteristic of UC framework is security under modular composition. This means a protocol ρ that realizes $\mathcal{F}$, can be used as a sub-protocol in π and written as π^ρ. Then we can form a hybrid protocol $\pi^{\mathcal{F}}$, where calls to ρ are replaced with calls to $\mathcal{F}$. If π securely realizes some ideal functionality $\mathcal{G}$ then π^ρ securely realizes $\mathcal{G}$.

In our non-interactive zero-knowledge protocol, the voter computer commits to a value (either 0 or 1) of each ballot share to the counting servers. Since this is non-interactive protocol, there is no challenge string from the counting servers. But, the voter computer responds based on the common random string provided by a trusted third party. And then the counting servers verify the ballots non-interactively. So we need ideal functionalities for commitment scheme, common random string, and the NIZK protocol. We use modular composition theorem and work with hybrid protocol where we assume that we have protocols for realizing commitment scheme and common random string functionalities.

5.2   Ideal Functionalities

The ideal functionalities for the commitment scheme $\mathcal{F}_{\text{COM}}^{1:\text{M}}$ (one-to-many commitment scheme), the common random string $\mathcal{F}_{\text{CRS}}$, and the NIZK protocol $\mathcal{F}_{\text{NIZK}}^{1:\text{M}}$ are as follows:

Ideal Functionality for Commitment Scheme: We first define the commitment scheme ideal functionality for our NIZK protocol. Our commitment scheme is one-to-many UC commitment scheme in which the committer is a voter computer commits to the value of the ballot to j counting servers. Here, a ballot B consists of j ballot shares $(b_1, b_2, \ldots, b_j)$. Each of these ballot shares is either 0 or 1, and B contains only one ballot share with value 1.

Functionality 1: $\mathcal{F}_{\text{COM}}^{1:\text{M}}$
$\mathcal{F}_{\text{COM}}^{1:\text{M}}$ runs with Voter Computer VC and Counting Servers $CS1, CS2, \ldots,$ CSj, and adversary S

1. Upon receiving an input (*commit, sid, $b_1, b_2, \ldots, b_j$*) from Voter Computer VC, verify that $sid = (VC, CS1, CS2, \ldots, CSj, sid')$ for Counting Servers $CS1, CS2, \ldots, CSj$, else ignore the input. Record $(sid, b_1, b_2, \ldots, b_j, VC, CS1, CS2, \ldots, CSj)$ and send public output (*receipt, sid, $VC, CS1, CS2, \ldots, CSj$*) to $CS1, CS2, \ldots, CSj$, and S. Ignore subsequent commit inputs with same sid from VC to $CS1, CS2, \ldots, CSj$.
2. Upon receiving an input (*reveal, sid*) from VC, if there is a recorded $(sid, b_1, b_2, \ldots, b_j, VC, CS1, CS2, \ldots, CSj)$ then generate public output (*reveal, sid, $b_1, b_2, \ldots, b_j, VC, CS1, CS2, \ldots, CSj$*) to VC and S. Otherwise do nothing.
3. Upon receiving a message (*corrupt – committer, sid*) from the adversary, send $(b_1, b_2, \ldots, b_j)$ to the adversary. If the adversary provides a value $(b'_1, b'_2, \ldots, b'_j)$, and the *receipt* is not yet written on CSs tape, then change the recorded value to $(b'_1, b'_2, \ldots, b'_j)$.

Ideal Functionality for Common Random String: We assume that P contains the valid voter computer and counting server identities. The voter computer invokes this functionality as a committer; in reply this functionality sends the common random string c to all parties. The random string c is used as the challenge bit string for both voter computer and counting servers in the non-interactive zero-knowledge proof scheme.

Functionality 2: $\mathcal{F}_{\mathrm{CRS}}$

$\mathcal{F}_{\mathrm{CRS}}$ runs with Voter Computer VC and Counting Servers $CS1$, $CS2,\ldots$, CSj, and adversary S

1. Upon receiving an input (CRS, sid, VC, $CS1$, $CS2,\ldots,CSj$) from Voter Computer VC, verify that $sid = (\mathcal{P}, sid')$. Also verify that $VC \in \mathcal{P}$, and ($CS1$, $CS2,\ldots,CSj$) $\in \mathcal{P}$.
2. If string c is not recorded, then choose and record c (c is a random challenge string). Send output (CRS, sid, VC, $CS1$, $CS2,\ldots,CSj$, c) to VC, $CS1$, $CS2,\ldots,CSj$, and S.

Program for the Voter Computer and Counting Server: Voter Computer chooses the random string R, and computes the ballot $B = (b_1, b_2,\ldots,b_j)$ as described in Section 4. Each of $b_1, b_2,\ldots,b_j$ is either 0 or 1, and B contains only one ballot share with value 1 and all other ballot shares contain 0 values. The programs for voter computer ($\mathcal{P}_{\mathrm{VC}}$) and counting servers ($\mathcal{P}_{\mathrm{CS}}$) are briefly presented in the following:

Program 1: $\mathcal{P}_{\mathrm{VC}}$

$\mathcal{P}_{\mathrm{VC}}$ proceeds as follows:

1. The VC invokes $\mathcal{F}_{\mathrm{COM}}^{1:M}$
2. The VC generates the random string R, and computes the ballot B
3. The VC also picks α and β values, and generates *pairs*
4. The VC sends the ballot B, and the *pairs* to the counting servers via the Authentication Server (AS)
5. The VC invokes $\mathcal{F}_{\mathrm{CRS}}$ and gets random challenge string c
6. The VC computes the d values (responses) based on the challenge string c
7. The VC sends the d values, and the string R to the counting servers via the AS

Program 2: $\mathcal{P}_{\mathrm{CS}}$

$\mathcal{P}_{\mathrm{CS}}$ proceeds as follows:

1. The counting servers receive B, *pairs*, d, and R from the VC via the AS. The counting servers also receive the random challenge string c from $\mathcal{F}_{\mathrm{CRS}}$
2. The counting servers verify each of the ballot shares by verifying d and *pair* values based on the challenge string c
3. The counting servers also verify B by verifying $\sum_{i=1}^{j} r_i = 1 \pmod{e}$, and $g_i^{r_i} = \prod_{i=1}^{j} b_j[\mathrm{i}]$ (from R value)

Ideal Functionality for NIZK Protocol: Our ideal functionality for NIZK protocol $(\mathcal{F}_{\text{NIZK}}^{1:M})$ is one-to-many UC zero-knowledge protocol in that a voter computer proves the validity of the ballot to j counting servers.

Functionality 3: $\mathcal{F}_{\text{NIZK}}^{1:M}$

$\mathcal{F}_{\text{NIZK}}^{1:M}$ runs with Voter Computer VC and Counting Servers $CS1$, $CS2$,..., CSj, and adversary S

1. Upon receiving an input (*prove, sid, VC, CS*1, *CS*2,...,*CSj, B, pairs, d, R*) from Voter Computer VC, verify that $sid = (VC, CS1, CS2,...,CSj, sid')$ for Counting Servers $CS1, CS2,...,CSj$, else ignore the input. Verify the ballot using ($\mathcal{F}_{\text{COM}}^{1:M}$ and $\mathcal{F}_{\text{CRS}}$). If B is valid, display output (*accept, B, sid, VC, CS*1, *CS*2,...,*CSj*) to $VC, CS1, CS2,...,CSj$ and S, else do nothing. Ignore future (*prove,...*) inputs.
2. Upon receiving an input from (*corrupt − prover, sid*) from the adversary, send B to the adversary. If the adversary provides a value B' and counting servers prove it as valid, and no output is yet written to CSs tape, then output (*accept, B', sid, VC, CS*1, *CS*2,...,*CSj*) to VC and S.

5.3 Universally Composable NIZK Protocol

The NIZK protocol $\pi_{\text{NIZK}}^{\mathcal{F}_{\text{COM}}^{1:M},\mathcal{F}_{\text{CRS}}}$ for the Voter Computer (VC) and the Counting Servers (CS) with access to ideal functionalities $\mathcal{F}_{\text{COM}}^{1:M}$, $\mathcal{F}_{\text{CRS}}$, and $\mathcal{F}_{\text{NIZK}}^{1:M}$ is described here.

Protocol $\pi_{\text{NIZK}}^{\mathcal{F}_{\text{COM}}^{1:M},\mathcal{F}_{\text{CRS}}}$ proceeds as follows:

1. The VC invokes $\mathcal{F}_{\text{COM}}^{1:M}$, generates the random string R, computes ballot shares $(b_1, b_2,...,b_j)$ to generate the ballot $B = (b_1, b_2,...,b_j)$
2. The VC picks α and β values, and generates $k − pairs$ (k is the security parameter of the system)
3. The VC sends B, and these $k − pairs$ to the counting servers via the authentication server
4. The VC invokes $\mathcal{F}_{\text{CRS}}$ to receive the random challenge string c
5. The VC computes response d based on the c values
6. The VC sends the d values, and the string R to the counting servers via the authentication server
7. The counting servers receive B, *pairs*, d, and R values from the VC via the authentication server, and the challenge string c from $\mathcal{F}_{\text{CRS}}$
8. The counting servers verify each of the ballot shares by verifying d and *pair* values based on the c values
9. The counting servers also verify the ballot B by verifying the string R
10. The counting servers count the ballot (accept the ballot) B if it is valid

A non-interactive protocol that UC realizes the two-party zero-knowledge functionality $\mathcal{F}_{\text{ZK}}$ [8], can directly be used to realize our $\mathcal{F}_{\text{NIZK}}^{1:M}$ functionality [6].

Proposition 1. *The non-interactive protocol* $\pi_{\text{NIZK}}^{\mathcal{F}_{\text{COM}}^{1:M},\mathcal{F}_{\text{CRS}}}$ *UC-realizes* $\mathcal{F}_{\text{NIZK}}^{1:M}$ *in the* $(\mathcal{F}_{\text{COM}}^{1:M}, \mathcal{F}_{\text{CRS}})$-*hybrid model, in the presence of malicious and adaptive adversaries.*

Proof. If we can prove that the Voter Computer (VC) can separately prove the validity of the ballot to all the Counting Servers (CS), then the protocol $\pi_{\text{NIZK}}^{\mathcal{F}_{\text{COM}}^{1:M},\mathcal{F}_{\text{CRS}}}$ for realizing $\mathcal{F}_{\text{NIZK}}^{1:M}$ will work fine. In this case, the protocol for each of these pairwise proofs (the proof between the voter computer and each of the counting servers) is exactly the two-party protocol of [6], with the exception that commitments are one-to-many commitments rather than two-party commitments. A counting server accepts a ballot if and only if all the pairwise proofs are accepted, that is, if all counting servers accept that ballot.

The protocol $\pi_{\text{NIZK}}^{\mathcal{F}_{\text{COM}}^{1:M},\mathcal{F}_{\text{CRS}}}$ uses only $\mathcal{F}_{\text{COM}}^{1:M}$ and $\mathcal{F}_{\text{CRS}}$, no cryptographic primitives are used in it. Thus, the security of the protocol in the $(\mathcal{F}_{\text{COM}}^{1:M}, \mathcal{F}_{\text{CRS}})$-hybrid model is unconditional [8].

It is possible for the counting servers to know whether all the pairwise proofs are accepted or not, since the commitments and messages are seen by all the counting servers and the zero-knowledge proof is publicly verifiable. That is, it is enough to see the transcript of VC/CS messages to know whether or not the proof was accepted by the counting servers.

To prove the universal composability of $\mathcal{F}_{\text{NIZK}}^{1:M}$, we need an ideal-process adversary (a simulator) that simulates the proofs for two cases. The first case is that the voter computer is not corrupted and the counting servers are corrupted. The second case is that the simulator is able to extract the witness from an adversarially generated proof, that is, if the voter computer is corrupted.

We can run the simulator of the two-party protocol of [8] for every pairwise proof to simulate a proof for a corrupted counting server.

It is possible to run the two-party extractor for any pairwise proof in which the counting servers are not corrupted to extract the witness from a corrupted voter computer. Here, we consider the case that the voter computer is corrupted and at least one counting server is not corrupted. Otherwise, all parties (the voter computer and the counting servers) are corrupted and simulation is straightforward. This implies that there exists one pairwise proof in which a counting server is not corrupted. We can run the extractor for the protocol of [8] in this purpose. The simulator delivers the output of $\mathcal{F}_{\text{NIZK}}^{1:M}$ to the counting servers if and only if all counting servers accept the ballot in the simulation. So, the parties' outputs in the ideal process are the same as in a real execution. □

Theorem 1. *Protocol* $\pi_{\text{NIZK}}^{\mathcal{F}_{\text{COM}}^{1:M},\mathcal{F}_{\text{CRS}}}$ *securely realizes* $\mathcal{F}_{\text{NIZK}}^{1:M}$ *in the* $(\mathcal{F}_{\text{COM}}^{1:M}, \mathcal{F}_{\text{CRS}})$-*hybrid model.*

Proof. We assume that $\mathcal{A}$ is an adversary that operates against the protocol $\pi_{\text{NIZK}}^{\mathcal{F}_{\text{COM}}^{1:M},\mathcal{F}_{\text{CRS}}}$ in the $(\mathcal{F}_{\text{COM}}^{1:M}, \mathcal{F}_{\text{CRS}})$-hybrid model. We can construct an ideal-process adversary or simulator $\mathcal{S}$ such that no environment $\mathcal{Z}$ can tell whether it is interacting with $\mathcal{A}$ and $\pi_{\text{NIZK}}^{\mathcal{F}_{\text{COM}}^{1:M},\mathcal{F}_{\text{CRS}}}$ in the $(\mathcal{F}_{\text{COM}}^{1:M}, \mathcal{F}_{\text{CRS}})$-hybrid model or with $\mathcal{S}$ in the ideal process for $\mathcal{F}_{\text{NIZK}}^{1:M}$.

We also assume that $\mathcal{S}$ runs a simulated copy of $\mathcal{A}$. Also, messages received from $\mathcal{Z}$ are forwarded to the simulated $\mathcal{A}$, and messages sent by the simulated $\mathcal{A}$ to its environment are forwarded to $\mathcal{Z}$.

1. Suppose $\mathcal{A}$ on behalf of a corrupted Voter Computer VC' starts an interaction as a prover with the uncorrupted counting servers, then $\mathcal{S}$ records the values that $\mathcal{A}$ sends to $\mathcal{F}_{\text{COM}}^{1:M}$ and $\mathcal{F}_{\text{CRS}}$, plays the role of the counting servers, and records $\mathcal{A}$'s responses. $\mathcal{S}$ simulates counting servers' decision algorithm and if the counting servers accept the ballot, then $\mathcal{S}$ finds a ballot B and sends B to $\mathcal{F}_{\text{NIZK}}^{1:M}$. Else $\mathcal{S}$ sends an invalid ballot B' to $\mathcal{F}_{\text{NIZK}}^{1:M}$.
2. Suppose an uncorrupted Voter Computer VC starts an interaction with the corrupted counting servers CS' then $\mathcal{S}$ learns from $\mathcal{F}_{\text{COM}}^{1:M}$ whether counting servers accept or reject a ballot, and simulates the view of $\mathcal{A}$. $\mathcal{S}$ has no problem carrying out the simulation since it simulates for $\mathcal{A}$ an interaction with $\mathcal{F}_{\text{COM}}^{1:M}$ and $\mathcal{F}_{\text{CRS}}$, where $\mathcal{F}_{\text{COM}}^{1:M}$ and $\mathcal{F}_{\text{CRS}}$ are played by $\mathcal{S}$. Thus, $\mathcal{S}$ is not bound by the "commitments" and can "reveal" them [8].
3. Suppose uncorrupted Voter Computer VC and uncorrupted Counting Servers CS interact, then $\mathcal{S}$ simulates for $\mathcal{A}$ the appropriate protocol messages.
4. If the counting servers are corrupted, the counting servers provide the adversary with no extra information. If the voter computer is corrupted, $\mathcal{S}$ corrupts the voter in the ideal process for the zero-knowledge proof.   □

6   Conclusions

In this paper, we present an Internet voting scheme that is voter verifiable and satisfies all the basic requirements for a secure and practical voting system. We describe the Non-Interactive Zero-Knowledge (NIZK) protocol to verify the validity of the ballot and the universal composability of the protocol. We see that the NIZK protocol used in the voting scheme is very efficient.

We find that the protocol $\pi_{\text{NIZK}}^{\mathcal{F}_{\text{COM}}^{1:M},\mathcal{F}_{\text{CRS}}}$ presented in this paper UC-realizes $\mathcal{F}_{\text{NIZK}}^{1:M}$ in the $(\mathcal{F}_{\text{COM}}^{1:M}, \mathcal{F}_{\text{CRS}})$-hybrid model, in the presence of malicious and adaptive adversaries. The protocol also securely realizes $\mathcal{F}_{\text{NIZK}}^{1:M}$ in the $(\mathcal{F}_{\text{COM}}^{1:M}, \mathcal{F}_{\text{CRS}})$-hybrid model. In the ideal functionalities, we use one-to-many UC commitment scheme and one-to-many UC zero-knowledge proof protocol.

References

1. Canetti, R.: Universally Composable Security: A New Paradigm for Cryptographic Protocols. Electronic Colloquium on Computational Complexity, Revision 3 of Report N0. 16 (2001), ISSN: 1443-8092 (2005), http://eprint.iacr.org/2000/067
2. Groth, J.: Evaluating Security of Voting Schemes in the Universal Composability Framework. Springer, Heidelberg (2004) ISBN: 978-3-540-22217-0
3. Iversen, K.R.: The Application of Cryptographic Zero-Knowledge Techniques in Computerized Secret Ballot Election Schemes. Ph.D. dissertation, IDT-report, 1991:3, Norwegian Institute of Technology (February 1991)

4. Schoenmakers, B.: A simple publicly verifiable secret sharing scheme and its application to electronic voting. In: Wiener, M. (ed.) CRYPTO 1999. LNCS, vol. 1666, pp. 148–164. Springer, Heidelberg (1999)
5. Damgard, I., Groth, J., Salomonsen, G.: The Theory and Implementation of an Electronic Voting System. In: Gritzalis, D. (ed.) Secure Electronic Voting, pp. 77–100. Kluwer Academic Publishers, Dordrecht (2003)
6. Canetti, R., Lindell, Y., Ostrovsky, R., Sahai, A.: Universally Composable Two-Party and Multi-Party Secure Computation. In: 34th STOC, pp. 494–503 (2002)
7. Wikström, D.: A universally composable mix-net. In: Naor, M. (ed.) TCC 2004. LNCS, vol. 2951, pp. 317–335. Springer, Heidelberg (2004)
8. Canetti, R., Fischlin, M.: Universally composable commitments. In: Kilian, J. (ed.) CRYPTO 2001. LNCS, vol. 2139, pp. 19–40. Springer, Heidelberg (2001)
9. Based, M.A., Mjølsnes, S.F.: A Non-interactive Zero Knowledge Proof Protocol in an Internet Voting Scheme. In: Proceedings of the the 2nd Norwegian Security Conference (NISK 2009), Tapir Akademisk Forlag, pp. 148–160 (2009) ISBN: 978-82-519-2492-4
10. Based, M.A.: Security Aspects of Internet based Voting. In: Sobh, et al. (eds.) Proceedings of the International Conference on Telecommunications and Networking (TeNe 2008), Novel Algorithms and Techniques in Telecommunications and Networking, pp. 329–332. Springer, Heidelberg (2010) ISBN: 978-90-481-3661-2
11. Santis, A.D., Persiano, G.: Zero-Knowledge Proofs of Knowledge Without Interaction. In: Proceedings of the 33rd Symposium on Foundations of Computer Science 1992 (FOCS 1992), Pittsburgh, PA, pp. 427–437 (October 24-27, 1992)
12. Feige, U., Lapidot, D., Shamir, A.: Multiple Non-Interactive Zero-Knowledge Proofs Based on a Single Random String. In: Proceedings of the 22th Annual Symposium on the Theory of Computing, pp. 308–317 (1990)
13. Blum, M., Feldman, P., Micali, S.: Non-Interactive Zero-Knowledge and its Applications. In: Proceedings of STOC 1988, pp. 103–112 (1988)
14. Meng, B.: Analyzing and Improving Internet Voting Protocol. In: Proceedings of the IEEE International Conference on e-Business Engineering, pp. 351–354. IEEE Computer Society, Los Alamitos (2007) ISBN 0-7695-3003-6

Protocol Analysis Modulo Combination of Theories: A Case Study in Maude-NPA[*]

Ralf Sasse[1], Santiago Escobar[2], Catherine Meadows[3], and José Meseguer[1]

[1] University of Illinois at Urbana-Champaign, USA
{rsasse,meseguer}@illinois.edu
[2] DSIC-ELP, Universidad Politécnica de Valencia, Spain
sescobar@dsic.upv.es
[3] Naval Research Laboratory, Washington DC, USA
catherine.meadows@nrl.navy.mil

Abstract. There is a growing interest in formal methods and tools to analyze cryptographic protocols *modulo* algebraic properties of their underlying cryptographic functions. It is well-known that an intruder who uses algebraic equivalences of such functions can mount attacks that would be impossible if the cryptographic functions did not satisfy such equivalences. In practice, however, protocols use a collection of well-known functions, whose algebraic properties can naturally be grouped together as a union of theories $E_1 \cup \ldots \cup E_n$. Reasoning symbolically modulo the algebraic properties $E_1 \cup \ldots \cup E_n$ requires performing $(E_1 \cup \ldots \cup E_n)$-unification. However, even if a unification algorithm for each individual E_i is available, this requires combining the existing algorithms by methods that are highly non-deterministic and have high computational cost. In this work we present an alternative method to obtain unification algorithms for combined theories based on *variant narrowing*. Although variant narrowing is less efficient at the level of a single theory E_i, it does not use any costly combination method. Furthermore, it does not require that each E_i has a dedicated unification algorithm in a tool implementation. We illustrate the use of this method in the Maude-NPA tool by means of a well-known protocol requiring the combination of three distinct equational theories.

Keywords: Cryptographic protocol verification, equational unification, variants, exclusive or, narrowing.

1 Introduction

In recent years there has been growing interest in the formal analysis of protocols in which the crypto-algorithms satisfy different algebraic properties [10,13,29,16]. Applications such as electronic voting, digital cash, anonymous

[*] R. Sasse and J. Meseguer have been partially supported by NSF Grants CNS-0716638, CNS-0831064 and CNS-0904749. S. Escobar has been partially supported by the EU (FEDER) and the Spanish MEC/MICINN under grant TIN 2007-68093-C02-02. C. Meadows has been partially supported by NSF Grant CNS-0904749.

J. Cuellar et al. (Eds.): STM 2010, LNCS 6710, pp. 163–178, 2011.

communication, and even key distribution, all can profit from the use of such cryptosystems. Thus, a number of tools and algorithms have been developed that can analyze protocols that make use of these specialized cryptosystems [29,28,6,2,14].

Less attention has been paid to combinations of algebraic properties. However, protocols often make use of more than one type of cryptosystem. For example, the Internet Key Exchange protocol [23] makes use of Diffie-Hellman exponentiation (for exchange of master keys), public and private key cryptography (for authentication of master keys), shared key cryptography (for exchange of session keys), and exclusive-or (used in the generation of master keys). All of these functions satisfy different equational theories. Thus it is important to understand the behavior of algebraic properties in concert as well as separately. This is especially the case for protocol analysis systems based on unification, where the problem of combining unification algorithms [3,35] for different theories is known to be highly non-deterministic and complex, even when efficient unification algorithms exist for the individual theories, and even when the theories are disjoint (that is, share no symbols in common).

The Maude-NPA protocol analysis tool, which relies on unification to perform backwards reachability analysis from insecure states, makes use of two different techniques to handle the combination problem. One is to use a general-purpose approach to unification called *variant narrowing* [20], which, although not as efficient as special purpose unification algorithms, can be applied to a broad class of theories that satisfy a condition known as the *finite variant property* [12]. A second technique applicable to special purpose algorithms, or theories that do not satisfy the finite variant property, uses a more general framework for combining unification algorithms.

One advantage of using variant narrowing is that there are well-known methods and tools for checking that a combination of theories has the finite variant property, including checking its local confluence and termination, and also its satisfaction of the finite variant property itself [17]. Furthermore, under appropriate assumptions some of these checks can be made modularly (see, e.g., [33] for a survey of modular confluence and termination proof methods). This makes variant narrowing easily applicable for unification combination and very suitable for experimentation with different theories. Later on, when the theory is better understood, it may be worth the effort to invest the time to apply the framework to integrate more efficient special purpose algorithms.

In this paper we describe a case study involving the use of variant narrowing to apply Maude-NPA to the analysis of a protocol that involves three theories: (i) an associative-commutative theory satisfied by symbols used in state construction, (ii) a cancellation theory for public key encryption and decryption, and (iii) the equational theory of the exclusive-or operator. This theory combination is illustrated in the analysis of a version of the Needham-Schroeder-Lowe protocol [28], denoted NSL⊕, in which one of the concatenation operators is replaced by an exclusive-or [8].

The rest of this paper is organized as follows. In Section 2 we give some necessary background. In Section 3 we give an overview of Maude-NPA. In Sections 4 and 5 we describe variant narrowing and how it is used in Maude-NPA. In Section 6 we describe our use of Maude-NPA on the NSL⊕ protocol. In Section 7 we discuss related work, and Section 8 concludes the paper.

2   Background on Term Rewriting

We follow the classical notation and terminology from [36] for term rewriting and from [30,31] for rewriting logic and order-sorted notions. We assume an *order-sorted signature* Σ with a finite poset of sorts $(S, \leq)$ (such that each connected component of $(S, \leq)$ has a top sort) and a finite number of function symbols. We assume an S-sorted family $\mathcal{X} = \{\mathcal{X}_s\}_{s \in S}$ of disjoint variable sets with each $\mathcal{X}_s$ countably infinite. $\mathcal{T}_\Sigma(\mathcal{X})_s$ denotes the set of terms of sort s, and $\mathcal{T}_{\Sigma,s}$ the set of ground terms of sort s. We write $\mathcal{T}_\Sigma(\mathcal{X})$ and $\mathcal{T}_\Sigma$ for the corresponding term algebras. We write $Var(t)$ for the set of variables present in a term t. The set of positions of a term t is written $Pos(t)$, and the set of non-variable positions $Pos_\Sigma(t)$. The subterm of t at position p is $t|_p$, and $t[u]_p$ is the result of replacing $t|_p$ by u in t. A *substitution* σ is a sort-preserving mapping from a finite subset of $\mathcal{X}$ to $\mathcal{T}_\Sigma(\mathcal{X})$.

A Σ-*equation* is an unoriented pair $t = t'$, where $t \in \mathcal{T}_\Sigma(\mathcal{X})_s$, $t' \in \mathcal{T}_\Sigma(\mathcal{X})_{s'}$, and s and s' are sorts in the same connected component of the poset $(S, \leq)$. For a set E of Σ-equations, an E-*unifier* for a Σ-equation $t = t'$ is a substitution σ s.t. $\sigma(t) =_E \sigma(t')$. A *complete* set of E-unifiers of an equation $t = t'$ is written $CSU_E(t = t')$. We say that $CSU_E(t = t')$ is *finitary* if it contains a finite number of E-unifiers. A *rewrite rule* is an oriented pair $l \to r$, where $l \notin \mathcal{X}$ and $l, r \in \mathcal{T}_\Sigma(\mathcal{X})_s$ for some sort $s \in S$. An *(unconditional) order-sorted rewrite theory* is a triple $\mathcal{R} = (\Sigma, E, R)$ with Σ an order-sorted signature, E a set of Σ-equations, and R a set of rewrite rules. The rewriting relation $\to_{R,E}$ on $\mathcal{T}_\Sigma(\mathcal{X})$ is $t \xrightarrow{p}_{R,E} t'$ (or $\to_{R,E}$) if $p \in Pos_\Sigma(t)$, $l \to r \in R$, $t|_p =_E \sigma(l)$, and $t' = t[\sigma(r)]_p$ for some σ. Assuming that E has a finitary and complete unification algorithm, the narrowing relation modulo on $\mathcal{T}_\Sigma(\mathcal{X})$ is $t \xrightarrow{p}_{\sigma,R,E} t'$ (or $\leadsto_{\sigma,R,E}$, $\leadsto_{R,E}$) if $p \in Pos_\Sigma(t)$, $l \to r \in R$, $\sigma \in CSU_E(t|_p = l)$, and $t' = \sigma(t[r]_p)$.

We say that the relation $\to_{R,E}$ is *terminating* if there is no infinite sequence $t_1 \to_{R,E} t_2 \to_{R,E} \cdots t_n \to_{R,E} t_{n+1} \cdots$. We say that the relation $\to_{R,E}$ is *confluent* if whenever $t \to^*_{R,E} t'$ and $t \to^*_{R,E} t''$, there exists a term t''' such that $t' \to^*_{R,E} t'''$ and $t'' \to^*_{R,E} t'''$. An order-sorted rewrite theory (Σ, E, R) is confluent (resp. terminating) if the relation $\to_{R,E}$ is confluent (resp. terminating). In a confluent, terminating, order-sorted rewrite theory, for each term $t \in \mathcal{T}_\Sigma(\mathcal{X})$, there is a unique (up to E-equivalence) R, E-irreducible term t' obtained from t by rewriting to canonical form, which is denoted by $t \to^!_{R,E} t'$ or $t\downarrow_{R,E}$ (when t' is not relevant). The relation $\to_{R,E}$ is E-*coherent* [24] if $\forall t_1, t_2, t_3$ we have $t_1 \to_{R,E} t_2$ and $t_1 =_E t_3$ implies $\exists t_4, t_5$ such that $t_2 \to^*_{R,E} t_4$, $t_3 \to^+_{R,E} t_5$, and $t_4 =_E t_5$.

3   Protocol Specification and Analysis in Maude-NPA

Given a protocol $\mathcal{P}$, we first explain how its states are modeled algebraically. The key idea is to model such states as elements of an initial algebra $T_{\Sigma_{\mathcal{P}}/E_{\mathcal{P}}}$, where $\Sigma_{\mathcal{P}}$ is the signature defining the sorts and function symbols for the cryptographic functions and for all the state constructor symbols and $E_{\mathcal{P}}$ is a set of equations specifying the *algebraic properties* of the cryptographic functions and the state constructors. Therefore, a state is an $E_{\mathcal{P}}$-equivalence class $[t] \in T_{\Sigma_{\mathcal{P}}/E_{\mathcal{P}}}$ with t a ground $\Sigma_{\mathcal{P}}$-term. However, since the number of states $T_{\Sigma_{\mathcal{P}}/E_{\mathcal{P}}}$ is in general infinite, rather than exploring concrete protocol states $[t] \in T_{\Sigma_{\mathcal{P}}/E_{\mathcal{P}}}$ we explore *symbolic state patterns* $[t(x_1, \ldots, x_n)] \in T_{\Sigma_{\mathcal{P}}/E_{\mathcal{P}}}(X)$ on the free $(\Sigma_{\mathcal{P}}, E_{\mathcal{P}})$-algebra over a set of variables X. In this way, a state pattern $[t(x_1, \ldots, x_n)]$ represents not a single concrete state but a possibly infinite set of such states, namely all the instances of the pattern $[t(x_1, \ldots, x_n)]$ where the variables $x_1, \ldots, x_n$ have been instantiated by concrete ground terms.

Let us introduce a motivating example that we will use to illustrate our approach based on exclusive–or. We use an exclusive–or version borrowed from [8] of the Needham-Schroeder-Lowe protocol [28] which we denote NSL⊕. In our analysis we use the protocol based on public key encryption, i.e., operators pk and sk satisfying the equations $pk(P, sk(P, M)) = M$ and $sk(P, pk(P, M)) = M$ and the messages are put together using concatenation and exclusive–or. Note that we use a representation of public-key encryption in which only principal P can compute $sk(P, X)$ and everyone can compute $pk(P, X)$. For exclusive–or we have the associativity and commutativity (AC) axioms for $\oplus$, plus the equations[1] $X \oplus 0 = X$, $X \oplus X = 0$, $X \oplus X \oplus Y = Y$.

1. $A \to B : pk(B, N_A; A)$
   A sends to B, encrypted under B's public key, a communication request containing a nonce N_A that has been generated by A, concatenated with its name.
2. $B \to A : pk(A, N_A; B \oplus N_B)$
   B answers with a message encrypted under A's public key, containing the nonce of A, concatenated with the exclusive–or combination of a new nonce created by B and its name.
3. $A \to B : pk(B, N_B)$
   A responds with B's nonce encrypted under B's public key.

A and B agree that they both know N_A and N_B and no one else does.

In the Maude-NPA [15,16], a *state* in the protocol execution is a term t of sort state, $t \in T_{\Sigma_{\mathcal{P}}/E_{\mathcal{P}}}(X)_{state}$. A state is a multiset built by an associative and commutative union operator $\_\&\_$. Each element in the multiset can be a strand or the intruder knowledge at that state (intruder knowledge is wrapped by $\{\_\}$). A *strand* [21] represents the sequence of messages sent and received by a principal executing the protocol and is indicated by a sequence of messages $[msg_1^-, \ msg_2^+, \ msg_3^-, \ldots, \ msg_{k-1}^-, \ msg_k^+]$ where each msg_i is a term of sort Msg (i.e., $msg_i \in T_{\Sigma_{\mathcal{P}}}(X)_{\mathsf{Msg}}$), msg^- represents an input message,

---

[1] The third equation follows from the first two. It is needed for coherence modulo AC.

and msg^+ represents an output message. In Maude-NPA, strands evolve over time and thus we use the symbol $|$ to divide past and future in a strand, i.e., $[msg_1^\pm, \ldots, msg_{j-1}^\pm \mid msg_j^\pm, msg_{j+1}^\pm, \ldots, msg_k^\pm]$ where $msg_1^\pm, \ldots, msg_{j-1}^\pm$ are the past messages, and $msg_j^\pm, msg_{j+1}^\pm, \ldots, msg_k^\pm$ are the future messages ($msg_j^\pm$ is the immediate future message). The *intruder knowledge* is represented as a multiset of facts unioned together with an associative and commutativity union operator $\_,\_$. There are two kinds of intruder facts: positive knowledge facts (the intruder knows m, i.e., $m \in \mathcal{I}$), and negative knowledge facts (the intruder *does not yet know* m but *will know it in a future state*, i.e., $m \notin \mathcal{I}$), where m is a message expression. Facts of the form $m \notin \mathcal{I}$ make sense in a backwards analysis, since one state can have $m \in \mathcal{I}$ and a prior state can have $m \notin \mathcal{I}$.

The strands associated to the three protocol steps above are given next. There are two strands, one for each principal in the protocol. Note that the first message passing $A \rightarrow B : pk(B, N_A; A)$ is represented by a message in Alice's strand sending $(pk(B, n(A, r); A))^+$, together with another message in Bob's strand that receives $(pk(B, N; A))^-$. When a principal cannot observe the contents of a concrete part of a received message (e.g., because a key is necessary to look inside), we use a generic variable for such part of the message in the strand (as with variable N of sort *Nonce* above, and similarly for X, Y below). We encourage the reader to compare the protocol in strand notation to the presentation of the protocol above. We also omit the initial and final *nil* in strands, which are needed in the tool but clutter the presentation.

- (Alice) $:: r :: [(pk(B, n(A, r); A))^+, (pk(A, n(A, r); B \oplus Y))^-, (pk(B, Y))^+]$
- (Bob) $:: r' :: [(pk(B, X; A))^-, (pk(A, X; B \oplus n(B, r')))^+, (pk(B, n(B, r')))^-]$

Note that r, r' are used for nonce generation (they are special variables handled as *unique constants* in order to obtain an infinite number of available constants).

There are also strands for initial knowledge and actions of the intruder, such as concatenation, deconcatenation, encryption, decryption, etc. For example, concatenation by the intruder is described by the strand $[(X)^-, (Y)^-, (X; Y)^+]$. We will show the full list of intruder capabilities in Section 6.

Our protocol analysis methodology is then based on the idea of *backward reachability analysis*, where we begin with one or more state patterns corresponding to *attack states*, and want to prove or disprove that they are *unreachable* from the set of initial protocol states. In order to perform such a reachability analysis we must describe how states change as a consequence of principals performing protocol steps and of intruder actions. This can be done by describing such state changes by means of a set $R_{\mathcal{P}}$ of *rewrite rules*, so that the rewrite theory $(\Sigma_{\mathcal{P}}, E_{\mathcal{P}}, R_{\mathcal{P}})$ characterizes the behavior of protocol $\mathcal{P}$ modulo the equations $E_{\mathcal{P}}$. The following rewrite rules describe the general state transitions, where each state transition implies moving rightwards the vertical bar of one strand:

$$SS \,\&\, [L \mid M^-, L'] \,\&\, \{M \in \mathcal{I}, IK\} \rightarrow SS \,\&\, [L, M^- \mid L'] \,\&\, \{IK\}$$
$$SS \,\&\, [L \mid M^+, L'] \,\&\, \{IK\} \qquad\;\; \rightarrow SS \,\&\, [L, M^+ \mid L'] \,\&\, \{IK\}$$
$$SS \,\&\, [L \mid M^+, L'] \,\&\, \{M \notin \mathcal{I}, IK\} \rightarrow SS \,\&\, [L, M^+ \mid L'] \,\&\, \{M \in \mathcal{I}, IK\}$$

variables L, L' denote lists of input and output messages (m^+, m^-) within a strand, IK denotes a set of intruder facts $(m \in \mathcal{I}, m \notin \mathcal{I})$, and SS denotes a set of strands. An unbounded number of sessions is handled by another rewrite rule introducing an extra strand $[m_1^\pm, \ldots, m_{j-1}^\pm \mid m_j^+, msg_{j+1}^\pm, \ldots, m_k^\pm]$ for an intruder knowledge fact of the form $m_j \in \mathcal{I}$. See [15] for further information.

The way to analyze *backwards* reachability is then relatively easy, namely to run the protocol "in reverse." This can be achieved by using the set of rules $R_{\mathcal{P}}^{-1}$, where $v \longrightarrow u$ is in $R_{\mathcal{P}}^{-1}$ iff $u \longrightarrow v$ is in $R_{\mathcal{P}}$. Reachability analysis can be performed *symbolically*, not on concrete states but on symbolic state patterns $[t(x_1, \ldots, x_n)]$ by means of *narrowing modulo* $E_{\mathcal{P}}$ (see Section 2 and [24,32]).

$E_{\mathcal{P}}$-unification precisely models all the different ways in which an intruder could exploit the algebraic properties $E_{\mathcal{P}}$ of $\mathcal{P}$ to break the protocol; therefore, if an initial state can be shown unreachable by backwards reachability analysis modulo $E_{\mathcal{P}}$ from an attack state pattern, this ensures that, even if the intruder uses the algebraic properties $E_{\mathcal{P}}$, the attack cannot be mounted. This means that efficient support for $E_{\mathcal{P}}$-unification is a crucial feature of symbolic reachability analysis of protocols modulo their algebraic properties $E_{\mathcal{P}}$.

4   A Unification Algorithm for $XOR \cup pk\text{-}sk \cup AC$

In general, combining unification algorithms for a theory $E = E_1 \cup E_2 \cup \ldots \cup E_n$ is computationally quite expensive, and typically assumes that the symbols in E_i and E_j are pairwise disjoint for each $i \neq j$. This is due to the substantial amount of non–determinism involved in the inference systems supporting such combinations (see [3]). In our NSL⊕ example, $E = E_1 \cup E_2 \cup E_3$, where E_1 is the XOR theory, E_2 is the theory *pk-sk* given by the two public key encryption equations $pk(K, sk(K, M)) = M$ and $sk(K, pk(K, M)) = M$, and E_3 is the AC theory for each of the state constructors $\_,\_$ and $\_\&\_$ explained in Section 3. To further complicate the matter, we need to combine not just *untyped* unification algorithms, but typed, and more precisely *order-sorted* ones.

Fortunately, the variant–narrowing–based approach that we use in this paper avoids all these difficulties by obtaining the $(XOR \cup pk\text{-}sk \cup AC)$-unification algorithm as an instance of the *variant narrowing* methodology supported by Maude-NPA. The point is that if an equational theory E has the *finite variant property* [12], then a *finitary* E-unification algorithm can be obtained by *variant narrowing* [20,19], as further explained in Section 5. In our case, the equations in the theory *pk-sk* are confluent and terminating and, furthermore, have the finite variant property. Likewise, the equations in the XOR theory presented in Section 3 are confluent, terminating and coherent modulo the AC axioms of $\oplus$ and also have the finite variant property. Finally, the theory of AC for the state-building constructors $\_,\_$ and $\_\&\_$ is of course finitary and can be viewed as a trivial case of a theory with the finite variant property (decomposed with no rules and only axioms). Note that all these three equational theories are disjoint, i.e., they do not share any symbols. The good news is that the following disjoint union theory $XOR \cup pk\text{-}sk \cup AC$ with $\Sigma_{NSL\oplus}$ being the entire (order-sorted) signature of our NSL⊕ protocol example is also confluent, terminating and coherent modulo the AC axioms[2], and satisfies the finite variant property:

1. *Rules*:
   - $pk(K, sk(K, M)) = M$, $sk(K, pk(K, M)) = M$,
   - $X \oplus 0 = X$, $X \oplus X = 0$, $X \oplus X \oplus Y = Y$,
2. *Axioms*: AC for $\oplus$, AC for $\_,\_$ and AC for $\_\&\_$

Therefore, Maude-NPA can analyze the NSL⊕ protocol using variant narrowing. In the following we explain variant narrowing in more detail.

5   Variant Narrowing and Variant Unification

Suppose that an equational theory $\mathcal{E}$ is decomposed according to the following definition.

Definition 1 (Decomposition [19]). *Let $(\Sigma, \mathcal{E})$ be an order-sorted equational theory. We call (Σ, Ax, E) a decomposition of $(\Sigma, \mathcal{E})$ if $\mathcal{E} = E \uplus Ax$ and (Σ, Ax, E) is an order-sorted rewrite theory satisfying the following properties.*

1. *Ax is regular, i.e., for each $t = t'$ in Ax, we have $Var(t) = Var(t')$, and sort-preserving, i.e., for each substitution σ, we have $t\sigma \in \mathcal{T}_\Sigma(\mathcal{X})_s$ iff $t'\sigma \in \mathcal{T}_\Sigma(\mathcal{X})_s$; furthermore all variables in $Var(t)$ have a top sort.*
2. *Ax has a finitary and complete unification algorithm.*
3. *For each $t \to t'$ in E we have $Var(t') \subseteq Var(t)$.*
4. *E is sort-decreasing, i.e., for each $t \to t'$ in E, each $s \in S$, and each substitution σ, $t'\sigma \in \mathcal{T}_\Sigma(\mathcal{X})_s$ implies $t\sigma \in \mathcal{T}_\Sigma(\mathcal{X})_s$.*
5. *The rewrite rules E are confluent and terminating modulo Ax, i.e., the relation $\to_{E,Ax}$ is confluent and terminating.*
6. *The relation $\to_{E,Ax}$ is Ax-coherent.*

Given a term t, an *E,Ax-variant* of t is a pair (t', θ) with t' an *E,Ax*-canonical form of the term $t\theta$. That is, the variants of a term intuitively give us all the irreducible *patterns* that instances of t can reduce to. Of course, some variants are *more general* than others, i.e., there is a natural preorder $(t', \theta') \sqsubseteq_{E,Ax} (t'', \theta'')$ defining when variant (t'', θ'') is *more general* than variant (t', θ'). This is important, because even though the set of *E,Ax*-variants of a term t may be infinite,

---

[2] All these conditions are easily checkable. Indeed, coherence modulo the combined AC axioms is immediate, and we can use standard methods and tools to check the local confluence and termination of the combined theory; similarly, the method described in [17] can be used to check the finite variant property of the combined theory. Alternatively, one can use *modular* methods to check that a combined theory satisfies all these properties under certain assumptions: see [33] for a good survey of modularity results for confluence and termination. Likewise, the finite variant property can also be checked modularly under appropriate assumptions, but a discussion of this topic is beyond the scope of this paper.

the set of *most general variants* (i.e., maximal elements in the generalization preorder up to Ax-equivalence and variable renaming) may be finite.

The intimate connection of variants with $\mathcal{E}$-unification is then as follows. Suppose that we add to our theory decomposition $E \uplus Ax$ a binary equality predicate eq, a new constant $\mathtt{tt}^3$ and for each top sort $[s]$ and x of sort $[s]$ an extra rule $eq(x, x) \to \mathtt{tt}$. Then, given any two terms t, t', if θ is a $\mathcal{E}$-unifier of t and t', then the E, Ax canonical forms of $t\theta$ and $t'\theta$ must be Ax-equal and therefore the pair $(\mathtt{tt}, \theta)$ must be a variant of the term $eq(t, t')$. Furthermore, if the term $eq(t, t')$ has a finite set of most general variants, then we are *guaranteed* that the set of most general $\mathcal{E}$-unifiers of t and t' is *finite*.

For any theory $E \cup Ax$ with E confluent, terminating, and coherent modulo Ax, the *folding variant narrowing* of [20] is a general and effective *complete* strategy. Complete both in the sense of computing a complete set of $E \cup Ax$-unifiers, and of computing a minimal and complete set of variants for any input term t.

In the following, we characterize a notion of variant semantics for equational theories.

Definition 2 (Variant Semantics [20]). *Let* (Σ, Ax, E) *be a decomposition of an equational theory and t be a term. We define the set of variants of t as* $[\![t]\!]^{\star}_{E, Ax} = \{(t', \theta) \mid \theta \in Subst(\Sigma, \mathcal{X}), t\theta \to^{!}_{E, Ax} t'', \text{ and } t'' =_{Ax} t'\}.$

Example 1. Let us consider the equational theory $XOR \cup pk\text{-}sk$, which, together with AC for $\_,\_$ and $\_\&\_$ is used for our NSL$\oplus$ protocol presented in Section 3. This equational theory is relevant because none of our previously defined unification procedures is directly applicable to it, e.g. unification algorithms for exclusive–or such as [22] do not directly apply if extra equations are added.

For (Σ, Ax, E) a decomposition of $XOR \cup pk\text{-}sk$, and for terms $t = M \oplus sk(K, pk(K, M))$ and $s = X \oplus sk(K, pk(K, Y))$, we have that $[\![t]\!]^{\star}_{E, Ax} = \{(0, id), \ldots\}$ and

$$[\![s]\!]^{\star}_{E, Ax} = \{(X \oplus Y, id),$$
$$(Z, \{X \mapsto 0, Y \mapsto Z\}), (Z, \{X \mapsto Z, Y \mapsto 0\}),$$
$$(Z, \{X \mapsto Z \oplus U, Y \mapsto U\}), (Z, \{X \mapsto U, Y \mapsto Z \oplus U\}),$$
$$(0, \{X \mapsto U, Y \mapsto U\}), (Z_1 \oplus Z_2, \{X \mapsto U \oplus Z_1, Y \mapsto U \oplus Z_2\}),$$
$$(0, \{X \mapsto V \oplus W, Y \mapsto V \oplus W\}), \ldots\}$$

We write $(t_1, \theta_1) \sqsubseteq_{E, Ax} (t_2, \theta_2)$ to denote that variant (t_2, θ_2) is *more general* than variant (t_1, θ_1).

Definition 3 (Variant Preordering [20]). *Let* (Σ, Ax, E) *be a decomposition of an equational theory and t be a term. Given two variants* $(t_1, \theta_1), (t_2, \theta_2) \in [\![t]\!]^{\star}_{E, Ax}$, *we write* $(t_1, \theta_1) \sqsubseteq_{E, Ax} (t_2, \theta_2)$, *meaning* (t_2, θ_2) *is more general than* (t_1, θ_1), *iff there is a substitution ρ such that* $t_1 =_{Ax} t_2 \rho$ *and* $\theta_1 \downarrow_{E, Ax} =_{Ax} \theta_2 \rho$. *We write* $(t_1, \theta_1) \sqsubset_{E, Ax} (t_2, \theta_2)$ *if for every substitution ρ such that* $t_1 =_{Ax} t_2 \rho$ *and* $\theta_1 \downarrow_{E, Ax} =_{Ax} \theta_2 \rho$, *then ρ is not a renaming.*

---

[3] We extend Σ to $\widehat{\Sigma}$ by adding a new sort Truth, not related to any sort in Σ, with constant $\mathtt{tt}$, and for each top sort $[s]$ of a connected component, an operator $eq : [s] \times [s] \to$ Truth.

Example 2. Continuing Example 1 we have $v_1 = (0, \{X \mapsto U, Y \mapsto U\})$ as a valid variant of s. Also, $v_2 = (0, \{X \mapsto V \oplus W, Y \mapsto V \oplus W\})$ is a valid variant of s but clearly $v_2 \sqsubseteq_{E,Ax} v_1$, and thus v_2 should not be included in the most general set of variants. On the other hand for $u_1 = (X \oplus Y, id)$ and $u_2 = (Z, \{X \mapsto 0, Y \mapsto Z\})$, we have that neither $u_1 \sqsubseteq_{E,Ax} u_2$ nor $u_2 \sqsubseteq_{E,Ax} u_1$ hold.

We are, indeed, interested in equivalence classes for variant semantics and provide a notion of equivalence of variants up to renaming, written $\approx_{Ax}$.

Definition 4 (Ax-Equivalence [20]). *Let (Σ, Ax, E) be a decomposition of an equational theory and t be a term. For $(t_1, \theta_1), (t_2, \theta_2) \in [\![t]\!]^{*}_{E,Ax}$, we write $(t_1, \theta_1) \approx_{Ax} (t_2, \theta_2)$ if there is a variable renaming ρ such that $t_1 \rho =_{Ax} t_2 \rho$ and $\theta_1 \rho =_{Ax} \theta_2 \rho$. For $S_1, S_2 \subseteq [\![t]\!]^{*}_{E,Ax}$, we write $S_1 \approx_{Ax} S_2$ if for each $(t_1, \theta_1) \in S_1$, there exists $(t_2, \theta_2) \in S_2$ s.t. $(t_1, \theta_1) \approx_{Ax} (t_2, \theta_2)$, and for each $(t_2, \theta_2) \in S_2$, there exists $(t_1, \theta_1) \in S_1$ s.t. $(t_2, \theta_2) \approx_{Ax} (t_1, \theta_1)$.*

The preorder of Definition 3 allows us to provide a most general and complete set of variants that encompasses all the variants for a term t.

Definition 5 (Most General and Complete Variant Semantics [20]). *Let (Σ, Ax, E) be a decomposition of an equational theory and t be a term. A most general and complete variant semantics of t, denoted $[\![t]\!]_{E,Ax}$, is a subset $[\![t]\!]_{E,Ax} \subseteq [\![t]\!]^{*}_{E,Ax}$ such that: (i) $[\![t]\!]^{*}_{E,Ax} \sqsubseteq_{E,Ax} [\![t]\!]_{E,Ax}$, and (ii) for each $(t_1, \theta_1) \in [\![t]\!]_{E,Ax}$, there is no $(t_2, \theta_2) \in [\![t]\!]_{E,Ax}$ s.t. $(t_1, \theta_1) \not\approx_{Ax} (t_2, \theta_2)$ and $(t_1, \theta_1) \sqsubseteq_{E,Ax} (t_2, \theta_2)$.*

Example 3. Continuing Example 1 it is obvious that the following variants are most general w.r.t. $\sqsubseteq_{E,Ax}$: $[\![t]\!]_{E,Ax} = \{(0, id)\}$ and

$$[\![s]\!]_{E,Ax} = \{(X \oplus Y, id),$$
$$(Z, \{X \mapsto 0, Y \mapsto Z\}), (Z, \{X \mapsto Z, Y \mapsto 0\}),$$
$$(Z, \{X \mapsto Z \oplus U, Y \mapsto U\}), (Z, \{X \mapsto U, Y \mapsto Z \oplus U\}),$$
$$(0, \{X \mapsto U, Y \mapsto U\}), (Z_1 \oplus Z_2, \{X \mapsto U \oplus Z_1, Y \mapsto U \oplus Z_2\})\}.$$

Note that, by definition, all the substitutions in $[\![t]\!]_{E,Ax}$ are E,Ax-normalized. Moreover, $[\![t]\!]_{E,Ax}$ is unique up to $\approx_{Ax}$ and provides a very succinct description of $[\![t]\!]^{*}_{E,Ax}$. Indeed, up to Ax-equality, $[\![t]\!]_{E,Ax}$ characterizes the set of *maximal elements* (therefore, most general variants) of the preorder $([\![t]\!]^{*}_{E,Ax}, \sqsubseteq_{E,Ax})$.

Again, let us make explicit the relation between variants and $\mathcal{E}$-unification.

Proposition 1 (Minimal and Complete $\mathcal{E}$-unification [20]). *Let (Σ, Ax, E) be a decomposition of an equational theory $(\Sigma, \mathcal{E})$. Let t, t' be two terms. Then, $S = \{\theta \mid (\mathtt{tt}, \theta) \in [\![eq(t, t')]\!]_{\widehat{E},Ax}\}$ is a minimal and complete set of $\mathcal{E}$-unifiers for $t = t'$, where eq and tt are new symbols defined in Footnote 3 and $\widehat{E} = E \cup \{eq(X, X) \to \mathtt{tt}\}$.*

The *finite variant property* defined by Comon-Lundh and Delaune [12], provides a useful sufficient condition for finitary $\mathcal{E}$-unification. Essentially, it determines whether every term has a finite number of most general variants.

Definition 6 (Finite variant property [12]). *Let (Σ, Ax, E) be a decomposition of an equational theory $(\Sigma, \mathcal{E})$. Then $(\Sigma, \mathcal{E})$, and thus (Σ, Ax, E), has the finite variant property iff for each term t, the set $[\![t]\!]_{E,Ax}$ is finite. We will call (Σ, Ax, E) a finite variant decomposition of $(\Sigma, \mathcal{E})$ iff (Σ, Ax, E) has the finite variant property.*

In [18] a technique is proposed to check whether an equational theory has the finite variant property. Using this technique it is easy to check that Example 1 has the finite variant property, as every right–hand side is a constant symbol or a variable. See [18, Example 2] for more details.

Finally, it is clear that when we have a finite variant decomposition, we also have a finitary unification algorithm.

Corollary 1 (Finitary $\mathcal{E}$-unification [20]). *Let (Σ, Ax, E) be a finite variant decomposition of an equational theory $(\Sigma, \mathcal{E})$. Then, for any two given terms t, t', $S = \{\theta \mid (\mathtt{tt}, \theta) \in [\![\mathtt{eq}(t, t')]\!]_{\widehat{E}, Ax}\}$ is a finite, minimal, and complete set of $\mathcal{E}$-unifiers for $t = t'$, where $\widehat{E}$, eq, and tt are defined as in Proposition 1.*

Note that the opposite does not hold: given two terms t, t' that have a finite, minimal, and complete set of $\mathcal{E}$-unifiers, the equational theory $(\Sigma, \mathcal{E})$ may not have a finite variant decomposition (Σ, Ax, E). An example is the unification under homomorphism (or one-side distributivity), where there is a finite number of unifiers of two terms but the theory does not satisfy the finite variant property (see [12,18]); the key idea is that the term $\mathtt{eq}(t, t')$ may have an infinite number of variants even though there is only a finite set of most general variants of the form $(\mathtt{tt}, \theta)$. We refer the reader to [20] for further information.

Currently, Maude-NPA restricts itself to a subset of theories satisfying the finite variant property:

1. The axioms Ax can declare some binary operators in Σ to be commutative (with the `comm` attribute), or associative-commutative (with the `assoc` and `comm` attributes).
2. The set of rewrite rules E is *strongly right irreducible*, that is no instance of the right-hand side of a rule in E by a normalized substitution can be further simplified by the application the equations in E modulo Ax.

The reasons for restricting ourselves in this way is for efficiency and ease of implementation. Maude currently supports unification modulo commutative and associative-commutative theories, as well as syntactic unification, so this is what drives our choice of Ax. Furthermore, the restriction of E to strongly right irreducible theories means that the depth of the narrowing tree is bounded by the number of symbols in a term. Moreover, many of the finite variant theories that arise in cryptographic protocol analysis satisfy strong right irreducibility. These include encryption-decryption cancellation, exclusive-or, and modular exponentiation. The major exception is Abelian groups (other than those described by exclusive-or). We are currently working on implementing full variant narrowing in Maude-NPA to handle these and other cases not currently covered by strong right irreducibility.

6   Finding Attacks Modulo $XOR \cup pk\text{-}sk \cup AC$ Using Maude-NPA

We have analyzed the NSL⊕ protocol presented in Section 3 modulo its equational theory $XOR \cup pk\text{-}sk \cup AC$ in Maude-NPA using variant narrowing.

We now explain in more detail all the operations available to the intruder. Its capabilities are all given in strand notation. Note that we are omitting the position marker | which is assumed to be at the beginning.

(s1) $[(X)^-, (Y)^-, (X;Y)^+]$ Concatenation
(s2) $[(X;Y)^-, (X)^+]$ Left-deconcatenation
(s3) $[(X;Y)^-, (Y)^+]$ Right-deconcatenation
(s4) $[(X)^-, (Y)^-, (X{\oplus}Y)^+]$ Exclusive–or
(s6) $[(X)^-, (sk(i, X))^+]$ Encryption with i's private key
(s7) $[(X)^-, (pk(A, X))^+]$ Encryption with any public key
(s8) $[(0)^+]$ Generate the exclusive–or neutral element
(s9) $[(A)^+]$ Generate any principal's name.

The attack state pattern from which we start the backwards narrowing search in this example is given by one strand, representing Bob (b) wanting to communicate with Alice (a)

$$:: r :: [(pk(b, X; a))^-, (pk(a, X; b{\oplus}n(b, r)))^+, (pk(b, n(b, r)))^- | nil]$$

together with requiring the intruder (i) to have learned Bob's nonce, i.e., $n(b, r){\in}\mathcal{I}$. What this represents is an attack in which Bob has properly executed the protocol and believes to be talking to Alice, while the intruder has obtained the nonce that Bob created and considers a secret shared between Alice and him.

See Figure 1 for a pictorial representation of the strand space and messages sent and received, depicting the attack found by Maude-NPA. This attack agrees with the one described in [8]. The figure has been created with the help of the Maude-NPA GUI [34], with the exclusive–or symbol ⊕ textually represented as * in the figure.

7   Related Work

There is a substantial amount of research on formal verification of cryptographic protocols. Much of it abstracts away from any equational theories obeyed by the cryptographic operators, but there is a growing amount of work addressing this

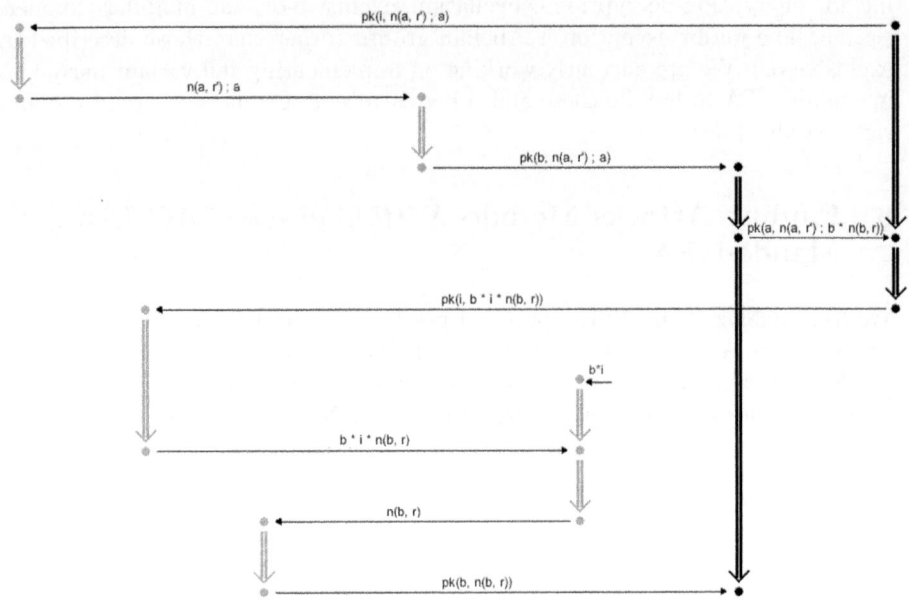

Fig. 1. Pictorial representation of the initial state, leading to an attack

problem. The earliest was the NRL Protocol Analyzer [29], which, like Maude-NPA, was based on unification and backwards search, implemented via narrowing over confluent equational theories. This was sufficient to handle, for example, the cancellation of encryption and decryption, although there were many theories of interest it did not address, such as exclusive-or and other Abelian group operators.

More recently, tools have begun to offer support for specification and, to some degree, analysis of protocols involving equational theories. These tools include, for example, ProVerif [6], OFMC [4], and CL-Atse [37]. Both OFMC and CL-Atse work in the bounded session model, while ProVerif uses abstraction and unbounded sessions. Both OFMC and CL-Atse support exclusive-or and Diffie-Hellman exponentiation. ProVerif can also be used to analyze these, but the equational theories it is known to work well with are more limited, e.g. not supporting associativity-commutativity or Diffie-Hellman exponentiation. However, Küsters and Truderung [25,26] have developed algorithms that can translate protocols using exclusive-or or Diffie-Hellman exponentiation to protocols that can be analyzed by ProVerif in a free algebra model; for exclusive-or they can handle protocols satisfying the $\oplus$-linearity property. According to a study by Lafourcade et al. [27], this produces analysis times that are only slightly slower than analyses by OFMC and CL-Atse, mainly because of the translation time.

There is also a growing amount of theoretical work on cryptographic protocol analysis using equational theories, e.g. [1,9,7,11,5]. This concentrates on the decidability of problems of interest to cryptographic protocol analysis, such as deducibility, which means that it is possible (e.g. for an intruder) to deduce a term from a set of terms, and static equivalence, which means that an intruder cannot tell the difference between two sets of terms. However, there is much less work on the combination of different theories, although Arnaud, Cortier, and Delaune [13] have considered the problem in terms of decidability of the problem for combination of disjoint theories, showing that if any two disjoint theories have decidable static equivalence problems, then so does their combination. More recently Chevalier and Rusinowitch analyze the security of cryptographic protocols via constraint systems and have also studied composition of theories. In [10], they give a general method for combining disjoint theories that is based on the Baader-Schulz combination algorithm for unification algorithms for different theories [3]. This can be thought of as a constraint-based analogue of the Maude-NPA combination framework, which is also based on the Baader-Schulz combination algorithm [3].

8   Conclusions and Future Work

To gain high assurance about cryptographic protocols using formal methods requires reasoning modulo the algebraic properties of the underlying cryptographic functions. In symbolic analyses this typically necessitates performing unification *modulo* such algebraic properties. However, since a protocol may use a variety of different functions —so that different protocols typically require reasoning modulo different theories— it is unrealistic to expect that a fixed set of unification algorithms will suffice for such analyses. That is, *combination methods* that obtain unification algorithm for a composition of theories out of a family of such algorithm for each of them, are unavoidable. Standard methods for obtaining a unification algorithm for a combined theory $E_1 \cup \ldots \cup E_n$ [3] are computationally costly due to the high degree of non-determinism in the combination method; furthermore, they require the existence of a unification algorithm for each individual theory E_i, which in practice may not be available in a tool's infrastructure. In this work we have proposed an alternative method based on *variant narrowing* to obtain a $(E_1 \cup \ldots \cup E_n)$-unification algorithm under simpler requirements. Specifically, dedicated implementations of unification algorithms for each of the theories E_i are not needed: in our example, only a dedicated *AC*-unification algorithm was used: no dedicated algorithms for *XOR* of *pk-sk* were needed. Furthermore, even though narrowing is less efficient than a dedicated algorithm for each individual theory E_i, the costly computational overhead of a standard combination method is avoided. The case study presented has shown that variant narrowing, as supported by the Maude-NPA, is indeed an effective method to deal with nontrivial combinations of equational theories; and for analyzing many protocols with even a modest infrastructure of built-in unification algorithms. The case study was chosen as a well-known protocol for illustration purposes, but many other examples could have been given.

We should emphasize that standard combination methods such as those described in [3], and the alternative variant narrowing method presented here are not "rival" methods. Instead they are highly *complementary* methods which, when used *in tandem*, allow a tool to analyze a much wider range of protocols than those analyzable by each method in isolation. Let us use our example theory $XOR \cup pk\text{-}sk \cup AC$ to illustrate this important point. Variant narrowing decomposed this combined theory into: (i) three rewrite rules for XOR and two rewrite rules for $pk\text{-}sk$ plus, (ii) three instances of AC: one for $\oplus$, another for $\_,\_$ and another for $\_\&\_$. That is, variant narrowing with the rules in (i) was performed *modulo* the axioms in (ii). But the axioms in (ii) are themselves a *combined theory* (in fact, also combined with all the other function symbols in the protocol specification as free function symbols). The Maude infrastructure used by Maude-NPA has in fact used an order-sorted version of a standard combination method in the style of [3] to support unification with the combined axioms of (ii). Therefore, the advantage of using standard combination methods and variant narrowing in tandem is the following:

1. A given tool infrastructure can only have a finite number of predefined (finitary) unification algorithms for, say, theories $T_1, \dots, T_k$; however, it should also be able to support any combination of such built-in theories by a standard combination method.
2. A given protocol may require performing unification modulo a combination of theories $E_1 \cup \dots \cup E_n$, but some of the E_i may not belong to the library $T_1, \dots, T_k$, so that the standard combination method cannot be used.
3. However, if $E_1 \cup \dots \cup E_n$ can be *refactored* as a theory decomposition (Σ, B, R) that: (i) it has the finite variant property; and (ii) B is a combination of the theories $T_1, \dots, T_k$ supported by the current library, then a *finitary* $(E_1 \cup \dots \cup E_n)$-unification algorithm can be obtained by variant narrowing.

A very important direction for future work in formal tools supporting symbolic protocol analysis modulo equational properties consists in: (i) developing methods for expanding a tool's built-in unification infrastructure as described in (1) above to make it as efficient and extensible as possible; and (ii) improving and optimizing the methods for efficient variant narrowing modulo such infrastructure. Good candidates for new theories T_j to be added to the built-in infrastructure include commonly used theories, with high priority given to theories that lack the finite variant properties. For example, the theory of homomorphic encryption, which lacks the finite variant property, has been recently added to Maude-NPA for exactly this purpose.

References

1. Abadi, M., Cortier, V.: Deciding knowledge in security protocols under equational theories. Theoretical Computer Science 367(1-2), 2–32 (2006)
2. Armando, A., Basin, D.A., Boichut, Y., Chevalier, Y., Compagna, L., Cuéllar, J., Drielsma, P.H., Héam, P.-C., Kouchnarenko, O., Mantovani, J., Mödersheim, S., von Oheimb, D., Rusinowitch, M., Santiago, J., Turuani, M., Viganò, L., Vigneron, L.: The avispa tool for the automated validation of internet security protocols and applications. In: Etessami, K., Rajamani, S.K. (eds.) CAV 2005. LNCS, vol. 3576, pp. 281–285. Springer, Heidelberg (2005)

3. Baader, F., Schulz, K.U.: Unification in the union of disjoint equational theories: Combining decision procedures. In: Kapur, D. (ed.) CADE 1992. LNCS, vol. 607, pp. 50–65. Springer, Heidelberg (1992)

4. Basin, D.A., Mödersheim, S., Viganò, L.: An on-the-fly model-checker for security protocol analysis. In: Snekkenes, E., Gollmann, D. (eds.) ESORICS 2003. LNCS, vol. 2808, pp. 253–270. Springer, Heidelberg (2003)

5. Baudet, M., Cortier, V., Delaune, S.: YAPA: A generic tool for computing intruder knowledge. In: Treinen, R. (ed.) RTA 2009. LNCS, vol. 5595, pp. 148–163. Springer, Heidelberg (2009)

6. Blanchet, B.: An efficient cryptographic protocol verifier based on prolog rules. In: CSFW, pp. 82–96. IEEE Computer Society, Los Alamitos (2001)

7. Bursuc, S., Comon-Lundh, H.: Protocol security and algebraic properties: Decision results for a bounded number of sessions. In: Treinen, R. (ed.) RTA 2009. LNCS, vol. 5595, pp. 133–147. Springer, Heidelberg (2009)

8. Chevalier, Y., Küsters, R., Rusinowitch, M., Turuani, M.: An NP decision procedure for protocol insecurity with XOR. In: LICS, pp. 261–270. IEEE Computer Society, Los Alamitos (2003)

9. Chevalier, Y., Rusinowitch, M.: Hierarchical combination of intruder theories. Inf. Comput. 206(2-4), 352–377 (2008)

10. Chevalier, Y., Rusinowitch, M.: Symbolic protocol analysis in the union of disjoint intruder theories: Combining decision procedures. Theor. Comput. Sci. 411(10), 1261–1282 (2010)

11. Ciobâcă, Ş., Delaune, S., Kremer, S.: Computing knowledge in security protocols under convergent equational theories. In: Schmidt, R.A. (ed.) CADE-22. LNCS, vol. 5663, pp. 355–370. Springer, Heidelberg (2009)

12. Comon-Lundh, H., Delaune, S.: The finite variant property: How to get rid of some algebraic properties. In: Giesl, J. (ed.) RTA 2005. LNCS, vol. 3467, pp. 294–307. Springer, Heidelberg (2005)

13. Cortier, V., Delaitre, J., Delaune, S.: Safely composing security protocols. In: Arvind, V., Prasad, S. (eds.) FSTTCS 2007. LNCS, vol. 4855, pp. 352–363. Springer, Heidelberg (2007)

14. Cremers, C.J.F.: The scyther tool: Verification, falsification, and analysis of security protocols. In: Gupta, A., Malik, S. (eds.) CAV 2008. LNCS, vol. 5123, pp. 414–418. Springer, Heidelberg (2008)

15. Escobar, S., Meadows, C., Meseguer, J.: A rewriting-based inference system for the NRL protocol analyzer and its meta-logical properties. Theoretical Computer Science 367(1-2), 162–202 (2006)

16. Escobar, S., Meadows, C., Meseguer, J.: Maude-NPA: Cryptographic protocol analysis modulo equational properties. In: Aldini, A., Barthe, G., Gorrieri, R. (eds.) FOSAD 2007/2008/2009 Tutorial Lectures. LNCS, vol. 5705, pp. 1–50. Springer, Heidelberg (2009)

17. Escobar, S., Meseguer, J., Sasse, R.: Effectively checking or disproving the finite variant property. Technical Report UIUCDCS-R-2008-2960, Department of Computer Science - University of Illinois at Urbana-Champaign (April 2008)

18. Escobar, S., Meseguer, J., Sasse, R.: Effectively checking the finite variant property. In: Voronkov, A. (ed.) RTA 2008. LNCS, vol. 5117, pp. 79–93. Springer, Heidelberg (2008)

19. Escobar, S., Meseguer, J., Sasse, R.: Variant narrowing and equational unification. Electr. Notes Theor. Comput. Sci. 238(3), 103–119 (2009)

20. Escobar, S., Sasse, R., Meseguer, J.: Folding variant narrowing and optimal variant termination. In: Ölveczky, P.C. (ed.) WRLA 2010. LNCS, vol. 6381, pp. 52–68. Springer, Heidelberg (2010)
21. Fabrega, F.J.T., Herzog, J., Guttman, J.: Strand Spaces: What Makes a Security Protocol Correct? Journal of Computer Security 7, 191–230 (1999)
22. Guo, Q., Narendran, P.: Unification and matching modulo nilpotence. In: CADE-13. LNCS, vol. 1104, pp. 261–274. Springer, Heidelberg (1996)
23. Harkins, D., Carrel, D.: The Internet Key Exchange (IKE), IETF RFC 2409, (November 1998)
24. Jouannaud, J.-P., Kirchner, C., Kirchner, H.: Incremental construction of unification algorithms in equational theories. In: Díaz, J. (ed.) ICALP 1983. LNCS, vol. 154, pp. 361–373. Springer, Heidelberg (1983)
25. Küsters, R., Truderung, T.: Reducing protocol analysis with xor to the xor-free case in the Horn theory based approach. In: ACM Conference on Computer and Communications Security, pp. 129–138 (2008)
26. Küsters, R., Truderung, T.: Using ProVerif to analyze protocols with Diffie-Hellman exponentiation. In: CSF, pp. 157–171. IEEE Computer Society, Los Alamitos (2009)
27. Lafourcade, P., Terrade, V., Vigier, S.: Comparison of cryptographic verification tools dealing with algebraic properties. In: Degano, P., Guttman, J.D. (eds.) FAST 2009. LNCS, vol. 5983, pp. 173–185. Springer, Heidelberg (2010)
28. Lowe, G.: Breaking and fixing the Needham-Schroeder public-key protocol using FDR. In: Margaria, T., Steffen, B. (eds.) TACAS 1996. LNCS, vol. 1055, pp. 147–166. Springer, Heidelberg (1996)
29. Meadows, C.: The NRL protocol analyzer: An overview. J. Log. Program. 26(2), 113–131 (1996)
30. Meseguer, J.: Conditional rewriting logic as a united model of concurrency. Theor. Comput. Sci. 96(1), 73–155 (1992)
31. Meseguer, J.: Membership algebra as a logical framework for equational specification. In: Parisi-Presicce, F. (ed.) WADT 1997. LNCS, vol. 1376, pp. 18–61. Springer, Heidelberg (1998)
32. Meseguer, J., Thati, P.: Symbolic reachability analysis using narrowing and its application to verification of cryptographic protocols. Higher-Order and Symbolic Computation 20(1–2), 123–160 (2007)
33. Ohlebusch, E.: Advanced Topics in Term Rewriting. Springer, Heidelberg (2002)
34. Santiago, S., Talcott, C.L., Escobar, S., Meadows, C., Meseguer, J.: A graphical user interface for Maude-NPA. Electr. Notes Theor. Comput. Sci. 258(1), 3–20 (2009)
35. Schmidt-Schauß, M.: Unification in a combination of arbitrary disjoint equational theories. J. Symb. Comput. 8(1/2), 51–99 (1989)
36. Terese (ed.): Term Rewriting Systems. Cambridge University Press, Cambridge (2003)
37. Turuani, M.: The CL-atse protocol analyser. In: Pfenning, F. (ed.) RTA 2006. LNCS, vol. 4098, pp. 277–286. Springer, Heidelberg (2006)

Defamation-Free Networks through User-Centered Data Control

Nadim Sarrouh, Florian Eilers, Uwe Nestmann, and Ina Schieferdecker

Technische Universität Berlin, Germany
{n.sarrouh,f.eilers,uwe.nestmann}@tu-berlin.de,
ina.schieferdecker@fokus.fraunhofer.de

Abstract. Existing online social networks hardly care about users' privacy rights. In particular, they do not permit users to keep control over "their" data. By "their" data, we denote data that refers to the respective user as an identifiable object within (textual, audio, image or video) media. The well-known concept of "usage control" employs a usage rights' perspective (e.g. DRM), but it does not explicitly deal with privacy. In this paper, we instead propose the concept of "data control", which exactly focusses on privacy rights and therefore employs a control rights' perspective. Based on data control, we propose a defamation-free network (DFN) in which control rights are not only manifest and visible, but can also be exercised. We examine the main usage scenarios of such a network, and discuss the possible approaches for implementing it. Finally, we sketch a solution with an underlying P2P architecture and highlight the basic technological challenges and requirements.

Keywords: Privacy, Social Networks, Usage Control, P2P, Web of Trust.

1 Introduction

Today it is common for employers to search the web for crediting or discrediting information about prospective employees. *Google*'s new mobile phone "Nexus One" proposes applications, through which users may get all the online information available concerning the person that you took a picture of, using the internal camera. Google-CEO Eric Schmidt states, not as ironically as one would hope: "If you have something that you don't want anyone to know, maybe you shouldn't be doing it in the first place." [1]

This kind of user transparency is undesirable in many cases. It is obvious that the liability for these circumstances cannot simply be seen with the data storage or search providers such as *Google*. Users themselves have to become sensible concerning their own privacy. They have to be made aware of possible dangers of unconditional personal exposure on the web. However, apart from these social aspects, the technology itself should provide better means not only to raise awareness but also to provide tools to deal with threatening exposure or defamation.

---

[1] For this statement watch Eric Schmidt on privacy on *Youtube*:
http://www.youtube.com/watch?v=A6e7wfDHzew\&feature=player_embedded
Last checked: 25.03.10.

J. Cuellar et al. (Eds.): STM 2010, LNCS 6710, pp. 179–193, 2011.

Several existing online services such as "DeinGuterRuf.de"[2] offer to help the user with finding and erasing this kind of data from the Internet on a commercial basis. These companies enforce the erasing of the data and relieve the user of the stressful and complicated communication with responsible website owners. If the Web site owner does not yield to the demand, legal steps may be taken in most countries in order to force him to delete this data. However, considering the distributed content-centric architecture of the web, there is up to date no technical solution to enforce those rights at an infrastructural level.

We believe that, considering these rising challenges of privacy, it is necessary to develop a new infrastructure in which the user not only has control over the distribution and usage of user-owned data (usage rights) but also over associated data (data that identifies the user in some way) posted by others (privacy rights). To this end, it is essential to investigate new technologies that enforce rights of the individual at a technical level.

Within this paper, following the summary of related work in section 2, we define data control in this privacy context in section 3. We derive four levels of data control and examine the main scenarios that an architecture with privacy control would have to stand up to. We conclude the third section with a list of basic technological requirements for implementing such an architecture. In section 4 we discuss the suitability of centralized and decentralized approaches. Finally, in section 5, we propose the development of a defamation-free P2P online social network and sketch the main basic challenges of such a Defamation-Free Network (DFN) before we come to our conclusion and outline future work in section 6 and 7.

2   Related Work

The nearest approach to our proposal is Castelluccia's "Owner-Centric Network" [4]. He considers a novel network architecture in which users may track where they stored data themselves, so that it may easily be retrieved and if necessary modified or deleted by the owner. Users would then be able to control the flow of their own data and access control mechanisms would prevent other users to download or change this data. However, Castellucia's approach does not consider any degree of control over personal data, which is spread by others and therefore does not satisfy our requirements for enhanced data control.

Research concerning P2P social networks has been lately very popular. The two approaches most suitable to our data control requirements are *Safebook* [5] and the *Peerson Project* [2]. Among these two platforms, the *Safebook* platform seems slighty further developed; therefore, it also looks more promising as a potential basis for an implementation of a DFN. For a concrete solution proposal see section 5.

Usage control concepts, platforms and enforcement mechanisms exist in a variety too big to cover in this paper. The most common model for usage control is the *UCONabc*-model [9], which proposes a novel view on data objects,

---

[2] http://deinguterruf.de/ Last checked: 25.03.10.

consisting not only of the data itself, but of usage rights, obligations and conditions. Several researchers have tried to implement this concept or a variation of it. Pretschner et al. invented a policy language and formal means to express usage control mechanisms in a verifiable way. Based on these formalizations they have proposed a usage control architecture based on an *X11* and data flow tracking [11]. Alam et al. suggested a *SElinux* with *mandatory access control (MAC)* in order to enforce policies concerning data [1].

3   Data Control

In this section, we provide our view of data control. We start by pointing out the difference to the concept of traditional usage control and formulate an approach for possible data control levels. Finally, we motivate which data control level we want to enforce with our conceptual architecture.

3.1   Data Control vs. Usage Control

The concept of usage control consists of data-object specific authorization and access monitoring and enforcement mechanisms, which are to enable the constraining of future usage of data after it is released from its own environment into a different control domain. In order to get data from the data provider negotiations concerning the usage of this data take place. These negotiations result in a usage policy which is transferred together with the data, assuming the client is indeed able to enforce this policy through a local usage control platform. The usage control platform transfers the policies and (by monitoring the access and usage of the data) ensures that its constraints are enforced properly[10].

This concept is relevant for commercial online data distribution, e.g. in *digital rights management (DRM)*. An example scenario could be: "viewing this movie is permitted 5 times only and will be denied after 48 hours". Also medical applications especially considering Electronic Health Records may benefit from usage control mechanisms. Hafner et al. propose a usage control architecture in order to provide patients with the means to enforce their privacy in scenarios like: "Access to a medical record is allowed for 5 times only and should last for 48 hours, after its first access"[8].

As opposed to usage control's provider-consumer scheme, we propose the concept of data control. Just like usage control this notion is a collection of mechanisms. However, it does not exclusively deal with usage rights, but focusses on privacy rights. It provides mechanisms and tools that allow control over personal data spread throughout a network. Users have the possibility to get an overview of data that identifies them no matter if published by them or by others. They may even get the rights to unpublish it. We point out that such rights do not only apply to user-owned data. Associated data published by others which involves the user or in the worst case defames or discredits him, has to be controlled in the same manner.

The data control concept is relevant for personal use, but also suitable for groups or cooperations since actors do not have to be natural but can also be

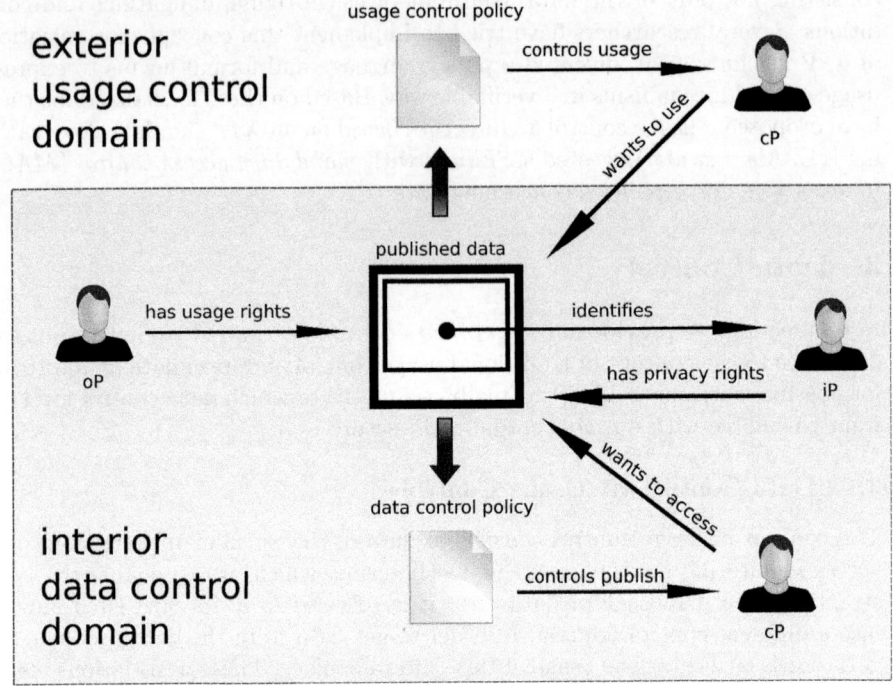

Fig. 1. Data control and usage control perspectives

legal bodies. One basic scenario would be: "How can I prevent that my employer gets hold of compromising data about me?"

Summarizing, the main differences of usage control and data control are based on different perspectives. While usage control is content-centered and focuses on the enforcement of usage rights, after data has been delivered from the owners domain to another environment, user-centered data control focusses on a user's privacy rights inside a social network and delivers tools and means to enforce his privacy inside this domain. Usage control and data control are therefore complementary concepts. Figure 1 visualizes a scenario where usage control is used as an extension of data control. Users are categorized into three roles: Owning persons (oP) may enforce usage and privacy rights on the data they own. Persons identified in published data (iP) may enforce their own privacy rights. Consuming persons (cP) may want to view or use the data and to do so must accept the terms of data control or usage control policies.

We identify four levels of data control, focusing on different aspects of data:

Data Control Level I. This basic level deals with the bare linking of data to users. Links are publicly visible associations of data to users, normally made manually by the user himself or by his friends. This level describes the possibility to get an overview over which data in the network is linked to the user's profile and the ability to unlink it. (e.g. Facebook photo links). The main motivation of establishing this data control level would be the argument that only data that is linked to a user can be found by using a name, dates, etc. Therefore it may be enough to delete these links in order to establish control over defaming or discrediting data.

Data Control Level II. Like level I, but including the possibility to not only overview data that is linked to a user's profile but also to find unlinked data associated to them. Associations fundamentally differ from links: They are automatically generated relations from data to users and are not publicly displayed. The only person aware of associations to data is the actual associated user. To get an overview of these associations, the infrastructure has to be equipped with content recognition algorithms. The content recognition would be triggered during the publishing of the data. This content recognition will be a mixture of automated and interactive processes (e.g. "Is that you?"). Associated users would then be informed about new data available about them. With data control level II comes also the ability to prohibit a future linking of this data to a user's profile. However, since it only focusses on linkage, this level does not grant any unpublishing rights to the user. In order to actually unpublish data, we define the next level. To our knowledge there exists no social network application today that provides this kind of functionality.

Data Control Level III. Like level II, but including the possibility to unpublish data about a user from network. In order to provide these features the associated users will have to be provided with rights so that even users who do not own the data are able to enforce their rights upon the data.

Data Control Level IV. Like level III, but including usage control mechanisms that extend the control over user-owned data to the control over usage outside of the infrastructure (e.g. on offline machines etc.). These mechanisms would provide the possibility to constrain the usage of personal data in scenarios like: view, change or copy. This includes the necessity for trusted platforms, monitors, signalers and a rigid policy management. Policies could be generated from configurations, which the data owner applies to his data.

The relation between usage control and data control can be derived from these data control levels. While the first three levels focus on data control of the system's interior, the fourth level considers data that leaves the system onto the platform of a cP in an exterior domain. It is obvious that usage control mechanisms extend the control over personal data; However, only the oP may enforce the usage of his data and no iP will get those exclusive usage control rights. This is no technical short-coming but a social one: If somebody took a picture of the Eiffel Tower, with another person in it, this person is not able to force the photographer to not use this picture for his private purpose or even show or give it to his friends. This fact depicts a fundamental difference to data control levels I-III.

Hence we focus on data control level III leaving the implementation of level IV as optional, in order to establish even more control over personal data. Several usage control architectures have been proposed in literature [1][10][11], which could help to establish data control level IV as an addition to the first three levels.

It is important to acknowledge that our concept of Data Control has to deal with questions of privacy opposed to the right of expression or the right of information, which could be severly limited by our proposed architecture. Although we believe that privacy in an online context is of particular importance and therefor legitimate the use of Data Control tools, it might be necesarry to discuss this matter in future work. However we focus on the conceptional implementation of A DFN and therefor do not particularly discuss moral, ethic or law issues.

3.2   Data Control Scenarios

In this section we describe the basic scenarios to which a data control platform would have to stand up to as well as the main technical components to support these scenarios. After these descriptions, we summarize the conceptional needs in order to implement this data control platform.

Scenario I: Publish Data. The first scenario is in fact the most important one because it deals with the publishing process of data. The analyzing, associating, and categorizing of this data is essential in order to establish data control level III.

We propose a data publish control mechanism. This mechanism, in fact an aggregation of several content recognition and data control mechanisms, comes into action as soon as a user publishes to the network.[3] Before that, the data publish control checks the data for associations to other persons (e.g. face-recognition, names, etc). If the mechanisms find iPs in the data it checks if the iPs are part of the network and in this case notifies the user in question.

If the iP can not be found, because he is (not yet) part of the network, the meta–information will be stored in a database for unknown associations in order to make it possible to link this data at a later date. It is advisable to implement a fine-grained categorization of this meta–information (e.g. gender, eye-color, etc) so the needed resources to search the unknown entries are disburdened. As soon as a new user joins the network his profile would be categorized in the same way and could then be compared to the respective meta–information categories.

The data publish control will also have to deal with different types of data, for example, photos, videos or textual references. While it is conceivable that photo and video recognition algorithms may recognize the simple fact that there is a person in a photo or video, the semantic interpretation of textual data is still impossible. This fact is particularly important when considering the unknown associations: If the algorithm identifies a person is not yet part of the network, then this meta-information can be stored in the database for unknown entries. While it is possible to search textual data for associations to existing users (e.g.

---

[3] Integration of content recognition mechanisms is desirable but not obligative. A manual check of submitted data through content assignement and a moderator system could replace the automated content recognition, even if this would arise novel questions of practicability.

by name search) it is impossible to find associations to unregistered users. Therefore there will be no unknown associations for textual references. The platforms of newly joined users will have to search all existing textual data (e.g. with their name) to find existing associations to them.

In a DFN, data is first published, and may then be removed by an identified person if she thinks it exposes her privacy. There are various alternatives to schedule the publication of data with respect to its potential later removal. As an extreme, publication may just be immediate, while its removal might take place whenever afterwards requested. This would leave identified persons no time for reaction. As another extreme, publication maybe delayed until all identified persons have agreed. This would hardly be acceptable from the publisher's point of view. As a compromise, one might consider some latency before the actual publishing of the data. In an implementation, the publication control mechanism may adjust the specific latency value depending on the number of identified persons who are currently offline.

If all the published data gets analyzed upon publishing, this means that there will not exist any unchecked data so that given a certain reliability of the content recognition mechanisms all data is associated with its possible iPs. It is easy to see that the whole concept of data control relies heavily on Scenario I and the implied data publish control mechanisms. Correctly implemented, these mechanisms would set the cornerstone for later scenarios like "unpublish" or "control usage".

Scenario II: Find data. There is no need to search the network for associated data that was published after the associated user joined the network: Users may choose to be notified on a push-basis as soon as new associations have been recognized. However, one of the problems of data publish control arises as soon as no existing user name can be found. Consider a defaming commentary about a person who is not yet part of the network. The question now is: How is a newly joined user made aware of associated data that already existed in the network before his arrival. We propose a pull-mechanism here: As soon as a new user arrives, his client could trigger an overview request, and thereby flood the network in search for existing associations (not only the unknown entries but also all textual data). Since the unknown associations are stored by using a fine-grained categorization and processing textual search queries is of relatively low complexity this pull mechanism would not stress the resources in an unaccountable way. Nevertheless, DoS-attacks might be an immanent danger of this process. Therefore this overview request will be only permitted once upon registering, since all later published data will be analyzed by the data publish control.

Scenario III: Confirm Data Association. The third scenario deals with the confirmation of associations to data. If some data is unwanted and the user wants to unpublish, he will first have to confirm his association. Through this confirmation of his association to the data he will also be able to change the privacy settings of the data (e.g. "Only my friends may view this photo").

Obviously this would not prevent malicious users from gaining deletion rights over data that has been falsely connected to them. In order to avoid falsely claimed rights, one could think of a four-eyed confirmation process: the iP himself as well as a third not-involved person would have to testify that the generated associations are true. To make sure that the claimed rights are based on true and trustful associations we therefore suggest the implementation of a "web of trust" [3] in which the authenticy of certificates gets validated through mutual affirmation. Trust levels could be assigned to every user to evaluate the trustworthiness of the user in question [7]. Persons with a high trust level, called notaries, could be consulted to confirm claimed rights of users. In such a network the confirmation of the associated user alone would not be enough to answer the "Is that you"- question .

To get the desired rights, users will have to contact notaries, who would then approve or reject the request. As soon as this confirmation is made the user would get the right to change privacy settings or unpublish the data in question.

The web of trust principles could also be extended to place the discussion about the borderlin between privacy and right of expression in the hand of the users themselves. For example one can think of a system in which the user is not able to directly delete confirmed associated content but has to contact another notary in order to do so. If this notary finds that the content is not offensive he might deny the deletion request. Because of the limited space, we leave this interesting discussion for future work.

Scenario IV: Unpublish Data. Scenario IV uses the same backend described in scenario III. In this backend the user would be able to get an overview of all the associations to him that have been found by the publish control mechanism. Given the correct and trustworthy confirmation of an association to a piece of data in the network (assured during the confirmation process) the user would now be able to hit a "delete"-button and thereby force the publisher's platform to unpublish the data. The implementation of this unpublish process itself should be relatively trivial. By implementing this possibility to unpublish data, data control level III would be established.

Unpublishing the data does not necessarily imply the actual deletion of the data from the network. It may be desired to change the privacy settings of the data in question and thereby manipulate it's visibility or access conditions. The oP will of course have to notified of any change in publish or privacy settings of his data.

3.3   Data Control Requirements

Our main goal is to establish data control level III, thus enabling the user to get an overview over data about him published in the network and the possibility to unpublish. To achieve this goal we formulate the following needs:

- Need for data publish control mechanism that analyzes all published data for associations to existing users through various existing or yet-to-be-developed content recognition mechanisms.

- Need for interactive confirmation process in order to verify that found associations are true.
- Need for processes that confirm claimed associations and make them trustworthy (e.g. web of trust).
- Need to implement a user interface in which he can get an overview of all data associated with him (confirmed or unconfirmed).
- Need to deliver deletion rights to the user for data that has been confirmed to be associated with him.
- Need to categorize unknown associations and store them in a database for later association to newly arrived users.
- Need to couple an automated overview request with the registration process in order to search unknown associations and textual references for connections to the newly arrived user.

4   Solution Proposal

In this section we propose conceptual technical solutions for the data control paradigm. We discuss the pros and cons of two different approaches: a centralized server-client-architecture opposed to a decentralized P2P network. After this discussion we conclude in a general recommendation as well as brief description about necessary next steps.

It is importantion to note, that we intent to publish our architecture under a Open Source License in order to intensify community participation and facilitate integration with other existing approaches.

4.1   Centralized Architecture

It is conceivable to enhance existing server-client architectures such as the *Facebook Open Platform* with data control mechanisms in order to improve the control over personal data in the network. Therefore our proposal in this section is to use the Facebook Open platform and extend it with those mechanisms to provide additional functionality. In a centralized architecture all data is stored on a single server which is usually managed by a service provider. In order to achieve data control levels in an architecture of this kind the following measures will have to be taken:

Data Control Backend. A user interface has to be implemented in which users are provided with an overview of their own data, data about them and possible associations to data. This backend will have to provide the functionality to modify the privacy settings of data belonging to a user or about a user as well as unpublishing of the content in question. Also it will serve as a notification board for newly recognized associations. From this backend the user will be able to confirm associations and thereby claim his rights to modify the privacy settings of this content or completely unpublish it.

Server-Side Data Publish Control. Each piece of data submitted to the network will have to pass through a server-side data publish control before being published. This data publish control consists of several mechanisms, including the content-recognition algorithms as well as categorization of unknown content. Also this data publish control will deal with the associations to existing users and notify them of possible references. Unknown associations (for example to persons who are not yet part of the network) will be stored in a database for later processing.

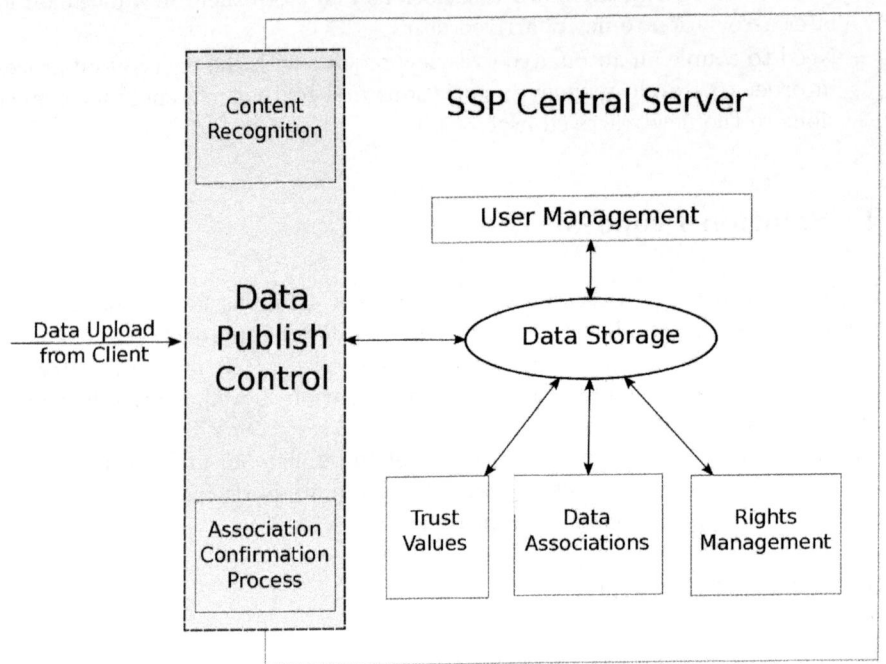

Fig. 2. Structural Components of a centralized DDFN

Confirming associations through web of trust. In order to confirm and verify the associations that have been found by the data publish control, it is necessary to implement a web of trust[4] in which users are assigned to trust levels. Users with high trust levels, so called notaries, will be required to verify associations to pieces of data and thereby enable users to claim their rights upon content that does not belong to them but references them in some way.

Search the network after registration. To make newly arrived users aware of pre-existing data about them, that has been published before they joined the network, the registration process has to be modified. Firstly, the user would have to provide the platform with information (e.g. with fotos, names, etc) that can be

---

[4] One can think of alternatives, however the principle of a web of trust fits the purpose very well here.

used to search the network for similar data entries. Secondly, this information will be used just after registration in order to search the unknown entries database and all textual references in the network. This search request is only triggered once upon registering, since afterward all newly published data will be recognized by the data publish control.

Usage Controlled Clients. If it is desired to establish data control level IV all clients will have to be equipped with a usage control platform. For example, Zhang et al.'s approach consisting of a SELinux as a trusted platform combined with mandatory access control policies (MAC-policies), would ensure that data belonging to users would not be used in an undesired way as soon as it leaves the network.

5   Decentralized P2P Architecture

The popular term "P2P" describes a decentralized infrastructure in which peers directly and autonomously exchange data with other peers of their choice. In a P2P network there is no single service provider and no central server on which all data is stored. To the contrary all information is stored on the peers themselves and made available from there.

In the past this structure has been particularly successful in file sharing domains. One of the most popular representatives of the P2P file sharing platforms is *Gnutella*[5], a specific network protocol on which many popular file sharing clients (e.g. *LimeWire*)[6] are based on.

However in the last years, research has also considered P2P infrastructures for various other fields of application such as consumer-to-consumer (C2C) infrastructures for platforms like eBay or Amazon [6]. *Tribler*[7] uses a P2P infrastructure for video-on-demand services. Recently there have also been several approaches considering a decentralized P2P infrastructure as the base for a privacy-enabling social network.

A promising approach is *Safebook* by Cutillo et al. [5], in which a three component architecture is proposed: a trusted service for identification, a P2P infrastructure and a setting of matryoshkas, which are trust rings of friends (peers) surrounding a user on which the user may then store of publish data.

We propose an extension of *Safebook* by adding functionalities, which establish data control over personal data. In order to do so we need to address the following issues:

Data publish controlled peers. In a P2P network there is no central computing instance, which may detect data associations to other users. Hence, the data publish control, including the content recognition mechanisms must be applied on a local client software located on the peer itself. Newly published data will be checked for associations to friends of the publisher. If the data identifies

---

[5] http://rfc-gnutella.sourceforge.net/ Last checked: 25.03.10.

[6] http://www.limewire.com/ Last checked: 25.03.10.

[7] http://www.tribler.org/ Last checked: 25.03.10.

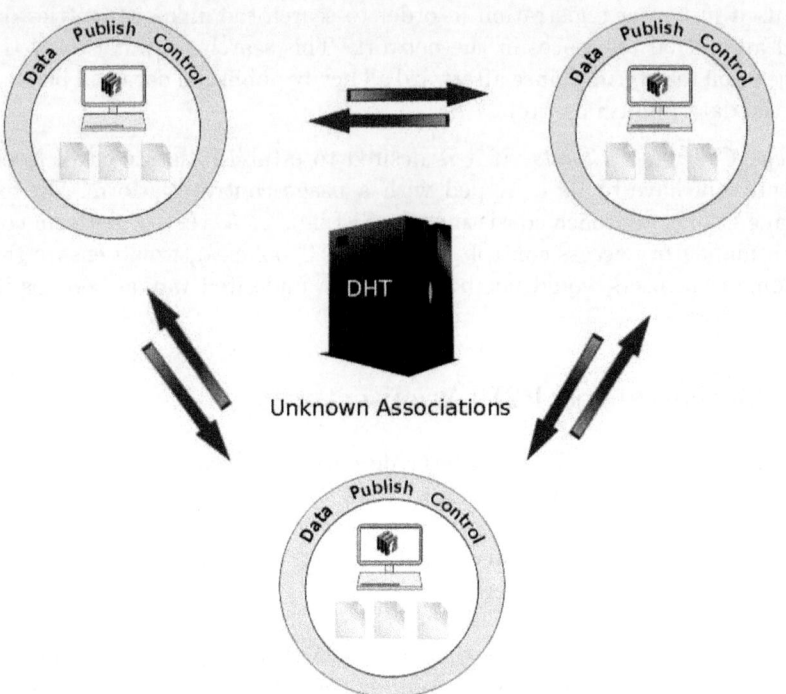

Fig. 3. Conceptional sketch of data control in a P2P network

some of the publisher's friends, these friends will be instantly notified of the new association and may then claim rights of this data.

However it might be possible that the submitted data holds associations to users that are not directly connected to the publisher herself. In a privacy-enabling P2P environment there is no way to check for associations of all users in the network instantly. Only those peers directly or to some small degree connected to the own peer are known. Since there is no central storage device holding a list of all users in the network, these associations will have to be considered unknown and will therefore be treated the same as truly unknown associations to users who are actually not registered in the network as long as no iP has been found.

The unknown associations have to be made available for later processing both for users in the network who are not directly connected to one's peer as well as for newly arrived users. Therefore the metadata collected out of the content recognition mechanisms will be stored in a distributed hash table (DHT). In order to preserve privacy aspects of the network this DHT will only hold metadata with links to the data itself. No personal data will be made available in the DHT.

Search the DHT after registration. As soon as a new peer enters the network its user might want to know if there is already data about him spread in the network.

In order to find out, he will need to provide basic information about himself to his client during the registering process, such as name, biometrical data from photos etc. After the registration the client will then trigger an overview request.

Search the DHT continuously. In contrast to a centralized approach, the finding of new associations in a P2P environment, will not be a passive action solely. On the one hand, associations are collected passively, considering data that has been published by users that are connected to a user's peer (e.g. friends, friends-of-friends). However data that has been published by users that are not known to the user's peer may also contain associations to him. The metadata of these unknown associations is stored in a DHT, which will be searched continuously, and incrementally by the user's client itself. This search process might take a while for the first time; however, as soon as the DHT is searched completely the search algorithm may concentrate on updates and will therefore guarantee a timely reaction to newly published data with associations to oneself.

Confirming associations through web of trust. Similarly to a centralized data control approach each peer will have to be assigned with trust levels. In order to claim rights over associated data, the user will have to contact a highly trusted individual (notary) who may then accept or decline the right claim. After an acceptance by a notary, the user may send out requests to the publisher's peer in order to change privacy settings or unpublish the data in question.

External publish control on local clients. As soon as the user successfully claimed rights over data associated to him, he might want to change the privacy settings of the data in question or even be able to unpublish it. This task is not trivial, since the data and the privacy settings are not published to an external server control by a SSP. On the contrary the data will be located on the peer itself. In order to externally trigger the change of these local settings the client platform will have to be able to enforce external right applications from other users.

6   Centralized vs. Decentralized

It is imaginable to enhance existing server-client architectures such as the *Facebook Open Platform* with data control mechanisms in order to improve the control over personal data in the network. For example one could use the *Facebook Open platform* and extend it with those mechanisms and additional functionality.

Opposed to the advantages of central storage of data there are serious concerns of privacy due to the power of control of the single service provider. Even if most of the security-disadvantages of a centralized system such as intrusion attempts, DoS-Attacks, etc. could be handled, the single service provider (SSP) would still be able to use the accumulated data according their own discretion. Similarly to *facebook*, the SSP could sell data to parties outside of the network and would therefore undermine our described notion of data control. Even terms of usage, which forbid the sale of this information, would be no guarantee for the user's control over his data, since the SSP might change his terms of usage at any time.

Because of these main problems of any centralized architecture we conclude that a data controlled network established in a centralized manner would raise serious scalability, resource and privacy problems and is therefore not first choice in order to implement a DFN.

A decentralized P2P solution with a special focus on privacy (such as *Safebook*) promises solutions for the shortcomings of a centralized approach. Nevertheless further research has to take place concerning P2P-inherent questions and problems, such as scalability, availability and practicability (e.g. of search algorithms in a distributed network). However, these questions are orthogonal to our research and therefore not in our center of attention.

7   Conclusion

We propose the new paradigm of user-centered data control in order to address the rising challenges for privacy and security in social networks. This concept is opposed to traditional content-centric networks where users are not able to enforce their rights on personal data once it has been published.

We identify different data control levels reaching from simple linkage control as in existing online social networks to the possibility to actually unpublish unwanted data no matter who published it. Additionally, usage control mechanisms could be applied in order to extend this control to exterior domains after the data left the network domain.

Basic usage scenarios such as "publish data", "find data" or "unpublish data" are described in this paper through which basic technological challenges and necessary components are outlined.

We come to the conclusion that a defamation-free network (DFN), in which users have control over private data, no matter if published by them or by others, is realizable both in a centralized or decentralized manner. However centralized architectures come with serious privacy issues concerning the information sovereignty of the singel service provider. Therefore we suggest a P2P network architecture for our DFN and point out the main technological challenges and requirements.

8   Future Work

Following this work it is necessary to explore the possibility of implementing data control functions in a distributed environment such as *Safebook* [5]. It is imperative to provide a prototypical architecture based on one of the P2P network approaches. We will especially have to deal with questions of network scalability and availability of the data, with respect to the metadata as well as the data itself. In order to make the metadata available at all times distributed servers could be provided by some of the peers themselves. Questions about motivation and incentives for such a behavior arise and should be addressed. Tests, evaluations and simulations of this architecture have to be included as well as recommendations for the extension of the prototype. Formal and theoretical aspects are of high importance especially when considering the data control rights management as well as the verification of data control security intentions. Therefore, a formal specification of Data Control and it's functions in a defamation-free network are currently under development by the authors.

References

1. Alam, M., Seifert, J.-P., Li, Q., Zhang, X.: Usage control platformization via trustworthy selinux. In: ASIACCS, pp. 245–248 (2008)
2. Buchegger, S., Schiöberg, D., Vu, L.H., Datta, A.: PeerSoN: P2P Social Networking - Early Experiences and Insights. In: Second ACM Workshop on Social Network Systems Social Network Systems 2009, Nürnberg, Germany (March 31, 2009)
3. Caronni, G.: Walking the web of trust. In: WETICE 2000: Proceedings of the 9th IEEE International Workshops on Enabling Technologies, pp. 153–158. IEEE Computer Society, Washington, DC, USA (2000)
4. Castelluccia, C., Kaafar, M.A.: Owner-centric networking (ocn): Toward a data pollution-free internet. In: SAINT 2009: Proceedings of the 2009 Ninth Annual International Symposium on Applications and the Internet, pp. 169–172. IEEE Computer Society, Washington, DC, USA (2009)
5. Cutillo, L.A., Molva, R., Strufe, T.: Safebook: a privacy preserving online social network leveraging on real-life trust. To appear in IEEE Communications Magazine, Consumer Communications and Networking Series (December 2009)
6. Datta, A., Hauswirth, M., Aberer, K.: Beyond web of trust: Enabling p2p e-commerce. In: CEC, pp. 303–312 (2003)
7. Eilers, F., Nestmann, U.: Deriving trust from experience. In: Degano, P., Guttman, J.D. (eds.) FAST 2009. LNCS, vol. 5983, pp. 36–50. Springer, Heidelberg (2010)
8. Hafner, M., Breu, R.: Security Engineering for Service-Oriented Architectures. Springer, Heidelberg (2009)
9. Park, J., Sandhu, R.S.: The $ucon_{abc}$ usage control model. ACM Trans. Inf. Syst. Secur. 7(1), 128–174 (2004)
10. Pretschner, A.: An overview of distributed usage control. In: Proc. of KEPT 2009 International Conference, pp. 25–33 (July 2009)
11. Pretschner, A., Büchler, M., Harvan, M., Schaefer, C., Walter, T.: Usage control enforcement with data flow tracking for x11. In: 5th International Workshop on Security and Trust Management, STM 2009 (2009)

InDico: Information Flow Analysis of Business Processes for Confidentiality Requirements

Rafael Accorsi and Claus Wonnemann

Department of Telematics
University of Freiburg, Germany
{accorsi,wonnemann}@iig.uni-freiburg.de

Abstract. This paper presents InDico, an approach for the automated analysis of business processes against confidentiality requirements. InDico is motivated by the fact that in spite of the correct deployment of access control mechanisms, information leaks in automated business processes can persist due to erroneous process design. InDico employs a meta-model based on Petri nets to formalize and analyze business processes, thereby enabling the identification of leaks caused by a flawed process design.

Keywords: Business processes, compliance management, confidentiality requirements, information flow analysis.

1 Introduction

Managing compliance is the most challenging task in enterprise computing [15]. Over 70% of business processes deployed today rely on business process management systems for their automated execution [31]. The central entity here are workflow models that formalize the business processes. Despite the growing expenses in tool design for the compliant deployment and certification of workflows, e.g. according to CobiT and COSO, noncompliance incidents and the monetary damage they incur are still soaring [22].

Confidentiality violations constitute the major source of noncompliance in enterprise systems [12] and are particularly relevant for data privacy [9]. Even if correct access and usage policies and corresponding controls are in place, information leaks undermine the confidentiality of data items and workflow characteristics. The technical issue here is that policies and access control mechanisms are only effective for "legitimate" channels between subjects, whereas the so-called "covert-channels" are neglected, i.e. channels that are not meant to transfer information but are misused to do so [18].

This paper presents InDico (lat. to indicate), an approach for the automated information flow analysis of workflow models against confidentiality requirements. Specifically, InDico analyzes the control flow of a workflow to identify structural vulnerabilities that cause information leaks. To detect them, information flow (IF) analysis is a suitable verification technique that focuses on the information propagation throughout the system (*end-to-end*) rather than mere data access (*point-to-point*). IF analysis can identify leaks, so-called *interferences*, that circumvent access control mechanisms.

J. Cuellar et al. (Eds.): STM 2010, LNCS 6710, pp. 194–209, 2011.
© Springer-Verlag Berlin Heidelberg 2011

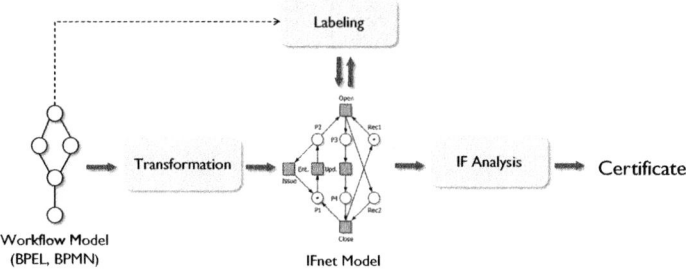

Fig. 1. Overview of the InDico-framework

Fig. 1 gives a high-level overview of InDico's operation. First, workflow models, e.g. in BPEL or BPMN specification languages, are mapped into IFnet, a specialization of colored Petri nets for workflow modeling and IF analysis. Second, as a precondition for IF analysis, the activities in the resultant IFnet are annotated with the security labels – typically "high" for confidential and "low" for public. Third, the labeled IFnet is analyzed against Petri net patterns formalizing IF properties, so-called *non-interference*. Detected leaks, i.e. interferences, are compiled in a certificate, which indicates the places and transitions that cause the leak and which properties they violate.

The use of a Petri net-based meta-model offers three advantages: first, it provides a uniform, modeling language-independent formalism for which translation tools are readily available [20]; second, it allows the well-founded formalization of structural IF properties as Petri net patterns [11]; and third, it provides a sound basis for the efficient IF analysis, which boils down to determining whether a Petri net encompasses a flawed pattern [14]. Moreover, the graphical notation and similarity with workflow models make Petri nets suitable for the practical use by compliance officers.

This paper makes, in summary, the following contributions:

- Present InDico, an approach based on Petri nets for the automated analysis of business processes for confidentiality requirements.
- Introduce IFnet, a meta-model based on colored Petri nets for the representation and IF analysis of processes as workflow models.
- Demonstrate the applicability of InDico in a running example. In particular, it applies preliminary labeling strategies and analysis methods for the identification of information leaks in a business process.

The overall goal of InDico is to provide automated tool support to identify potential violations of compliance requirements, especially confidentiality properties, caused by structural vulnerabilities in business processes. Currently, the transformation and the analysis are supported by independent tools and ongoing work addresses the uniform tool support throughout the three phases of InDico (see Fig. 1). Given the results of an InDico analysis and the risk put to confidentiality, the structure of the process could be changed, or the corresponding

196 R. Accorsi and C. Wonnemann

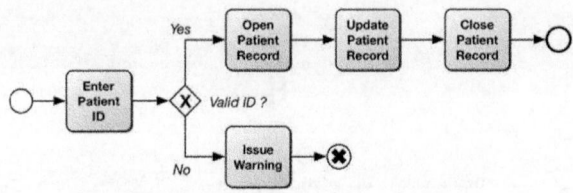

Fig. 2. "Update Patient Record" process

controls could be put at work to eliminate information leaks, or at least alleviate their impact. Defining such countermeasures, e.g. as safe process patterns,
is subject of future work.

Paper Structure. Following a brief introduction to colored Petri nets in §2, §3
defines IFnet, the workflow meta-model for IF analysis; §4 proposes strategies to
encode common confidentiality requirements as IF constraints and §5 presents
criteria for secure information flow which have been implemented in the analysis.
A discussion and related work are provided in §6 and §7 concludes the paper.

1.1 Running Example

Throughout the paper we employ the "Update Patient Record" process depicted
in Fig. 2 to illustrate InDico's operation. This process was obtained in a case
study carried out in cooperation with a German hospital. In this pilot project,
various deployed business processes have been analyzed for dataflows and information leaks. The goal is to show or refute processes' compliance with regulatory
requirements. In particular, InDico was deployed to check whether information
regarding the medical treatment of a patient is not disclosed to third parties,
which is a requirement stipulated by German privacy legislation.

Albeit simple, "Open Patient Record" is a central fragment that recurs as a
subprocess in several of the hospital's information systems, e.g. for accounting,
medical treatment and patient allocation, thereby making it attractive from
the analysis viewpoint. It consists of five activities (depicted as boxes) and an
exclusive choice (x-diamond) that represents an if-statement. The corresponding
BPEL code that models this process fragment is as follows:

```
<sequence name="main">
  <empty name="Enter_Patient_ID"/>
  <switch name="Switch_1">
    <case>
      <sequence>
        <empty name="Open_Patient_Record"/>
        <empty name="Update_Patient_Record"/>
        <empty name="Close_Patient_Record"/>
      </sequence>
    </case>
    <otherwise>
      <empty name="Issue_Warning"/>
    </otherwise>
  </switch>
</sequence>
```

The stipulated confidentiality of information regarding the treatment of patients is expressed as a process isolation requirement: there must be no information exchange between concurrently running instances of "Open Patient Record", as it might relate to the medical treatment and thus violate the compliance rule. The verification of this requirement with InDico is shown in detail along with the description of the corresponding components in the remainder of the paper.

2   Colored Petri Net

This section introduces a notion of Colored Petri Net (CPN), on top of which IFnet is defined. CPN generalizes standard Petri net to support distinguishable tokens and which is used as the basis for the IFnet workflow modeling formalism presented in Section 3. Following the terminology introduced by Jensen, tokens are distinguished by their *color* [16], which is an identifier from the universe $\mathcal{C}$ of token colors.

A CPN is a tuple $N = (P, T, F, C, I, O)$, where P is a finite set of *places*, T is a finite set of *transitions* such that $P \cap T = \emptyset$, and $F \subseteq (P \times T) \cup (T \times P)$ is a set of directed arcs, called the *flow relation*. Let $x, y \in (P \cup T)$, xFy denotes that there is an arc from x to y. The functions C, I and O define the *capacity* of places and the *input* and *output* of transitions, respectively:

- The capacity function C defines the number of tokens a place can hold at a time: $C \in P \rightarrow \mathbb{N}$.
- The input function I defines for each transition t, each place i with iFt and each token color c the number of tokens that is expected: $I \in T \times P \times C \rightarrow \mathbb{N}$.
- The output function O defines for each transition t, each place o with tFo and each token color c the number of produced tokens: $O \in T \times P \times C \rightarrow \mathbb{N}$.

Marking. At any time a place contains zero or more tokens. The *marking* (or *state*) is the distribution of tokens over places. A marking M is a *bag* over the Cartesian product of the set of places and the set of token colors, i.e. a function from $P \times C$ to the natural numbers: $M \in P \times C \rightarrow \mathbb{N}$. A partial ordering is defined to compare states with regard to the number of tokens in places. For any two states M_1 and M_2, $M_1 \leq M_2$ iff for all $p \in P$ and for all $c \in C$: $M_1(p, c) \leq M_2(p, c)$. The sum of two bags $(M_1 + M_2)$, the difference $(M_1 - M_2)$ and the presence of an element in a bag $(a \in M_1)$ are defined in a straightforward way. A *marked* CPN is a pair (N, M), where $N = (P, T, F, C, I, O)$ is a CPN and M is a bag over $P \times C$ denoting the marking of the net.

Nodes. Elements of $P \cup T$ are called *nodes*. A node x is an *input node* of another node y *iff* there is a directed arc from x to y (i.e. xFy). Node x is an *output node* of y *iff* yFx. For any $x \in P \cup T$, $\overset{N}{\bullet} x = \{y \mid yFx\}$ and $x \overset{N}{\bullet} = \{y \mid xFy\}$; the superscript N can be omitted if it is clear from the context.

Firing. The number of tokens may change during the execution of the net. Transitions are the active components in a CPN. They change the state of the net according to the following *firing rule*:

1. A transition $t \in T$ is *enabled* in state M_1 *iff* each input place contains sufficiently many tokens of each color and each output place has sufficient capacity to contain the output tokens:
   - $\forall i \in \bullet t, \forall c \in \mathcal{C} : I(t, i, c) \leq M_1(i, c)$ and
   - $\forall o \in t\bullet : \sum_{c \in \mathcal{C}} O(t, o, c) + \sum_{c \in \mathcal{C}} M_1(o, c) \leq C(o)$.
2. An enabled transition may *fire*. If transition t fires, then t *consumes* the designated number of tokens from each of its input places and *produces* the designated number of tokens for each of its output places. Firing of transition t in state M_1 results in some state M_2 which is defined as follows:
   - $\forall i \in \bullet t, \forall c \in \mathcal{C} : M_2(i, c) = M_1(i, c) - I(t, i, c)$ and
   - $\forall o \in t\bullet, \forall c \in \mathcal{C} : M_2(o, c) = M_1(o, c) + O(t, o, c)$ and
   - $\forall p \in P \setminus (\bullet t + t\bullet), \forall c \in \mathcal{C} : M_2(p, c) = M_1(p, c)$.

Reachability. Given a CPN N and a state M_1, the following notation is defined:

- $M_1 \xrightarrow{t} M_2$: transition t is enabled in M_1 and firing t in M_1 results in state M_2.
- $M_1 \longrightarrow M_2$: there is a transition t such that $M_1 \xrightarrow{t} M_2$.
- $M_1 \xrightarrow{\sigma} M_n$: the firing sequence $\sigma = t_1 t_2 t_3 ... t_{n-1}$ from state M_1 leads to state M_n via a (possibly empty) set of intermediate states $M_2, ..., M_{n-1}$, i.e. $M_1 \xrightarrow{t_1} M_2 \xrightarrow{t_2} ... \xrightarrow{t_{n-1}} M_n$.

A state M_n is *reachable* from M_1 (notation $M_1 \xrightarrow{*} M_n$) *iff* there is a firing sequence σ so that $M_1 \xrightarrow{\sigma} M_n$. The empty firing sequence is also allowed, i.e. $M_1 \xrightarrow{*} M_1$. The set of states that is reachable from state M_1 is denoted $[M_1]$.

3   IFnet: Modeling Business Processes for IF Analysis

IFnet refines CPN by adding constructs required for workflow modeling and IF analysis. An IFnet models workflow activities through transitions and data items (including documents, messages, variables) through tokens. Tokens with color `black` ("black tokens") have a special status. They do not stand for data items but indicate the triggering and termination of activities. The set of *colored tokens* (i.e. tokens that are not `black`) is denoted $\mathcal{C}_c$, i.e. $\mathcal{C}_c = \mathcal{C} \setminus \{\texttt{black}\}$.

Formally, an IFnet is a tuple $N = ((P, T, F, C, I, O), S_{\mathcal{U}}, A, G, L_{SC})$, where (P, T, F, C, I, O) is a CPN and the further elements are defined as follows:

- The function $S_{\mathcal{U}}$ assigns transitions *subjects* from a set $\mathcal{U}$: $S_{\mathcal{U}} \in T \to \mathcal{U}$. A subject denotes the acting entity on which behalf a corresponding workflow activity is performed.
- The function A defines whether a transition t reads or writes an input datum $i \in \bullet t$: $A \in T \times \mathcal{C}_c \to \{read, write\}$.

– The function G assigns predicates (guards) to transitions: $G \in T \rightarrow \mathsf{P}_\mathcal{C}$, where $\mathsf{P}_\mathcal{C}$ denotes the set of predicates over colored tokens. A predicate evaluates to either *true* or *false* and is denoted, for instance, $\mathsf{p}(\mathsf{red}, \mathsf{green})$, where p is the name of the predicate and the identifiers in brackets indicate the tokens needed for its evaluation. For an enabled transition to fire, its guard must evaluate to *true*.
– The function L_{SC} assigns security labels to transitions and colored tokens: $L_{SC} \in T \cup \mathcal{C}_\mathsf{c} \rightarrow \mathcal{SC}$. $\mathcal{SC}$ is a finite set of security labels which forms a lattice under the relation $\prec$. Every set $\mathcal{SC}$ contains an additional element $\mathsf{unlabeled}$, which denotes that a transition or token does not hold a label.

Furthermore, an IFnet must meet the following conditions:

1. *Source Place.* There is a nonempty set $P_I \subset P$ of places with $\bullet i = \emptyset, i \in P_I$. Each $i \in P_I$ can carry at most one black token and no colored tokens. P_I is the set of *source places*.
2. *Sink Place.* There is a nonempty set $P_O \subset P$ of places with $o\bullet = \emptyset, o \in P_O$. Each $o \in P_O$ can carry at most one black token and no colored tokens. P_O is the set of *sink places*.
3. *Connectedness.* For every node $x \in P \cup T$ there exists a source place $i \in P_I$ and a sink place $o \in P_O$ such that x is on a path from i to o.
4. *Black Tokens.* Every transition consumes at least one black token and produces at least one black token, i.e.
   – $\forall t \in T \; \exists i \in \bullet t : I(t, i, \mathsf{black}) \geq 1$ and
   – $\forall t \in T \; \exists o \in t\bullet : O(t, o, \mathsf{black}) \geq 1$.
5. *Colored Tokens.* Every colored token that is produced by a transition must either be an input token of that transition or be a *fresh* token, i.e. it must have a color that has not been used before.

The first two conditions ensure that a workflow has defined start and end points. The third condition prevents that there are "dangling" transitions or activities which do not contribute to the processing of the workflow. The fourth condition requires transitions to signal their triggering and termination through black tokens. The last condition ensures that data items are passed through the workflow according to the transitions.

Below, the following abbreviations are used:

Storage/Interface Place. A storage/interface place $p \in P$ is a place which cannot hold black tokens.

Initial State. An initial state is a marking where each source place holds a black token and where all colored tokens reside in storage/interface places. The set of all initial states of N is denoted $\mathcal{M}_I^N$.

Termination State. A termination state of IFnet N is a marking where each sink place holds a black token. $\mathcal{M}_O^N$ denotes the set of all termination states of N.

Marked IFnet. This is a pair $(N, M) = (((P, T, F, C, I, O), A, G, L_{SC}), M)$ where $((P, T, F, C, I, O), M)$ is a marked CPN with marking M. The set of all marked IFnet is denoted $\mathcal{N}$.

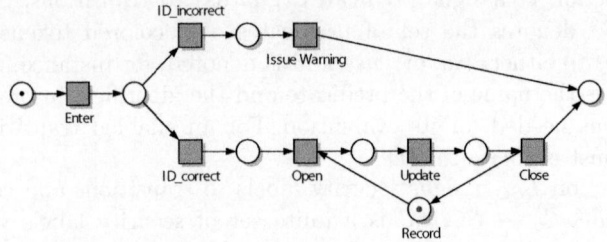

Fig. 3. IFnet model of "Open Patient Record" workflow

Automated Transformation to IFnet. Transformation of workflows specified in common industrial formats (such as BPEL and BPMN) into IFnet is carried out automatically by extending existing mapping functions [20]. For the BPEL case, there are at least two tools which provide a feature-complete mapping of a workflow's control flow to standard Petri nets, namely "BPEL2oWFN" [19] and "WofBPEL" [24]. Building upon these tools, generated Petri nets are subjected to a second transformation step that produces the correspondent IFnet models.

Example 1 (Modeling of "Open Patient Record"). Fig. 3 shows the IFnet model of the "Open Patient Record" workflow from the running example. For the sake of readability, the figure only displays the structure of the net. The activities of the workflow are modeled by transitions, which are depicted as filled boxes. Places – depicted as circles – represent conditions, tokens are depicted as dots and arcs are shown as arrows. The net is very simple and does not feature guards (i.e. all guards are implicitly *true*) and different subjects.

Except for the black token residing in an initial place, there is one colored (red) token in the interface/storage place Record. This token represents the patient record and is used by the activities Open, Update and Close. Open and Close have reading access to the record, and Update has write access.   ⊣

4   Labeling Strategies

InDico's labeling component encodes confidentiality requirements in an IFnet model by annotating transitions and tokens with labels from an ordered lattice $(SC, \prec)$. The labeling component operates according to a given *labeling strategy* which defines how a specific security requirement is translated into a labeled IFnet model.

Currently, two labeling strategies have been implemented in InDico. The first strategy extracts the *confidentiality of data items* from the access rights defined in an access control list (ACL). The goal of this labeling strategy is to define the confidentiality of data items as IF constraints according to the intentions expressed in the ACL, thereby enabling the ACL's verification with the additional capabilities of IF analysis. This strategy is useful when checking for dataflows across the execution of the workflow. The second strategy addresses the *isolation of concurrent workflow instances* and is described in detail below, as it is used for the running example "Open Patient Record".

4.1 Workflow Isolation

Several compliance requirements, such as HIPAA and Sarbanes-Oxley, demand that workflows with different security clearances are isolated from each other, i.e. that there must be no information exchange between instances of corresponding workflows. A well-known example for a corresponding policy is the Chinese-Wall security model [10]. It aims to prevent conflicts of interest in organizations dealing with clients, which are, for instance, direct competitors in the same market.

To check an isolation requirement with InDico, the labeling function combines the IFnet models of two workflows into a single IFnet which models their concurrent execution. (Here we refrain from showing that the corresponding operations produce IFnet models.) The workflows are connected at their shared storage/interface places. The labeling function subsequently annotates transitions and tokens of the composed model with different security labels corresponding to the workflow they originated from. The following describes this procedure in detail.

Disjoint. To be composed, two IFnet models must be separate from each other, so that they do not share transitions and subjects. Shared tokens may only reside in storage/interface places that are connected to both nets. Formally, two marked IFnet (N_1, M_1) and (N_2, M_2) are *disjoint, iff*:[1]

- $T_1 \cap T_2 = \emptyset$.
- There are no subjects performing activities in both nets, i.e. $\forall(t_1, t_2) \in T_1 \times T_2 : S_{\mathcal{U}}(t_1) \neq S_{\mathcal{U}}(t_2)$.
- All shared places are storage/interface places, i.e. $\forall p \in P_1 \cap P_2 : M_1(p, \texttt{black}) = M_2(p, \texttt{black}) = 0 \land \forall t \in \bullet p : O(t, p, \texttt{black}) = 0$.
- In their initial states, N_1 and N_2 hold tokens of the same color only in places shared by both nets, i.e. $\forall p_1 \in P_1 \forall p_2 \in P_2 \forall c \in \mathcal{C}_c : M_1(p_1, c) = M_2(p_2, c) = 1 \Rightarrow p_1 = p_2$.
- There is no pair of transitions $(t_1, t_2) \in T_1 \times T_2$, where t_1 and t_2 produce fresh tokens of the same color.

Workflow Composition. The composition operator $\Pi \in \mathcal{N} \times \mathcal{N} \to \mathcal{N}$ integrates two marked and disjoint IFnet (N_1, M_1) and (N_2, M_2) into a single model. The resulting IFnet (N_3, M_3) is defined as follows:

- Except for the labeling function, the capacity function and the marking, the elements of (N_3, M_3) are merged from their corresponding counterparts in (N_1, M_1) and (N_2, M_2): $P_3 = P_1 \cup P_2$, $T_3 = T_1 \cup T_2$, $F_3 = F_1 \cup F_2$, $I_3 = I_1 + I_2$, $O_3 = O_1 + O_2$, $S_{\mathcal{U},3} = S_{\mathcal{U},1} + S_{\mathcal{U},2}$, $A_3 = A_1 + A_2$ $G_3 = G_1 + G_2$.
- For the labeling of transitions, $L_{\mathcal{SC},3}$ is defined as follows:

$$L_{\mathcal{SC},3}(t) = \begin{cases} \texttt{high} & \text{if } t \in T_1 \\ \texttt{low} & \text{if } t \in T_2 \end{cases}$$

---

[1] The subscript of an element indicates its belonging to the corresponding net, e.g. T_1 denotes the set of transitions of N_1.

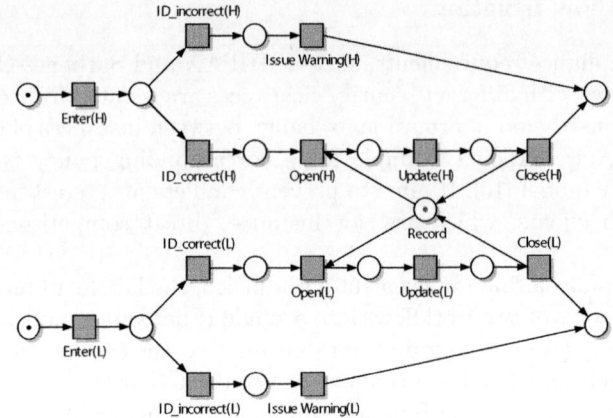

Fig. 4. Labeled and unfolded IFnet model

Colored tokens are labeled as follows:

$$L_{SC,3}(c) = \begin{cases} \text{high} & \text{if } \exists p \in P_1 \setminus P_2 : M_1(p,c) \geq 1 \\ \text{high} & \text{if } c \text{ is a fresh token produced by a transition from } T_1 \\ \text{low} & \text{otherwise} \end{cases}$$

– The capacity of places in the composed net is defined as follows:

$$C_3(p) = \begin{cases} C_1(p) & \text{if } p \in P_1 \setminus P_2 \\ C_2(p) & \text{if } p \in P_2 \setminus P_1 \\ max\left(C_1(p), C_2(p)\right) & \text{if } p \in P_1 \cap P_2 \end{cases}$$

– The marking M_3 is defined in an analogous way to the capacity:

$$M_3(p,c) = \begin{cases} M_1(p,c) & \text{if } p \in P_1 \setminus P_2 \\ M_2(p,c) & \text{if } p \in P_2 \setminus P_1 \\ max\left(M_1(p,c), M_2(p,c)\right) & \text{if } p \in P_1 \cap P_2 \end{cases}$$

Instance Cloning. A cloning operator $\Phi \in \mathcal{N} \to \mathcal{N}$ on (N_1, M_1) is defined as an auxiliary function to check whether two instances of the same workflow might interfere. Applied to a marked IFnet (N_1, M_1), it yields a marked IFnet (N_2, M_2) which is equivalent to (N_1, M_1), but with its elements renamed for distinction. Solely the naming of the storage/interface places is adopted by the cloned model.

Given a marked IFnet $N \in \mathcal{N}$, a model N' of concurrently running instances of N with different security classifications is constructed by cloning N and applying the composition operator, i.e. $N' = \Pi(N, \Phi(N))$.

Example 2 (Labeling of "Open Patient Record"). To check whether two instances of the "Open Patient Record" might interfere, the corresponding IFnet model is cloned and labeled according to the previously proposed labeling strategy. The resultant model is depicted in Fig. 4. The upper part of the figure shows the "High"-instance of the workflow and the lower part its "Low"-instance, indicated by the letters H and L attached to the transition names. The red token at the place Record is left unlabeled. ⊣

5   Analysis of IFnet Models

This section introduces a static analysis approach to determine whether a labeled IFnet model allows for information leaks. This boils down to checking whether the model exhibits interferences between the different security classes. Besides dataflow, IFnet can model the following workflow constructs which can act as covert-channels:[2]

1. Causality of activities.
2. Resource conflicts (usage and storage).
3. Conditional branching.

  The following proposes criteria for two types of covert-channels (causality of activities and resource conflicts). For both, checking algorithms have been implemented which are applied in the running example. The presentation omits the description of the criterion for conditional branching, as it has not yet been implemented and does not occur in the running example.

  The proposed notions of noninterference follow the ones proposed by Busi and Gorrieri for standard Petri nets [11]. They have shown that fulfillment of the established noninterference property *Bisimulation Non-Deducibility on Composition* (BNDC) [13] can be checked through a semi-structural analysis of a Petri net. The analysis inspects the net for the presence of certain patterns (see below), where their absence in a net implies BNDC. Specifically, models are analyzed in a hybrid, two-step manner: the first step inspects the net for the presence of structural patterns, which is an efficient, purely static procedure. The second step checks whether the identified structural patterns are *active*, i.e. whether they can be executed (technically: reached) within a run of the business process. Since this step requires the analysis of the dynamic behavior of the net, it exhibits an exponential worst-case complexity. Precisely: let p and f be the number of places and arcs of a net, the static check runs in $O(f + p)$ and the dynamic check in $O(2^{3p})$ [14]. §6 discusses the practical implications and scalability issues associated with such an exponential complexity.

  The notions described below adapt the established patterns (causality and resource *usage*) to the IFnet formalism and complement them by an additional pattern for the detection of resource *storage* conflicts (which cannot occur in standard Petri nets).

---

[2] There are further types of channels, such as the timing behavior or probability distributions of execution paths. However, these cannot be checked statically without further information on the workflow's runtime behavior.

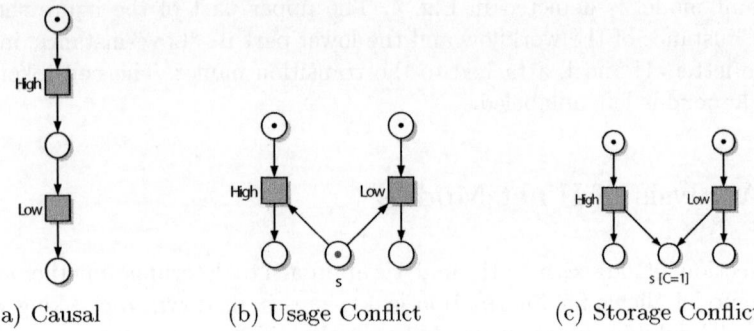

(a) Causal   (b) Usage Conflict   (c) Storage Conflict

Fig. 5. Examples for covert-channels in IFnet models

5.1   Causality of Activities

A workflow's control flow conveys information from "High" to "Low" if the occurrence of higher-level activities has an influence on the occurrence of lower-level activities. The following defines a notion of causality which captures IFnet patterns, where the firing of a higher-level transition is a prerequisite for the firing of a lower-level transition. An example is depicted in Fig. 5(a). The definition starts with a notion for *adjacent* transitions, which is taken from [11] and adapted to IFnet. Subsequently, we generalize this notion to also consider unlabeled places between the corresponding activities.

Let (N, M) be a marked IFnet and $t_a, t_b \in T$ transitions with $t_a \bullet \cap \bullet t_b \neq \emptyset$. Firing of t_a is *directly causal* for firing of t_b iff:

$$\exists p \in t_a \bullet \cap \bullet t_b \; \exists c \in C \; \exists M_1, M_2 \in [M] \; \exists \sigma \in T^* :$$
$$M_1 \xrightarrow{t_a \sigma t_b} M_2 \wedge$$
$$O(t_a, p, c) \geq 1 \; \wedge \; I(t_b, p, c) \geq 1 \; \wedge$$
$$O(t', p, c) = 0 \; \textit{for all } t' \in \sigma.$$

This definition states that there must be at least one token c which is produced by t_a and necessary for the firing of t_b. It is further ruled out that this token is produced by any other transition after firing of t_a and before firing of t_b. The following generalizes the notion for transitions that are not necessarily adjacent to each other. Here, it is required that on every path between t_a and t_b is a sequence of transitions that are directly causal.

For transitions $t_a, t_b \in T$, t_a is *causal* for t_b if:

$$\forall \sigma \in T^* \text{ with } \sigma = t_a \sigma' t_b \text{ and } M_1 \xrightarrow{\sigma} M_2, M_1, M_2 \in [M] :$$
$$\exists \delta = t_1 t_2 ... t_n \subseteq \sigma \text{ with } t_1 = t_a \text{ and } t_n = t_b \text{ such that}$$
$$t_i \text{ is directly causal for } t_{i+1}, \forall i \in \{1, ..., n-1\}.$$

Therefore, IFnet (N, M) is free from interferences induced by the causality of activities, if for all transition pairs $(t_H, t_L) \in T \times T$ with $L_{SC}(t_L) \prec L_{SC}(t_H)$, t_H is not causal for t_L. This property is checked in a two steps: the first identifies transition pairs, where a higher-level transition precedes a lower-level transition;

the second checks for each identified transition pair whether there is a causality between the transitions by exploring the net's state space.

5.2   Resource Conflicts

Illicit IF occurs when a higher-classified activity prevents a lower-classified activity from using a shared resource: from the fact that the access attempts fail, "Low" can deduce that "High" is using the resource. There are two types of resource conflicts in an IFnet model. First, concurrent attempts to use the same data item and, second, concurrent attempts to use limited storage space. The following defines noninterference criteria for both types in a marked IFnet.

Resource Usage Conflict. Fig. 5(b) illustrates a situation where the two transitions High and Low attempt to use the red token placed in token s. If High fires, Low is blocked and can infer that High is using the red token. Formally, for transitions $t_a, t_b \in T$, t_a prevents resource *usage* of t_b if:

$$\exists p \in \bullet t_a \cap \bullet t_b, \exists c \in \mathcal{C}, \exists M_1, M_2, M_3 \in [M], \sigma \in T^* :$$
$$I(t_a, p, c) \geq 1 \ \wedge \ I(t_b, p, c) \geq 1 \ \wedge \ M_1(p, c) \geq 1 \ \wedge$$
$$M_1 \xrightarrow{t_a} M_2 \ \wedge$$
$$M_1 \xrightarrow{\sigma t_b} M_3, \ where \ O(t', p, c) = 0 \ for \ all \ t' \in \sigma.$$

Resource Storage Conflict. Fig. 5(c) illustrates an analogous situation, where both High and Low attempt to place a token in storage place s, which has insufficient capacity to accommodate both. Consequently, firing High prevents Low from firing, causing an illicit IF. Formally, for transitions $t_a, t_b \in T$, t_a prevents resource *storage* of t_b iff:

$$\exists p \in t_a \bullet \cap t_b \bullet, \exists c_a, c_b \in \mathcal{C}, \exists M_1, M_2, M_3 \in [M], \sigma \in T^* :$$
$$O(t_a, p, c_a) \geq 1 \ \wedge \ O(t_b, p, c_b) \geq 1 \ \wedge$$
$$M_1 \xrightarrow{t_a} M_2 \ \wedge \ \sum_{c \in \mathcal{C}} M_2(p, c) = C(p) \ \wedge$$
$$M_2 \xrightarrow{\sigma t_b} M_3, \ where \ I(t', p, c') = 0 \ for \ all \ t' \in \sigma \ and \ for \ all \ c' \in \mathcal{C}.$$

An IFnet (N, M) is free from interferences induced by resource conflicts, if for all transition pairs $(t_H, t_L) \in T \times T$ with $L_{\mathcal{SC}}(t_L) \prec L_{\mathcal{SC}}(t_H)$, t_H neither prevents resource usage nor resource storage by t_L. The checking for resource conflicts is also implemented as a two-step procedure, which first identifies transition pairs where both a higher-level transition and a lower-level transition interact with the same place. Subsequently, the procedure checks whether there is an execution of the net that can lead to a conflict.

Example 3 (Analysis of "Open Patient Record"). The analysis of the labeled IFnet model from Fig. 4 yields as the result that there is both a covert-channel induced by conflicting resource usage and by the causality of activities:

– **Conflict.** By firing the transition Open(H), the patient record is removed from the storage place and transition Open(L) is blocked until the token is returned. Here, the "High" part of the net influences the "Low" part as it prevents the transition from firing. There is an information flow which allows the "Low" part to deduce that "High" is currently holding the patient record.

– **Causal.** With the firing of transition Close(H), the token representing the patient record is returned to its storage place and might be consumed by transition Open(L). Hence, opening the patient record on the "Low" side requires its preceding return on the "High" side: this causality reveals to "Low" the fact that "High" has returned the record.

InDico's certificate indicates these interferences as violations of the BNDC property and graphically points out the fragments of the IFnet model where they occurred. A critical assessment of the detected interferences with regard to the hospital's security requirements is currently left as a manual task to compliance officers. The appliaction of InDico for the verification of a more complex auction workflow can be found in [2]. As a future work, InDico aims for a better automation of this task through the deployment of filtering and *declassification* techniques [27].   ⊣

6   Discussion and Related Work

Two issues are central with regard to the practical use of InDico: the identification of *false positives* and the *exponential complexity* involved in verification of IFnet. The following discusses these issues and casts InDico into the related work.

Discussion. Being based on IF techniques, the analysis carried out by InDico is very powerful, identifying interference as an information leak. In consequence, InDico still delivers a large number of false-positives, i.e. hints to information leaks that are allowed and even required for process termination. InDico also identifies a number of leaks that are, from a security or compliance viewpoint, irrelevant. While very much welcome from the perspective of vulnerability management [21], an exhaustive enumeration of all possible leaks is an overkill for compliance management [4]. This "drawback" is not new and lies in the very nature of IF analysis [26]. To classify identified interferences according to their threat, further work will investigate the extent to which declassification rules [27], derived from policies and workflow models, provide a basis for the distinction.

As described in §5, the verification of an IFnet has an exponential worst-case complexity. Specifically: $O(2^{3p})$, where p stands for the number of places in the net. However, two aspects should be considered when interpreting this result and its implications for the applicability of InDico. First, best-practice business process modeling prescribes processes with at most ten activities [31]. This amounts to nets with $p = 11$, for which verification would still be feasible. Second, the worst-case complexity only occurs when the (linear time) static analysis identifies *every* place in the net as a potentially harmful pattern for which a dynamic check is required. In practice, the number of such places does not surpass five. Altogether, in spite of the exponential growth, the analysis technique of InDico based on IFnet is feasible for most industrial workflows.

Related Work. This paper presents the InDico framework for the verification of business processes for confidentiality properties and a corresponding meta-model IFnet. The following casts these contributions in the state of the art.

The verification of business processes traditionally focuses solely on plain access control models, thereby failing to address information leaks lying beyond the scope of reference monitors. In [8] Barletta et al. propose a method for verifying the interplay of policies and workflows in a service-oriented architecture. In [5], Atluri et al. propose an approach to verifying workflows against a Chinese Wall policy model. Similarly, Yang et al. propose an approach for dataflows (so-called "explicit information flows") in scientific workflows [32]. Namiri and Stojanovic propose a pattern-based methodology stipulating the construction of workflows from recurring patterns that are deemed secure [23]. While this includes several relevant organizational patterns, such as separation of duties and four-eye rule, it does not focus on information leaks. In [1], Accorsi and Wonnemann present an approach for the reconstruction of dataflows from logs, whereas their approach cannot capture the kinds of data leaks addressed here. Still focusing on dataflows, [17] presents an approach for the verification of multi-level security policies, such as Bell-LaPadula, in workflow models based on Petri nets. Sun et al. [28] and Trčka et al. [29] propose methodologies for the integration of the dataflow perspective into formal workflow models and the verification for sets of predefined error patterns. Wang and Li investigate the notion of workflow resilience [30], but neglect information leaks.

Petri nets (and their specialized dialects) are largely employed to reason about business processes. In [3], Adam et al. introduce the modeling and analysis of workflows using Petri nets. Here, only structural properties, e.g. leading to deadlock or inconsistencies, are considered. In turn, Atluri and Huang investigate the verification of an authorization model for workflows [6]. In these works, plain Petri nets are employed. The use of colored Petri nets for workflow modeling is suggested by Pesic and van der Aalst [25]. However, the proposed nets do not allow labeling and the modeling of data items, which are essential for information leak analysis. The meta-model presented by Atluri and Huang in [7] allows labeling, but cannot capture resource consumption.

7 Summary

This paper presented InDico, a formal technique for the automated IF analysis of business processes. InDico transforms business processes, formalized in the corresponding languages such as BPMN and BPEL, in specialized Petri nets and applies efficient verification techniques to detect structural vulnerabilities. Its applicability is illustrated in a running example throughout the paper, demonstrating the kinds of vulnerabilities it detects.

Overall, the static identification of IF in workflow models is a promising research direction to ensure formally-founded, rigorous security analyses of business processes. Through the formalization of properties as patterns and the extensive testing of InDico, we expect to collect a library of safe (as well as harmful) workflow patterns and to devise guidelines for building IF-safe and compliant workflows by design. In doing so, InDico would gain a constructive character, being not only useful for certification audits, but also for compliance officers and business processes development. To this end, we are not only addressing the open issues discussed in the paper, but also developing an improved tool-chain for push-button, fully automated analysis of business processes.

References

1. Accorsi, R., Wonnemann, C.: Auditing workflow executions against dataflow policies. In: Abramowicz, W., Tolksdorf, R. (eds.) BIS 2010. LNBIP, vol. 47, pp. 207–217. Springer, Heidelberg (2010)
2. Accorsi, R., Wonnemann, C.: Strong non-leak guarantees for workflow models. In: ACM Symposium on Applied Computing, pp. 308–314. ACM, New York (2011)
3. Adam, N., Atluri, V., Huang, W.: Modeling and analysis of workflows using Petri nets. Journal of Intelligent Information Systems 10(2), 131–158 (1998)
4. Allman, E.: Complying with compliance. ACM Queue 4(7), 19–21 (2006)
5. Atluri, V., Chung, S., Mazzoleni, P.: A Chinese Wall security model for decentralized workflow systems. In: ACM Conference on Computer and Communications Security, pp. 48–57. ACM, New York (2001)
6. Atluri, V., Huang, W.: An authorization model for workflows. In: Bertino, E., Kurth, H., Martella, G., Montolivo, E. (eds.) ESORICS 1996. LNCS, vol. 1146, pp. 44–64. Springer, Heidelberg (1996)
7. Atluri, V., Huang, W.: An extended Petri net model for supporting workflows in a multilevel secure environment. In: IFIP Conference Proceedings of Database Security, vol. 79, pp. 240–258. Chapman & Hall, Boca Raton (1996)
8. Barletta, M., Ranise, S., Viganò, L.: Verifying the interplay of authorization policies and workflow in service-oriented architectures. In: Conference on Computational Science, vol. 3, pp. 289–296. IEEE, Los Alamitos (2009)
9. Breaux, T., Antón, A.: Analyzing regulatory rules for privacy and security requirements. IEEE Transactions on Software Engineering 34(1), 5–20 (2008)
10. Brewer, D., Nash, M.: The Chinese-wall security policy. In: IEEE Symposium on Security and Privacy, pp. 206–214. IEEE, Los Alamitos (1989)
11. Busi, N., Gorrieri, R.: Structural non-interference in elementary and trace nets. Mathematical Structures in Computer Science 19(6), 1065–1090 (2009)
12. Bussmann, K.D., Krieg, O., Nestler, C., Salvenmoser, S., Schroth, A., Theile, A., Trunk, D.: Wirtschaftskriminalität 2009 – Sicherheitslage in deutschen Großunternehmen. In: Martin-Luther-Universität Halle-Wittenberg and PwC AG (2009)
13. Focardi, R., Gorrieri, R.: A taxonomy of security properties for process algebras. Journal of Computer Security 3(1), 5–34 (1995)
14. Frau, S., Gorrieri, R., Ferigato, C.: Petri net security checker: Structural non-interference at work. In: Degano, P., Guttman, J., Martinelli, F. (eds.) FAST 2008. LNCS, vol. 5491, pp. 210–225. Springer, Heidelberg (2009)
15. Hammer, M.: The process audit. Harvard Business Review 85(4), 119–142 (2007)
16. Jensen, K.: Coloured Petri nets: A high level language for system design and analysis. In: Rozenberg, G. (ed.) APN 1990. LNCS, vol. 483, pp. 342–416. Springer, Heidelberg (1991)
17. Knorr, K.: Multilevel security and information flow in Petri net workflows. In: Conference on Telecommunication Systems (2001)

18. Lampson, B.: A note on the confinement problem. Communications of the ACM 16(10), 613–615 (1973)
19. Lohmann, N.: A feature-complete petri net semantics for WS-BPEL 2.0. In: Dumas, M., Heckel, R. (eds.) WS-FM 2007. LNCS, vol. 4937, pp. 77–91. Springer, Heidelberg (2008)
20. Lohmann, N., Verbeek, E., Dijkman, R.: Petri net transformations for business processes – A survey. In: Jensen, K., van der Aalst, W.M.P. (eds.) Transactions on Petri Nets and Other Models of Concurrency II. LNCS, vol. 5460, pp. 46–63. Springer, Heidelberg (2009)
21. Lowis, L., Accorsi, R.: Vulnerability analysis in SOA-based business processes. IEEE Transactions on Services Computing (to appear 2010)
22. Müller, G., Accorsi, R., Höhn, S., Sackmann, S.: Sichere Nutzungskontrolle für mehr Transparenz in Finanzmärkten. Informatik Spektrum 33(1), 3–13 (2010)
23. Namiri, K., Stojanovic, N.: Using control patterns in business processes compliance. In: Weske, M., Hacid, M.-S., Godart, C. (eds.) WISE Workshops 2007. LNCS, vol. 4832, pp. 178–190. Springer, Heidelberg (2007)
24. Ouyang, C., Verbeek, E., van der Aalst, W.M., Breutel, S., Dumas, M., ter Hofstede, A.H.: WofBPEL: A tool for automated analysis of BPEL processes. In: Benatallah, B., Casati, F., Traverso, P. (eds.) ICSOC 2005. LNCS, vol. 3826, pp. 484–489. Springer, Heidelberg (2005)
25. Pesic, M., van der Aalst, W.M.P.: Modelling work distribution mechanisms using colored Petri nets. International Journal on Software Tools for Technology Transfer 9(3-4), 327–352 (2007)
26. Ryan, P., McLean, J., Millen, J., Gligor, V.: Non-interference: Who needs it? In: IEEE Computer Security Foundations Workshop, pp. 237–238. IEEE, Los Alamitos (2001)
27. Sabelfeld, A., Sands, D.: Dimensions and principles of declassification. In: IEEE Computer Security Foundations Workshop, pp. 255–269. IEEE, Los Alamitos (2005)
28. Sun, S., Zhao, L., Nunamaker, J., Sheng, O.L.: Formulating the data-flow perspective for business process management. Information Systems Research 17(4), 374–391 (2006)
29. Trčka, N., van der Aalst, W., Sidorova, N.: Data-flow anti-patterns: Discovering data-flow errors in workflows. In: van Eck, P., Gordijn, J., Wieringa, R. (eds.) CAiSE 2009. LNCS, vol. 5565, pp. 425–439. Springer, Heidelberg (2009)
30. Wang, Q., Li, N.: Satisfiability and resiliency in workflow systems. In: Biskup, J., López, J. (eds.) ESORICS 2007. LNCS, vol. 4734, pp. 90–105. Springer, Heidelberg (2007)
31. Wolf, C., Harmon, P.: The state of business process management. BPTrends Report (2010), http://www.bptrends.com/
32. Yang, P., Lu, S., Gofman, M., Yang, Z.: Information flow analysis of scientific workflows. Journal of Computer and System Sciences 76, 390–402 (2009)

Stateful Authorization Logic:
Proof Theory and a Case Study

Deepak Garg and Frank Pfenning

Carnegie Mellon University
{dg,fp}@cs.cmu.edu

Abstract. Authorization policies can be conveniently represented and reasoned about in logic. Proof theory is important for many such applications of logic. However, so far, there has been no systematic study of proof theory that incorporates system state, upon which access policies often rely. The present paper fills this gap by presenting the design and proof theory of an authorization logic BL that, among other features, includes direct support for external procedures to verify predicates on system state. We discuss design choices in the interaction between state and other features of the logic and validate the logic both foundationally, by proving relevant metatheoretic properties of the logic's proof system, and empirically, through a case study of policies that control access to sensitive intelligence information in the U.S.

Keywords: Authorization logic, proof theory, stateful policies, case study.

1   Introduction

Many authorization policies rely on conditions that are controlled by the environment and whose changes are not stipulated by the policies themselves. For example, a sensitive file may be accessible to the public **if the file is marked unclassified**; an employee may enter her office **if it is between 9 AM and 5 PM on a weekday**; a doctor may read any patient's health records **if there is a medical emergency**. Conditions such as "if the file is marked unclassified", written in boldface in the previous sentence, have the following characteristics: (a) They influence consequences of the authorization policy of interest, and (b) The authorization policy itself does not stipulate when or how such conditions change, although, in conjunction with other enforcement mechanisms in the system, it may constrain who may change them (e.g., the list of individuals who may mark a file unclassified may be stipulated by the authorization policy itself). We informally call conditions satisfying these two criteria *conditions of state*, and any authorization policy relying on them a stateful authorization policy.

Many formal proposals for representing, enforcing and reasoning about stateful authorization policies use logic to represent the policies. Central to such use of logic is *proof theory*, which is used both to enforce the authorization policies through proof-carrying authorization or PCA [3,4,5], and to facilitate logical inference to analyze their consequences [11,10]. Yet, despite several papers

J. Cuellar et al. (Eds.): STM 2010, LNCS 6710, pp. 210–225, 2011.
© Springer-Verlag Berlin Heidelberg 2011

on proof theory of authorization logics without state [15,1,12], to the best of our knowledge, there has been no systematic work on proof theory for logics that can represent stateful authorization policies. The main objective of this paper is to fill this gap: we examine in detail the proof theory of a new logic BL in which stateful authorization policies can be represented. We validate the logic's foundations by proving several metatheoretic properties of its proof system including cut-elimination, which is a proof-theoretic statement of the logic's soundness [28,22]. Empirically, we illustrate BL and justify its expressiveness through a case study of policies for access to sensitive U.S. intelligence information. (Owing to its length, we defer the entire case study to a separate technical report [17] and present here only illustrative examples from it.) Further, we discuss subtle design choices in the interaction between state and other components of the logic. Orthogonal to our main objective, we provide a new interpretation for the common access control connective k says s [2], which increases the logic's expressiveness.

At its core, BL is a first-order intuitionistic logic. To that we add the connective k says s, which means that principal k supports statement s, and *state predicates*, a subclass of predicates that can be established through decision procedures external to the logic that may refer to the system state. Finally, in order to represent real time, we include the connective s @ $[u_1, u_2]$ from our prior work with DeYoung [12]. s @ $[u_1, u_2]$ means that formula s holds in the time interval $[u_1, u_2]$, but possibly not outside of it. Through its combination of state predicates, explicit time (the @ connective), and the says connective, BL is a very expressive authorization logic.

There are two main challenges in incorporating state in an authorization logic like BL. The first is to decide the interaction between state predicates and other features of the logic, especially explicit time. For example, if s is a state predicate then depending on the values of u_1 and u_2, s @ $[u_1, u_2]$ may refer to a property of state in the *past* (or *future*) of the authorized access, which may be difficult (resp. impossible) for a reference monitor to enforce. In BL, we make a deliberate decision to eliminate such policies by interpreting s @ $[u_1, u_2]$ as "s at the time of access" irrespective of $[u_1, u_2]$ whenever s is a state predicate. Another central decision is whether or not to treat time as a part of the state (e.g., via a constant localtime that evaluates to the time of access), as in some prior work [4,7]. We argue in Section 3.3 that this choice results in a loss of expressiveness — any policy that refers to more than one point of time cannot be expressed if time is treated as a part of state. Thus, a treatment of time through the @ connective is useful even in the presence of state predicates.

The second challenge in incorporating state is the integration of external procedures for checking state predicates with the inference rules of the logic without breaking metatheoretic properties like cut-elimination. In this regard, our proof theory is guided by, and similar to, prior work on integrating decision procedures for constraint domains into a logic [29,20]. The key idea is to formally represent the external procedure for checking state predicates by an abstract judgment $E \models i$ (any environment which satisfies all state predicates in E, also satisfies

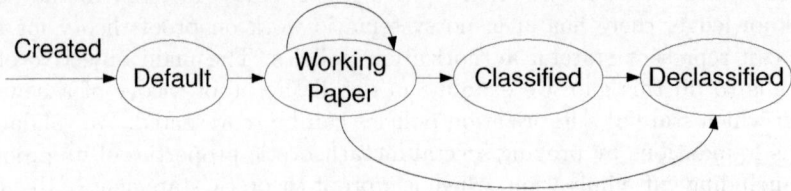

Fig. 1. Stages of a sensitive intelligence file in the US

state predicate i), and stipulating only a few, reasonable conditions on the judgment. We list these conditions in Section 3.2 and show that they are enough to obtain metatheoretic properties of interest, including cut-elimination.

The rest of this paper is organized as follows. In Section 2, we present our case study, thus motivating the need for stateful authorization policies and also illustrating, by way of example, the syntax and features of BL. In Section 3, we introduce the logic and its proof theory stepwise. We start with a first-order intuitionistic logic with the connective k says s, then add state predicates, and finally add explicit time. Section 4 presents metatheoretic properties of the proof system. Related work is discussed in Section 5 and Section 6 concludes the paper. A related paper [16] presents a file system, PCFS, capable of enforcing policies represented in BL, including those presented in this paper.

2   Case Study: Stateful Authorization by Example

As a canonical example of stateful authorization policies, we introduce our case study: U.S. policies for access to sensitive intelligence information.[1] We assume that the unit of sensitive information is a digital file that is already classified or will potentially be classified. It is often necessary to share such files (among intelligence agencies, for example) and, as a result, there are federal policies that mandate who may access such files. For the purpose of this section, there are two interesting points about these policies. First, any sensitive file goes through a life cycle consisting of up to four stages that are shown in Figure 1. Rules to access a file depend on the stage the file is in, as shown in Figure 2. Second, transitions between stages are dictated by non-mechanizable factors such as human intent and beliefs and are, therefore, not prescribed by the authorization policy itself. As far as the authorization policy is concerned, the stages can change unpredictably. Hence, for the purposes of formalization and enforcement, it is easiest to represent the stage of a file as an element of system state. In the specific encoding of policies described here, the stage of a file is represented as

---

[1] The primary sources of policies in this paper are interviews of intelligence personnel conducted by Brian Witten and Denis Serenyi of Symantec Corporation. Some parts of the policies are based on Executive Orders of the White House [26,25] or Director of Central Intelligence Directives (DCIDs) [24,23]. The policies presented here themselves unclassified, and may not represent official practices.

Value of extended attribute status on file F	Meaning	Who has access
default	F is in default stage	Owner
working T	F is a working paper, put into that stage at time T	Anyone, at the discretion of owner
classified T T'	F is classified from time T to time T'	Complex rules to decide access
declassified	F is declassified	Everyone

Fig. 2. Formalization of stages and permissions allowed in them

an extended attribute (file meta-data) called status, which is stored in the file system. The policy relies on this extended attribute to determine who may read the file but does not stipulate the conditions under which the attribute may change. Hence, the authorization policy is stateful in the sense mentioned in the introduction.

Formalizing state in BL. System state can be represented in BL through a special class of predicates called *state predicates*, denoted i. State predicates can be established in a proof through an external procedure, which may vary by application. For formalizing the policy at hand, we need two state predicates: (a) (**has_xattr** f a v), which means that file f has extended attribute a set to value v; in particular, a special attribute status determines the stage of a sensitive file, and (b) (**owner** f k), which means that file f is owned by principal k. We do not stipulate what principals are — they may be individuals, agencies, or groups. We assume that a procedure to check both predicates in the file system being used for implementation is available. A brief word on notation before we proceed further: we write state predicates in **boldface** to distinguish them from others and use Curried notation for applying arguments to predicates, e.g., we write (**owner** f k) instead of the more conventional **owner**(f, k).

The attribute status in our formalization can take four possible values corresponding to the four stages in Figure 1. These are listed in Figure 2, together with a description of principals who have access to the file in each stage. Technically, the words default, working, classified, and declassified are uninterpreted function symbols in BL having arities 0, 1, 2, and 0, respectively. The arguments T, T' represent time points (discussed later).

Formalizing policy rules in BL. Authorization is formalized in the logic as a predicate (may k f p), which means that principal k has permission p on file f. may k f p is *not* a state predicate because it must be established by logical deduction starting from the policy rules and valid credentials. Representative examples of formulas from our formalization of the policy are shown below:

admin claims ((may K F read) :-
        has_xattr F status default,
        owner F K).

admin claims (((may K F read) :-
          has_xattr F status (classified T T'),
          indi/has-clearances/file K F,
          owner F K',
          K' says (may K F read)) @ $[T, T']$).

admin claims (((may K F read) :-
          has_xattr F status (classified T T')) @ $[T', +\infty]$).

admin claims (((may K F read) :-
          has_xattr F status (working T),
          owner F K',
          K' says (may K F read),
          $T' = (T + 90d)$) @ $[T, T']$).

The notation s :- $s_1, \ldots, s_n$ means "formula s holds if formulas $s_1, \ldots, s_n$ hold", and is equal to $(s_1 \wedge \ldots \wedge s_n) \supset s$. Uppercase variables like K and F occurring in $s, s_1, \ldots, s_n$ are implicitly assumed to be universally quantified outside this formula. The prefix **admin claims** ... before each rule means that the rule is created by the principal **admin**, who is assumed to be the ultimate authority on access decisions. The prefix is formally discussed in Section 3. Accordingly, the first rule above states that (it is the admin's policy that) principal K may read file F if F is in stage default and K owns F. The latter two facts are determined by looking at the file's meta-data through the external procedure for state predicates.

The second rule illustrates two central, but possibly unfamiliar connectives of authorization logics including BL: k says s and s @ $[u_1, u_2]$. The former has been studied extensively in the context of authorization logics [2,15,1,3] and means that principal k supports formula s or declares that the formula is true. k says s can be established *a priori* in a proof through a digital certificate that contains formula s and is signed by principal k's private key. In fact, this is the *only* way to establish a priori any formula other than a state predicate, constraint (constraints are discussed below), or tautology. s @ $[u_1, u_2]$ captures real time in the logic; it means that formula s holds during the time interval $[u_1, u_2]$, but does not say anything about s outside this interval. The second rule above states that principal K may read file F if F is classified from time T to time T' (**has_xattr** F status (classified T T')), K has the right clearances to read file F (indi/has-clearances/file K F), and the owner K' of file F allows K to read the file (K' says (may K F read)). The suffix @ $[T, T']$ after the formula means that the entire formula and, hence, its consequence (may K F read) apply only in the interval $[T, T']$. Beyond T', the file is effectively declassified and accessible to everyone as captured in the third rule above, which means that during the interval $[T', +\infty]$, any principal K may read a file F that was classified from time T to time T'.

Our fourth rule highlights the need for another integral feature of BL — constraints, such as the atom $T' = (T + 90d)$ in the fourth formula. Constraints are similar to state predicates in that they are decided by an external procedure but different in that they are independent of state. Constraints are useful for reasoning about time. For instance, the fourth rule means that principal K may read file F if F is a working paper, the owner K' of F allows the access, and less than 90 days have elapsed since the file became a working paper. The last condition enforces a policy mandate that a file can remain a working paper for at most 90 days.

The second, third, and fourth rules above also exemplify an interesting interaction between state and time: they apply over time intervals that depend on time values T obtained through state predicates. There are other, more interesting interactions between state and time that do not show up in our case study but are described in Section 3.3. The remaining case study is devoted to formalizing the predicate (indi/has-clearances/file K F) from the second rule above. This predicate relates credentials of an individual K with attributes of a classified file F to determine whether or not K should have access to F. Besides the encoding of state and time, which we have described above, this is the most challenging part of the case study and involves 38 rules. However, these rules do not refer to state, so we defer their details to a technical report [17].

3 The Logic BL: Syntax and Proof Theory

We present the logic BL stepwise. The core of BL is sorted (typed) first-order intuitionistic logic. In the first stage of presentation (Section 3.1), we consider the core with one additional connective, k says s, calling the resulting logic BL_0. Then we add state predicates, calling the logic BL_1 (Section 3.2). Finally, we add explicit time through the connective s @ $[u_1, u_2]$ to obtain the full logic BL (Section 3.3). For brevity, we omit a description of sorts, disjunction, and existential quantification as well as proofs of theorems from this paper. These details may be found in the first author's thesis [14, Chapters 3&4].

3.1 BL_0: The says Connective

The first fragment of BL we consider, BL_0, has the following syntax:

Terms	$t, u, k ::=$	Alice | Bob | admin | ...
Predicates	$P ::=$	may | ...
Atoms	$p ::=$	$P\ t_1 \ldots t_n$
Formulas	$r, s ::=$	$p \mid s_1 \wedge s_2 \mid s_1 \supset s_2 \mid \top \mid \bot \mid \forall x.s \mid k$ says s

Although we do not stipulate the domain of terms, it must include at least principals who are authorized access and who create policies (Alice, Bob, admin, etc.). Formulas are either atomic p, or built from the usual connectives of first-order logic — $\wedge$ (conjunction), $\supset$ (implication), $\top$ (truth), $\bot$ (falsity), $\forall$ (universal quantification), and the access control specific connective k says s. As explained and illustrated in Section 2, k says s means that principal k supports or states formula s, without necessarily implying that s is true. Negation, $\neg s$, may be defined as $s \supset \bot$ if needed to represent a policy.

Proof theory. When using authorization logics in practice, access is granted only if there is a proof which justifies the access. Therefore, to understand the meaning of a proposition in authorization logic, we must understand how it can be proved. This naturally leads us to the proof theory of BL_0, i.e., a systematic study of its formal proofs. We adopt Gentzen's sequent calculus style [18] in describing the proof theory and follow Martin-Löf's judgmental approach [22], which has been used previously to describe other modal logics [28,15]. Briefly, a *judgment* J is an assertion that can be established through proofs. For BL_0 we need two kinds of judgments: s true, meaning that formula s is true, and k claims s, meaning that principal k claims or supports formula s (but s may or may not be true). The latter is needed to define the meaning of the says connective. A sequent has the following form, where Γ abbreviates a multi-set $J_1, \ldots, J_n$ of judgments and Σ is a set containing all first-order variables free in Γ, s, and k.

$$\Sigma; \Gamma \xrightarrow{k} s \text{ true}$$

The informal meaning of the sequent is: "Parametrically in the variables in Σ, assuming that everything that principal k claims is true, the judgment s true follows logically from the judgments in Γ." The principal k is called the *view* of the sequent, and can be roughly thought of as the principal relative to whose claims we wish to prove the sequent (hence the hypothesis "assuming that everything that principal k claims is true ..." in the meaning of the sequent).

Sequents are established through proofs that are trees of inference rules with axioms at leaves. The following two rules relate the judgments themselves. The first rule, (init), is standard and states that if atom p is assumed as a hypothesis, then it can be concluded. We restrict the rule to atoms, but it can be proved that a generalization to arbitrary formulas holds (we prove a similar theorem for the entire logic BL in Section 4). The second rule, (claims), captures the meaning of the view of a sequent: if k claims s is assumed and the view is k, then s true can also be assumed.

$$\frac{}{\Sigma; \Gamma, p \text{ true} \xrightarrow{k} p \text{ true}} \text{init} \qquad \frac{\Sigma; \Gamma, k \text{ claims } s, s \text{ true} \xrightarrow{k} r \text{ true}}{\Sigma; \Gamma, k \text{ claims } s \xrightarrow{k} r \text{ true}} \text{claims}$$

Other inference rules of the sequent calculus are directed by connectives. We list below rules for the says connective. The notation $\Gamma|$ in the first rule denotes the subset of Γ containing only judgments of the form k' claims s', i.e., $\Gamma| = \{(k' \text{ claims } s') \mid k' \text{ claims } s' \in \Gamma\}$. The first rule, (saysR), can be interpreted as follows: we can establish that k says s is true in hypotheses Γ in any view k_0 (conclusion of the rule) if we can prove only from $\Gamma|$ in view k that s is true (premise). Hypotheses of the form s' true are removed in the premise because they may have been introduced in Γ in the view k_0, but may not be claimed or trusted by k. The second rule (saysL) states that the judgment $(k \text{ says } s)$ true entails the judgment k claims s. In fact, the two judgments are equivalent in BL_0. (Technically, we say that the connective says internalizes the judgment claims into the syntax of formulas.)

$$\frac{\Sigma; \Gamma| \xrightarrow{k} s \text{ true}}{\Sigma; \Gamma \xrightarrow{k_0} k \text{ says } s \text{ true}} \text{saysR} \qquad \frac{\Sigma; \Gamma, k \text{ says } s \text{ true}, k \text{ claims } s \xrightarrow{k_0} r \text{ true}}{\Sigma; \Gamma, k \text{ says } s \text{ true} \xrightarrow{k_0} r \text{ true}} \text{saysL}$$

Rules for connectives of first-order logic ($\wedge$, $\supset$, $\top$, $\bot$, $\forall$) are standard so we refer the reader to existing work for details [28]. In all these rules, the view passes unchanged from the premises to the conclusion. Several standard metatheoretic properties including admissibility of cut and consistency hold of BL_0's proof theory but we refrain from presenting them here because we present similar properties for the larger logic BL in Section 4.

BL_0's says connective. The says connective in BL_0 has a different interpretation from that than in prior authorization logics containing says [15,1,2]. For the benefit of readers, we list below a rule and three axioms that completely characterize the says connective of BL_0 (in terms of the sequent calculus, $\vdash s$ means that $\Sigma; \cdot \xrightarrow{k} s$ true for any k and appropriate Σ):

From $\vdash s$ infer $\vdash k$ says s
$\vdash (k$ says $(s_1 \supset s_2)) \supset ((k$ says $s_1) \supset (k$ says $s_2))$
$\vdash (k$ says $s) \supset k'$ says k says s
$\vdash k$ says $((k$ says $s) \supset s)$

The reader may ask why we are considering a new interpretation for says, when there exist others that also have simpler proof theories, e.g., [15,1,2]. The answer lies in striking a delicate balance between having a good proof theory and having a usable meaning for the says connective, which we believe BL_0 achieves. As a case in the point for other interpretations of says with simpler proof theories, consider recent work that treats k says $\cdot$ as a family of lax modalities [15,1]. Even though these logics have a simpler proof theory, their ability to express delegation is limited. Consider the formula k says $((k'$ says $s') \supset s)$, which may intuitively mean that k supports s if k' supports s'. Interpreting k says s as a lax modality, it (counterintuitively) suffices for k, *not* k', to state s' in order to derive k says s from this rule. Technically, this happens because with a lax interpretation of k says s, the axiom $s \supset (k$ says $s)$ is admissible, which is not the case in BL_0. Such delegations arise in practical examples, as in the following rule from our case study.

admin claims $(((\text{indi/has-background } K \text{ topsecret}) \text{ :-}$
$\qquad\qquad\qquad BA \text{ says } (\text{indi/has-ssbi } K \text{ } T),$
$\qquad\qquad\qquad T' = (T + 5y)) @ [T, T']).$

In words, the principal admin agrees that principal K has topsecret clearance if a person certified to check others' background, BA, says that K has passed a SSBI (single scope background investigation). Although the predicate $(\text{indi/has-ssbi } K \text{ } T)$ has been delegated to BA by admin, the latter has no authority over this predicate. Comparison to the lax interpretation of says is merely an example, but the general point here is that obtaining an authorization logic that has a sound proof theory and high expressiveness is difficult. We justify BL_0 on both these counts — on its proof theory through metatheorems of Section 4 and on practical usability through our case study. Of course, this does not preclude the possibility of other logics that are also good on both counts.

Using BL_0 in practice. Like other authorization logics with a says connective, BL_0 can be used to authorize access in practice in a standard way. A fixed predicate such as may from Section 2 is used to represent permissions, and a fixed principal, e.g., admin, is assumed to be the ultimate authority in making access decisions. Access is allowed if the prevailing policy, represented as hypotheses Γ, entails admin says (may t) true for appropriate arguments t, i.e., if there is a proof of $\cdot; \Gamma \xrightarrow{k}$ (admin says (may t)) true (the view k is irrelevant at the top-level; it can be a fresh constant). Evidence for the assumed policy Γ comes in the form of signed certificates: a digital certificate (e.g., in X.509 format [19]) containing s signed by k is taken as a priori evidence of the judgment k claims s. Of course, not all parts of a policy can be established by certificates. For example, state predicates must be checked directly on system state. Reconciling such predicates with proof theory is the main objective of this paper, to which we turn next.

3.2   BL$_1$: State Predicates

To represent stateful policies, examples of which were shown in Section 2, we extend BL$_0$ with a special class of atomic formulas called stateful atoms, denoted i, and add a new form of hypotheses — a set of stateful atoms, E — to sequents. The resulting logic, BL$_1$, has sequents of the form $\Sigma; E; \Gamma \xrightarrow{k} s$ true, which informally mean that: "Parametrically in the variables in Σ, assuming that everything that principal k claims is true, the judgment s true follows logically from the judgments in Γ *in any environment that validates all stateful atoms in E*." In practice, a proof of authorization can be constructed as explained at the end of Section 3.1, except that now the stateful atoms E are also available in the proof. Assumptions in E may be discharged by an external procedure that has access to the environment or system state.

Syntax. The syntax of BL$_1$ formulas is shown below. The meta-variables p and t inherit their syntax from BL$_0$. State predicates I are assumed to be distinct from regular predicates P.

State predicates	$I ::=$ **has_xattr** $\mid$ **owner** $\mid \ldots$	
Stateful atoms	$i ::= I\ t_1 \ldots t_n$	
Formulas	$r, s ::= p \mid i \mid s_1 \wedge s_2 \mid s_1 \supset s_2 \mid \top \mid \bot \mid \forall x.s \mid k$ says s	

Proof theory. We incorporate relations between stateful atoms into the proof theory through an abstract judgment $\Sigma; E \models i$, which means that "for all ground instances of variables in Σ, any environment that satisfies all stateful atoms in E also satisfies atom i". We do not stipulate any rules to establish this judgment since they may vary from environment to environment. For instance, in an environment where some constraint forces that files a.txt and b.txt always have the same value for attribute status, it may be the case that $\Sigma;$ **has_xattr** a.txt status $v \models$ **has_xattr** b.txt status v, but this may not be case in other environments. In the simplest instance, the judgment may hold if and only if $i \in E$. Our metatheoretic results (Section 4) assume only the following properties of this judgment, all of which follow from its intuitive explanation.

$$\Sigma; E, i \models i \qquad \text{(Identity)}$$
$$\Sigma; E \models i \text{ implies both } \Sigma, x; E \models i \text{ and } \Sigma; E, E' \models i \qquad \text{(Weakening)}$$
$$\Sigma; E \models i \text{ and } \Sigma; E, i \models i' \text{ imply } \Sigma; E \models i' \qquad \text{(Cut)}$$
$$\Sigma, x; E \models i \text{ implies } \Sigma; E[t/x] \models i[t/x] \text{ if } \mathtt{fv}(t) \subseteq \Sigma \qquad \text{(Substitution)}$$

As explained earlier, BL_1 sequents have the form $\Sigma; E; \Gamma \xrightarrow{k} s$ true. BL_1 inherits all inference rules of BL_0 with the proviso that the new context E passes unchanged from the conclusion to premises in all rules. We do not reiterate these rules. Two new rules for reasoning about stateful atoms are added. The first rule states that the judgment i true holds if $E \models i$ for the assumed state E. The second rule means that a hypothesis i true implies that the stateful atom i holds. Together, the two rules imply that the judgment i true is equivalent to the atom i holding in the prevailing environment, which closely couples the stateful *formula* i to its intended interpretation.

$$\frac{\Sigma; E \models i}{\Sigma; E; \Gamma \xrightarrow{k} i \text{ true}} \text{stateR} \qquad \frac{\Sigma; E, i; \Gamma, i \text{ true} \xrightarrow{k} s \text{ true}}{\Sigma; E; \Gamma, i \text{ true} \xrightarrow{k} s \text{ true}} \text{stateL}$$

We list below admissible and inadmissible statements relating to stateful atoms and the says connective. The second and third statements mean that a false stateful atom signed by a principal does not contaminate the entire logic.

$$\vdash i \supset k \text{ says } i$$
$$\nvdash (k \text{ says } i) \supset i$$
$$\nvdash (k \text{ says } i) \supset (k' \text{ says } i) \text{ if } k \neq k'$$

3.3   BL: Explicit Time and the @ Connective

In our final increment to the logic, we add explicit time by including the connective $s @ [u_1, u_2]$. This treatment of time is very similar to that in our prior work with DeYoung for a different logic η [12] and, as a result, we describe the proof theory of the final extension only briefly. The reason for considering this extension is two-fold. First, explicit time is needed to correctly represent policy rules that have a pre-determined expiration, as well as other rules that limit the temporal validity of formulas (e.g., the second, third, and fourth rules of Section 2). Second, there are important design decisions in the interaction between state and time that we wish to highlight.

Since $s @ [u_1, u_2]$ means that s holds throughout the interval $[u_1, u_2]$, it also seems reasonable that $s @ [u_1, u_2]$ imply $s @ [u'_1, u'_2]$ if $u_1 \leq u'_1$ and $u'_2 \leq u_2$. To make such properties admissible in the logic, we need a theory of the total order $u_1 \leq u_2$ on time points and, for expressing certain policies (e.g., the fourth rule in Section 2), we also need a theory of arithmetic over time points. We include both by adding a single *constraint domain* of time points to the logic. From the perspective of proof theory, constraints are similar to state. However, the external procedure for solving constraints does not depend on state.

Syntax. Time points are integers or the elements $\{-\infty, +\infty\}$. The numbers represent time elapsed in seconds from a fixed point of reference. In the concrete syntax we often write time points in the format YYYY:MM:DD:hh:mm:ss. We also include the function symbol $+$ of arity 2. A new syntactic class of constraints, c, is also added. Constraints are predicates of one of two forms: $u_1 \leq u_2$ or $u_1 = u_2$.

Terms	$t, u, k ::=$ Alice | Bob | YYYY:MM:DD:hh:mm:ss | $-\infty$ | $+\infty$ |
	$u_1 + u_2$ | $\ldots$
Constraints	$c ::= u_1 \leq u_2$ | $u_1 = u_2$
Formulas	$r, s ::= p$ | i | c | $s_1 \wedge s_2$ | $s_1 \supset s_2$ | $\top$ | $\bot$ | $\forall x.s$ | k says s |
	$s @ [u_1, u_2]$

Proof theory. The addition of time requires a significant change to the logic's judgments [12]. Instead of the judgments s true and k claims s, we use refined judgments $s \circ [u_1, u_2]$ (s is true throughout the interval $[u_1, u_2]$) and k claims $s \circ [u_1, u_2]$ (k claims that s is true throughout the interval $[u_1, u_2]$). Sequents in BL have the form $\Sigma; \Psi; E; \Gamma \xrightarrow{k, u_1, u_2} s \circ [u'_1, u'_2]$. Here, Ψ is a set of constraints, much like E is a set of stateful atoms. The meaning of the sequent is: "Parametrically in the variables in Σ, assuming that everything that *principal k claims about intervals containing* $[u_1, u_2]$ is true, the judgment $s \circ [u'_1, u'_2]$ follows logically from the judgments in Γ in any environment that validates all stateful atoms in E, *if all constraints in Ψ hold.*" Besides the addition of constraints as hypotheses, another change is the addition of an interval of time to the view. This is not particularly important here since we could also have constructed a logic without time intervals in views (for details of the trade-offs involved in making this choice, see [14, Section 4.4]).

Relations between constraints are incorporated into the logic through an abstract judgment $\Sigma; \Psi \models c$, which is similar to $\Sigma; E \models i$. As for the latter judgment, our metatheoretic properties rely only on basic properties of $\Sigma; \Psi \models c$, which we borrow from prior work [12]. In particular, we require that $u_1 \leq u_2$ be reflexive and transitive. Inference rules of the sequent calculus for BL are derived from those of BL$_1$, taking into account carefully the interaction between time and the different connectives. Although this interaction is non-trivial in most cases, it is similar to that in prior work. Accordingly, we describe here rules for only the @ connective and state predicates (the latter reflect a key design choice), describe the interaction between @ and the remaining connectives through properties, and refer the reader to the first author's thesis for remaining details of the proof theory [14, Chapter 4].

The @ connective. In BL, $s @ [u_1, u_2]$ internalizes the judgment $s \circ [u_1, u_2]$ into the syntax of formulas. Because $s @ [u_1, u_2]$ means that s holds throughout $[u_1, u_2]$, a further qualification by adding $\circ [u'_1, u'_2]$ as in $s @ [u_1, u_2] \circ [u'_1, u'_2]$ does not add anything to the meaning, so the judgments $s \circ [u_1, u_2]$ and $s @ [u_1, u_2] \circ [u'_1, u'_2]$ are equivalent. This results in the following two rules for the @ connective. (ν denotes an arbitrary view k, u_1, u_2.)

$$\frac{\Sigma;\Psi;E;\Gamma \xrightarrow{\nu} s \circ [u_1,u_2]}{\Sigma;\Psi;E;\Gamma \xrightarrow{\nu} s @ [u_1,u_2] \circ [u_1',u_2']} @\mathrm{R}$$

$$\frac{\Sigma;\Psi;E;\Gamma,s @ [u_1,u_2] \circ [u_1',u_2'], s \circ [u_1,u_2] \xrightarrow{\nu} r \circ [u_1'',u_2'']}{\Sigma;\Psi;E;\Gamma,s @ [u_1,u_2] \circ [u_1',u_2'] \xrightarrow{\nu} r \circ [u_1'',u_2'']} @\mathrm{L}$$

State predicates and time. If i is a stateful atom, what should $i \circ [u_1,u_2]$ mean? One possibility (which we don't use in BL) is to apply the usual meaning of $s \circ [u_1,u_2]$, implying that $i \circ [u_1,u_2]$ mean that the stateful atom i holds throughout the time interval $[u_1,u_2]$. Although intuitive, this interpretation can result in policies that are impossible to enforce. Consider, for example, the policy $((T' = (T + 5)) \wedge (i @ [T,T'])) \supset ((\mathsf{may}\ K\ F\ \mathsf{read}) @ [T,T])$. Intuitively, the policy says that a principal K may read file F at time T if i holds in the interval $[T, T + 5]$. Thus, permission to access file F at time T refers to state at later points of time, which is, of course, impossible to enforce in a reference monitor.

To avoid such non-enforceable policies, we make a substantial design decision in BL: we assume that all stateful atoms are interpreted at exactly one point of time and $i \circ [u_1,u_2]$ simply means that i holds in the environment at this point of time (independent of u_1 and u_2). The logic does not stipulate what that point of time is, but it seems practical to use the time at which the access happens. In that interpretation, $i \circ [u_1,u_2]$ means that i holds at the time of access. Following this decision, the following rules for stateful atoms are self-explanatory:

$$\frac{\Sigma;E \models i}{\Sigma;\Psi;E;\Gamma \xrightarrow{\nu} i \circ [u_1,u_2]}\mathrm{stateR} \qquad \frac{\Sigma;\Psi;E,i;\Gamma,i \circ [u_1,u_2] \xrightarrow{\nu} r \circ [u_1',u_2']}{\Sigma;\Psi;E;\Gamma,i \circ [u_1,u_2] \xrightarrow{\nu} r \circ [u_1',u_2']}\mathrm{stateL}$$

Seemingly, we are limiting the logic's expressiveness because we are eliminating (enforceable) policies that refer to stateful atoms in intervals prior to access. However, this is not a significant limitation because such policies can still be encoded by requiring evidence of the stateful atom(s) having been true in the past (e.g., a trusted observer's certificate) to exist at the time of access. As a result, we consider this design decision reasonable.

Time as a special case of state? A different possibility for including time is to treat it as a part of state without explicitly including the connective $s @ [u_1,u_2]$, as in some prior work [7,4]. The idea is to have an interpreted constant, e.g., localtime, that evaluates to the time of access. Although this choice avoids the need for the @ connective, it also results in a loss of expressiveness: since there is no way to state that a formula holds at a time other than the time of access, we can only represent policies all of whose subformulas need to hold at the time of access. In particular, a policy like $((u' = (u + 5)) \wedge (p @ [u,u])) \supset (p' @ [u',u'])$ (if predicate p holds at time u, then p' holds at $u + 5$) is impossible to represent in such a setup. Thus, a representation of explicit time through the @ connective is useful even when state is included in the logic.

Other connectives and time. The following list of admissible and inadmissible properties highlights salient points of the interaction between @ and other connectives of BL. Notably, $(s_1 \supset s_2) @ [u_1, u_2]$ is equivalent to having a single proof of $(s_1 @ [x_1, x_2]) \supset (s_2 @ [x_1, x_2])$ for every subinterval $[x_1, x_2]$ of $[u_1, u_2]$ (property 8 below). In the following, $s \equiv r$ denotes $(s \supset r) \wedge (r \supset s)$, $\vdash s$ means that $\Sigma; \cdot; \cdot; \cdot \xrightarrow{\nu} s \circ [u_1, u_2]$ for all u_1, u_2, ν and appropriate Σ, and $\nvdash s$ means that the latter is not true for s in the stated generality.

1. $\vdash ((u_1 \leq u_1') \wedge (u_2' \leq u_2)) \supset ((s @ [u_1, u_2]) \supset (s @ [u_1', u_2']))$
2. $\vdash ((s @ [u_1, u_2]) @ [u_1', u_2']) \equiv (s @ [u_1, u_2])$
3. $\vdash ((s_1 \wedge s_2) @ [u_1, u_2]) \equiv ((s_1 @ [u_1, u_2]) \wedge (s_2 @ [u_1, u_2]))$
4. $\vdash ((\forall x.s) @ [u_1, u_2]) \equiv (\forall x.(s @ [u_1, u_2]))$ $\qquad (x \notin u_1, u_2)$
5. $\vdash \top @ [u_1, u_2]$
6. $\vdash (\bot @ [u_1, u_2]) \supset (s @ [u_1', u_2'])$
7. There is no interval $[u_1, u_2]$ such that $\vdash \bot @ [u_1, u_2]$
8. $\vdash ((s_1 \supset s_2) @ [u_1, u_2]) \equiv (\forall x_1. \forall x_2. (((u_1 \leq x_1) \wedge (x_2 \leq u_2) \wedge (s_1 @ [x_1, x_2]))$
   $\supset (s_2 @ [x_1, x_2])))$
9. $\vdash ((k \text{ says } s) @ [u_1, u_2]) \supset (k \text{ says } (s @ [u_1, u_2]))$
10. $\nvdash (k \text{ says } (s @ [u_1, u_2])) \supset ((k \text{ says } s) @ [u_1, u_2])$

4   Metatheory of BL

We prove several important metatheoretic properties of BL. The first lemma below states that proofs respect substitution of stateful atoms, which, in a sense, means that the proof theory preserves the meaning of the judgment $\Sigma; E \models i$. A similar property holds for constraints, but we do not state it explicitly.

Lemma 1. $\Sigma; E \models i$ and $\Sigma; \Psi; E, i; \Gamma \xrightarrow{\nu} r \circ [u_1, u_2]$ imply $\Sigma; \Psi; E; \Gamma \xrightarrow{\nu} r \circ [u_1, u_2]$.

Our main metatheoretic results are admissibility of cut — the proof of a judgment can be used to discharge the same judgment used as a hypothesis in another proof — and identity — any judgment assumed as hypothesis can be concluded. Admissibility of cut is a proof-theoretic statement of soundness of a logic. Dually, identity is a proof-theoretic statement of completeness of the logic's inference rules. Together, the proofs of the two theorems show that the rules of the logic fit well with each other [28].

Theorem 1 (Admissibility of cut). $\Sigma; \Psi; E; \Gamma \xrightarrow{\nu} s \circ [u_1, u_2]$ and $\Sigma; \Psi; E; \Gamma, s \circ [u_1, u_2] \xrightarrow{\nu} s' \circ [u_1', u_2']$ imply $\Sigma; \Psi; E; \Gamma \xrightarrow{\nu} s' \circ [u_1', u_2']$.

Proof. By simultaneous induction, first on the structure of s, and then on the depths of the two given derivations, as in prior work [27].

Theorem 2 (Identity). $\Sigma; \Psi; E; \Gamma, s \circ [u_1, u_2] \xrightarrow{\nu} s \circ [u_1, u_2]$.

Proof. By induction on s.

By an analysis of inference rules, it also follows that the logic is proof-theoretically consistent, i.e., $\bot$ cannot be proved a priori. Similarly, k says $\bot$ cannot be proved a priori.

Theorem 3 (Consistency). *(1)* $\Sigma; \cdot; \cdot; \cdot \nxrightarrow{\nu} \bot \circ [u_1, u_2]$, and *(2)* $\Sigma; \cdot; \cdot; \cdot \nxrightarrow{\nu} (k \text{ says } \bot) \circ [u_1, u_2]$.

5   Related Work

Several formal frameworks for authorization policies allow for representation of state, but no prior proposal has considered an integration of state and logic from a proof-theoretic perspective. Perhaps closest to BL's treatment of stateful atoms is the Nexus Authorization Logic (NAL) [30] that is used for authorizing access in several components of the Nexus operating system. NAL includes support for state predicates in a manner similar to that stipulated in Section 3.2, i.e., the reference monitor verifies certain predicates using trusted decision procedures that may refer to the system state. Several other logic-based frameworks for representing authorization policies [7,4,9,21] do not make a distinction between constraints and state predicates, and consequently support system state implicitly as part of their support for constraints. However, we believe that maintaining this distinction is important from the perspective of both implementation and reasoning about policies expressed in logic.

There has also been some work on declarative languages and logics in which authorization policies and *state transitions* can be represented and reasoned about simultaneously [6,8,13]. In contrast, BL's state predicates are meant to model situations where rules for state transitions are not specified. Some recent programming languages, e.g., [11,10], use type systems to enforce state-dependent authorization policies that are represented in first-order logic. Stateful atoms are not distinguished from others in the proof theory used in these languages.

The connective k says s has been included in several past proposals for writing access policies, starting with the work of Abadi et al [2]. The BL connective $s @ [u_1, u_2]$ is based on our prior work with DeYoung [12], and our treatment of constraints goes further back to work on reconciling constraint domains and proof theory of linear logic [29,20]. Study of proof theory for authorization logics was initiated in our prior work [15]. The present paper incorporates many ideas from that work, especially the use of intuitionistic first-order logic as a foundation for authorization policies.

6   Conclusion

A proof-theoretic treatment of state in an authorization logic requires careful design. Part of the complication arises due to the well-understood difficulty of reconciling decision procedures with proof theory, but most of the design choices arise in the interaction between state predicates and other features of authorization logic, in particular, explicit time. The logic BL strikes a good balance in this design space, as evident from its strong metatheoretic foundations and validation through a realistic case study.

Acknowledgments. This research was supported in part by the AFRL under grant no. FA87500720028, and the iCAST project sponsored by the National Science Council, Taiwan under grant no. NSC97-2745-P-001-001. The first author was also supported by the AFOSR MURI "Collaborative Policies and Assured Information Sharing." We thank Denis Serenyi and Brian Witten for providing textual descriptions of policies for the case study and for subsequent discussions on them, and anonymous referees for their helpful comments on this paper.

References

1. Abadi, M.: Access control in a core calculus of dependency. Electronic Notes in Theoretical Computer Science 172, 5–31 (2007); Computation, Meaning, and Logic: Articles dedicated to Gordon Plotkin
2. Abadi, M., Burrows, M., Lampson, B., Plotkin, G.: A calculus for access control in distributed systems. ACM Transactions on Programming Languages and Systems 15(4), 706–734 (1993)
3. Appel, A.W., Felten, E.W.: Proof-carrying authentication. In: 6th ACM Conference on Computer and Communications Security (CCS), pp. 52–62 (1999)
4. Bauer, L.: Access Control for the Web via Proof-Carrying Authorization. Ph.D. thesis, Princeton University (2003)
5. Bauer, L., Garriss, S., McCune, J.M., Reiter, M.K., Rouse, J., Rutenbar, P.: Device-enabled authorization in the grey system. In: Zhou, J., López, J., Deng, R.H., Bao, F. (eds.) ISC 2005. LNCS, vol. 3650, pp. 431–445. Springer, Heidelberg (2005)
6. Becker, M.Y.: Specification and analysis of dynamic authorisation policies. In: 22nd IEEE Computer Security Foundations Symposium (CSF), pp. 203–217 (2009)
7. Becker, M.Y., Fournet, C., Gordon, A.D.: Design and semantics of a decentralized authorization language. In: 20th IEEE Computer Security Foundations Symposium, pp. 3–15 (2007)
8. Becker, M.Y., Nanz, S.: A logic for state-modifying authorization policies. In: Biskup, J., López, J. (eds.) ESORICS 2007. LNCS, vol. 4734, pp. 203–218. Springer, Heidelberg (2007)
9. Becker, M.Y., Sewell, P.: Cassandra: Flexible trust management applied to health records. In: 17th IEEE Computer Security Foundations Workshop (CSFW), pp. 139–154 (2004)
10. Borgstrm, J., Gordon, A.D., Pucella, R.: Roles, stacks, histories: A triple for Hoare. Tech. Rep. MSR-TR-2009-97, Microsoft Research (2009)
11. Broberg, N., Sands, D.: Paralocks: Role-based information flow control and beyond. SIGPLAN Notices 45(1), 431–444 (2010)
12. DeYoung, H., Garg, D., Pfenning, F.: An authorization logic with explicit time. In: 21st IEEE Computer Security Foundations Symposium (CSF), pp. 133–145 (2009); extended version available as Carnegie Mellon University Technical Report CMU-CS-07-166
13. DeYoung, H., Pfenning, F.: Reasoning about the consequences of authorization policies in a linear epistemic logic, Workshop on Foundations of Computer Security, FCS (2009), http://www.cs.cmu.edu/~hdeyoung/papers/fcs09.pdf
14. Garg, D.: Proof Theory for Authorization Logic and Its Application to a Practical File System. Ph.D. thesis, Carnegie Mellon University, Technical Report CMU-CS-09-168 (2009)
15. Garg, D., Pfenning, F.: Non-interference in constructive authorization logic. In: 19th Computer Security Foundations Workshop (CSFW), pp. 283–293 (2006)
16. Garg, D., Pfenning, F.: A proof-carrying file system. In: Proceedings of the 31st IEEE Symposium on Security and Privacy, Oakland, pp. 349–364 (2010)

17. Garg, D., Pfenning, F., Serenyi, D., Witten, B.: A logical representation of common rules for controlling access to classified information. Tech. Rep. CMU-CS-09-139, Carnegie Mellon University (2009)
18. Gentzen, G.: Untersuchungen über das logische Schließen. Mathematische Zeitschrift 39, 176–210, 405–431 (1935); English translation in Szabo, M.E. (ed.) The Collected Papers of Gerhard Gentzen, pp. 68–131. North-Holland, Amsterdam (1969)
19. Housley, R., Ford, W., Polk, W., Solo, D.: Internet X.509 public key infrastructure (1999), http://www.ietf.org/rfc/rfc2459.txt
20. Jia, L.: Linear Logic and Imperative Programming. Ph.D. thesis, Department of Computer Science, Princeton University (2008)
21. Li, N., Mitchell, J.C., Winsborough, W.: Design of a role-based trust-management framework. In: 23rd IEEE Symposium on Security and Privacy, Oakland, pp. 114–130 (2002)
22. Martin-Löf, P.: On the meanings of the logical constants and the justifications of the logical laws. Nordic Journal of Philosophical Logic 1(1), 11–60 (1996)
23. Office of the Director of Central Intelligence: DCID 1/19: Security policy for sensitive compartmented information and security policy manual (1995), http://www.fas.org/irp/offdocs/dcid1-19.html
24. Office of the Director of Central Intelligence: DCID 1/7: Security controls on the dissemination of intelligence information (1998), http://www.fas.org/irp/offdocs/dcid1-7.html
25. Office of the Press Secretary of the White House: Executive order 12958: Classified national security information (1995), http://www.fas.org/sgp/clinton/eo12958.html
26. Office of the Press Secretary of the White House: Executive order 13292: Further amendment to executive order 12958, as amended, classified national security information (2003), http://nodis3.gsfc.nasa.gov/displayEO.cfm?id=EO_13292_
27. Pfenning, F.: Structural cut elimination I. Intuitionistic and classical logic. Information and Computation 157(1/2), 84–141 (2000)
28. Pfenning, F., Davies, R.: A judgmental reconstruction of modal logic. Mathematical Structures in Computer Science 11, 511–540 (2001)
29. Saranli, U., Pfenning, F.: Using constrained intuitionistic linear logic for hybrid robotic planning problems. In: International Conference on Robotics and Automation (ICRA), pp. 3705–3710 (2007)
30. Schneider, F.B., Walsh, K., Sirer, E.G.: Nexus Authorization Logic (NAL): Design rationale and applications. Tech. rep. Cornell University (2009), http://ecommons.library.cornell.edu/handle/1813/13679

Privacy-Friendly Energy-Metering via Homomorphic Encryption

Flavio D. Garcia and Bart Jacobs

Institute for Computing and Information Sciences,
Radboud University Nijmegen,
P.O. Box 9010, NL-6500 GL Nijmegen, The Netherlands
{flaviog,bart}@cs.ru.nl

Abstract. The first part of this paper discusses developments wrt. smart (electricity) meters (simply called E-meters) in general, with emphasis on security and privacy issues. The second part will be more technical and describes protocols for secure communication with E-meters and for fraud detection (leakage) in a privacy-preserving manner. Our approach uses a combination of Paillier's additive homomorphic encryption and additive secret sharing to compute the aggregated energy consumption of a given set of users.

Keywords: smart-metering, privacy, homomorphic encryption.

1 Introduction

Many countries, for instance in Europe and North America, are currently undergoing changes in their electricity infrastructure, in which a better match between production and consumption is one of the goals. Accurate usage data is important for such a better match. So-called smart meters, or advanced meters [LGGG07], or E-meters, for consumers are a basic element in building a "smart grid" for electricity production and distribution. Frequent meter readings can be used to optimise the grid, but also reveal behavioural patterns, for instance about whether the inhabitants are at home, or at what time they get up or go to bed. Refined data analysis/mining over longer periods may reveal further information, for instance about the kind of devices that are being used, at which time, *etc.*

Privacy concerns are thus highly relevant in this context, and should be taken seriously by the utility sector. For instance, in April 2009 the Senate in the Netherlands has refused to pass a bill that made it compulsory for consumers to accept E-meters in their homes, precisely because of privacy concerns—and more generally, data protection concerns. This blocking of mandatory roll-out worked as wake-up call for the utility sector, at least in the Netherlands.

The issues of privacy, data protection and computer security are being addressed by various parties, see for instance the report [CPW09] by the Canadian information and privacy commissioner, or [NIS10] by NIST in the US (see also [EPI09]). Most of the emphasis in these documents lies on regulation via standards, procedures, rules of conduct, auditing, independent oversight, *etc.*

J. Cuellar et al. (Eds.): STM 2010, LNCS 6710, pp. 226–238, 2011.

The emphasis in this paper will be on using technical means for achieving certain security and/or privacy goals, via privacy-protecting cryptographic techniques. In this way data minimalisation is enforced not only by design but also by implementation. The cryptographic techniques ensure that sufficient information is available to achieve certain goals, without revealing additional (privacy-sensitive) information. Specifically, Section 4 uses homomorphic (Paillier) encryption and additive secret sharing to make the aggregated consumption readings visible at the neighbourhood level, without revealing E-meter readings at the household level. By comparing the aggregated consumption with the measurement of the actual consumption at the neighbourhood level, electricity leakage (via fraud) can be detected.

The first part of the paper discusses general issues in (electricity) metering and argues towards the inclusion of a trusted element, like a smart card, in E-meters. This is reflected in the slogan "power to the meter!". Such a trusted element provides secure storage of meter readings (like the traditional meter does via hardware protection), and basic cryptographic primitives based on public key cryptography, for authentication and secure communication. The protocols later on in the paper are based on the availability of such primitives. They demonstrate how basic cryptographic techniques can be used to achieve justifiable monitoring aims of grid operators without violating privacy of consumers.

In particular, Section 4 describes a protocol whereby data concentrators at the neighbourhood level can obtain sums of the measurements of all the connected customers (typically a few hundred) without learning the individual measurements. By comparing this sum with its own measurement of the consumed amount, it becomes clear how much energy leaks in this neighboorhood. These protocols may be run frequently, say every 15 minutes, without affecting privacy. In case serious leakage levels are found, additional means of investigation will have to used to detect the reason. How to do this is beyond the scope of the current paper.

In Section 5 appropriate security notions are introduced for the protocol from Section 4. In essence they say that an adversary should not be able to notice the swapping of the measurements of two customers. A sketch of a security proof is included for our protocol.

2   Background on Smart Metering

This section discusses the main players, the concerns and architecture for E-metering. We shall not go deeply into the E-metering set-up, and abstract for instance from the technique for communication with E-meters (GSM, power line communication, . . .) and from the technique for the measurement of electricity consumption.

2.1   Stakeholders

The main stakeholders that we distinguish are:

- The electricity producer, *i.e.* the company that produces electricity and sells it to its customers. It needs accurate data about how much to produce at which moment, and how much (generation) capacity it needs to keep in reserve. Additionally, it needs cumulative usage data of individual customers for billing, on a monthly or bi-monthly basis.

- The grid operator, *i.e.* the company that controls the infrastructure for the distribution and transportation of electricity from producers to customers, and returns usage data to producers. In principle the metering can also be done by a separate party, but this is not what is assumed here for reasons of simplicity. Grid operators need accurate data about electricity flows and status information about essential grid components, in order to optimise their networks.
- The consumer of electricity, which is in the present setting a household consumer, and not a larger organisation (for which there are usually separate arrangements). European electricity regulation foresees 80% of consumers equipped with *E*-metering systems by 2020. Consumers must be regularly made aware of their energy consumption and its associated costs, in the hope that this leads to energy savings.

There are of course more stakeholders in this field, like regulators, (national) authorities, and *E*-meter producers. Their role will not be discussed here.

A fundamental question is: how much information do the operators and producers need to run their operations? For electricity producers this is relatively easy: they need cumulative and not continuous information for billing, and statistical information for usage patterns. This does not have serious privacy implications. Grid operators may need more information to efficiently run their network. From a privacy perspective, the question is whether they need usage information about individual households, or whether aggregated information from so-called substations at the neighbourhood level suffices. A stumbling block in the current debate is that no clear answers are given to this question. Therefor the operators seem to want all information, at the individual household level, with short intervals, down to quarter hour measurements, and they will see later how much information they will actually use.

From a data protection and privacy perspective this attitude is clearly unacceptable. First, justifiable goals for data gathering must be clearly defined, and subsequently data minimization techniques must be applied to achieve these goals, with not more (identifiable) data than strictly necessary.

Experience in the Netherlands shows that grid operators find it difficult, and are thus reluctant, to define their goals other than in very generic terms (optimisation of their grids). However, the existing level of resistance forces them to take these issues more seriously.

2.2   Privacy Concerns

Frequently measuring electricity consumption is privacy sensitive, because it reveals behavioural patterns that can be abused in various ways.

1. Daily measurements reveal any day whether a house is inhabited or not. It thus shows when the inhabitants are away for a weekend, or for a couple of

weeks, on holidays. This information is relevant for burglars, for instance. Out-of-context storage of such measurement data in the servers of grid operators creates vulnerabilities, because the servers may be hacked, or system managers may be bribed or blackmailed into handing the data over to malicious outsiders.

2. More frequent, hourly or even quarter-hourly measurements, reveal even more information. Devout muslims get up at five in the morning for their first prayers, and can thus be singled-out, with some level of certainty (possibly in combination with names). Whether or not people are staying over in one-person flats may be noticeable. For instance, Figure 1 displays hourly measurements of electricity, water and gas of a particular home[1]. It seems that the inhabitants arrive at home at five in the afternoon, and that one (or more?) of them is taking a shower or bath at one o'clock at night. These measurement data are collected within private homes, "behind the front door" and inside "my home as my castle". They may make people exposed.

3. Long-term detailed insight in power consumption enables data mining and profiling in various ways (see [Har89, Qui09]). For instance, the grid operators can observe certain patterns, like when the fridge switches on and how much electricity it uses. The operator can even observe if such a fridge becomes old (less efficient) and needs to be replaced soon. This information can be used, for instance, for targeted (fridge) advertisements, listing a particular brand of fridges only—for which the grid operator gets a commission with each sell. Consumers may view this positively as a service or negatively as a form of intrusion.

A recent report [CK08] commissioned by the consumer organisation in the Netherlands, argues that frequent reading of E-meters is problematic from a legal perspective, specifically because it violates article 8 on Privacy of the European Convention on Human Rights: a pressing need in a democratic society to force people to deliver privacy sensitive usage data is lacking. The setup which is foreseen may thus be challenged at some stage in (European) court. Hence a long-term perspective, building on trust and societal acceptance, is needed.

An additional sensitive issue is that remote reduction, or even shutdown, of electricity supply is foreseen, for instance in case of nonpayement. This creates a huge denial of service (DOS) risk, not only for individual customers, but also for national security (in case of cyber warfare, or as force multiplier in a terrorist attack)[2].

2.3   Centralised Trust

Traditional (legacy) electricity meters have a physical counter that moves forward due to a metallic disc that turns with a speed proportional to the electricity

---

[1] The homeowner(s) voluntarily put these data on the web, see `bwired.nl`.

[2] It thus makes sense to restrict this remote shutdown to a certain minimal level only, so that one can still switch on the light but not the whirlpool bath. This can be achieved physically by having two wires, and restricting the shutdown functionality to only one of them.

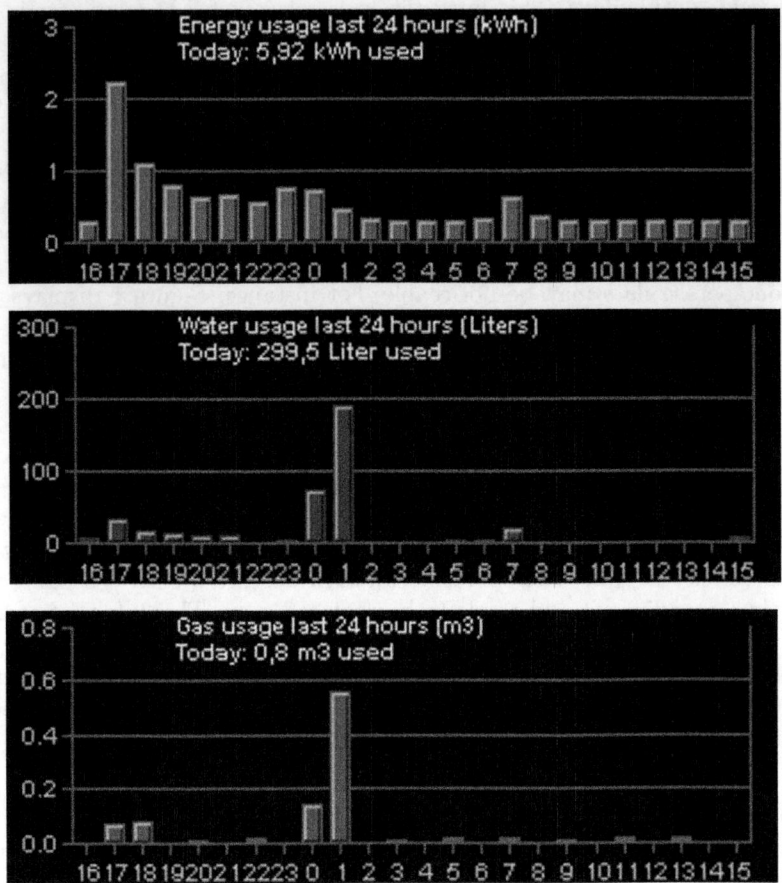

Fig. 1. Example hourly measurements of electricity, water and gas, from `bwired.nl`

consumption. This process takes place within a sealed container, so that tampering is not so easy and can be detected. It involves local storage of cumulative usage levels, in a way that is fairly reliable. Such domestic meters may last for decades. The hardware protection works in two directions: it prevents that customers (easily) manipulate (esp. decrease) the meter readings, so that they pay less than they should. But it also prevents that electricity suppliers (easily) manipulate (esp. increase) the meter readings so that customers pay more than they should. Additionally it protects against other possibly malicious actors. This set-up with protected local storage is essential for guaranteeing a reasonable level of trust, in two directions.

The focus of the current generation of *E*-meters is on protection against manipulation by customers. No (technical) protection is foreseen against manipulation by grid operators, since they can remotely update not only crucial values like timers and cryptographic keys, but also install new software and thus completely replace the functionality of the meters whenever they like. Grid operators thus need to be universally trusted. Customers are protected only by procedural guidelines, audits, codes of behaviour ("we do not read your meter surreptitiously"). Furthermore, the measurement data are no longer only locally securely stored, in-context, but they are stored (also) centrally, out-of-context in the database of the operator.

This change in responsibilities and in the balance of power is remarkable. Whether it is in the long term interest of the operators (and the utility sector at large) remains to be seen. When people are forced to trust a single party, this trust may suddenly collapse, like for voting machines [JP09]. Abuse will get media attention and the premiss of universal trust in the operator will then be questioned. Also, customers may contest their bills in court. If such a customer claims his bill is incorrect or even fabricated by the grid operator (or by someone else) because of software malfunctioning, the grid operator is in such a set-up in a weak position to defend itself. After all, the grip operator controls all software, timing, storage, and cryptographic keys of the E-meter.

2.4 Secure Authentication and Local Storage: "Power to the Meter"

Usually in the security architecture of a distributed system one identifies the different islands of trust, and provides each of them with their own trusted computing base (TCB), and with secure communication lines between them, going across security boundaries through untrusted territories. The current design does not have such a structure. Instead, there is only one party that is universally trusted (the grid operator) and has total control over the others (notably the E-meters and substations at the neighbourhood level), since it has the "divine" power to (remotely) replace the software and cryptographic keys of the others.

A more robust and trustworthy design gives the E-meters (and probably also the substations) a certain level of autonomy via trusted elements, providing secure storage and autonomous cryptographic functionality. These trusted elements should lie outside the reach of the operators. In particular, it should not be possible to remotely change their software or change their cryptographic keys. The software of the device in which the trusted element resides may then be updated remotely, because the device is not part of the trusted computing base[3]. A similar, but more elaborate form of local autonomy, is proposed in [LGGG07] via the Trusted Platform Module (TPM), hypervisors, and several separate Virtual Machines (VMs).

Via such trusted elements, like smart cards or secure USB sticks, E-meters can digitally sign the messages they send, including the meter readings. This provides confidentiality and integrity, but also non-repudiation, which should be the basis of conflict resolution, see Section 3.

In a rather predictable future scenario electric cars will be used more extensively. A domestic E-meter could be provided with several such USB sticks for mobile electricity consumption. When visiting a friend by (electric) car, charging

---

[3] Admittedly, this architecture is more complicated than sketched here, because the trusted computing base must also include the measurement sensor and a clock.

the batteries over there can be billed to my own account via such a USB stick for secure authentication. It thus makes sense to build secure authentication deep into the architecture of E-meters, certainly if this infrastructure is meant to last for decades[4].

In the remainder of this paper we shall thus assume that E-meters have secure elements providing a trusted computing base with secure storage and basic cryptographic functionality, including public key cryptography. We assume that the software of these trusted elements cannot be changed remotely by the operators. Also, the private keys of, or generated by, these trusted elements are inaccessible from the outside. They do have a number of certificates (with public keys), for instance of the grid operator, of a number of electricity producers, and possibly of additional service providers. New certificates may be sent to the trusted element, provided with appropriate signatures, for instance after expiry of the old ones, or when new parties arrive on the market. Ideally, these trusted elements also have their own clock and power supply, for instance embedded in a USB stick. In case of a major security break down these trusted elements will have to be replaced (physically).

Current E-meters, as far we know, do not have such separate trusted elements and rely mostly on symmetric key cryptography (if any). The security level that they provide is limited, see for instance [KR08]. The E-meter market is not very mature yet, making early large scale roll-out risky.

3   Basic Protocols

This section sketches some protocols for basic communication with E-meters, using elementary cryptographic operations. They ensure that messages are authentic, fresh (to prevent replay), and confidential. Moreover, they provide integrity protection and non-repudiation. These protocols are fairly obvious but are included to demonstrate how basic cryptographic primitives can secure the communication and provide authenticity. Their implementation with existing technology is unproblematic. For instance, we have our own prototype implementation using cheap Java-enabled smart cards.

This protocol involves three parties:

- the smart-meter $\mathcal{M}$;
- the grid operator GO;
- the supplier $\mathcal{S}$.

Notation. We write $\{m\}_{\mathcal{A}}$ to denote the encryption of message m under $\mathcal{A}$'s public key; $\mathcal{K}$ is the key generation algorithm; $[m]_{\mathcal{A}}$ denotes the signature produced by $\mathcal{A}$ on the message m.

Initially, $\mathcal{M}$ holds the public key of GO and the key of the certification authority CA. The grid operator GO might initiate the interactive protocols **set_supplier**

---

[4] Such non-domestic electricity consumption introduces additional location-sensitive privacy issues which form a topic on its own.

and **switch_power** with $\mathcal{M}$. In contrast to the current setup where the grid operator can access the meter readings at will, we propose a setting where grid operators can set a reading policy, indicating who is the energy supplier and how often the meter is supposed to report the meter readings for billing purposes. This time period P, typically 2 months, can be shown to the consumers on the meter's display, and then it is the meter itself who initiates the **meter_report** protocol.

Concretely, in the **set_supplier** protocol, the grid operator GO says hello, I want to set a new supplier. Then the meter sends a challenge nonce n in order to ensure freshness. Then GO sends an encrypted and signed message containing the new policy, *i.e.*, the identity of the new supplier and its public key, the time period P for the reports and a time-stamp ts determining when the new supplier takes over.

set_supplier:

$GO \rightarrow \mathcal{M}$: hi, init set_supplier

$\mathcal{M} \rightarrow GO$: nonce n

$GO \rightarrow \mathcal{M}$: $\{\,[\,\text{set\_supplier}, \mathcal{M}, n, \mathcal{S}, \text{pk}_{\mathcal{S}}, \text{ts}, P\,]_{GO}\,\}_{\mathcal{M}}$

In emergency situations or in case of nonpayment, there is the requirement that grid operators can unplug a household from the grid or there is also the possibility of a partial disconnect where the meter allows only a few kW/h for basic needs. The following **switch_power** protocol implements this functionality, where power $\in [0,1]$ represents the permitted consumption, being 0 totaly unplugged and 1 fully operational.

switch_power:

$GO \rightarrow \mathcal{M}$: hi, init switch_power

$\mathcal{M} \rightarrow GO$: nonce n

$GO \rightarrow \mathcal{M}$: $\{\,[\,\text{switch\_power}, \mathcal{M}, n, \text{ts}, \text{power}\,]_{GO}\,\}_{\mathcal{M}}$

Starting from the time ts from the **set_supplier** protocol and for every period of time P, the meter $\mathcal{M}$ will report the meter readings to the supplier $\mathcal{S}$. This message, in fact, is being relayed by the grid operator to the supplier, but we abstract from that since end-to-end encryption is used.

meter_report:

$\mathcal{M} \rightarrow \mathcal{S}$: $\{\,[\,\mathcal{M}, \text{time}, \text{meter readings}\,]_{\mathcal{M}}\,\}_{\mathcal{S}}$

These protocols are sufficient for billing purposes and, provided that the time period P is large enough, the privacy sensitive information revealed is minimal.

There is one issue though, for leakage or fraud detection and smart-grid optimization, grid operators claim that they need much more frequent readings, more in the order of every 15 minutes. On the positive side, for this tasks they do not need the specific readings of each meter, but it is enough to know the aggregated consumption at block or neighborhood level. Section 4 describes a protocol that achieves such goals in a privacy-friendly manner.

4   The No-Leakage Protocol

We assume a local substation SSt that is connected to several customer meter devices $\mathcal{M}_1, \ldots, \mathcal{M}_N$, as in Figure 2. Typically N is in the order of a few hundred. The number of meter devices connected to SSt may change over time, due to addition or removal of meters.

The SSt supplies electricity / gas / water, to the $\mathcal{M}_i$, and measures these total supplies m_{SSt} at regular intervals, for instance every 15 minutes. The $\mathcal{M}_i$ have their own (regular) measurements m_i, and report these measurements back to the SSt.

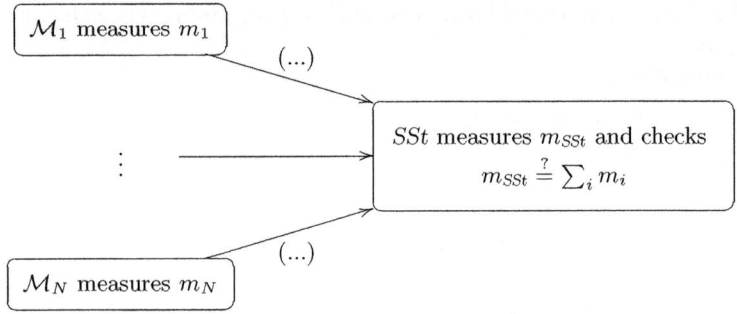

Fig. 2. Neighboorhood set-up, with supplies to the $\mathcal{M}_i$ going via SSt, and protected measurements m_i sent back at regular intervals. The total supply m_{SSt} measured by SSt should equal the sum of the m_i, at each interval.

The goal of the no-leakage protocol is to learn the aggregated energy consumption of N consumers (think of a neighborhood) without revealing any information about the individual consumption of the users, even when the data concentrator is malicious, *i.e.*, does not necessarily follow the protocol.

The security of this protocol relies on the assumption that at least two out of N users in the neighborhood are uncorrupted, *i.e.*, they behave according to the protocol specification. More precisely, we assume that there is a trusted certification authority that issues certificates and that the adversary is unable to obtain a large number of public key certificates for which he knows the private key. This assumption seems unavoidable since it is inherent in the problem that when the adversary knows the consumption of all-but-one consumers then she can trivially learn the consumption of the last consumer by simply running the protocol and subtracting.

Let $\{ \cdot \}$. be an IND-CPA secure, additively homomorphic encryption scheme satisfying $\{ m_1 \}_k \cdot \{ m_2 \}_k = \{ m_1 + m_2 \}_k$ like Paillier [Pai99]. Assume that each meter $\mathcal{M}_i$ has a public key certificate $cert_{\mathcal{M}_i}$ of his public key pk_i, and he also has knowledge of the corresponding private (decryption) key.

The no-leakage protocol is depicted in Figure 3. The data concentrator initiates the protocol by sending the public key certificates of all users in the neighborhood. If the number of certificates is smaller than the minimum neighborhood

$SSt \longrightarrow \mathcal{M}_i$: no-leakage; $cert_{\mathcal{M}_1}, \ldots, cert_{\mathcal{M}_N}$

$\mathcal{M}_i \longrightarrow SSt$: $y_{i1}, \ldots, y_{ii-1}, y_{ii+1}, \ldots, y_{iN}$

where $\mathcal{M}_i$ picks random numbers $a_{i1}, \ldots, a_{iN}$ s.t. $m_i{=}\sum_j a_{ij} \mod n$

and sets $y_{ij} := \{a_{ij}\}_{\text{pk}_j}$ for $j = 1, \ldots, i-1, i+1, \ldots, N$.

If $N < N_{\min}$ then $\mathcal{M}_i$ aborts.

$SSt \longrightarrow \mathcal{M}_i$: $\prod_{j \neq i} y_{ji} = \{\sum_{j \neq i} a_{ji}\}_{\text{pk}_i}$ (due to the homomorphic property of $\{\cdot\}$.)

$\mathcal{M}_i \longrightarrow SSt$: $\sum_{j \neq i} a_{ji} + a_{ii} = \sum_j a_{ji} \mod n$

SSt sets $m := \sum_i \sum_j a_{ji} \mod n$.

Fig. 3. No-leakage protocol

size allowed N_{min}, then the participants abort the protocol. This prevent information leakage when the neighborhood is too small, ultimately of size one. Then, each $\mathcal{M}_i$ prepares N shares $a_{i1}, \ldots, a_{iN}$ of its measurement m_i s.t. $m_i = \sum_j a_{ij}$ mod n, for a large n. $\mathcal{M}_i$ encrypts each of these shares a_{ij} with the public key pk_j of user $\mathcal{M}_j$ and sends them back to SSt, except for the share a_{ii}, which is simply remembered locally by $\mathcal{M}_i$. Next, SSt multiplies all $N - 1$ ciphertexts intended to user $\mathcal{M}_i$ and sends the resulting ciphertext to him to decrypt. Due to the aforementioned homomorphic property of the cipher, this equals the sum of these $N - 1$ shares. Next, $\mathcal{M}_i$ decrypts the received ciphertext, adds a_{ii} to the plaintext and sends back the result to SSt. This later addition of a_{ii} results crucial (i.e., prevents an attacker from using this step of the protocol as a decryption oracle) to the security (and soundness) of the protocol. Finally, SSt collects the contributions from all users and adds them to obtain the aggregated consumption m which can be compared to m_{SSt}.

5   Security Notions

This section elaborates precise security notions for metering protocols. We first recall the standard IND-CPA security for encryption schemes and then we introduce two new security notions for metering protocols: correctness and no-leakage.

Definition 5.1 (IND-CPA-Game).

$$
\begin{array}{l}
\textit{\textbf{IND-CPA-Game}}_{\Pi,\mathcal{A}}(\eta) \; : \\[4pt]
(sk, pk) \leftarrow \mathcal{K}(1^\eta) \\[2pt]
p_0, p_1 \leftarrow \mathcal{A}_0(pk) \\[2pt]
b \leftarrow \{0,1\} \\[2pt]
b' \leftarrow \mathcal{A}_1(\{p_b\}_{pk}) \\[2pt]
\textit{\textbf{winif}} \; \textit{if } b = b'.
\end{array}
$$

Adversaries implicitly pass state i.e., from $\mathcal{A}_0$ to $\mathcal{A}_1$.

Definition 5.2 (IND-CPA). *An encryption scheme Π is said to be* IND-CPA *secure if for all probabilistic polynomial-time adversaries $\mathcal{A} = (\mathcal{A}_0, \mathcal{A}_1)$*

$$\mathbb{P}[\textbf{IND-CPA-Game}_{\Pi,\mathcal{A}}(\eta)] - 1/2$$

is a negligible function of η.

Definition 5.3 (correctness). *A protocol Π is said to be correct if it indeed outputs the aggregated consumption of all N participants, i.e., a value $m = \sum_{i=0}^{N} m_i$.*

Next we want to define what does it mean for a protocol to be non-leaking. We will do so in the style of what IND-CCA is for an encryption scheme. For that we first define an indistinguishability game and then we concretely define no-leakage. The intuition behind the definition is that if an adversary cannot even distinguish the swapping of the consumptions of two arbitrary users, then the protocol does not reveal information about the individual consumptions of the users.

The game proceeds as follows. First, the key generation algorithm is invoked to create a public/private key pair (sk, pk) for the certification authority CA and for each meter. Then, the certification authority CA outputs the corresponding public key certificates and these are given to the adversary $\mathcal{A}_0$, together with the public key pk_{CA} of the CA. At this point the adversary is able to query the corruption oracle $\mathcal{O}$ in order to retrieve the private keys of a number of meters. At some point the adversary $\mathcal{A}_0$ stops and outputs two uncorrupted target meters $\mathcal{M}_0^{\star}$ and $\mathcal{M}_1^{\star}$ and two challenge consumption measurements m_0 and m_1. Then, the environment chooses a random bit b which determines a permutation of m_0 and m_1. Then, $\mathcal{A}_1$ can interact with the challenge meters and try to learn information about their consumption. At any time $\mathcal{A}_1$ might query the corruption oracle, but the restriction over the target meters still apply. Eventually $\mathcal{A}_1$ stops and outputs a guess b' for the bit b. We say that the adversary wins the game if $b = b'$.

Definition 5.4 (No-Leakage-Game).

$$\boxed{\begin{aligned}
&\textbf{\textit{No-Leakage-Game}}_{\Pi,\mathcal{A}}(\eta) \; : \\
&(sk_{CA}, pk_{CA}) \leftarrow \mathcal{K}(1^\eta) \\
&(sk_0, pk_0) \ldots (sk_N, pk_N) \leftarrow \mathcal{K}(1^\eta) \\
&\text{cert}_0 \ldots \text{cert}_N \leftarrow CA(sk_{CA}, pk_0 \ldots pk_N) \\
&\mathcal{M}_0^{\star}, \mathcal{M}_1^{\star}, m_0, m_1 \leftarrow \mathcal{A}_0^{\mathcal{O}}(pk_{CA}, \text{cert}_0 \ldots \text{cert}_N) \\
&b \leftarrow \{0,1\} \\
&b' \leftarrow \mathcal{A}_1^{\mathcal{O}}(\mathcal{M}_0^{\star}(sk_0^{\star}, m_b), \mathcal{M}_1^{\star}(sk_1^{\star}, m_{1-b})) \\
&\textbf{\textit{winif}} \text{ if } b = b'.
\end{aligned}}$$

were the adversary $\mathcal{A}$ has access to a corrupting oracle $\mathcal{O}$ that on input the identity of a meter $\mathcal{M}_i$ returns its corresponding private key sk_i. The target meters $\mathcal{M}_0^{\star}$ and $\mathcal{M}_1^{\star}$ must be uncorrupted, which means that no $\mathcal{O}(\mathcal{M}_{\{0,1\}}^{\star})$ query is made. Adversaries implicitly pass state i.e., from $\mathcal{A}_0$ to $\mathcal{A}_1$.

Definition 5.5 (No-Leakage). *A protocol Π is said to be* non-leaking *if for all probabilistic polynomial-time adversaries $\mathcal{A} = (\mathcal{A}_0, \mathcal{A}_1)$*

$$\mathbb{P}[\textbf{\textit{No-Leakage-Game}}_{\Pi,\mathcal{A}}(\eta)] - 1/2$$

is a negligible function of η.

6 Security Analysis

This section shows correctness and no-leakage properties of the protocol proposed in Section 4.

Theorem 6.1. *The protocol depicted in Fig. 3 is correct.*

Proof. The proof of correctness is trivial, observe that

$$m = \sum_i \sum_j a_{ji} = \sum_i \sum_j a_{ij} = \sum_i m_i. \qquad \square$$

Theorem 6.2. *The protocol depicted in Fig. 3 is non-leaking.*

Proof. Assume that there is an adversary $\mathcal{B}$ that wins the **No-Leakage-Game** with probability significantly larger than $1/2$. Then we build the following adversary $\mathcal{A}$ against the IND-CPA security of the encryption scheme. For simplicity of the exposition and without loose of generality, assume that $N = 2$. If the no-leakage property holds for $N = 2$ then it holds for $N > 2$.

The adversary $\mathcal{A}$ will first simulate the environment for $\mathcal{B}$, this is, it will create a public key pair for the CA and a public key pair (pk_2, sk_2) for $\mathcal{M}_2$ by calling $\mathcal{K}$. The public key pair (pk_1, sk_1) of $\mathcal{M}_1$ will not be generated by $\mathcal{A}$ but the challenge public key pk from the INC-CPA game will be used instead of pk_1. Following the structure of the **No-Leakage-Game**, $\mathcal{A}$ will create the corresponding certificates $cert_{\mathcal{M}_1}$ and $cert_{\mathcal{M}_2}$. Then it calls $\mathcal{B}_0$ which will eventually output two target meters and two consumption measurements m_0 and m_1. Assume w.l.o.g that it outputs $\mathcal{M}_1$ and $\mathcal{M}_2$. Next $\mathcal{B}_1$ is called.

If at any point of the simulation $\mathcal{B}$ initiates a non-leakage protocol, then $\mathcal{A}$ will proceed as the protocol indicates choosing random $a_{11} + a_{12} = m_1$ and $a_{21} + a_{22} = m_2$. Then, instead of sending $y_{21} := \{\, a_{21}\,\}_{K_1}$ it will send $p_0 := a_{21}$ and $p_1 := a_{12}$ as challenge plaintexts for the IND-CPA game and it will get the challenge ciphertext $\{\, p_b\,\}_{k_1}$ in return, for a random bit b. $\mathcal{A}$ will choose a random bit $t \leftarrow \{0,1\}$ of its own and set $y_{21} := \{\, p_b\,\}_{k_1}$ and $y_{12} := \{\, p_t\,\}_{k_2}$. When $t = 0$ it will also swap the values of a_{11} and a_{22} to keep a consistent protocol run. Observe that due to the later addition of a_{ii}, this does not affect $\mathcal{B}$'s view of the protocol. For the rest of the protocol $\mathcal{A}$ follows the protocol description. At some point $\mathcal{B}$ stops and outputs a guess b'. Then $\mathcal{A}$ also finishes and outputs the same guess b'. Note that, when $t = 1 - b$, $\mathcal{A}$ has the same distinguishing advantage than $\mathcal{B}$, and this happens with probability $\frac{1}{2}$. $\qquad \square$

7 Conclusions

This paper discussed several privacy issues in the current smart metering infrastructure. We conclude that this structure has to be rethought in order to replace a unilateral trust assumption by a more multilateral architecture where *E*-meters have a trusted component and enjoy a certain level of autonomy. A trustworthy system should provide guarantees about the measurements for both grid operators *and* consumers. We have shown how to realize several tasks like billing, grid optimization and notably leakage detection in a privacy-friendly manner. The protocols proposed here are practical and can be straightforwardly implemented using inexpensive smart cards.

There is still much more research to be done in this area, but we hope that the concerns raised here will ignite fruitful discussions in an application area that is not yet up-to-date with the state of the art in cryptography.

References

[CK08]   Cuijpers, C., Koops, B.-J.: Het wetsvoorstel slimme meters: een privacytoets op basis van art. 8 EVRM. Technical report, Tilburg University, Report (October 2008) (in Dutch)

[CPW09]   Cavoukian, A., Polonetsky, J., Wolf, C.: SmartPrivacy for the Smart Grid: Embedding Privacy into the Design of Electricity Conservation (November 17, 2009), http://www.ipc.on.ca/images/Resources/pbd-smartpriv-smartgrid.pdf

[EPI09]   EPIC. Comments of the Electronic Privacy and Information Center on the NIST Smart Grid Standards (December 1, 2009), http://epic.org/privacy/smartgrid/EPIC_Smart_Grid_Cybersecurity_12-01-09.2.pdf

[Har89]   Hart, G.: Residential energy monitoring and computerized surveillance via utility power flows. IEEE Technology and Society Magazine 8(2), 12–16 (1989)

[JP09]   Jacobs, B., Pieters, W.: Electronic voting in The Netherlands: From early adoption to early abolishment. In: Aldini, A., Barthe, G. (eds.) FOSAD 2007/2008/2009. LNCS, vol. 5705, pp. 121–144. Springer, Heidelberg (2009)

[KR08]   Keemink, S., Roos, B.: Security Analysis of Dutch Smart Metering Systems. Technical report, Amsterdam: UvA (July 7, 2008), https://www.os3.nl/2007-2008/students/bart_roos/rp2

[LGGG07] LeMay, M., Gross, G., Gunter, C., Garg, S.: Unified architecture for large-scale attested metering. In: HICSS 2007: Proceedings of the 40th Annual Hawaii International Conference on System Sciences, pp. 115–125. IEEE Computer Society, Washington, DC, USA (2007)

[NIS10]   NIST. Smart Grid Cyber Security Strategy and Requirements (February 2, 2010), http://www.itl.nist.gov/div893/csrc/publications/drafts/nistir_7628/draft-nistir-7628_2nd-public-draft.pdf.

[Pai99]   Paillier, P.: Public-key cryptosystems based on composite degree residuosity classes (chapter 16). In: Stern, J. (ed.) EUROCRYPT 1999. LNCS, vol. 1592, pp. 223–238. Springer, Heidelberg (1999)

[Qui09]   Quinn, E.L.: Privacy and the New Energy Infrastructure (2009), http://ssrn.com/abstract=1370731

Extending an RFID Security and Privacy Model by Considering Forward Untraceability*

Mete Akgün[1,2] and Mehmet Ufuk Çağlayan[2]

[1] Tübitak UEKAE, 41470, Kocaeli, Turkey
makgun@uekae.tubitak.gov.tr
[2] Computer Engineering Department, Boğaziçi University, İstanbul, Turkey
caglayan@boun.edu.tr

Abstract. There are numerous works on the privacy and the security problems for RFID systems. However, many of them have failed due to the lack of formal security proof. In the literature, there are a few formal models that consider forward untraceability. In ASIACRYPT 2007, Vaudenay presented an new security and privacy model for RFID that combines early models to more understandable one. In this paper, we revisit Vaudenay's model and modify it by considering the notion of forward untraceability. Our modification considers all message flows between RFID reader and tags before and after compromising secrets of tag. We analyze some RFID schemes claiming to provide forward untraceability and resistance to server impersonation. For each scheme, we exhibit attacks in which a strong adversary can trace the future interactions of the tag and impersonate the valid server to the tag. Further, we show that a previously proposed attack claiming to violate forward untraceability of an existing RFID scheme does not violate forward untraceability.

Keywords: RFID, privacy, formal proof model, forward untraceability, server impersonation, authentication schemes.

1 Introduction

Radio Frequency Identification (RFID) technology that enhances ubiquitous computing environment is used to identify many types of objects. Some of the main applications are asset management, tracking, access control and automated payment scheme [1],[5],[6],[14]. Many of us can see RFID applications implemented for different purposes in daily life. However, privacy and security issues of RFID system are still the most prominent obstacle to make this technology widespread in various areas [14]. A bewildering number of privacy and security schemes have been proposed to eliminate security and privacy threats to RFID systems. However, there have been a few schemes providing formal security proof, therefore much existing work offer ad hoc notions of security and privacy [7].

RFID systems have many privacy concerns. One of the most important problems of RFID systems is traceability. Most previous studies consider backward

---

* This work has been partially funded by FP7-Project ICE under the grant agreement number 206546.

J. Cuellar et al. (Eds.): STM 2010, LNCS 6710, pp. 239–254, 2011.

untraceability that means a strong adversary compromising a tag at time t cannot trace the past interactions of the tag that occurred at time $t' < t$. Lim and Kwon have introduced the concept of forward untraceability meaning that a strong adversary compromising a tag at time t cannot trace the future interactions of the tag that occurred at time $t' > t$ [8]. They also show that forward untraceability is important for perfect ownership transfer of RFID tags.

In this paper, we revisit Vaudenay's security and privacy model [16] by considering forward untraceability and describe the notion of forward untraceability. The modified model defines the minimum restrictions for forward untraceability by considering all message flows between RFID reader and tags. We further apply the modified model to some existing RFID schemes: the scheme by Lim and Kwon [8] at ICICS'06, the scheme by Song and Mitchell [13] at WISEC'08, and the scheme by Cai et al. [4] at WISEC'09. Lim and Kwon's scheme provides forward untraceability, resistance to server impersonation and other security and privacy features. Song and Mitchell's scheme provides the same security and privacy features as Lim and Kwon's scheme with improved performance in memory space, computation time and communication overhead [10]. Cai et al.'s scheme is the revised version of Song and Mitchell's scheme that eliminates its some vulnerabilities.

2   RFID Privacy Models

RFID privacy model defines following attributes formally: RFID schemes, security and privacy requirements of RFID schemes and abilities of an adversary. RFID scheme must have security properties to provide tag-reader authentication and must have privacy properties to resist adversaries aiming to identify, trace or link tags [16]. Privacy models are used to determine the privacy level of RFID schemes. There are several proposed RFID privacy models in the literature. In this section, we give brief information about these models.

Avoine has proposed strong cryptographic model and defined the strong privacy notion of untraceability in RFID schemes [2]. This model has different level of privacy and defines different abilities for an adversary. Privacy is formalized by the ability to distinguish two known tags. Juels and Weis extend Avoine's model by considering side-channel information [7]. They find a powerful desynchronization attack on Avoine's model. Avoine shows OSK scheme [9] is secure under his model. However, according to Juels and Weis' model, this scheme is considered as insecure. Lim and Kwon propose a privacy model for untraceability by making Avoine's model more general and flexible by considering various possible restriction in terms of access time of the adversary and the frequency that the adversary uses [8]. This model defines the strong privacy notion of untraceability especially forward and backward untraceability.

Vaudenay proposes a new model that classifies privacy in RFID [16]. This model has eight classes of privacy levels. Avoine et al. modify Vaudenay's model [16] considering a side channel that leaks computational time of the reader [3]. They model a new attack based on the time required for a tag authentication.

3 Extended RFID Security and Privacy Model

In this section, we present a modification to a general RFID security and privacy model [16] proposed by Vaudenay in ASIACRYPT 2007. We extend the model in [16] by defining the notion of forward untraceability by considering some restrictions on RFID systems in terms of accessing possibility of an adversary to each communication round. Generally, in privacy models it is assumed that the adversary accesses all communication round of a scheme if she calls an execute query. In real life, the adversary has the probability of missing some communication rounds, therefore, we can say that she has some limitations in the number of communication rounds of a valid session that can be read by the adversary.

In this model, the tag $\mathcal{T}$ is considered as a passive transponder that has some limitations in terms of power, memory and computation. It can communicate with the reader $\mathcal{R}$ up to the limited distance and has a unique ID to be identified by the reader $\mathcal{R}$. It does not provide resistance to tampering. The reader $\mathcal{R}$ consists of one or more transceivers and a backend database. The communication channel between the transceiver and the backend database is considered secure. The reader stores all tag identifiers ID and other secrets related to tags in the backend database in order to identify legitimate tags when interacting them.

3.1 System Model

An RFID scheme is defined by the following procedures:

- SetupReader(1^s) $\rightarrow$ (K_S, K_P) is used to generate the public parameter K_P which is available to all players and the private parameter K_S which is only known by the reader with security parameter s. It also creates a database to store all identifiers of valid tags.
- SetupTag^{K_P}(ID) $\rightarrow$ (K, S) takes K_P and ID as input. It is used to generate a tag with unique identifier ID. The tag is generated with a key K and an updateable memory states S. The (ID, K) is added to the backend database when the tag is legitimate.
- IdentTag $\rightarrow$ out is an interactive scheme that determines how scheme parties a $\mathcal{T} \in Tags$ and a $\mathcal{R} \in Readers$ interact each other in scheme sessions. At the end of the scheme session, if the reader identifies the tag, it outputs the identifier of the tag; otherwise it rejects the tag and outputs $\bot$.

3.2 Adversarial Model

The features of an adversary denoted $\mathcal{A}$ are determined by considering the actions she is allowed to perform, why she wants to attack the system and how she performs her attack.

At the beginning of each experiment, the SetupReader(1^s) procedure is already executed so 1^s, K_P and K_S are already generated and 1^s and K_P are already given to $\mathcal{A}$. Furthermore, it is considered that there is no tag in the system when $\mathcal{A}$ begins an experiment. $\mathcal{A}$ is allowed to use CreateTag^b(ID) oracle to create a tag. In the Vaudenay's model, a tag is considered as either a *free* tag or a *drawn* tag. Drawn tags are the set of tags that are in the reading range of the adversary so that the adversary can interact with them. Free tags are other tags that are not accessible by the adversary.

The following oracles are defined to represent the abilities of the adversary.

- CreateTag^b(ID) is used to create a free tag with unique identifier ID. This oracle calls SetupTag^{K_P}(ID) to create (K, S) for the tag. If $b = 1$, the tag is legitimate and (ID, K) is added to backend database; otherwise it is not legitimate and (ID, K) is not added to backend database.
- DrawTag(distr, n) $\rightarrow$ (vtag$_0$, b$_0$, ..., vtag$_{n-1}$, b$_{n-1}$) is used to choose a set of tags to which the adversary is allowed to access from the set of free tags with distribution probability $distr$. The oracle changes the status of tags from $free$ to $drawn$ and returns an array of fresh identifiers (vtag$_0$,...,vtag$_{n-1}$) of the tags. The adversary may access to drawn tags for one single session because vtag is temporary identifier. The oracle returns $\perp$ for already drawn or not existing tags. The relation between the real identifier ID$_i$ and temporary identifier vtag$_i$ is kept in hidden table T such that T(vtag$_i$) = ID$_i$. Furthermore, the oracle returns array of bits (b$_0$,...,b$_{n-1}$) telling whether drawn tags are legitimate or not.
- Free(vtag) is used to make a tag inaccessible by the adversary thus the adversary cannot interact with the tag. The oracle changes the status of tags from $drawn$ to $free$.
- Launch() $\rightarrow$ π is used to start a new IdentTag scheme instance at the reader side.
- SendReader(m, π) $\rightarrow$ m' sends a message m to the reader in IdentTag scheme session π. The reader responds with message m'.
- SendTag(m, vtag) $\rightarrow$ m' sends a message m to the virtual tag vtag. The tag responds with message m'.
- Execute(vtag) $\rightarrow$ (π, $transcript$) is used to execute a complete scheme between vtag and the reader. The oracle starts with a Launch() query and continues with the successive use of SendReader and SendTag queries. It returns the transcript of the scheme that is the list of successive scheme messages.
- Result(π) $\rightarrow$ x returns either 1 if the scheme instance π is completed successfully that means the reader identifies a legitimate tag. In other case in which the reader does not identify the tag and outputs $\perp$, the oracle returns 0.
- Corrupt(vtag) $\rightarrow$ S is used to get the current state S of the vtag. If vtag is no longer used by the adversary after this oracle is called, vtag is considered as destroyed.

3.3   Privacy Classes

Vaudenay defines the different classes of adversaries by putting some restrictions to the adversary in the use of oracle queries. The eight privacy classes are distinguished by different oracles sets and restrictions on accessing Corrupt(vtag) according to the attack strategies of the adversary.

- WEAK: It is the weakest privacy class which allows to access to all the oracles except Corrupt(vtag). An adversary cannot obtain the internal state of the tag.

- FORWARD: It is allowed to access Corrupt(vtag) under the condition that after it is called, the adversary can only access more Corrupt(vtag). An adversary can obtain the internal state of a tag when the system is already corrupted.
- DESTRUCTIVE: It is allowed to access Corrupt(vtag) under the condition that after it called for the given tag, the adversary cannot call queries for the same tag. After an adversary obtains the internal state of a tag, the tag is destroyed and cannot be used again.
- STRONG: It is the strongest privacy class in which there is no restriction on accessing to all the oracles. This privacy class corresponds to many real-life systems in which there is no tag resisting to tampering.

There are also NARROW − STRONG, NARROW − DESTRUCTIVE, NARROW− FORWARD and NARROW − WEAK privacy classes that have the same restrictions with the above privacy classes but they cannot use Result(π).

3.4 Security Properties

Correctness (Completeness). This property requires that the reader always accepts a legitimate tag and returns its identifier with overwhelming probability. If the reader interacts with non-legitimate tag, it returns $\perp$ at the end of the scheme session.

Definition 1. *Correctness (Completeness).* An RFID scheme is said to be *correct if the reader $\mathcal{R}$ returns the tag identifier* ID *with overwhelming probability at the end of the* IdentTag *scheme.*

After an adversary interacts with a legitimate tag to make it rejected, the reader also accepts a legitimate tag and returns its identifier with overwhelming probability. We give the notion of strong correctness below.

Definition 2. *Strong Correctness (Strong Completeness).* An RFID *scheme is said to be correct if the reader $\mathcal{R}$ returns the tag identifier* ID *with overwhelming probability after interacting with a legitimate tag T that could have subjected to an attack.*

The security of an RFID scheme also depends on the fact that the adversary that can use all oracle except Corrupt(vtag) oracle cannot impersonate a legitimate tag. Vaudenay says that the security is a critical property and it must be provided in the presence of the strongest adversary. If the strongest adversary is allowed to use Corrupt(vtag) oracle, it is impossible to prevent impersonation because Corrupt(vtag) oracle makes impersonation trivial.

Definition 3. *Soundness.* An RFID *is said sound if the probability that an adversary impersonates a legitimate tag T is negligible [3].*

3.5 Privacy

The definition of privacy is given by classifying the adversary according to its power. In Vaudenay's model, there is a blinded adversary called as blinder $\mathcal{B}$. Blinder $\mathcal{B}$ is a polynomial-time algorithm which simulates Launch(), SendReader(m, π), SendTag(m, vtag) and Result(π) without carrying any secret. There is no interaction between $\mathcal{B}$ and $\mathcal{A}$. $\mathcal{B}$ can only observe inputs and outputs of oracle queries that are called by $\mathcal{A}$. An RFID scheme is said to private if the success probability of $\mathcal{A}$ that interacts with the whole system using oracles is similar with the success probability of $\mathcal{B}$.

The adversary runs a privacy experiment (game) on an RFID scheme to see whether the adversary guesses the target tag correctly. In the first phase, the adversary can use any oracles that she is allowed to use. After that, the adversary can see the hidden table to the tags. The adversary uses the information obtained in the first phase to analyze the table. If the adversary outputs True, then she wins the game.

3.6   The Notion of Forward Untraceability for RFID

Forward untraceability means that a strong adversary compromising a tag at time t cannot trace the future interactions of the tag that occurred at time $t' > t$. Only strongest adversary described in Vaudenay's model can violate the forward untraceability of an RFID scheme because there is no restriction for accessing Corrupt(vtag) in STRONG privacy class. That means the adversary can use other oracle queries to trace the tag after she corrupts it. In [16], Vaudenay shows that strong privacy cannot be achieved and narrow-strong privacy does not imply strong privacy. Furthermore, he shows that narrow-strong private RFID scheme can be transformed into a key agreement protocol that can be achieved by using public-key algorithm.

We observe that, in the real world, an adversary that is trying to eavesdrop communication between a reader and a tag can miss some communication rounds because of the following reasons: the signal can be corrupted by noise, the signal power can be low, the adversary cannot be close enough to listen signals and interference from other signals. In Vaudenay's model, Execute(vtag) oracle does not model the real world settings because Execute(vtag) oracle is assumed to return the list of successive scheme messages. If all communication rounds of the scheme carries a valuable information that are needed to update or refresh secrets of tag, this assumption increases the success probability of adversary when tracing a specific tag. We now define a new oracle called ExecuteOne(vtag, r) and give the definition below.

Definition 4. ExecuteOne(vtag, r) $\rightarrow$ (π, *transcript*) *is used to execute one communication round* r *of scheme between* vtag *and the reader. The oracle starts with a* Launch() *query if* $r = 1$ *and continues with the use of* SendReader *or* SendTag *query according to the value of* r. *It returns the transcript of the communication round* r *of the scheme that is the list of messages.*

Untraceability is formally described using the game $\mathcal{G}$ between an adversary and a set of readers and tags. We describe below the notion of untraceability.

At the beginning of the experiment, $\mathcal{A}$ creates two legitimate tags using CreateTag^b(ID).

Learning:

    a. $\mathcal{A}$ gets access to one of these two tags by calling $\mathsf{DrawTag}(1/2, 1)$ and gets the fresh identifier of tag vtag_c where $c \in \{0, 1\}$.

    b. $\mathcal{A}$ is able to send any oracle queries to the tag vtag_c during the chosen time interval I and gets $(\pi_c, transcript_c)$ for the chosen time interval I

    c. $\mathcal{A}$ frees a chosen tag by calling $\mathsf{Free}(\mathsf{vtag}_c)$.

Challenge:

    a. $\mathcal{A}$ gets access to both tags by calling $\mathsf{DrawTag}(1/2, 2)$ and gets the fresh identifiers of tag vtag_0 and vtag_1.

    b. $\mathcal{A}$ is able to send any oracle queries to the tags vtag_0 and vtag_1 during the chosen time intervals I_0 and I_1 such that $(I_0 \cup I_1) \cap I = \oslash$ and gets $(\pi_0, transcript_0)$ and $(\pi_1, transcript_1)$.

    c. $\mathcal{A}$ frees both tags by calling $\mathsf{Free}(\mathsf{vtag}_0)$ and $\mathsf{Free}(\mathsf{vtag}_1)$.

Guess: Eventually, $\mathcal{A}$ terminates the game simulation and outputs a bit c' which is its guess of the value of c.

If $\mathcal{A}$ does not use the $\mathsf{Corrupt}(\mathsf{vtag})$ query during the time interval of challenge phase, the advantage of $\mathcal{A}$ in distinguishing whether $\mathcal{A}$ receives vtag_0 or vtag_1 is defined by $Adv_P^{UNT}(\mathcal{A}) = 2Pr(c' = c) - 1$ [2]. If $\mathcal{A}$ can use $\mathsf{Corrupt}(\mathsf{vtag})$ query during the time interval of challenge phase, the untraceability is determined by the choice of experiment time interval. If the choice of time intervals is that $I > I_0$ and $I > I_1$, then the protocol is resistant to backward traceability. In [8], the minimum restriction for forward untraceability is defined such that there should exist some non-empty gap not accessible by $\mathcal{A}$ between the time of $\mathsf{Corrupt}(\mathsf{vtag})$ query and the attack time. If $\mathcal{A}$ chooses the time intervals such that $I < I_0$ and $I < I_1$ and there are time intervals J_0 and J_1 such that $I < J_0 < I_0$ and $I < J_1 < I_1$ which $\mathcal{A}$ does not access, then the protocol is resistant to forward traceability.

In some schemes, such as the scheme in [13], after corrupting secrets of the tag, $\mathcal{A}$ does not need to access some exchanged messages between scheme parties since these messages do not contain information required to refresh or update secrets of the tag. If a single communication round of the scheme consists of such messages entirely, $\mathcal{A}$ is not under the necessity of accessing this communication round of the scheme. In case in which $\mathcal{A}$ uses $\mathsf{ExecuteOne}(\mathsf{vtag}, \mathsf{r})$ oracle, this situation increases the success probability of $\mathcal{A}$ because the number of communication rounds that $\mathcal{A}$ has to access decreases.

Our analysis reveals a nice design criterion for RFID authentication schemes, namely all communication rounds of the scheme must contain necessary information to refresh or update secrets of the tag. Thus, $\mathcal{A}$ has to access all communication rounds of the scheme to trace the tag. Now, we can change the minimum restriction for forward untraceability. That is; there should exist at least a single session which $\mathcal{A}$ does not access at least a single communication round of it between the time of $\mathsf{Corrupt}(\mathsf{vtag})$ query and the attack time. Formally, to provide forward untraceability we only need scheme sessions S_0 and S_1 such that $I < S_0 < I_0$ and $I < S_1 < I_1$ which $\mathcal{A}$ does not access at least a single communication round of them.

246   M. Akgün and M.U. Çağlayan

4   Analysis of the Song and Mitchell's Scheme

The S-M scheme was proposed at WISEC'08 [13]. In the scheme, the following notations are used. $h()$ $\{0,1\}^l \rightarrow \{0,1\}^l$ is a hash function. $f_k()$ $\{0,1\}^l \times \{0,1\}^l \rightarrow \{0,1\}^l$ is a keyed hash function with key k. $x \gg y$ is a right circular shift operator, which rotates all bits of x to the right by y bits and $x \ll y$ is a left circular shift operator, which rotates all bits of x to the left by y bits. l is the length of the parameters in the scheme.

For each tag T_i, the reader R stores its current identifier and its previous identifier $(u_i, t_i)_{new}, (u_i, t_i)_{old}$. u_i is an unique secret for T_i and $t_i = h(u_i)$. T_i only stores the value t_i. The S-M scheme is described in Figure 1.

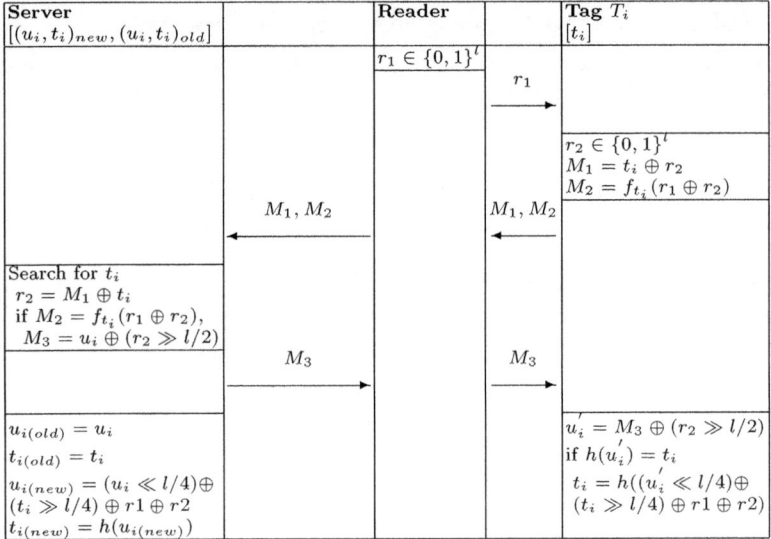

Fig. 1. Song and Mitchell's scheme

Deursen et al. show how an active adversary impersonates a tag to a legitimate server when the adversary does not have any secrets of the tag [15]. This attack does not result in de-synchronized updating of the secret information between the tag and the server. The adversary can fool the legitimate reader. Cai et al. present a server impersonation attack [4]. In this attack an active adversary can impersonate a legitimate server to a tag when the adversary does not have any secrets of the tag. This attack results in de-synchronized updating of the secret information between the tag and the server.

4.1   Violating the Forward Untraceability

In the S-M scheme the forward untraceability is preserved under an assumption if a strong attacker misses M_3 just once in a single successful authentication session after compromising T_i's secret. That is, if the attacker cannot prevent T_i from receiving the last message M_3, or does not have access to all the values r_1, r_2 and u_i that are needed to update t_i, then she cannot compute the new identifier and trace future transactions. Authors claim that the only potential attack to trace future transactions is to access all the values r_1, r_2 and u_i. Formally, the attack works as follows. At the beginning of the attack, $\mathcal{A}$ creates two legitimate tags using CreateTag^b(ID).

1. **Learning:**
   a) $\mathcal{A}$ gets access to one of these two tags by calling DrawTag$(1/2, 1)$ and gets the fresh identifier of tag vtag$_c$ where $c \in \{0, 1\}$.
   b) $\mathcal{A}$ chooses a time interval $I = [l_1, l_2]$. Firstly $\mathcal{A}$ issues a Corrupt(vtag$_c$) .
   c) During the time interval I, $\mathcal{A}$ calls an Execute(vtag$_c$) query, gets r_1, M_1, M_3 and computes vtag$_c$'s new identifier t_c.
   d) $\mathcal{A}$ frees a chosen tag by calling Free(vtag$_c$).
2. **Challenge:**
   a) $\mathcal{A}$ gets access to both tags by calling DrawTag$(1/2, 2)$ and gets the fresh identifiers of tag vtag$_0$ and vtag$_1$.
   b) $\mathcal{A}$ chooses a time interval $J = [l_3]$ where $l_3 = l_2 + 1$.
   c) $\mathcal{A}$ calls SendTag$(r_1,$ vtag$_0)$ and SendTag$(r_1,$ vtag$_1)$ and obtains their responses $(M_1^{\text{vtag}_0}, M_2^{\text{vtag}_0})$ and $(M_1^{\text{vtag}_1}, M_2^{\text{vtag}_1})$.
   d) $\mathcal{A}$ frees both tags by calling Free(vtag$_0$) and Free(vtag$_1$).
3. **Guess:** $\mathcal{A}$ computes $r_2' = M_1^{\text{vtag}_0} \oplus t_c$ and checks if $f_{t_c}(r_1 \oplus r_2') = M_2^{\text{vtag}_0}$. If so, the adversary knows vtag$_c$ = vtag$_0$ else knows vtag$_c$ = vtag$_1$.

Now, we show that after calling Corrupt(vtag$_c$), the attacker does not need to eavesdrop M_3 and access u_c for each session to trace future transactions. Formally, the attack works as follows:

At the beginning of the attack, $\mathcal{A}$ creates two legitimate tags using CreateTag^b(ID).

1. **Learning:**
   a) $\mathcal{A}$ gets access to one of these two tags by calling DrawTag$(1/2, 1)$ and gets the fresh identifier of tag vtag$_c$ where $c \in \{0, 1\}$.
   b) $\mathcal{A}$ chooses a time interval $I = [l_1, l_2]$. Firstly $\mathcal{A}$ issues a Corrupt(vtag$_c$).
   c) In the first session l_1, $\mathcal{A}$ calls an Execute(vtag$_c$), eavesdrops r_1, M_1, M_3, gets the values r_1, r_2, u_c and computes the current values of $u_c = (u_c \ll l/4) \oplus (t_c \gg l/4) \oplus r_1 \oplus r_2, t_c = h(u_c)$.
   d) During the time interval $[l_1 + 1, l_2]$, $\mathcal{A}$ calls an ExecuteOne(vtag$_c$, 1) to eavesdrop r_1 and Execute(vtag$_c$, 2) to eavesdrop M_1, gets the values r_1, r_2 and computes the current values of $u_c = (u_c \ll l/4) \oplus (t_c \gg l/4) \oplus r_1 \oplus r_2, t_c = h(u_c)$.
   e) $\mathcal{A}$ frees a chosen tag by calling Free(vtag$_c$).
2. **Challenge:**
   a) $\mathcal{A}$ gets access to both tags by calling DrawTag$(1/2, 2)$ and gets the fresh identifiers of tag vtag$_0$ and vtag$_1$.
   b) $\mathcal{A}$ chooses a time interval $J = [l_3]$ where $l_3 = l_2 + 1$.

    c) $\mathcal{A}$ calls SendTag(r_1, vtag$_0$) and SendTag(r_1, vtag$_1$) and obtains their responses $(M_1^{vtag_0}, M_2^{vtag_0})$ and $(M_1^{vtag_1}, M_2^{vtag_1})$.

    d) $\mathcal{A}$ frees both tags by calling Free(vtag$_0$) and Free(vtag$_1$).

3. **Guess:** $\mathcal{A}$ computes $r_2' = M_1^{vtag_0} \oplus t_c$ and checks if $f_{t_c}(r_1 \oplus r_2') = M_2^{vtag_0}$. If so, the adversary knows vtag$_c$ = vtag$_0$ else knows vtag$_c$ = vtag$_1$

$\mathcal{A}$ gets M_3 in the session l_1, she can compute the new identifier t_c and the new value of u_c. She does not need M_3 to compute the current value of identifier during the time interval $[l_1 + 1, l_2]$ because she already knows the current value of u_c sent in M_3. We can see that $\mathcal{A}$ misses M_3 during the time interval $[l_1 + 1, l_2]$ (not only in a single session) but the S-M scheme does not preserve the forward untraceability as claimed.

4.2 Server Impersonation Attack after Corrupting the Tag

An adversary impersonating the valid server can trace the future transactions of the tag without eavesdropping all the future transactions of the tag. The attack works as follows:

1. $\mathcal{A}$ creates a legitimate tag using CreateTag[b](ID).
2. $\mathcal{A}$ gets access to the tag by calling DrawTag(1, 1) and gets the fresh identifier of tag vtag$_0$
3. An adversary $\mathcal{A}$ issues a Corrupt(vtag$_0$) query.
4. In the first session after corrupting, $\mathcal{A}$ calls Execute(vtag$_0$), eavesdrops r_1, M_1, M_3 and gets the values r_1, r_2, u_0.
5. $\mathcal{A}$ computes the current values of $u_0 = (u_0 \ll l/4) \oplus (t_0 \gg l/4) \oplus r_1 \oplus r_2$, $t_0 = h(u_0)$ because she knows the previous values of t_0, u_0 and the latest values of r_1, r_2.
6. Right after interaction between vtag$_0$ and $\mathcal{R}$, $\mathcal{A}$ initiates a session with vtag$_0$ by calling SendTag(r_1', vtag$_0$). Since she knows the current values of t_0, u_0, she impersonates the valid server and passes the check by the tag vtag$_0$ successfully.
7. After this session, $\mathcal{A}$ can trace all future interactions of the tag vtag$_0$ and valid readers cannot successfully interact with the tag vtag.

We can see that a strong adversary $\mathcal{A}$ compromising the tag can easily impersonate the valid server so the valid server becomes invalid for the tag. This is because the value u_0 used for server validation is updated with values t_0, r_1 and r_2 known by $\mathcal{A}$. Thus, $\mathcal{A}$ can behave like the valid server.

5   Analysis of the Cai et al.'s Scheme

At WISEC'09, Cai et al. [4] analyzed Song's scheme [13] and presented reader impersonation attack, which enables an adversary to impersonate any legitimate reader. This attack can result in de-synchronized updating of the secret information between the tag and the server. Inexpensive security operations such as

$\ll$ and $\oplus$ are extensively used in the design of Song's scheme. Although these operations can help to reduce the cost of RFID tags, they lead to various security vulnerabilities. Authors also propose their revised scheme that eliminates the vulnerabilities of the S-M scheme. They increase the computation cost of the tag to eliminate proposed attack. They revise $M_2 = f(r_1 \oplus r_1)$ to $M_2 = f(r_1||r_1)$ and $M_3 = u_i \oplus (r_2 \gg l/2)$ to $M_3 = u_i \oplus h(r_2)$. However, this revised scheme does not resist to attacks described in Section 4.1 and Section 4.2. The Cai et al's scheme is described in Figure 2.

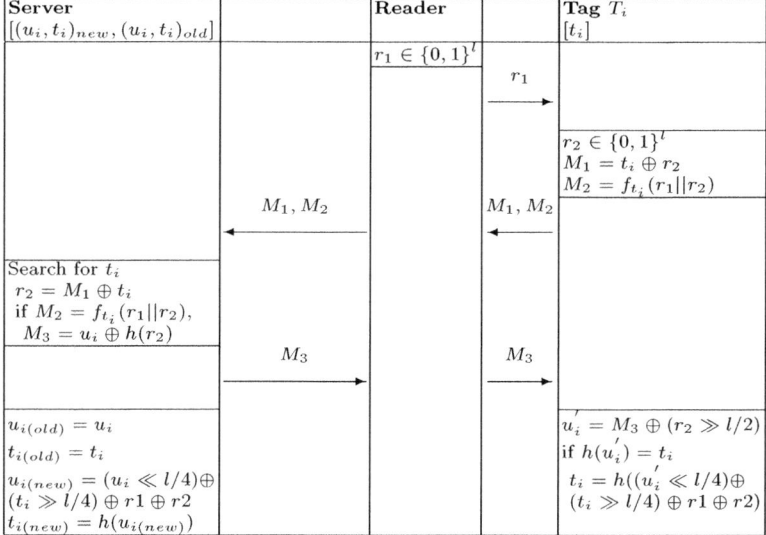

Fig. 2. Cai et al.'s scheme

Like S-M scheme, Cai et al.'s scheme provides forward untraceability under the same assumption described in Section 4.1. Authors claim that the only potential attack to trace future transactions is to access all the values r_1, r_2 and u_i. The same attack described in Section 4.1 can be applicable to Cai et al.'s scheme. Due to the page limit, we cannot explain the attack in detail.

An adversary impersonating the valid server can trace the future transactions of the tag without eavesdropping all future transactions of the tag. The same attack described in Section 4.2 can be applicable to Cai et al.'s scheme. Due to the page limit, we cannot explain the attack in detail.

6   Analysis of the Lim and Kwon's Scheme

Lim and Kwon introduce the concept of forward untraceability and its importance in designing RFID security schemes. Based on these observations, they proposed a new authentication scheme in [8]. This scheme provides forward untraceability under an assumption that a strong adversary compromising a tag cannot eavesdrop all the future interactions of the tag. The secrets of the tag are updated after

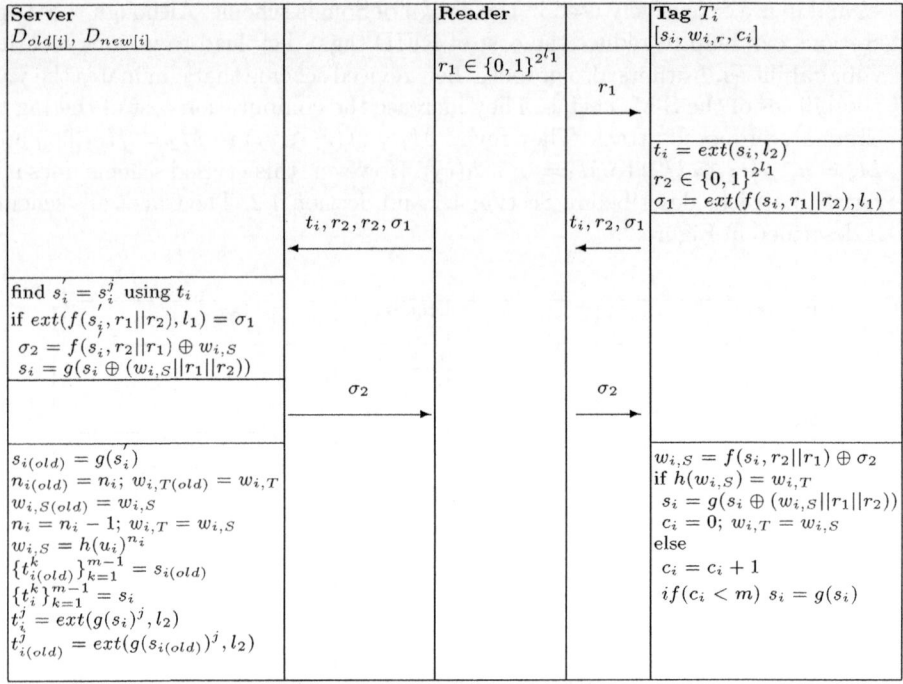

Fig. 3. Lim and Kwon's Scheme

each successful authentication session and thus a compromised tag becomes untraceable from the moment that the adversary misses even a single valid session of the tag. This scheme is also secure against server impersonation. It uses two hash key chains: a forward key chain for tag secret evolution, and a backward key chain, used in reverse order, for the server validation.

The initialization phase of the scheme is as follows:

1. The server chooses a random secret s_i for the tag T_i, evaluates $(m-1)$ evolutions of s_i, $s_i^0 = s_i$ and $s_i^j = g(s_i^{j-1})$ for $1 \leq j \leq m-1$ where m is the maximum number of allowable authentication failures between two valid sessions, and g is a pseudo random function. It computes a key identifier $t_i = ext(s_i^j, l_2)$ where l_2 is some bit length and $ext(x, l)$ is a extraction function returning l bits of x.

2. The server also chooses a random u_i for each tag T_i and computes a key chain of length n, $\{w_i^j\}_{j=0}^{n-1}$, such that $w_i^n = u_i$ and $w_i^j = h(w_i^{j+1})$ for $0 \leq j < n$. This key chain is used in reverse order for the server validation.

3. The tag stores $\langle$ tag secret, server validator$\rangle = \langle s_i, w_{i,T}\rangle$ where $w_{i,T} = w_i^0$ and initializes a failure counter $c_i = 0$.

4. The server stores two entry for the tag T_i: $D_{old[i]}$ that is empty initially and $D_{new[i]} = \langle s_i, \{t_i^j\}_{j=0}^{m-1}, u_i, n_i, w_{i,T}, w_{i,S}\rangle$ where $w_{i,S} = w_i^1$ and $n_i = n$.

Authentication phase of the scheme is described in Figure 3.

In [11,10], authors show how to trace a tag in this scheme without corrupting it so this scheme does not provide location privacy. The same attack is described in [12].

6.1 Analysis of the Forward Untraceability

Forward untraceability is provided under the assumption that the adversary compromising a tag cannot eavesdrop all the future interactions of the tag. The tag secret is refreshed after every successful interaction with the server and thus a compromised tag becomes untraceable from the moment that the adversary misses even a single valid session of the tag. The only way to trace future transactions is to access all the values r_1, r_2 and σ_2. Formally the attack works as follows:

At the beginning of the attack, $\mathcal{A}$ creates two legitimate tags using CreateTag^b(ID).

1. **Learning:**
   a) $\mathcal{A}$ gets access to one of these two tags by calling DrawTag$(1/2, 1)$ and gets the fresh identifier of tag vtag$_c$ where $c \in \{0, 1\}$.
   b) $\mathcal{A}$ chooses a time interval $I = [l_1, l_2]$. Firstly $\mathcal{A}$ issues a Corrupt(vtag$_c$) .
   c) During the time interval I, $\mathcal{A}$ calls an Execute(vtag) query, gets r_1, r_2, σ_2 and computes vtag$_c$'s new identifier s_c.
   d) $\mathcal{A}$ frees a chosen tag by calling Free(vtag$_c$).
2. **Challenge:**
   a) $\mathcal{A}$ gets access to both tags by calling DrawTag$(1/2, 2)$ and gets the fresh identifiers of tag vtag$_0$ and vtag$_1$.
   b) $\mathcal{A}$ chooses a time interval $J = [l_3]$ where $l_3 = l_2 + 1$.
   c) $\mathcal{A}$ calls SendTag(r_1, vtag_0) and SendTag(r_1, vtag_1) and obtains their responses $(t_0^{\text{vtag}_0}, r_2^{\text{vtag}_0}, \sigma_1^{\text{vtag}_0})$ and $(t_1^{\text{vtag}_1}, r_2^{\text{vtag}_1}, \sigma_1^{\text{vtag}_1})$
   d) $\mathcal{A}$ frees both tags by calling Free(vtag$_0$) and Free(vtag$_1$).
3. **Guess:** $\mathcal{A}$ checks if $ext(f(s_c, r_1 || r_2), l_1) = \sigma_1^{\text{vtag}_0}$. If so, the adversary knows vtag$_c$ = vtag$_0$ else knows vtag$_c$ = vtag$_1$

This scheme resists to attacks described in Section 4.1. A strong adversary $\mathcal{A}$ having s_c and $w_{c,T}$ must monitor all communication rounds of a single session to trace a tag because she does not compute the new value of $w_{c,S}$ sent in the value σ_2 in the third communication round. All communication rounds have fresh values r_1, r_1 and σ_2 that $\mathcal{A}$ must access to compute the refreshed value of tag secret s_c.

Attack of Quafi and Phan: At ACNS'08 Quafi and Phan presented an attack that violates the forward untraceability of Lim and Kwon's scheme. The attack does not violate the assumption under which the scheme provides forward untraceability [11]. They claim that after the attack an adversary can trace the tag in all future sessions, and legitimate readers can no longer successfully interact with the tag. The attack works as follows:

At the beginning of the attack, $\mathcal{A}$ creates a legitimate tags using CreateTag^b(ID).

1. $\mathcal{A}$ gets access to the tag by calling $\mathsf{DrawTag}(1,1)$ and gets the fresh identifier of tag vtag_0.
2. $\mathcal{A}$ issues a $\mathsf{Corrupt}(\mathsf{vtag}_0)$ query and gets the stored secrets s_0, c_0 and $w_{0,T}$.
3. $\mathcal{A}$ calls $\mathsf{Execute}(\mathsf{vtag}_0)$. She gets a r_1, r_2 and $\sigma_2 = f(s_0, r_2 || r_1) \oplus w_{0,S}$. After this session, vtag_0 and the legitimate reader updates $w_{0,T} = w_{0,S}$ and $s_0 = g(s_0 \oplus (w_{0,T} || r_1 || r_2))$.
4. Right after the interaction between vtag_0 and the legitimate reader, $\mathcal{A}$ starts a session with vtag_0 by calling $\mathsf{SendTag}(r_1', \mathsf{vtag}_0)$. Since she knows the latest values of r_1, r_2 and $w_{0,T}$ and the previous s_0, she can compute the latest $s_0 = g(s_0 \oplus (w_{0,T} || r_1 || r_2))$. *The adversary can pass the check by the tag without any problem and trace all future interaction of the tag.*

However, this attack does not work correctly because the adversary cannot pass the check by the tag. In Step 1, the adversary can get s_0, c_0 and $w_{0,T}$ by corrupting the tag. In Step 2, she can get r_1, r_2 and $w_{0,S}$ from the value $\sigma_2 = f(s_0, r_2 || r_1) \oplus w_{0,S}$. In Step 3, she computes the latest value of $w_{0,T} = w_{0,S}$ and $s_0 = g(s_0 \oplus (w_{0,T} || r_1 || r_2))$ and initiates a session with vtag_0 as follows:

1. $\mathcal{A}$ calls $\mathsf{SendTag}(r_1', \mathsf{vtag})$.
2. vtag_0 picks a random number r_2', computes t_0 and σ_2 and sends r_2', t_0, σ_2 to $\mathcal{A}$.
3. Now $\mathcal{A}$ must compute the valid $\sigma_2 = f(s_0, r_2 || r_1) \oplus w_{0,S}$ to pass the check by vtag_0. However she cannot compute the valid σ_2 because she does not know the current $w_{0,S}$. She only knows the current $w_{0,T}$ which equals to $h(w_{0,S})$. It is infeasible to compute the current $w_{0,S}$ that equals to $h(u_0)^{n_0}$ where u_0 is the seed of backward key chain used for server validation.

6.2   Analysis of Server Impersonation

A strong adversary $\mathcal{A}$ can make a tag invalid for the legitimate server. However, she cannot interact the tag after this attack. The attack works as follows:

At the beginning of the attack, $\mathcal{A}$ creates a legitimate tags using $\mathsf{CreateTag}^b(\mathsf{ID})$.

1. $\mathcal{A}$ gets access to the tag by calling $\mathsf{DrawTag}(1,1)$ and gets the fresh identifier of tag vtag_0.
2. $\mathcal{A}$ issues a $\mathsf{Corrupt}(\mathsf{vtag}_0)$ query and gets the stored secrets s_0, c_0 and $w_{0,T}$.
3. $\mathcal{A}$ calls $\mathsf{Execute}(\mathsf{vtag}_0)$. She gets a r_1, r_2 and $\sigma_2 = f(s_0, r_2 || r_1) \oplus w_{0,S}$ and invalidate a message σ_2 by modifying it so the legitimate reader cannot pass the check by the tag vtag_0.
4. Right after the interaction between vtag_0 and the legitimate reader, $\mathcal{A}$ starts a session with the tag vtag_0 by calling $\mathsf{SendTag}(r_1', \mathsf{vtag}_0)$. She knows the value of $w_{0,S}$ and can compute the current value of $s_0 = g(s_0)$. Therefore, she can compute the valid $\sigma_2 = f(s_0, r_2' || r_1') \oplus w_{0,S}$ and pass the check by the tag vtag_0. After this interaction, valid readers cannot interact with the tag vtag_0.

The above attack does not result in privacy problem such as traceability. After the attack, the strong adversary $\mathcal{A}$ cannot trace the future interactions of the tag vtag$_0$ because she does not know the current value of $w_{0,S}$ and it is infeasible to compute it. The adversary can impersonate the valid server only once. After this attack, the tag vtag$_0$ cannot interact any reader which is legitimate or not.

7   Conclusion

In this paper, we revisited and modified an RFID security and privacy model proposed by Vaudenay in ASIACRYPT 2007 by defining the notion of forward untraceability. In this model, we emphasized the importance of conveying valuable information on each communication round of the scheme. We introduced a new oracle to model eavesdropping close to the real world. We applied our revised model to analyze the forward untraceability of some existing schemes and their resistance to server impersonation. We showed that the scheme of Song and Mitchell, and Cai et al. do not provide forward untraceability and resistance to server impersonation as claimed. We found that Lim and Kwon's scheme provides the best security against forward traceability and server impersonation attack. We also showed that the attack of Quafi and Phan claiming to violate forward untraceability of the scheme of Lim and Kwon does not violate forward untraceability.

References

1. Ahson, S., Ilyas, M.: RFID Handbook: Applications, Technology, Security, and Privacy. CRC Press, Boca Raton (2008)
2. Avoine, G.: Adversarial Model for Radio Frequency Identification. Cryptology ePrint Archive, Report 2005/049 (2005), http://eprint.iacr.org/
3. Avoine, G., Coisel, I., Martin, T.: Time Measurement Threatens Privacy-Friendly RFID Authentication Protocols. In: Ors Yalcin, S.B. (ed.) RFIDSec 2010. LNCS, vol. 6370, pp. 146–165. Springer, Heidelberg (2010)
4. Cai, S., Li, Y., Li, T., Deng, R.H.: Attacks and improvements to an RFID mutual authentication protocol and its extensions. In: WiSec 2009: Proceedings of the second ACM conference on Wireless network security, pp. 51–58. ACM, New York (2009)
5. Cole, P.H., Ranasinghe, D.C.: Networked RFID Systems and Lightweight Cryptography. Springer, Heidelberg (2008)
6. Garfinkel, S., Rosenberg, B.: RFID: Applications, Security, and Privacy. Addison-Wesley, Reading (2005)
7. Juels, A., Weis, S.: Defining Strong Privacy for RFID. In: International Conference on Pervasive Computing and Communications – PerCom 2007, pp. 342–347. IEEE Computer Society Press, New York (2007)
8. Lim, C.H., Kwon, T.: Strong and Robust RFID Authentication Enabling Perfect Ownership Transfer. In: Ning, P., Qing, S., Li, N. (eds.) ICICS 2006. LNCS, vol. 4307, pp. 1–20. Springer, Heidelberg (2006)
9. Okhubo, M., Suzuki, K., Kinoshita, S.: Cryptographic approach to "privacy-friendly" tags. In: RFID Privacy Workshop. MIT, Massachusetts (2003)
10. Ouafi, K., Phan, R.C.W.: Privacy of Recent RFID Authentication Protocols. In: Chen, L., Mu, Y., Susilo, W. (eds.) ISPEC 2008. LNCS, vol. 4991, pp. 263–277. Springer, Heidelberg (2008)

11. Ouafi, K., Phan, R.C.W.: Traceable Privacy of Recent Provably-Secure RFID Protocols. In: Bellovin, S.M., Gennaro, R., Keromytis, A.D., Yung, M. (eds.) ACNS 2008. LNCS, vol. 5037, pp. 479–489. Springer, Heidelberg (2008)
12. Paise, R.I., Vaudenay, S.: Mutual Authentication in RFID: Security and Privacy. In: Proceedings of the 3rd ACM Symposium on Information, Computer and Communications Security – ASIACCS 2008, pp. 292–299. ACM Press, Tokyo (2008)
13. Song, B., Mitchell, C.J.: RFID authentication protocol for low-cost tags. In: WiSec 2008: Proceedings of the first ACM conference on Wireless network security, pp. 140–147. ACM, New York (2008)
14. Thornton, F., Hanies, B., Das, A.M., Bhargava, H., Campbell, A., Kleinschmidt, J.: RFID Security. Syngress (2006)
15. van Deursen, T., Radomirović, S.: Attacks on RFID Protocols. Cryptology ePrint Archive, Report 2008/310 (2008)
16. Vaudenay, S.: On Privacy Models for RFID. In: Kurosawa, K. (ed.) ASIACRYPT 2007. LNCS, vol. 4833, pp. 68–87. Springer, Heidelberg (2007)

Protecting Privacy of Sensitive Value Distributions in Data Release

Michele Bezzi[1], Sabrina De Capitani di Vimercati[2], Giovanni Livraga[2], and Pierangela Samarati[2]

[1] SAP Research, Sophia-Antipolis, France
michele.bezzi@sap.com
[2] Università degli Studi di Milano, 26013 Crema, Italy
{sabrina.decapitani,pierangela.samarati}@unimi.it,
giovanni.livraga@guest.unimi.it

Abstract. In today's electronic society, data sharing and dissemination are more and more increasing, leading to concerns about the proper protection of privacy. In this paper, we address a novel privacy problem that arises when non sensitive information is incrementally released and sensitive information can be inferred exploiting dependencies of sensitive information on the released data. We propose a model capturing this inference problem where sensitive information is characterized by peculiar distributions of non sensitive released data. We also discuss possible approaches for run time enforcement of safe releases.

1 Introduction

Sharing and dissemination of information play a central role in today's information society. Governmental, public, and private institutions are increasingly required to make their data electronically available, as well as to offer services and data access over the Internet. This implies disclosing to external parties or sharing information once considered classified or accessible only internally, that must now be made partially available to outside interests. Such information release, publication and dissemination are clearly selective. Data maintained by any organization may in fact considerably differ with respect to the needs for sharing with external parties as well as for their sensitivity. Data publication and sharing must then ensure on one hand the satisfaction of possible needs for data to be fed to external parties and on the other hand, proper protection of sensitive data to preserve the confidentiality and/or the privacy of involved individuals. The problem is notably complex, since the possible correlations and dependencies existing among data can introduce inference channels causing leakage of sensitive information even if such information is not explicitly released. The problem has been under the attention of researchers for decades and a large body of research has addressed different facets of the problem with different settings and assumptions. Such a large body of research includes: statistical databases and statistical data publications [1]; multilevel database systems with the problem of establishing proper classification of data, capturing data relationship and corresponding inference channels [5,13]; novel privacy problems introduced by the release of

J. Cuellar et al. (Eds.): STM 2010, LNCS 6710, pp. 255–270, 2011.

data referring to individuals whose identities or whose associated sensitive information should be maintained private [3,4]; protection of associations among data due to possible mining [2]. Different approaches have then been proposed addressing all these aspects of the complex privacy problem and offering solutions to block or limit the exposure of possible sensitive or private information. Still new data publication scenarios together with richness of published data and available data sources raise novel problems that need to be addressed.

In this paper, we address a specific problem related to inferences arising from the dependency of sensitive (not released) information referred to some entities, which can be enabled by the observation of other properties regarding such entities. In particular, we are concerned with the possible inferences that can be withdrawn by observing the distribution of values of non sensitive information associated with the entities. For instance, the distribution of soldiers' age in a military location can allow inferring the nature of the location itself, whether it is a headquarter (hosting old officials) or a training campus (hosting young privates). Intuitively, such a problem of sensitive information derivation becomes more serious as the amount of released data increases. In fact, as the amount of data released increases, the confidence in the external observations will increase; also, external observations will tend to be more representative of the real situations. Our problem resembles in some aspects the classical, and much complex, problem of controlling horizontal aggregation of data but it differs from it in several assumptions. In particular, we assume a scenario where an external observer could gather the data released to legitimate users and inference is due to peculiar data values distributions. Also, we are not only concerned with protecting sensitive information associated with specific entities, but also avoiding possible false positives, where sensitive values may improperly be associated (by the observers) with specific entities.

The remainder of this paper is organized as follows. First, we characterize a novel scenario of inference in data publication raising from a real case study that needed consideration (Section 2). Second, we provide a model for capturing when inference can occur in such scenario, providing metrics for evaluating information exposure (Sections 3 and 4). Third, we discuss possible approaches to control data disclosure to ensure that releases are safe with respect to inference channels improperly exposing sensitive information (Section 5).

2   Motivation and Reference Scenario

We consider a scenario (see Figure 1) where a *data holder* maintains a collection of records stored in a trusted environment. Each record contains different attributes and can be released to authorized parties requiring it. While the records individually taken are not sensitive, their aggregation is considered sensitive since it might enable inferring sensitive information not appearing in the records and not intended for release. We assume all requests for records to be genuine and communication of responses to record release requests to be protected. However, once records are released the data holder has no control on them and therefore

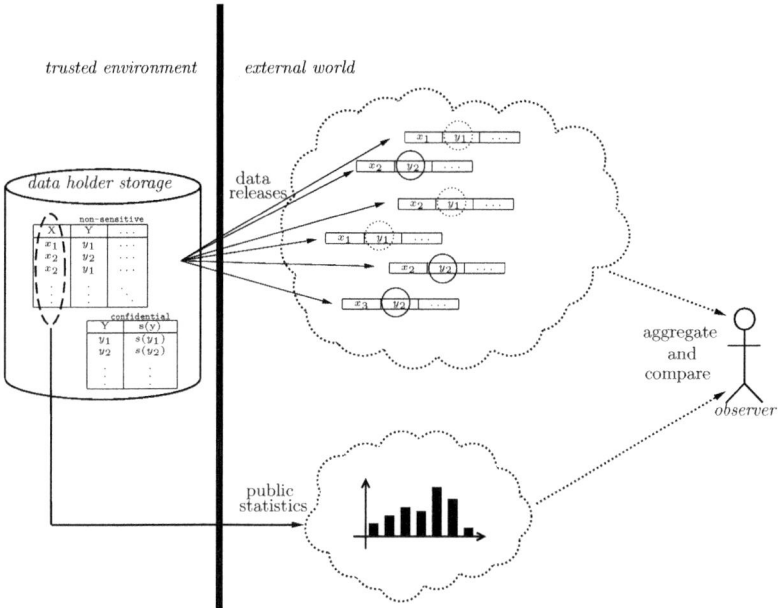

Fig. 1. Reference scenario

external observers can potentially gather all the records released. We then consider the worst case assumption of an observer that could be able to retrieve the complete collection of released records (which can happen, for example, if parties to which records are released would make use of a third party provider for storage). We assume that an observer is not aware of the requests submitted to the data holder for retrieving records as well as of the number of records stored at the data holder site.

Our problem is ensuring that the collection of records released to the external world be safe with respect to potential inference of sensitive (not released) information that could be possible by aggregating the released records. We consider a specific case of horizontal aggregation and inference channel due to the distribution of values of certain attributes with respect to other attributes. In particular, inference is caused by a distribution of values that deviates from expected distributions, which are considered as typical and are known to the observers.

In the paper, we refer our examples to a real case scenario characterized as follows. The data holder is a military organization which maintains records on its personnel. Each record refers to a soldier and reports the attributes Name, Age, and Location where the soldier is on duty. Some of the military locations are headquarters of the army. The information that a location is a headquarter is considered sensitive and neither appears in the soldiers' records nor it is released in other forms. Soldiers' records can be released upon request of the soldiers as well as of external parties (e.g., an external hospital). In addition, the data holder, to be compliant with legal requirements, publicly makes available statistics on the age of the soldiers. The age distribution publicly released, computed on the overall population regardless of the specific locations where soldiers are based, is a distribution that can be considered common and, in general, typically expected at each location. However, locations where headquarters are based show a different age distribution, characterized by an unusual peak of soldiers middle age or older. Such a distribution clearly differs from the expected age distribution, where the majority of soldiers are in their twenties or thirties. The problem is therefore that while single records are considered non sensitive, an observer aggregating all the released records could retrieve the age distribution of the soldiers in the different locations and determine possible deviations from the expected age distribution for certain locations, thus inferring that a given location hosts a headquarter. Our problem consists in ensuring that the release of records to the external world be safe with respect to such inferences.

3   Data Model and Problem Definition

In this section, we provide the notation and formalization of our problem. While our approach is applicable to a generic data model with which the data stored at the data holder site could be organized, for concreteness, we assume data to be maintained as a relational database. The data collection is therefore a table T characterized by a given set A of attributes, and each record is a tuple t in the table. Among the attributes contained in the table, we distinguish a set $Y \subset A$ of attributes corresponding to entities that we call *targets*.

Example 1. With respect to our scenario, table T is defined on the set A={Name, Age, Location} of attributes and Y={Location}. In our examples, we assume five different locations L_1, L_2, L_3, L_4, and L_5 are represented in the table.

While the identity (values) of entities Y is non sensitive, such entities are also characterized by *sensitive properties*, denoted $s(Y)$, which are not released. In other words, for each $y \in Y$ the associated sensitive information $s(y)$ does not appear in any released record. However, inference on it can be caused by the distribution of the values of some other attributes $X \subseteq A$ for the specific y. We denote with $P(X)$ the set of *relative frequencies* $p(x)$ of the different x values in the domain of X appearing in table T. Also, we denote with $P(X|y)$ the relative frequency of each value in the domain of X appearing in table T and restricted to the tuples for which Y is equal to y. We call this latter the *y-conditioned distribution* of X in T.

Example 2. In our scenario, $s(Y)$ is the type of the location (e.g., headquarter). The sensitive information $s(y)$ of whether a location y is a headquarter can be inferred from the distribution of the soldier age given the location. Figure 2(a) shows how tuples stored in table T are distributed with respect to the values of attributes Age and Location. For instance, over the 10000 tuples, 2029 refer to location L_1, 72 of which are of soldiers with age lower than 18. Figure 2(b) reports the corresponding relative frequency of age distributions. In particular,

	Number of tuples							P(Age|Location)							Loc	P(Loc)
Age	L1	L2	L3	L4	L5	Total	Age	L1	L2	L3	L4	L5	any		
<18	72	26	38	47	73	256	<18	3.55	2.00	2.31	2.34	2.42	2.56	L_1	20.29
18-19	151	53	82	140	223	649	18-19	7.44	4.08	4.96	6.98	7.40	6.49	L_2	12.99
20-24	539	147	449	505	736	2376	20-24	26.56	11.32	27.18	25.16	24.44	23.76	L_3	16.52
25-29	452	114	370	418	613	1967	25-29	22.28	8.78	22.40	20.83	20.35	19.67	L_4	20.07
30-34	335	213	234	318	501	1601	30-34	16.51	16.40	14.16	15.84	16.63	16.01	L_5	30.13
35-39	321	238	277	332	538	1706	35-39	15.82	18.32	16.77	16.54	17.86	17.06		
40-44	128	219	122	162	220	851	40-44	6.31	16.86	7.38	8.07	7.30	8.51		
45-49	20	205	50	49	76	400	45-49	0.99	15.78	3.03	2.44	2.52	4.00		
50-54	9	71	28	34	31	173	50-54	0.44	5.46	1.69	1.69	1.03	1.73		
≥55	2	13	2	2	2	21	≥55	0.10	1.00	0.12	0.11	0.05	0.21		
Total	2029	1299	1652	2007	3013	10000									
	(a)							(b)							(c)	

Fig. 2. Number of tuples in table T by Age and Location (a), loc-conditioned distributions P(Age\|Location) over table T (b), and location frequencies (c)

each column loc, with $loc \in \{L_1, \ldots, L_5\}$ reports the loc-conditioned distribution $P(\texttt{Age}|loc)$ (for convenience expressed in percentage). For instance, it states that 3.55% of the tuples of location L_1 refer to soldiers with age lower than 18. The last column of the table reports the distribution of the age range regardless of the specific location and then corresponds to $P(\texttt{Age})$ (expressed in percentage). Figure 2(c) reports the distribution of soldiers in the different locations regardless of their age (again expressed in percentage). For instance, 20.29% of the 10000 soldiers are based at L_1.

The existence of a correlation between the distribution of values of attributes X for a given target y and the sensitive information $s(y)$ is captured by the definition of *dependency* as follows.

Definition 1 (Dependency). *Let T be a table over attributes A, let X and Y be two disjoint subsets of A, and let $s(Y)$ be a sensitive property of Y. There is a dependency between X and Y, denoted $X \leadsto Y$, if there is a relationship between the conditional distribution $P(X|y)$ and the sensitive information $s(y)$.*

The existence of a dependency between the y-conditioned distribution of X and the sensitive information $s(y)$ introduces an inference channel, since the visibility on $P(X|y)$ potentially enables an observer to infer the sensitive information $s(y)$ even if not released. For instance, with respect to our running example, Age$\leadsto$Location.

Definition 1 simply states the existence of a dependency and does not say anything about when a given data distribution causes leakage of the sensitive information. In this paper, we consider the specific case of leakage caused by *peculiar* value distributions that differ from what is considered typical and expected. We then start to characterize the expected distribution, formally defined as *baseline distribution* as follows.

Definition 2 (Baseline distribution). *Let A be a set of attributes, and let X and Y be two disjoint subsets of A. The baseline distribution of X with respect to Y, denoted $B_Y(X)$ is the expected distribution of the different values (or range thereof) of X with respect to Y.*

The baseline distribution is the distribution publicly released by the data holder and can correspond to the real distribution of the values of attributes X in

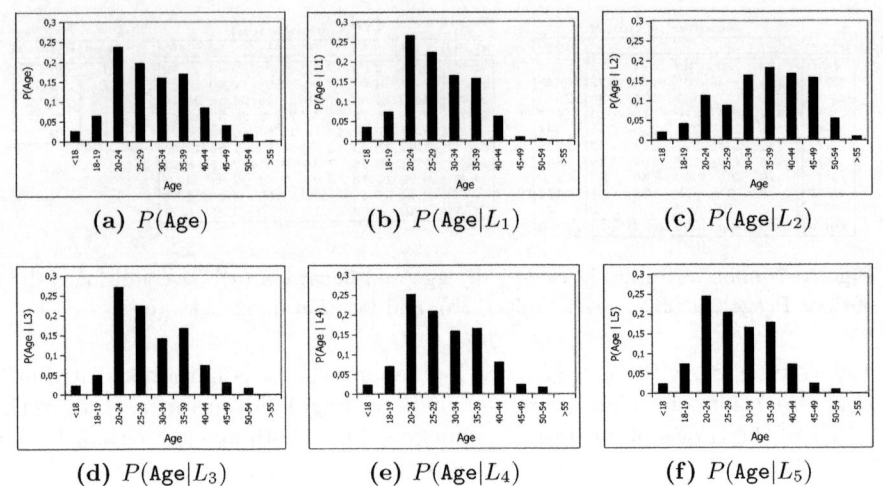

Fig. 3. Baseline distribution (a) and histogram representation of the *loc*-conditioned distributions P(Age|Location) in Figure 2(b)

the table T or can be any distribution that the data holder decides to publicly release. We assume the data holder to release truthful data and therefore assume the baseline distribution to coincide with the distribution of the values of X in T, that is, $B_Y(X) = P(X)$. This being said, in the following we simply use $P(X)$ when referring to the baseline distribution.

Example 3. With reference to our example, the baseline distribution $P(\text{Age})$ corresponds to the values (expressed in percentage) in the last column of Figure 2(b), which is also graphically reported as a histogram in Figure 3(a). Figures 3(b)-3(f) report the histogram representations of the *loc*-conditioned distributions for the different locations. As clearly visible from the histograms locations, while locations L_1, L_3, L_4, and L_5 enjoy a value distribution that resembles the expected baseline, location L_2 (the headquarter) shows a distribution considerably different.

Inference of sensitive information in our context is therefore caused by unusual distribution of values of X that the observer can learn from viewing released tuples. In the following section, we characterize unusual distributions and propose an approach to ensure released tuples be protected against such inference. In particular, our goal consists in providing the data holder with a means for assessing whether the release of a tuple (in conjunction with those already released) is safe with to respect to inference or should be denied[1].

4   Assessing Exposure

The first step for determining whether the release of a tuple t concerning a target y (i.e., $y = t[Y]$) is safe consists in characterizing when the y-conditioned

---

[1] Remember that the party requesting the release of the tuple is trusted and the communication is protected. Hence, denying a release does not cause any inference.

distribution of X (i.e., $P(X|y)$) is *peculiar*. In our framing of the problem, this happens when the difference, denoted $\Delta(X, y)$, between $P(X|y)$ and the baseline distribution $P(X)$ characterizes y as an *outlier*, that is, an entity that has a distribution of values of X different from what expected (and from the majority of the other targets). The problem is then how to define such a difference $\Delta(X, y)$. In practice, we would like to quantify how much information an observer can gain comparing $P(X|y)$ with $P(X)$ (which is known). Intuitively, if these two distributions are very *different* this information gain would be large and y represents an outlier. To this purpose, we adopt the classical notion of Kullback-Leibler distance between distributions, D_{KL} , which has a straightforward interpretation in terms of information theory, and define $\Delta(X, y)$ as follows.

$$\Delta(X, y) = D_{KL}(P(X|y), P(X)) = \sum_{x \in X} p(x|y) \log_2 \frac{p(x|y)}{p(x)} \qquad (1)$$

Example 4. Consider the distributions of the Age values for the different locations and $P(\text{Age})$ in Figure 2(b). We have:

$$\Delta(\text{Age}, L_1) = p(< 18|L_1) \log_2 \frac{p(< 18|L_1)}{p(< 18)} + \ldots + p(\geq 55|L_1) \log_2 \frac{p(\geq 55|L_1)}{p(\geq 55)} =$$
$$0.0355 \log_2 \frac{0.0355}{0.0256} + \ldots + 0.0010 \log_2 \frac{0.0010}{0.0021} = 0.12.$$

Similarly, we obtain: $\Delta(\text{Age}, L_2) = 0.42$, $\Delta(\text{Age}, L_3) = 0.07$, $\Delta(\text{Age}, L_4) = 0.06$, and $\Delta(\text{Age}, L_5) = 0.06$.

Translating the concept above to the whole table T, we aim at determining the average among the distances of the different y's, each weighted by y's frequency in the table. Such a formula nicely corresponds to the statistical concept of *mutual information*, for which D_{KL} represents a possible decomposition [8]. Intuitively, the mutual information between X and Y characterizes the *average* amount of knowledge about X an observer can have observing Y, or vice versa. The mutual information captures the weighted average of the Kullback-Leibler distance for the different targets as follows.

$$I(X, Y) = \sum_{x \in X, y \in Y} p(y)p(x|y) \log_2 \frac{p(x|y)}{p(x)} = \sum_{y \in Y} p(y)\Delta(X, y) \qquad (2)$$

Example 5. With respect to our running example, consider the values $p(loc)$, and $\Delta(\text{Age}, loc)$, with $loc = L_1, \ldots, L_5$, reported in Figure 2(c) and in Example 4, respectively. We have:
$I(\text{Age}, \text{Location}) = p(L_1)\Delta(\text{Age}, L_1) + p(L_2)\Delta(\text{Age}, L_2) + p(L_3)\Delta(\text{Age}, L_3) + p(L_4)\Delta(\text{Age}, L_4) + p(L_5)\Delta(\text{Age}, L_5) = 0.2029 \cdot 0.12 + 0.1299 \cdot 0.42 + 0.1652 \cdot 0.07 + 0.2007 \cdot 0.06 + 0.3013 \cdot 0.06 = 0.12$

The sensitive information $s(y)$ associated with a target $y \in Y$ is considered exposed if $\Delta(X, y)$ deviates from its average $I(X, Y)$ more than a standard deviation σ_Δ. In such a case we say that y is an X-outlier, as defined by the following definition.

Definition 3 (X-outlier). *Let T be a table over attributes A and let X and Y be two subsets of A such that $X \rightsquigarrow Y$. We say that $y \in Y$ is an X-outlier if and only if $\Delta(X, y) > I(X, Y) + \sigma_\Delta$, where σ_Δ is the standard deviation of $\Delta(X, y)$.*

Example 6. With respect to our running example, suppose that $\sigma_\Delta = 0.02$ and consider the values of $\Delta(\texttt{Age}, L_1), \ldots, \Delta(\texttt{Age}, L_5)$ in Example 4 and of $I(\texttt{Age}, \texttt{Location})$ in Example 5. L_2 is the unique location that is an Age-outlier since $\Delta(\texttt{Age}, L_2) = 0.42$ is greater than $I(\texttt{Age}, \texttt{Location}) + \sigma_\Delta = 0.14$.

Definition 3 characterizes the actual outliers in the original table T. However, external observers can only see and learn the distribution of values computed on tuples that have been released. By denoting with T_r the set of released tuples and with P_r the value distributions observable on T_r (in contrast to the P observable on T), the knowledge of an external observer can be expressed as the different observations $P_r(X|y)$ she can learn by collecting all the tuples released and the baseline distribution $P(X)$ publicly released by the data holder. We therefore need to characterize the exposure of a target y in terms of how much the observable y-conditioned distribution of X differ from the one expected.

A first term to characterize such exposure is the distance $\Delta_r(X, y)$ of the y-conditioned distribution of X over the released tuples T_r (i.e., $P_r(X|y)$) and the expected baseline distribution (i.e., $P(X)$). A second term that comes into play is the frequency of the specific y in the released dataset T_r. The rational is that since external observers do not have any information about the content of the original table T, they also do not know the number of tuples related to a given y in T: the only information observers can have about a target y is the one observable in T_r. Targets having small frequencies in T_r are then intrinsically more protected than ones having greater frequencies. In fact, if a target y appears with only few occurrences in T_r, an observer is likely not to put great confidence on its distribution, observed over few tuples. For instance, consider a released dataset T_r of 1000 tuples, where 10 tuples refer to y_1 and 990 to y_2, with $P(X|y_1) = P(X|y_2)$. While $\Delta_r(X, y_1)$ will be the same as $\Delta_r(X, y_2)$, an observer might not grant much confidence on the observations on y_1 since they result a limited number of tuples compared to the size of T_r. This aspect is captured by considering the frequency $p_r(y)$ of y in T_r as a weight for the Kullback-Leibler distance when computing the *exposure* of y. We therefore evaluate the exposure for a target y given a set of released tuples T_r as follows.

Definition 4 (Exposure). *Let T_r be a set of released tuples over attributes A, let X and Y be two subsets of A such that $X \rightsquigarrow Y$, and let $y \in Y$ be a target. The exposure for y over T_r due to the dependency on X is $\mathcal{E}_r(X, y) = p_r(y)\Delta_r(X, y)$.*

Example 7. With reference to our running example, consider the evaluation of the exposure for target L_2, and suppose that $\Delta_r(\texttt{Age}, L_2) = 0.22$. If T_r is composed by 10 tuples on L_2 and 90 tuples of different locations, then $p_r(L_2) = 0.1$, and the exposure for L_2 is $\mathcal{E}_r(\texttt{Age}, L_2) = p_r(L_2)\Delta_r(\texttt{Age}, L_2) = 0.1 \cdot 0.22 = 0.02$. If, otherwise, T_r is composed by 10 L_2 tuples and 10 tuples of different locations, then $p_r(L_2) = 0.5$, and the exposure for L_2 is $\mathcal{E}_r(\texttt{Age}, L_2) = p_r(L_2)\Delta_r(\texttt{Age}, L_2) = 0.5 \cdot 0.22 = 0.11$.

Having characterized the exposure for y over a given release T_r, we now need to characterize when the release of a tuple t is safe or when the corresponding target $y = t[Y]$ is considered too exposed and the privacy of its associated sensitive information $s(y)$ at risk. Adapting Definition 4, we consider the release of a given target y safe if its exposure is not above the average exposure plus one standard deviation, $\sigma_{\mathcal{E}}$. The average exposure is $\frac{I_r(X,Y)}{|Y_r|}$, with $I_r(X,Y)$ the mutual information between attributes X and Y computed on T_r, and $|Y_r|$ the different values of Y in T_r. The average exposure is computed on T_r instead of T since the original table T is not known to external observers, who can only see and learn distributions from the released dataset T_r. Note that, clearly, the average exposure differs from the average of $\Delta(X, y)$ of Definition 3.

Definition 5 (Safe release). *Let T_r be a set of released tuples over attributes A, let X and Y be two subsets of A such that $X \leadsto Y$, let t be a tuple to be released, with $y = t[Y]$. The release of t is safe if $\mathcal{E}_{r'}(X, y) = p_{r'}(y) \cdot \Delta_{r'}(X, y)$ over $T_{r'} = T_r \cup t$ is less than $\frac{I_{r'}(X,Y)}{|Y_{r'}|} + \sigma_{\mathcal{E}}$, where $|Y_{r'}|$ is the number of different values of Y in $T_{r'}$.*

According to Definition 5, a tuple t, with $y = t[Y]$, can be released if the exposure $\mathcal{E}_{r'}(X, y)$ for $y = t[Y]$ over $T_{r'} = T_r \cup t$ (Definition 4) is less than the threshold $\frac{I_{r'}(X,Y)}{|Y_{r'}|} + \sigma_{\mathcal{E}}$.

5   Controlling Exposure and Regulating Release

In the previous section we have characterized when a release is safe with respect to inference, which is when the distribution of values observable in the external world does not define the involved target as an X-outlier. The remaining aspect to consider is when to start enforcing such control. As a matter of fact, we are considering a scenario of incremental releases where the control needs to operate at run time and tuples can be requested one by one. We can clearly imagine that the release of the first few tuples will produce random distribution of values that will usually not resemble the actual distribution existing in the database, thus corresponding to an exposure of the different targets that can considerably differ from their real exposures. Typically, such a random exposure will characterize the targets as X-outliers, thus blocking any release. Enforcing the control on the safe release at the start time of the system can therefore cause a denial of service in the system raising many false alarms (since also targets that are not X-outliers will have a random initial distribution that will differ from the baseline). In addition we note that clearly no observer could put confidence on statistics computed over a few releases as they cannot be considered accurate and their distribution can be completely random. There is therefore a starting time at which the data holder should allow the release of tuples regardless of whether the safety condition (Definition 5) is satisfied. After a sufficient amount of information has been released for a given target, subsequent releases should be controlled and allowed only if the release is safe. There is not a unique way to specify when the amount of information released should be considered sufficient. In the following, we discuss some possible approaches, which we are further investigating, performing experiments to evaluate their pros and cons in different settings.

- *Exposure accuracy.* A first approach consists in evaluating the accuracy of the exposure known to the observer with respect to the real exposure, which corresponds to the release of all the tuples of the target. Once the exposure approximates for the first time the real exposure (i.e., when the amount of released data is such that the corresponding exposure approximates the real exposure), the external knowledge can be considered accurate enough and a control can be triggered. Exposure accuracy is particular intuitive as a control on real X-outliers. In fact, exposure accuracy would trigger the control when the external observations would essentially leak the information that the target is close to its real distribution (which is a distribution corresponding to an X-outlier). Also, for targets which are not X-outliers it intuitively captures the fact that the external knowledge is not accurate.
- *Number of releases.* Another possible alternative solution is based on the number of tuples released for each given target. Intuitively this approach captures the fact that a limited number of tuples offers little knowledge to the observer since the distributions of values on them can be completely random and rarely correspond to the distribution actually existing in the database. The threshold on the number of tuples to be applied could be the same for the different targets or specific for each of them (e.g., targets with smaller occurrences could have a smaller threshold). The consideration of the number of released tuples naturally captures the confidence that the observer can put on the distributions based on the amount of data released: the more the data, the more the confident in the statistics.
- *Number of releases for different values of X.* While starting the control after a given number of tuples has been released for a given target can perform usually well, especially for targets that are not X-outliers, in few cases (and in particular for outliers) it may not suffice. For instance, with reference to our example, the first few tuples could all be referred to the same range value for Age, then exposing a peak for that range. To illustrate, consider our running example in Figure 2 and Figure 3. For our outlier location L_2, the release of tuples in such a way that the distribution resembles the baseline distribution forces a maximum number of tuples that could be released for each age range. For instance, in the baseline distribution almost 19.67% of the soldiers are in the range [25-29], while in L_2 only 8.78% of tuples (140 tuples) fall in such range. Respecting the baseline distribution requires, even in the case where all tuples in the range [25-29] of L_2 are released to not release tuples in other ranges (so that the 140 tuples above actually correspond to 19.67%). Figure 4 graphically depicts this reasoning fitting the baseline distribution (in black) within the $L2$-conditioned distribution (gray going over the black). For each value range, no more than the number reached by the baseline distribution should be released.

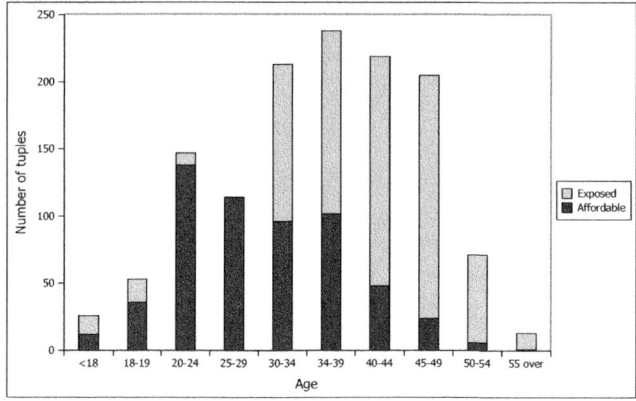

Fig. 4. Fitting the baseline distribution within the L_2-conditioned distribution

The different approaches above have all an intuitive nature, providing different kinds of controls that perform well in different scenarios. They could therefore be applied individually or in conjunction to control releases of data in different settings. We have conducted some experiments to assess the impact and guarantees of the different types of controls. We have considered a table T as described in Example 1, where the 10000 tuples in the table have been randomly generated to respect the baseline distribution illustrated in Figure 3(a), which corresponds to the age distribution of the UK Regular Forces as at 1 March 2006. The distribution of the age ranges for each location are illustrated in Figure 2, characterizing location L_2 as the only Age-outlier. We performed five simulations, where each simulation consists in randomly releasing all the tuples in T. Before each simulation, the content of table T has been shuffled, so to produce different orders of release (and therefore different incremental observations over time). Figures 5(a)-(e) show for the five simulations how the exposure $\mathcal{E}_r(\texttt{Age}, L_i)$ varies with the number of released tuples for the five locations $L_1, \ldots, L_5$. The horizontal dashed lines represent the actual exposure $\mathcal{E}(\texttt{Age}, L_i)$ and the continuous lines represent the final value of the threshold (i.e., the threshold computed in correspondence of the last tuple released) introduced in Definition 5, which varies as a new tuple is released. We report the final threshold value since in our experiments, after the release of a relatively small number of tuples (200 tuples on average), the released global distribution resembles the genuine distribution over table T, thus producing a threshold that quickly converges to the final value. Figure 5(f) illustrates, for each location, the average of the exposures $\mathcal{E}_r(\texttt{Age}, L_i)$ and of the threshold evaluated in the five simulations. In the graphs, we use a logarithmic scale for the ordinate axis to make the plot easier to view.

All the graphs in Figure 5 show that, for all locations and simulations, in the first releases there is a high exposure with fluctuations. The exposure then decreases and becomes stable (apart again small fluctuations) as the number of tuples released increases until the actual exposure is reached. The graphs confirm the intuition that the false positives happen mainly at the beginning of the

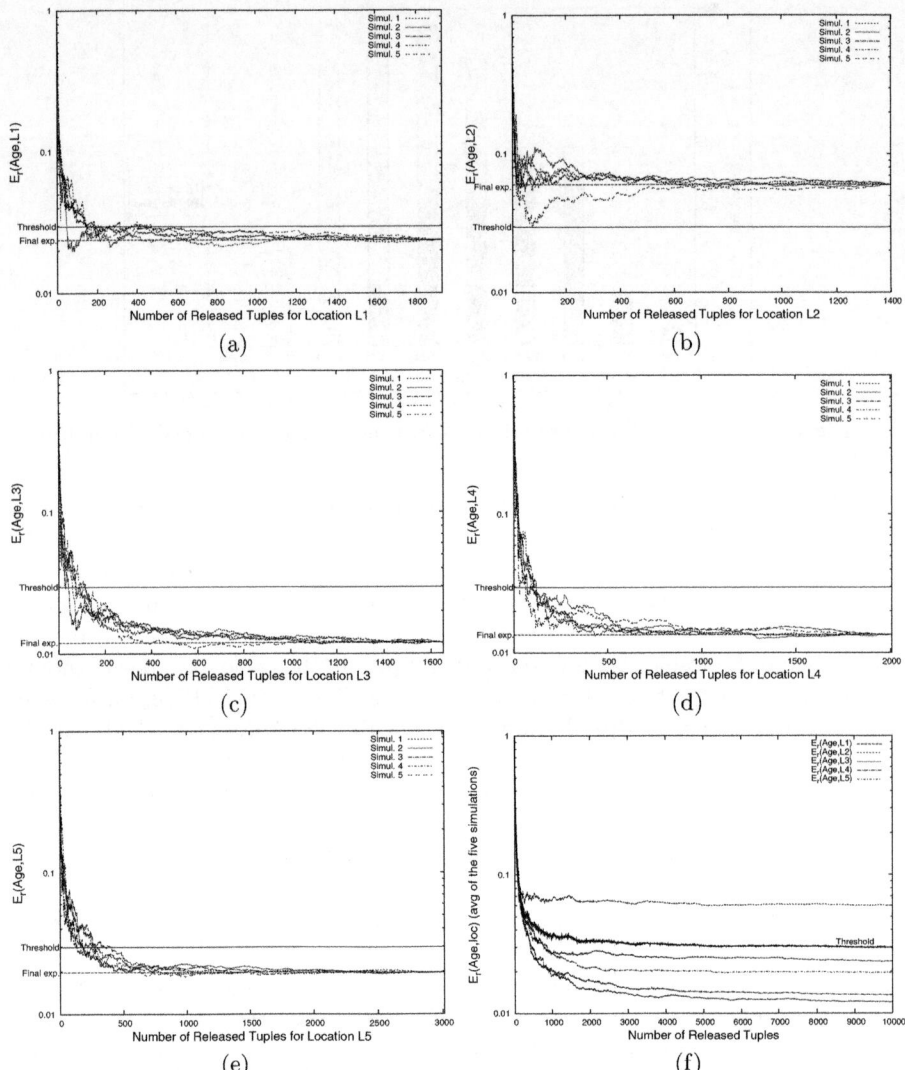

Fig. 5. Exposure variation for each location and simulation (a)-(e), and average on the five simulations of the exposure and threshold for each location (f)

releases (since distributions over a few tuples cannot be considered reliable). In fact, after a certain number of releases, for all locations but L_2 the exposure $\mathcal{E}_r(\mathtt{Age}, L_i)$ computed by an observer typically is less than the threshold represented by the continuous horizontal lines, meaning that the tuples related to such locations can be safely released.

The different thresholds discussed above, when individually applied, have different impact on the control. In particular, the accuracy of the exposure with respect to actual exposure would start the control the first time the lines of the exposure of the releases come close to the actual exposure. While performing usually well and being intuitive, such a threshold has the side effect of not triggering the control for releases that show an anomalous distribution for targets that in fact are not X-outlier, that is, for false positives that remain such for a considerable number of releases. This is, for example, the case of the fifth simulated release for location L_1, where the exposure remains for a very long time above the threshold but the release is allowed since the exposure does not correctly reflect the actual exposure (in other words, it is a false positive). Whether such situation is legitimate or not depends on the kind of controls one wants to apply and whether releases of false positives should be considered as harmful. In such case, another threshold should be applied in alternative or in conjunction with the accuracy metrics. The threshold based on the number of tuples released would start the control after a given number of tuples are released, blocking any release considered unsafe according to our definition. In such case, in the specific case of the fifth simulation of location L_4, the release of tuples would be blocked after the threshold number of tuples has been reached.

6   Related Work

Several research efforts have been recently dedicated to the problem of protecting privacy in data publication (e.g., [3,9,15,21]). In particular, considerable attention has been devoted to the problem of protecting the respondents' identities and the sensitive information associated with the respondents to whom the published data refer. Such proposals use the notion of k-anonymity [21] as a starting point or adopt some extensions of k-anonymity (e.g., [9,14,15,17]), and others are based on the idea of fragmenting data and publishing associations at the group level (e.g., [6,25]). Among them, t-closeness [15] and (α_i, β_i)-closeness [9] present some similarities with our work. t-closeness protects attribute disclosure by imposing that the distribution of sensitive values in the equivalence classes of the released table (i.e., in the groups of tuples with the same value for the quasi-identifying attributes) must be similar to the distribution in the private table. To this purpose, the t-closeness approach applies the Earth Mover's Distance (EMD) for measuring the distance between the global distribution computed on the private table and the distributions computed within each equivalence classes. The distance between these distributions should be no more than t. In [9], the authors present an extension of t-closeness that overcomes some of its limitations (e.g., the difficulty in choosing a correct value for t and the impossibility to specify that there are some attribute values more sensitive than others). With this approach, the data publisher defines a different range $[\alpha_i, \beta_i]$ associated with each value v_i of a sensitive attribute. A released table is then acceptable when for each equivalence class the proportion of tuples in the class with a given sensitive value v_i falls in the corresponding range $[\alpha_i, \beta_i]$. Although our proposal and these two approaches have in common the fact that they consider inference issues caused by anomalous value distributions, our work addresses a different and more complex scenario characterized by incremental releases of detailed data. Also, in our scenario the sensitive information is not released but can be inferred due to a value distribution dependency between a set of attributes appearing in the released data and the sensitive property itself.

Inference problems have been studied extensively in the context of multilevel database systems (e.g., [13,16,18]). Most inference research addresses detection of inference channels within a database or at query processing time. In the first case, inference channels are removed by upgrading selected schema components or redesigning the schema (e.g., [20]). In the second case, database transactions are evaluated to determine whether they lead to illegal inferences and, if so, deny the query (e.g., [10,12,19,23]). Neither approach is however applicable to the problem under consideration. As a matter of fact, the inference problem we address is due to a dependency existing between the value distribution observable aggregating all the released tuples and the sensitive information that we want to protect. Previous work on inference focuses instead on locating inference channels based on semantic relationships between attributes or on queries submitted to the systems.

Our problem also has common aspects with the aggregation problem that arises when the aggregation of two or more data items is considered more sensitive than the single data items. A well-known example is the Secret Government Agency (SGA) Phonebook [22]: the entire phonebook is classified as confidential and it is accessible only by users with the appropriate clearance but single entries are unclassified and available to any requester. Although our problem is conceptually similar, the classical solutions developed for addressing the aggregation problem (e.g., [7,11,13]) are not directly applicable in our context. These approaches define a threshold on the amount of data that can be released to each user and focus on maintaining history and establishing how to control collusion among users.

Other related proposals are those used to assess the *interestingness* of association rules in knowledge discovery problems. In [24], the authors introduced the J-measure to assess the relevance of an association rule. In some sense, these proposals are complementary to ours, as they can be used for assessing dependencies among the attributes characterizing a data collection. The information they produce can then be used as input to our approach for the definition of appropriate dependencies.

7 Conclusions

We considered the problem of protecting sensitive information in an incremental data release scenario, where the data holder releases non sensitive data on demand. As more and more data are released, an external observer can aggregate such data and infer the sensitive information by exploiting a dependency between the distribution of the non sensitive released data and the sensitive information itself. In this paper, we presented an approach for characterizing when data can be released without incurring to such inference. To this purpose, we defined when a distribution can be considered unusual and exploited for inference, and introduced the concept of safe release. Our work represents only a first step in the investigation of the problem and leaves space for further investigations, including: the experimental evaluations of the different approaches outlined in this paper for enforcing information release at run-time, the extension of the model to the consideration of inferences arising from information other than value distributions differing from a given pre-defined one, and the consideration of different types of knowledge that observers can exploit for inference.

Acknowledgments. This work was supported in part by the EU within the 7FP project "PrimeLife" under grant agreement 216483 and by the Italian Ministry of Research within the PRIN 2008 project "PEPPER"(2008SY2PH4).

References

1. Adam, N.R., Wortmann, J.C.: Security-control methods for statistical databases: A comparative study. ACM Computing Surveys 21(4), 515–556 (1989)
2. Aggarwal, C., Yu, P.S. (eds.): Privacy-Preserving Data Mining: Models and Algorithms. Springer, Heidelberg (2008)
3. Ciriani, V., De Capitani di Vimercati, S., Foresti, S., Samarati, P.: k-Anonymity. In: Yu, T., Jajodia, S. (eds.) Secure Data Management in Decentralized Systems, Springer, Heidelberg (2007)
4. Ciriani, V., De Capitani di Vimercati, S., Foresti, S., Samarati, P.: Microdata protection. In: Yu, T., Jajodia, S. (eds.) Secure Data Management in Decentralized Systems. Springer, Heidelberg (2007)
5. Dawson, S., De Capitani di Vimercati, S., Lincoln, P., Samarati, P.: Maximizing sharing of protected information. Journal of Computer and System Sciences 64(3), 496–541 (2002)
6. De Capitani di Vimercati, S., Foresti, S., Jajodia, S., Paraboschi, S., Samarati, P.: Fragments and loose associations: Respecting privacy in data publishing. In: Proc. of the VLDB Endowment, vol. 3(1) (2010)
7. Denning, D.D., Lunt, T.F., Schell, R.R., Heckman, M., Shockley, W.R.: The seaview security model. IEEE Transactions of Software Engineering 16(6), 593–607 (1990)
8. Fano, R.M.: Transmission of Information; A Statistical Theory of Communications. MIT University Press, New York (1961)
9. Frikken, K.B., Zhang, Y.: Yet another privacy metric for publishing micro-data. In: Proc. of the 7th ACM Workshop on Privacy in the Electronic Society (WPES 2008), Alexandria, VA, USA (October 2008)
10. Goguen, J.A., Meseguer, J.: Unwinding and inference control. In: Proc. of the IEEE Symposium on Security and Privacy, Oakland, CA, USA (May 1984)
11. Haigh, J.T., O'Brien, R.C., Thomsen, D.J.: The LDV secure relational DBMS model. In: Jajodia, S., Landwehr, C.E. (eds.) Database Security, IV: Status and Prospects, pp. 265–279. Elsevier Science Publishers, North-Holland (1991)
12. Hinke, T.H., Delugach, H.S., Chandrasekhar, A.: A fast algorithm for detecting second paths in database inference analysis. Journal of Computer Security 3(2/3), 147–168 (1995)
13. Jajodia, S., Meadows, C.: Inference problems in multilevel secure database management systems. In: Information Security: an Integrated Collection of Essays, pp. 570–584. IEEE Computer Society Press, Los Alamitos (1995)

14. LeFevre, K., DeWitt, D.J., Ramakrishnan, R.: Mondrian multidimensional k-anonymity. In: Proc. of the 22nd IEEE International Conference on Data Engineering (ICDE 2006), Atlanta, GA, USA (April 2006)
15. Li, N., Li, T., Venkatasubramanian, S.: t-closeness: Privacy beyond k-anonymity and ℓ-diversity. In: Proc. of the 23rd IEEE International Conference on Data Engineering (ICDE 2007), Istanbul, Turkey (April 2007)
16. Lunt, T.F.: Aggregation and inference: facts and fallacies. In: IEEE Symposium on Security and Privacy, Oakland, CA, USA (May 1989)
17. Machanavajjhala, A., Gehrke, J., Kifer, D.: ℓ-density: Privacy beyond k-anonymity. In: Proc. of the 22nd IEEE International Conference on Data Engineering (ICDE 2006), Atlanta, GA, USA (April 2006)
18. Marks, D.G., Motro, A., Jajodia, S.: Enhancing the controlled disclosure of sensitive information. In: Martella, G., Kurth, H., Montolivo, E., Hwang, J. (eds.) ESORICS 1996. LNCS, vol. 1146, Springer, Heidelberg (1996)
19. Morgenstern, M.: Controlling logical inference in multilevel database systems. In: Proc. of the IEEE Symposium on Security and Privacy, Oakland, CA, USA (May 1988)
20. Qian, X., Stickel, M.E., Karp, P.D., Lunt, T.F., Garvey, T.D.: Detection and elimination of inference channels in multilevel relational database. In: Proc. of the 1993 IEEE Symposium on Research in Security and Privacy, Oakland, CA, USA (May 1993)
21. Samarati, P.: Protecting respondents identities in microdata release. IEEE Transactions on Knowledge and Data Engineering 13(6), 1010–1027 (2001)
22. Schaefer, M. (ed.): Multilevel data management security. Air Force Studies Board Committee on Multilevel Data Management Security (1983)
23. Smith, G.W.: Modeling security-relevant data semantics. IEEE Transactions on Software Engineering 17(11), 1195–1203 (1991)
24. Smyth, P., Goodman, R.M.: An information theoretic approach to rule induction from databases. IEEE Transactions on Knowledge and Data Engineering 4(4), 301–316 (1992)
25. Xiao, X., Tao, Y.: Anatomy: Simple and effective privacy preservation. In: Proc. of the 32nd International Conference on Very Large Data Bases (VLDB 2006), Seoul, Korea (September 2006)

Author Index